THE SHORTSTOP FROM KALAMAZOO

THE SHORTSTOP FROM KALAMAZOO

THE LIFE AND TIMES OF NEIL BERRY

by

William Christiansen

Book Design by Deb Christiansen

ISBN: 978-0-578-77228-8

Published by
Out of The Zoo
P.O. Box 563
Schoolcraft, MI 49087
outofthezoo.com

Printed in the United States of America

DEDICATION

For My Girls

Wife, Deb (who does not suffer fools gladly but lovingly
suffers me and my passions)

Angela, Serena, Desiree, and Chantal

Also for The Kalamazoo Tennis Mafia (you know who
you are) for lending a collective ear to my telling of Neil's
stories during our bar time deliberations

TABLE OF CONTENTS

PREFACE 1

INTRODUCTION..5

1. THE EARLY YEARS
   Growing Up in Kalamazoo
   1922 to 1929.. 11

2. THE JUVENILE YEARS
   From Tom Sawyer to Organized Sports
   1930 to 1935.. 24

3. A STAR IS BORN
   Kalamazoo Central High School
   1936 to 1937.. 42

4. FOOTBALL CHAMPIONS
   Kalamazoo Central High School
   1938... 64

5. THE LEGION MAROONS
   American Legion Baseball
   1936 to 1939.. 86

6. SUTHERLAND PAPER CO.
   Kalamazoo City League Baseball
   1940... 112

7. COLLEGE FRESHMAN
   Western State Teachers College
   1940 to 1941.. 136

8. WAR WORRIES

Kalamazoo City League Baseball

1941 148

9. PRO BALL

The Winston-Salem Twins

1942 156

10. THE WAR YEARS

A Base Without Baseball

1942 to 1946 200

11. THE BUFFALO BISON YEARS

Back to Baseball

1946 to 1947 220

12. MAJOR LEAGUE BASEBALL

When Neil Berry Played the Game

1948 to 1954 250

13. THE DETROIT TIGERS

Making the Majors

1948 256

14. NEIL'S FAVORITE GAME

Extending Clevelands Season

1948 280

15. THE DETROIT TIGERS

Red Rolfe Takes Over

1949 290

16. THE DETROIT TIGERS

Pennant Contenders

1950 314

17. THE DETROIT TIGERS

Back to Mediocrity

1951 332

18. THE DETROIT TIGERS

Detroit's First 100 Loss Season

1952 348

19. TRADED TO THE BROWNS

St. Louis Browns & Chicago White Sox

1953 366

20. TRADED TO THE ORIOLES

Baltimore Orioles & Kansas City Blues

1954 390

21. BERRY REPLACES ROWE

Managing the Montgomery Rebels

1958 402

EPILOGUE 410

BIBLIOGRAPHY 420

INDEX 422

PREFACE

I had the good fortune of meeting Neil Berry in October 2013. I had been recruited by a friend to use my limited tennis ability to help with the newly formed Kalamazoo Wheelchair Tennis Association. My wife, Deb, was already helping with her considerable non-tennis abilities as a board member and communication director, so it was an offer that was hard to refuse. I showed up that first Tuesday night wearing a Detroit Tigers tee shirt, and when I met Linda Spann, the program's teaching pro, she saw that I was a Tiger fan and told me her father, Neil Berry, is the oldest living Detroit Tiger. I learned later that he had recently gained this milestone with the passing of Tiger pitching great Virgil "Fire" Trucks at the age of 95. Trucks debuted with the Tigers in September 1941 and threw two no-hitters in 1952. Neil Berry started his Major League career with the Tigers in 1948, debuting at shortstop on opening day. He was a teammate of Virgil Trucks until both were traded after the 1952 season.

With Linda's assurance that she would bring her dad to a future wheelchair tennis session, I searched eBay and found a vintage action photo of No. 36 Neil Berry sliding home as the ball got away from the catcher. I carefully carried the photo in my tennis bag anticipating the autograph that I would soon be able to add to my man-cave collection of baseball memorabilia. Three weeks later Linda brought her dad along and we were introduced. I chatted with Neil along with a few other people who were there with wheelchair tennis players. It was immediately evident that Neil enjoyed talking baseball and with plenty of volunteer racket help there that night, I never took mine out of the bag. Neil shared his opinions about the current Tiger team and told stories from his playing days. While talking about clubhouse chemistry, Neil shared an unfavorable opinion about a former Tiger teammate, but he was reluctant to give the teammate's name. When I got Neil to share the teammate's position I correctly identified George Kell as the player he was referring to, demonstrating that I had a bit of historical knowledge about the Tigers.

Toward the end of the hour and a half session, I took out the vintage photo I'd been carrying in my tennis bag, "Recognize this?" I asked, handing Neil the black and white photo from September, 1948. He did.

"Well, that's me sliding and the catcher's Birdie Tebbetts. Birdie was playin' for Boston at the time."

I was amazed. Birdie Tebbetts had his mask off in the picture but his chest protector covered the Boston team name. Neil Berry simply recognized the face of a player he had played against 65 years ago.

Well I got my autograph and my wife got an iPhone picture of me and with the oldest living Detroit Tiger. Neil and I shook hands, and I told him how much I enjoyed his stories. I thought that was that, but Neil, who was living with his daughter, Linda, asked me if I would visit him there. I said I would.

Two weeks later Neil was back at wheelchair tennis practice with Linda. I needed to feed and pick up tennis balls that night so I didn't get a chance to say hello until after the session.

"I thought you said you were gonna to stop and see me," Neil said, calling me on my earlier promise. We settled on a Thursday afternoon visit.

That Thursday Neil and I began going through the amazing scrapbooks his wife Gloria had put together. She clipped the first picture from the newspaper in 1936 when they were both sophomores in high school. Gloria continued to clip photos and articles for the next 22 years documenting Neil's sports career including high school football, American Legion baseball, and his entire professional baseball career.

That first visit lasted over four hours. Neil carried the

conversation telling me stories prompted by a picture or a newspaper article from one of the three large scrapbooks we were looking through. The scrapbook pages and many of the newspaper clippings, some of which were over 70 years old, were fragile and some were torn, so I brought tape with me on my next visit and repaired the tears while we looked through more pages.

At some point early on during our visits, Neil told me his favorite subject in school was history, "because history tells a story." Neil could also tell a pretty good story.

Neil went on to explain, "history is not a direct subject which is good. A direct subject is math and chemistry. History is not direct, you could say so and so did such and such—no he didn't—how can you prove it? But if you say two and two is four, that's four! History is not a direct subject, there's a lot of leeway, that's another thing I like about history. Even biology is direct, cut a frog open and that's it. It's still a frog."

Neil was a living treasure trove of stories about his life and his time, from childhood memories while growing up in Kalamazoo's Upjohn Park neighborhood, through his rise to prominence in high school sports to his path to the Major Leagues. We decided his stories—his history—needed to be written down and shared. I told Neil I would do that and, with his permission, I started recording our talks. Neil also carried those conversations. I would ask an occasional question, but for the most part, Neil just told his stories. Neil seldom used the leeway that history grants the storyteller. He didn't need to. His mind was sharp and his memory was remarkable.

Neil and I met almost every week since that first visit in October 2013, only missing when I was out of town or when one of us was sick. I was often told how nice it was that I visited the old ballplayer every week, but I was getting as much out of those visits as Neil was. In many ways, Neil was the grandfather I never knew, and the father I hadn't had for

3

20 years. A highlight of all those visits was when I brought my mother along. She was also a Kalamazoo Central alumni and had known Neil's younger sister, Joyce. I just sat back and listened to them reminisce about old times and the people they both knew.

Many of the stories from Neil's youth sounded eerily similar to my own—minus the athletic ability—that occurred three decades later. Stories that will likely not register a hint of recognition with younger generations unless they experienced something similar in a video game. They grew up in a different world with available technology that Neil, and myself for that matter, never dreamed of. This is definitely a history book for those readers.

The last time I spoke with Neil was August 23, 2016, at Bronson Hospital, the day before he passed away. Neil carried that conversation too. I told him I would finish this book, but not realizing this would be our last conversation, I left other things unsaid.

After nearly three years of weekly visits, I had what I needed to tell Neil Berry's story. I had over 200 hours of recordings. I had his scrapbooks with 22 years of newspaper clippings. I had everything I needed to finish this book, everything except Neil.

INTRODUCTION

The Game of Baseball

Baseball is 90% mental and the other half is physical.

~ Yogi Berra

Baseball is a unique game. A game with some significant differences from the other major team sports (basketball, football, and hockey). Professional baseball teams play a game nearly every day and play the same opponent two, three or four days in a row. Baseball managers—they're not called coaches—wear a uniform. Cornelius McGillicuddy (Connie Mack), with his suit and top hat, was the notable exception while he managed the Philadelphia Athletics' first 50 seasons of play. A manager has 25 players at his disposal to *use* during a baseball game and when a player comes out of the game he has been *used up* and can't go back in the game.

In the other major sports, the offense has control of the ball (or puck), but in a baseball game, the defense (starting with the pitcher) controls the ball. The offense—hitters and base runners—have coaches on the field (at first and third base) to coach the players during the game.

Contrary to the rules of other sports the ball is playable in foul territory. Both outs and runs can actually be recorded from a play in foul ground. Baseball is also the only sport where the defense can attempt to make plays in the stands, amongst the crowd.

Unlike a basketball court, a football field, or a hockey rink, the dimensions of a baseball park are different from park to park due to varying amounts of foul territory and different outfield configurations and distances.

Boston's Fenway Park (1912-present) has a 37 foot left field wall only 310 feet from home plate. That wall has turned what would have been routine fly-outs in other parks, into Fenway doubles.

New York's horseshoe-shaped Polo Grounds (1890-1963) with its expansive 480-foot center field was enough room for Willie Mays to make what has come to be known as "The Catch" in the 1954 World Series. Mays would have run out of room in most other parks. Conversely foul line distances of only 280 feet (left field) and 259 feet (right field) enabled a game winning home run in the same World Series game. The ball would likely not have reached the seats in any other major league park.

Unrelated to the demensions or shape, the Polo Grounds was also the site of the "Merkle Boner" in 1908.

It ain't over till it's over. ~ *Yogi Berra*

While baseball is the national pastime, you never know how much time will pass to complete a baseball game. Baseball—with the exception of some recent pace-of-play rules—is not ruled by a clock. Weather permitting, games are nine-inning affairs with extra innings played if necessary to decide the outcome. The umpires don't blow a whistle to stop play. There is no clock governing the length of a play, an inning or the length of a baseball game.

When three-time American League MVP ('51, '54, '55) and Hall-of-Famer Yogi Berra famously quipped, "It ain't over till it's over," he was talking about the Mets' chances in the 1973 pennant race, but he just as easily could have been talking about the game itself. A famous example that demonstrates a play and the game isn't over until it's over occurred during the 1908 National League pennant race. The New York Giants and the Chicago Cubs were just percentage points apart at the top of the standings when they faced off at the

Polo Grounds—the Giants home park—on September 23.

The game was tied 1-1 when the Giants came to bat in the bottom of the ninth. With two out and Moose McCormick on first base, Fred Merkle—the Giants 19-year-old first baseman—starting the first game of his career—lined the ball to right field. McCormick hustled to third base and Merkle stopped at first with a single. The next batter— Giant shortstop Al Birdwell—lined the first pitch he saw up the middle to drive in the winning run for the Giants, but as Yogi said many years later, "It ain't over till it's over," and it wasn't over.

Why wasn't it over? McCormick clearly touched home plate and Birdwell touched first base before he was mobbed by teammates and fans rushing onto the field. The apparent winning pitcher, Christy Mathewson, ran out of the dugout and embraced young Fred Merkle as he ran off the field. While all of this was going on the Cubs second baseman, Johnny Evers, was screaming at center fielder "Circus Solly" Hofman to throw him the ball. Evers—of "Tinker to Evers to Chance" fame—saw Fred Merkle cut off his run to second base and start celebrating when what should have been the winning run crossed the plate. Evers knew the run wouldn't count and the inning would be over if Merkle was forced out at second base regardless of when he was forced out relative to the runner crossing the plate. Apparently Joe McGinnity, a Giants pitcher who was coaching first base that day, realized what was going on, raced onto the field, commandeered the ball before it got to second base, and threw it into the stands. Cub players then retrieved the game ball (or a ball) and threw it to Evers. When Evers finally got the ball he got the attention of the field umpire, touched second base and asked the umpire to call Merkle out. After claiming he hadn't seen the play, the field umpire deferred to the home plate umpire who called Merkle out. The game remained tied. The game wasn't over, but it was called for darkness before the umpires could reconvene the teams.

Two weeks later the Cubs beat the Giants in a playoff game to win the National League pennant, a game that would not have been necessary had Fred Merkle touched second base. The play came to be known as the Merkle Boner and Merkle was forever stuck with the nickname, Bonehead.

The Cubs beat the Detroit Tigers in the 1908 World Series but would not reign as World Series champs again for 108 years.

"It's like déjà vu all over again." It's not clear when Yogi Berra first spoke those words of wisdom but they certainly applied on July 1, 2013 when the Lansing Lugnuts and Great Lakes Loons played a minor league game at Lugnuts Stadium. The game featured a "Merkle Boner" when the apparent game-winning single for the Lugnuts was nullified when the runner at first joined the celebration instead of advancing to second base. The Lugnuts lost in extra innings.

If the world were perfect, it wouldn't be. ~ Yogi Berra

The same can be said of baseball. Baseball is the perfect game played by imperfect people.

More so than any other major team sport, baseball is a team game reliant on individual performances. Baseball action starts with a battle between two athletes, the pitcher, and the batter. The pitcher delivers a pitch chosen in collaboration with his catcher. In a split second the batter has to decide whether or not to swing at the pitch. If he doesn't swing (and the pitch doesn't hit him), the catcher has to catch the pitch and the umpire has to decide if the pitch was in the strike zone. If the batter hits the pitched ball he has to run to first base and try to beat the fielder's throw if he hit a ground ball. He has to decide whether or not to attempt to go to second or third base on a ball that lands safely in the outfield. The wrong decision, along with proper execution by the defense, could result in an out instead of a base runner for his team.

Each fielder and base runner must be ready to react to a batted ball by the hitter. Knowing where to go and what to do when a batted ball is put in play is part of the mental aspect of the game. Be it the pitcher covering first base on a ball fielded by the first baseman, or the cutoff man being in position for an outfielder's throw, or the base runner advancing or staying on the base he occupies.

You can observe a lot by just watching. ~ *Yogi Berra*

Baseball is also a game that is conducive to keeping individual statistics. Every time the pitcher throws a pitch multiple stats are recorded; the pitch was a ball, called strike, swinging strike, hit foul, or put into play. Pitch count for the game is also tracked and is often used by the manager to determine when to change pitchers.

When the ball is put in play by the batter, the outcome for the batter and the individual performances by the defensive players are scrutinized—hit or error—by the game's official scorer. Outstanding defensive plays are not recorded differently than common outs. Could have been—should have been—double plays that only result in one out are not assigned an error because the official scorer cannot assume a double play. The fans know and will always have an opinion, but each game's official scorer makes the decisions that stand in the official record of the game and the player's career.

Neil Berry's seven-year major league career stats:

1087 at-bats, 265 hits, 0 home runs, 74 RBI, .244 batting average, 148 runs, 11 stolen bases.

Neil's speed, defense, and versatility—he could play second base, third base, and shortstop—kept him in the major leagues, playing for the Detroit Tigers (1948 - 1952), St. Louis Browns (1953), Chicago White Sox (1953), and

Baltimore Orioles (1954). A career that included highs and lows for both Neil personally, and for the Detroit Tiger teams he played on.

Before Neil Berry took the field as Detroit's opening day shortstop in 1948, he starred in High School football, and American Legion and City League Baseball while growing up and coming of age in Kalamazoo, Michigan. Neil grew up in Kalamazoo and he also grew up *with* Kalamazoo as the city evolved from the "Celery City" to the "Paper City" during periods of prosperous growth, the great depression, and pre-war anxiety.

After one year at Western State Teachers College and one year of pro ball at Winston-Salem in the Piedmont League, Neil—being part of America's greatest generation—served his country during World War II before continuing his baseball career. Neil Berry made it to the major leagues just after Jackie Robinson broke the color barrier—a turbulent period for the sport and the nation—but this isn't just a baseball history book. It is a book about a young man who enjoyed life's experiences to the fullest and played baseball.

Sportswriter Grantland Rice said it best in this verse, written 14 years before Neil Berry was born.

For when the One Great Scorer comes
To write against your name,
He marks not that you won or lost,
But how you played the Game

What follows is how Neil Berry—the shortstop from Kalamazoo—played the game.

When I was a little kid I could tell ya the exact spot where I was on Sundays. On Sundays . . . I went to church. The afternoon session was English, the rest were Dutch.

~ Neil Berry

1

The Early Years

Growing Up in Kalamazoo

1922 to 1929

Walter Street, in Kalamazoo, Michigan is only two blocks long, running between Lake Street to the south, and East Vine Street to the north. Today some businesses and few residential properties are located on the east side of the street. Railroad tracks run behind these properties, forming their east boundary. Upjohn Park, an eighteen-acre playground with a swimming pool; basketball, volleyball, and tennis courts; and softball and rugby fields, occupies the west side of Walter Street. During the decades of the 1920s and 30s, this predominantly Dutch residential area boasted five children named Cornelius living in the Upjohn Park neighborhood that included those two blocks of Walter Street. Cornelius Berry was one of them. His boyhood home still stands, a simple two-story, wood-frame house with a one-car garage. When the house was first occupied by the Berry family, and through much of the 1920s, there was a city dump across the street. Their backyard garden ended at the railroad tracks and the recurrent rumble of trains was part of the background noise of the Berry household.

Cornelius John Berry was born on January 11, 1922, in a house on John Street, in Kalamazoo. His great aunt Kate served as midwife, a common practice for the time. He was his mother's first child and, according to Neil, her favorite son. Neil's father, Hazen Berry, was an English/Irish widower with two children when he married Neil's mother, Lydia Brand in 1920. She was a Dutch girl, born in Holland, from a strict Dutch Christian upbringing. Those strict Dutch ways were only slightly relaxed

Two-year-old Neil Berry

Photo courtesy of Linda Spann

in the Berry household that included Neil's half-sister Alleen and half-brother Carl, seven and four respectively when Neil was born. Sister, Joyce (1925), brother, Gordon (1928), and a sister, Marilyn (1932) eventually completed the Berry family. Neil's Dutch grandfather, Cornelius (Casey) Brand, a veteran of the Dutch army, was also part of the Berry household.

Neil Remembered, "When I was a little kid I could tell ya the exact spot where I was on Sundays. On Sundays, we had to sit on the porch all day long, and I went to church. The First Christian Reformed Church, that's where I went to church. Went there at nine o'clock in the morning and stayed for Sunday school, came home about eleven, walked home because we were that close; went there at two o'clock in the afternoon, came home, went there again at seven o'clock at night—every Sunday. The afternoon session was English, the rest were Dutch."

Neal and his younger siblings were born into a rapidly changing world. The decade that followed World War I brought widespread prosperity and progress to a nation that was ready to return to what President Warren G. Harding called "normalcy." Harding asserted, "America's present need is not heroics but healing; not nostrums but normalcy; not revolution but restoration."

When Harding took office in 1921, the nation was in the midst of a postwar recession but by late 1922, the economic

13. SOUTH BURDICK STREET, KALAMAZOO, MICH.

outlook was improving. Unemployment was trimmed from its 1921 high of 12% to an average of 3.3% for the remainder of the decade. Wages, profits, and productivity all made significant gains during the 1920s and tax cuts actually increased the money flowing into the U.S. treasury.

The decade known as the Roaring Twenties was marked by a general good feeling and also breaks with tradition. Young women, known as flappers, wore short skirts, bobbed their hair, and flaunted their disdain for acceptable behavior, while jazz and dancing rose in popularity. The decade was also a time of American ingenuity and modernization. The mass production of the motor car invigorated other industries with highway construction, rubber, steel, and building, all prospering and a prosperous America needed roads built, and hotels erected to accommodate the newly mobile American tourist.

In 1922, President Harding proclaimed that America was in the age of the "motor car," which "reflects our standard of living and gauges the speed of our present-day life."

The industries in the city of Kalamazoo and surrounding areas participated in the growth, and their employees

CELERY FIELDS, KALAMAZOO, MICH.—"THE CELERY CITY"

shared in the prosperity that came with it. Most, in and around Kalamazoo, who wanted to work were employed during this time. With a growing family to support, Hazen Berry wanted to work and found employment in paper manufacturing, Kalamazoo's largest industry.

Kalamazoo was known as the Celery City because the crop grew so well in the muck of the surrounding floodplains, but it was also called the Paper City because paper making was the economic backbone of Kalamazoo in the first half of the

Machine Room, Mill No. 2 of the Kalamazoo Vegetable Parchment Company, Parchment, Kalamazoo, Michigan

twentieth century. The twenties was a decade of substantial growth by the paper industry, with increased demand for established paper products, and new demand for specialty paper cartons. During the decade the long-established Kalamazoo Paper Company and KVP (Kalamazoo Vegetable Parchment) added mills to meet the demand.

In 1925 Kalamazoo Paper was employing over a thousand workers, while the Bryant Paper Company was producing 75,000 tons of paper annually and employing 1,200 workers. The paper industry also saw the merger of the King Paper, Monarch Paper, and Bardeen Paper companies to form the Allied Paper Corporation in 1922. By 1925 Allied was shipping 2,725 boxcars of paper annually. Sutherland Paper Company, formed by brothers Louis and Frederick Sutherland in 1917, specialized in carton manufacturing. By 1925 it's folding box-board mill was turning out 2,000,000 cartons a day. In 1928 Sutherland acquired the Standard Paper Company, making Sutherland Paper one of the largest companies in the industry.

The strong paper industry in Kalamazoo resulted in a variety of paper related ventures that included paper users; Kalamazoo Stationery, Illinois Envelope, Kalamazoo Paper Box, and Kalamazoo Label. Other companies supplied chemicals, brushes, and other items necessary to support paper production.

Kalamazoo's form printing companies; Ihling Brothers Everard, and Doubleday Brothers and Company, also benefited from being located at the center of the paper industry.

Author's note: Doubleday Bros. was founded by the sons of Kalamazoo's Abner Doubleday who was a cousin of the Abner Doubleday who was, for a time, credited with being the originator of baseball in America.

Paper wasn't the only game in the diverse Kalamazoo economy of the 1920s. The Henderson-Ames Company supplied military uniforms during World War I and also manufactured regalia, costumes, and paraphernalia for fraternal organizations. The company's five-story factory occupied the corner of Michigan Avenue and N. Park Street.

By the mid-1920s, the Henderson-Ames Company was doing over a million dollars a year in business. Some of that business stayed close to home with a strong presence of fraternal organizations in Kalamazoo. A Kalamazoo Gazette survey in 1925 reported eighty-two fraternal, patriotic, and veteran orders in Kalamazoo, with a combined membership estimated to be between eighteen and twenty thousand.

In the 1890s Henderson-Ames owner, Frank Henderson,

built a Queen Anne style house on a West Main Hill location that his wife Mary had inherited. The ornate, 25-room Henderson Castle, with an excellent view of the city skyline, remains a Kalamazoo icon and is currently a bed and breakfast inn, fine dining restaurant, and wedding venue. During the decade the automobile almost completely replaced the horse and buggy on the streets of Kalamazoo. After becoming fully motorized, the Kalamazoo fire department sold their last horses in 1924. The more flexible motorbus led to the rapid decline of the city-to-city electric interurban lines and eventually rendered Kalamazoo's trolley cars obsolete.

The coming of the automobile doomed Kalamazoo's once prosperous carriage and buggy business, but automobile manufacturing in Kalamazoo did not take hold. Cars produced for a time in Kalamazoo include; The Cornelian, The Cannon Flyer, The Mighty Michigan, The Roamer, the Barley Special, and the Handley-Knight. All the companies behind these cars failed. The only exception was the success of Checker Cab Manufacturing which relocated from Chicago to Kalamazoo in 1923.

Several Kalamazoo based companies supported automobile production including Allen Electric and Equipment, Durametallic, Fuller Manufacturing, and the Limousine Body Company.

Kalamazoo Stove Company with its direct marketing approach, and famous, "A Kalamazoo direct to you" slogan was a major manufacturer and employer during the 1920s and beyond.

The Upjohn Company was establishing itself as a major industry in Kalamazoo during the 1920s with Phenolax wafers, a candied laxative, representing 20 percent of company revenue in 1924. Citrocarbonate, an effervescent salt, was first introduced in 1921 and also sold well. A cod-liver-oil vitamin product called Super D, was introduced in 1928, and was the first of many vitamin products that, along with their reputation for quality, would help fuel Upjohn's modest growth in the decade. The company's substantial growth would come later. During the 1920s and early 1930s the Upjohn Company employed fewer than 700 workers.

Among other Kalamazoo based industries operating in the 1920s — Gibson Guitar and Mandolin Company produced strung, fretted instruments; Eckrich and Sons processed meat; American Aggregate Corporation supplied rock for railway and highway construction, and Globe Construction Company built the highways.

With the return of City League baseball in 1924, many Kalamazoo businesses fielded teams and offered employment based solely on an applicant's baseball talent.

The land for the airport was purchased by the city in 1926 and by 1929 sixty tons of airmail a year were passing through the Kalamazoo airport. The Kalamazoo airport was the first municipal airport in Michigan, receiving Michigan Airport License No. 1 on December 14, 1929.

Amidst this decade of prosperity and growth, Neil Berry spent his early years oblivious to most of what was going on outside the sphere of his Walter Street home and Upjohn Park neighborhood. Young Neil had a nice blue tricycle that he would ride on the sidewalk in front of his house and sometimes he would greet neighbors who happened by. One of Neil's early childhood memories is when he did just that.

As Neil told it, "Where I lived, down the street was a real nice, elderly, black couple who you didn't even know they lived there, that's how quiet they were. I don't know if his name was George or not, but he would go by our house and walk down to 3rd Street to a little green icehouse, to get 50 lbs of ice in his wheelbarrow to take home and put in his icebox. So one day I'm riding [my tricycle] in front of our house on the sidewalk and down the street comes the colored guy with his wheelbarrow. I was right in front of our house and I don't know if he said something to me first or not, but I looked up at him and said, 'Hello nice n_ _ _ _r [n-word] man.' Well, he set his wheelbarrow down and was going to say something to me and I thought, 'Oh God, here he comes after me!' I fell off that bike more or less, and I tried to run but our driveway was gravel. I musta fell down 15 times in the gravel before I got to the back of the house. I'd run a few steps then see [in my mind] that big colored guy right on my butt, but he wasn't after me, he never moved. I was throwing cinders and stones all around, tryin' to run, half screamin', half cryin'. My mother thought someone was going to kill me, 'What's the matter! What's the matter!' I told her and she said, 'You should never say that.' So she went out to see him. I was scared to death, wouldn't come out. That scared the livin' poop out of me, but I thought I was bein' nice when I said it."

Author's note: Neil learned his lesson that day. The only time I've heard Neil use the n-word during two and a half years of weekly discussions is when he told that story or stories where others used the word and it was pertinent to the story.

Neil's dad took him fishing and hunting even before Neil was old enough to own his own gun. Neil recalled, "When I was real little, when my dad took me squirrel hunting, he was using me as a dog, 'Go around that bush and shake it . . . go around that tree and make some noise'"

Little Neil proved to be reasonably successful at flushing out squirrels for his dad's shotgun.

Kalamazoo schools completed extensive school construction projects during the decade, building Parkwood in 1921; Lincoln in 1922; Washington in 1923; Burdick Street, Hillcrest, and McKinley in 1924; a new Central High School in 1923-24, and Wilson in 1929. Schools that weren't replaced, were improved with additions. Parochial schools also grew during this prosperous time with four rooms added to the John Street School (later renamed Ebenezer Christian School), and the cornerstone of St. Augustine High School laid on August 30, 1925.

Neil started school a year early in 1926, when he was four years old, so most of his classmates were a year or more older. He attended Lake Street Elementary while many of his Dutch friends in the neighborhood attended the Ebenezer Christian School. Neil was on the small side and some winter afternoons when he walked home from kindergarten, the snow piled up along the path home by the railroad tracks was higher than he was.

Neil recalled the circumstances surrounding one of his elementary school pictures, "They used to take school pictures in the class that didn't mean anything, gym class. Well that particular day, my friends and I played a game with a rope where you [tied] it in back of your belt, and you'd run, and the guys would pull you back, just playin' horse. Well just before they blew the whistle to take the team picture, we were doin' that and a guy jerked the rope and broke my belt. My pants came down. I'm taking that picture and everybody wonders why my hands are in my pockets like this, with my legs folded like this, trying to look suave. That was a tragedy. There I sat like a little peacock, they didn't know my pants would come down if I stood up."

Neil's favorite classes were gym class and recess, but he also liked music and art class.

"Miss Pritchard had one of those silver dresses, made out of metal, she looked just like a big canary. Her face had a little pinky nose. I liked her [music] class.

"My art teacher's name was Artis, that was her last name. Well, we had to make a drawing and a painting, water paint, of whatever. So she says, 'Now if you could take your geography work and think of a country, you could make a picture from that country.' So I say, 'Okay, I'm going with Mexico and I'm gonna have a guy sell a sombrero to somebody in a store.' So I [draw] the guy behind the counter, and stacks of sombreros and this guy was standin' there buyin' one.

"By God they put it in the art museum downtown, it was there for a long time. Sombreros were easy to draw."

In the summer the dump on the west side of Walter Street was a popular playground for Neil and the other neighborhood boys. Saturday would bring trucks loaded with junk and treasures to the dump for their exploration. Neil's mother was lucky to get shoes on him before he got out the door to play and explore on summer mornings.

Sports were very popular in Kalamazoo in the 1920s. Baseball fans rooted for their favorite local teams and also followed the Detroit Tigers and/or the Chicago Cubs.

The Detroit Tigers replaced manager Hughie Jennings with their star player, the Georgia Peach, Ty Cobb in 1921.

Also starring for the Tigers in the 1920s was right fielder Harry Heilmann. The right-handed hitting Heilman beat out his manager for the 1921 American League batting title with a .394 average (Cobb was second at .389). Heilmann credited Cobb's mentoring for his improved hitting. He won three more batting championships during the decade, also winning honors in 1923, 1925 and 1927.

Ty Cobb had his greatest offensive day on May 5, 1925, at Sportsman's Park in St. Louis with three home runs, a double, and two singles in his six plate appearances. His sixteen total bases set a modern-day record. Cobb hit two more home runs the next day. His five home runs in two days also set a record, surpassing Babe Ruth and two others, and moved Cobb past Honus Wagner for the all-time record for extra-base hits. Ty Cobb retired after 24 seasons following the 1928 season with an all-time best career batting average of .366.

Twenty years and another World War later, a 5 ft-10 inch, 168 lb. shortstop from Kalamazoo, Michigan's Upjohn Park neighborhood, would play in an American League contest with historical implications on the last day of the 1948 baseball season.

Western State Teachers College (today's Western Michigan University) was undefeated and unscored upon in their 1922 football campaign under the direction of coach

Milton Olander. Coach Judson Hyames started a tradition of baseball excellence at Western in the twenties that carried on for decades and "Buck" Read did the same for basketball.

In the 1921-22 collegiate seasons Kalamazoo College won Michigan Intercollegiate Athletic Association championships in football, basketball, baseball, tennis, and track.

The Gateway golf course, Kalamazoo's first municipal course, opened in 1924 and forty acres were added to Milham Park for a golf course in 1927, that same year a zoo was opened at the park with two buffaloes donated by William P. Engelman.

In 1921 the city built supervised playgrounds for the summer months and the first baseball diamond was laid out at Upjohn Park. Eleven city blocks would be added to Upjohn Park during the decade and in the late '20s, the city started filling in the dump and a nearby pond. Soon they would build the athletic fields that would also become popular playgrounds for Neil and the neighborhood boys.

Kalamazoo Central High had outstanding football and basketball teams in the early '20s, led by coach Jim Fleugel. Some of the outstanding prep athletes from Central in that era included Fred Spurgeon, Glen Righter, John Westgate, Merle Baker, and Louie Gilbert to name a few. Central suffered through some down years in football in 1924, 1925, and 1926 when they only won four games in those three years. Their four-win, five loss, season of 1927 was "perhaps one of the most successful that Central has had in a good many seasons," according to *The Delphian*, Central's yearbook.

Neil Berry was six years old when Kalamazoo Public Schools hired Eugene "Gene" Thomas as a Social Science teacher and varsity football and basketball coach in 1928. Thomas was only 28 years old but had already coached the Marion, Indiana basketball team to its first state title in 1926. An outstanding prep athlete, Thomas had been recruited by

Knute Rockne to play at Notre Dame but declined in favor of Indiana University and became the Hoosiers' only four-sport letterman (football, baseball, basketball, and track) during his 1920 to 1923 college career. After college Thomas became the athletic director and coached in Marion, Indiana. Thomas had turned down Knute Rockne's offer to play at Notre Dame but the two remained friends and it was rumored that Rockne sent a letter of recommendation to the Kalamazoo schools when Thomas applied for the open teaching and coaching position.

Kalamazoo Central hired Coach Thomas and he brought the single-wing offense to Central football, Upjohn field, and the watchful eyes of a young Neil Berry.

We had a whole neighborhood of Tom Sawyers.

~ Neil Berry

2

The Juvenile Years

From Tom Sawyer to Organized Sports

1930 to 1935

As the decade of the 20s came to an end so did the prosperity and growth. The October 1929 crash of the New York stock market was the initiating factor in what would become the new normalcy of the great depression of the 1930s.

The Henderson-Ames Company was one of the local companies hard hit by the depression. With a significant drop off in demand, the company merged with the Lilley Company of Columbus, Ohio, another regalia firm, in 1933. Shortly after the merger, the Lilley-Ames Company moved the Kalamazoo operation and associated jobs to Ohio.

With business failures and family breadwinners out of work, city relief costs skyrocketed in 1931 to $188,000, up from $50,000 in 1930. The relief was provided through work, with every able-bodied man on assistance required to work for the city. Only 4% of the city budget went to relief in 1928, but by 1932 the relief effort took 32% of the budget. In 1932 a total of 3,218 families, representing 11,840 individuals, needed assistance. This was over 20% of the city of Kalamazoo's population.

Coach Mike Gary led Western State Teachers College to another undefeated football season in 1932 providing a welcome diversion for sports fans in the city. But in 1933 Western State was having trouble meeting payroll and Governor William Comstock considered closing the school. Only intense lobbying by Western President Dwight Waldo and his assistant (and eventual successor) Paul Sangren kept the school open.

In 1933 the federal government started a work program called the Civil Works Administration (CWA) which provided work for 2,500 men in Kalamazoo.

The city was able to complete major improvement projects during the depression years thanks to the federal government work programs and the city's own contributions.

Projects included street repairs and removal of obsolete trolley car tracks; building stone gutters, sewer additions, and sidewalks; and park improvements, including completion of an eighteen hole golf course at Milham Park. Major projects included the addition of runways at the airport and a new county building.

Money was tight during the depression years. Neil remembered, "The people next door had six or seven kids, none of them played any sports but they all became good carpenters. The old man was a carpenter and during the depression, he used to build boats, wooden boats. He built one a week and he'd sell 'em for like fifteen bucks, twenty bucks. All brass screws, I remember, just a wooden eight foot, ten foot boat, no oars, just the boat. That's the only thing he did on the side. I don't know if he worked for a company or worked on his own. A lot of those old guys were so damn ornery, those Dutchmen, they wanted to be independent, they didn't like to work for people.

"My mother couldn't understand why people, during the depression, they had to go to a parochial school, they had to pay tuition. Why they did that when right down the street was a public school. They went to a Dutch school, Ebenezer."

The paper industry remained strong and helped bring Kalamazoo through the depression years. Most paper workers kept their jobs and were able to work at least four days a week. In this respect the Berry household was luckier than many of the other neighborhood families—Neil's father, Hazen, worked for the Sutherland Paper Company and remained employed throughout the depression.

Neil recalled, "[My father] told me one time that he had a chance to go to Elkhart, Indiana, to a diesel school. Diesel had just scratched the surface and he had a chance to go to a diesel school, [but] he had a pretty good job at the paper mill and he didn't want to give that up because the depression was starting to come on. So he had that [job] and it was steady, never missed a day during the depression, never. Never missed a day and worked all the time. Didn't make the big bucks but we always had decent clothes, clean clothes, plenty of food, we didn't have to wear hand-me-downs or anything like that. He did a good job that way."

The Berry kids had dogs while growing up. Some fared better than others.

As Neil told it, "Over at the mill one day some guy brought a box with four or five pups, hounds, Heinz-57 variety, and my dad brought one home. He was a little brown one, so we called him Brownie. He was a good dog, grew up a good hunter, a good dog for us kids. [Later on] he got hit by a car, didn't hurt him, just rolled him over a few times, and then kids down the street started shooting him with a Beebee gun. So my dad said he was getting a little old and I know a guy that would really like to have him down on the farm, so we gave him to a farmer, it was great, the dog loved it.

"Then my sister had a dog and I killed him. Accidentally. A little tiny dog, a cocker spaniel. Well around the fourth [of July] we used to be able to get pretty good firecrackers. I was sitting on my back steps and the dog was behind me. I lit it and threw it out there, and the dog did like dogs do. He saw me throw it and he ran out, ran out and got to it, and it went 'boom!' Just like that he ran and banged into the garage, went back and banged into the garage again, and he kept banging himself into the side of the garage until he died. He killed himself. It almost killed my sister.

"When I got a little older I read in the paper, a guy had an ad in the paper, 'Cocker Spaniel, five bucks, come take your pick.' It was cold this time of year but on Saturday I took my bicycle [with one of my buddies] and we rode from here almost to Paw Paw [on an abandoned interurban line]. Colder than heck, pulled into the farmyard, 'you got dogs for sale?' He took me out to the barn and he had four or five of 'em in a pen. 'Take your pick.' So I took a little guy. I had a suede jacket on, and I zipped it down, put my dog in there, zipped it up, and rode him home. So that was my sister's dog. I had to give it to her 'cause I killed the other one."

During the 1920s and '30s, sports were very popular in Kalamazoo but not so much in the Berry family. Neil became interested in sports as a youngster because Kalamazoo Central High School's football team, the Maroons (later called the Maroon Giants), practiced and played at the newly constructed Upjohn field, right across the street from his house.

As Neil told it, "I was born and raised, you might say, on an athletic field. Down there, there were two baseball fields, one of them—when I was a little kid—was right in my backyard and the best teams in Kalamazoo played there. So I was a spectator, as I grew up the thing that awed me was sports. Sports—and right across was a football field— Kalamazoo Central practiced from here to the road from me, for all my life when I was a little kid. St. Augustine's practiced just across the creek right there too, so the whole thing was sports."

The Berry family owned a radio for indoor entertainment, as did most families in the time before television revolutionized home entertainment. For Neil growing up, that indoor entertainment was Chicago Cubs baseball, one of the first teams to broadcast all their home games. Neil would grab a pillow off the couch and curl up next to the furniture sized radio and listen to Cubs announcer Bob Elson's play-by-play.

"It used to be when I was younger, the Cubs were almost like a hometown team here. Billy Jurges was my baseball hero because—in those days—the only contact you had with professional sports was the Chicago Cubs. Detroit didn't announce their games on the radio. The Cubs announced every one, everyday the Chicago Cubs. Their shortstop at the time was Billy Jurges. I never saw Billy Jurges in my life but he was their shortstop. They used to describe him— little Billy Jurges—he did this and he did that.

"[The Cubs] had Jurges to Herman to Grimm—that was their double-play combo—and Woody English played third base, that was their infield. Gabby Hartnett caught. They had [Pitchers Lon] Warneke and Pat Malone, and Kiki Cyler and Hack Wilson in the outfield, but Jurges was my hero."

Billy Jurges started his professional career as an outfielder with the Newark Bears in 1927. He was sent to the Manchester Blue Sox of the New England League where he was converted to a shortstop. After hitting .332 in 1929 he was signed by the Chicago Cubs.

Jurges made it to the majors with the Cubs in 1931 at the age of 23 and played 88 games. In 1932 Jurges became the Cubs regular shortstop and raised his batting average from .201 in his rookie campaign to .253 his second year.

At ten years old, Neil may not have missed his baseball

hero during a 17 day stretch in July 1932, but if he did he likely wasn't privy to the reason he was out of the lineup.

On July 6, 1932, Violet Popovich Valli, a pretty brunette showgirl entered the Hotel Carlos (now the Sheffield House) a few blocks north of Wrigley Field and called Jurges from the front desk. Jurges had recently dated Valli and when he came down to the lobby the scorned woman fired three shots from her .25-caliber pistol hitting Jurges in the little finger of his left hand, and then in a rib with a bullet that ricocheted out his right shoulder. Valli shot herself in the arm with the third shot. Billy Jurges—not seriously hurt—didn't press charges.

The incident—and a similar incident involving Eddie Waitkus in 1947—likely provided inspiration for Bernard Malamud's 1952 novel The Natural, the basis for the classic 1984 baseball movie that starred Robert Redford as Roy Hobbs. It took the fictional Hobbs 16 years to return to professional baseball. It took Billy Jurges 16 games.

Jurges teamed with future Hall of Famer (1975) Billy Herman, to form the double-play combo that led Cubs teams to three World Series appearances in the 1930s. In the 1935 series against Detroit, Jurges set a record for putouts by a shortstop in a six-game series, with 16.

Jurges was traded to the New York Giants after the 1938 season and spent seven seasons with the Giants before completing his playing days back with the Cubs in 1946 and 1947. Jurges was a three-time National League All-Star (1937, 1939, 1940) during his career.

He coached for the Cubs in 1948 but rejected an offer to coach the Cincinnati Reds in 1949, choosing instead to accept a position with A.G. Spalding and Brothers.

During Billy Jurges' days with the Chicago Cubs young Neil could only visualize his shortstop play based on the play-by-play descriptions from the family radio, but Jurges was the baseball hero Neil tried to emulate when he was on the ball diamond.

Neil also listened to Detroit Tiger games on WKZO when Harry Heilman started broadcasting games in 1934. Tiger stars from that era included Hammerin' Hank Greenberg at first base, Charlie Gehringer—The Mechanical Man—at second base, catcher Mickey Cochrane, catcher/first baseman Rudy York, outfielder Goose Goslin and pitcher Schoolboy Rowe.

Neil recalled, "My grampa, he got mad because we spent all our time listening to the radio—until I started playin' [Legion ball]. Then you couldn't walk through the room when Hank Greenberg or Rudy York or one of those guys was up to bat. You couldn't even move because he had his ear right up to the radio. He started to like baseball and the radio was all you had."

Without realizing it Neil Berry began preparing for his sports career very early. Neil and his neighborhood peers were always throwing something at something, in all sorts of impromptu competitions.

As Neil told it, "When I was a little guy, the big guys used to have snowball fights. That's when I was seven or eight and they were twelve, the big guys. They used to want me on their side 'cause I could throw good, even though I was younger. I could make a good snowball and I could really throw. What we used to do was choose up sides and have some real battles, snow battles, and they always wanted me on their side."

When snowballs weren't in the forecast, Neil and his Upjohn Park friends came up with other things to throw, and other targets.

"When we were kids—not only me but six or seven of my friends—hell, we could throw within a limited area. It was no big deal, boom, throw the thing. We'd throw at birds, throw at bottles, we'd throw every day.

"We even threw at the brakeman when tomatoes got good

in the garden. You'd get a bunch of them that are green but aren't real good tomatoes. Those guys used to come by and they slowed down when they came down the tracks from Milham Park. It's downhill. Downhill all the way downtown and the train would make a big long curve to the east. They would be slowing down to make that curve and the brakeman would be on top of the car, you'd see him walking on top of the cars, he was a sucker. We had tomatoes from the garden, 'here he comes!' We'd be kinda ducking there and we'd throw tomatoes at the brakeman up there.

"Later on, a guy that used to be a brakeman worked with a guy on the east side, up on East Main hill. His name was Green, he managed a little baseball team for a grocery store. This guy that worked on the railroad, retired and became one of his coaches. When we were in the [American] Legion Blues, not the Maroons, [you're in] the Blues when you're ten, eleven years old, he found out where we lived . . . 'You little bastards,' he said 'you're the ones who used to throw tomatoes at me when I worked for the railroad. When we used to go from Lake Street to Vine Street down through there, there was always some young kids out there throwing snowballs or tomatoes while we were up on top of the car.'

"'That's us.' He remembered that and so did we.

"But anyway, throwing, throwing, throwing—that's what I wanted to get at."

Neil and his neighborhood gang didn't limit their throwing to rocks, snowballs, and tomatoes, they were also throwing and kicking footballs, or throwing and batting baseballs. They would emulate what the older kids were doing on Upjohn field—when they could get their hands on the equipment.

Neil recalled, "At Central's practice, the coach would let us kids throw and kick footballs off to one side as long as we didn't get in the way. Well, a football would end up in the bushes, we'd hide it in the bushes, and when the student manager collected the footballs, he never found that one.

So after they all went in, took their showers and went home, we'd go get the ball and we had a football. We never used to steal a brand new one, 'Don't get a new one, but don't get an old one either. Get a pretty good one,' we'd say, and we'd end up with a pretty good football.

"We did the same thing with baseball bats. When the guys played baseball we'd try to sneak their bats. I've seen a kid sitting on the bench dig a hole with his heel, way down at the end of the bench where nobody could see what he was doing, he'd dig a hole. Pretty soon it was big enough you could lay a bat in there and cover it up with dirt. End of the game, 'got all the bats?' They'd look around, 'yeah, okay,' and they'd take off in their cars.

"Then there were cracked bats, we'd see how bad they were cracked. If it was just a crack but still together we knew we could put some screws in, wrap it with tape, and use it.

"Balls were plentiful, we had so many ways to get baseballs. We even had the dog, Major. The Stoups family had this big dog, he was part Great Dane and part something else, but he was big. His name was Major and they trained Major to go get balls. He was behind the backstop, laid right behind the backstop down there. That backstop was [practically] in their backyard. That baseball field was in their backyard like the other one was in my front yard. I was on Walter Street, they were on John Street, we had the place surrounded. Anyway Major would go over and lay behind the backstop and when there was a foul ball . . . well you're not going to beat a dog to the ball. He'd go get the ball and run home. They had a basket on the front porch and he'd drop the ball in the basket, and go back and lay behind the backstop, and do it again."

During the depression years the neighborhood kids would do what they had to do to keep themselves entertained with little or no money. During the summer months the elementary schools showed free movies during the week, probably to keep the kids out of mischief and to give the parents a weeknight break. Neal recalled that "they had a popcorn wagon that always came to get the kids money but we'd sit there and watch, one of 'em was 'The Wolfman.' Others were just cheap cowboy shows and always a serial to keep you coming back. A guy'd fall off a cliff and when he's halfway down, the end, [to be] continued."

When they did have a little money they would sometimes pool it and rent gym time from the YMCA. Ten or fifteen cents each would buy them a couple of hours of basketball.

Neil would get what little money he needed from his mother, twenty-five cents would get him into a matinee at the Capitol Theater on South Street, or the much newer State Theater on the corner of Burdick and Lovell. Neil didn't have to work, but his father did assign him one regular chore. According to Neil, "the only thing he ever said to do was make sure you clean the ashes out of the furnace, that's the only thing I ever had to do."

Neil did take a spur-of-the-moment job in the summer of 1936, when he was 14.

As Neil told it, "A pretty good-sized store burnt down in Kalamazoo. On the corner of Walter Street and Vine Street, there was a house there, and a guy by the name of Homer Leland lived there. Behind Homer Leland's house, going towards Portage, was a big empty lot, nothing there. And the first house on the other side of the empty lot, a girl lived there, her name was Ester Corstange, and she had a brother named Louie. Well, when this store burnt downtown they took big dump truck loads of red brick and dumped 'em there in piles. The whole field was full. Someone said, 'hey, you wanna make some money?' I said, 'How's that?' . . . 'You can go over there and pile those bricks up.'

"So me and my friend from next door, Bennie Terpstra, we went over there and Ester Corstange, she was 16 years old, she was boss. Some guy came down from whoever dumped the bricks and told her, 'you be the boss, keep those kids workin'.'

"I think you got 50 cents a thousand or something like that, but you had to put them in a nice pile and the bricks couldn't have any mortar on 'em. We all got a hammer, we could all sneak a hammer from home, knock it off, pile 'em up, this way, then this way, then this way until you got a thousand. There musta been 15 of us there doin' this.

"What [Bennie and I] did, when a new load came in, we picked all the ones that didn't have any mortar on 'em. We didn't have to pound that way, just pile 'em up. The other guys were sayin', 'you can't do that, you have to take 'em as they come.' [We yelled back] 'Okay,' then we'd turn around and [keep getting] the ones without mortar on 'em. We'd get a fifty-cent pile here, fifty cents there, another fifty cents. We were millionaires.

"That afternoon, we started in the morning, that afternoon about three o'clock here comes a guy in a shiny car with a seal on the side says, 'State of Michigan.'

"[He said] 'who's the boss?' [Someone said] 'Ester Corstange.'

"[He said to her] 'Do you know how old these kids are?' She says, 'no, why?'

"[He asks] 'how old are you?' She tells him. [Then he tells us], 'None of you are allowed to work.' [We were] too young. Didn't pay us a lick. That was the one day I worked."

Other than his one day boyhood career, summer days would find Neil at Upjohn Park competing in whatever impromptu game was being played. When the neighborhood kids played a tag game they called "dart-ass," Neil was always the hardest one to tag, artfully dodging most attempts. He seemed to be a natural at all the games he and his friends would dream up, easily out jumping, out running, or out throwing his competition.

"We'd play games, run, run, run until it got dark. All day, every day. There was one, 'Hunt the Gray' I guess it was, probably down south they called it, 'Hunt the Blue,' but we'd hunt the gray. [It was] a derivative from the civil war, that's why they called it that. Anyway you'd line up, choose up sides, then see who could capture the most from the other side."

Neil's older, half-brother Carl would spend much of his summer at his aunt's house in Climax where he was raised before his father remarried and moved the family to Kalamazoo. But when Carl was home on weekends he would join in the fun.

"There was a guy, lived two houses down, a Dutch guy, lived all by himself. Well . . . he had a barn, a big red country barn, which was good because we used the side of it to throw balls at. We'd throw tennis balls and use the barn as a backstop. Anyway, he went from his house to the corner of the barn with a fence, metal fence, not chicken wire, fence with about four-inch squares. The only thing he had was a stake post in between [the house and the garage]. It was about five feet high. He put it up during the week and my brother didn't know that fence was there.

"It got dark and he went flyin' around the corner of that house, he hits that fence . . . geez. Like keystone cops, he hit that fence and flew back, knocked him on his butt. 'Why didn't you tell me that fence was there?' he said.

"We said, 'What, we're gonna advertise Al Klempt's fence?'

"We always said it was a lucky thing he didn't hit where the post was."

On summer nights after dinner, Neil and the six or eight neighborhood kids he hung out with on a regular basis, would meet at Upjohn Park and decide what adventure to tackle that night.

"In our neighborhood down there, it was in the city, fine, but it was fairly agricultural. Down Belmont Street, back in there, and down further, [there was] muck [with] pansies, celery, and berries. A lot of people had plum trees, apple trees, it was kind of rural that way.

"We had a whole neighborhood of Tom Sawyers, but they were all good. We never did anything that hurt anybody, really. We never stole anything that really counted, we stole a lot of fruit, vegetables, stuff like that. We had plenty of diversions there at night . . .

"I got cut one night stealing watermelon. I got my arm cut on the barbwire fence because I had a watermelon under each arm and I wasn't going to drop 'em. The right elbow is where the barb wire caught me, the scar's still there.

"Over on Hays Park, Washington Square area, they all get to their houses from the back alley. Well, you go down that back alley, they can't see you from the house. They have their garage between their house and you. If they had a good apple tree, plum tree, or something you'd sneak around the garage and jump over a little fence. There it is and they couldn't even see you. We used to go over there quite a bit, had some easy pickin'."

The picking wasn't always that easy, but that just created a challenge that needed a creative approach to their fruit tree larceny. Neil and two accomplices had their eye on a prime, but seemingly inaccessible, plum tree in a yard that backed up to Portage Creek.

Neil recalled, "The little creek, Portage Creek, and Lime Creek met at a point down in Upjohn Park, that's where it intersected, then it went toward Vine Street. From there on it was dominated by the lime [from the paper mills] so you didn't want to get in there."

The boys were smart enough not to wade in paper waste and clever enough to build a raft using salvaged and, no doubt, 'borrowed' lumber.

"So we built that raft. When you go under Vine Street there was only yeah-much room (Neil indicates yeah-much). You had to lay down on the raft to get under and you could look underneath and there was a bunch of re-rod hanging down through the cement. Just as you get underneath on the creek, the first house, that guy had a fence along his house right down to the creek so you couldn't get in there. But on the raft, you could go around that fence and pull up to his backyard. There was a plum tree that hung over the creek a little bit. We had it made. We had three guys and we had some big bags. We anchored that baby under that tree and unloaded those plums."

Sometimes forbidden fruit comes with unforeseen consequences.

"Boy were they good. We sat and ate 'em because we stole 'em. We had to get rid of 'em, we didn't want to throw them away, so we ate them. And when you do that you eat 'em all of course, but he sprayed them and we didn't wipe the spray off. Well, the next morning I was sicker than a dog, my mother didn't know what the scoop was."

Neil and his fellow Tom Sawyers would also climb trees. When they needed the just right, Y shaped, branch for a new beanie crotch (slingshot handle), they would simply cut it out of a tree, anybody's tree. The local filling station would supply the junk inner tube to slice up for the beanie rocket firing straps, and rebar mill ends or rocks from the railroad bed worked well as projectiles. Empty cans and bottles were handy targets for beanie rocket shooting competitions.

"We'd sneak out, just before it got dark at night, take a saw . . . right down the street in Mrs. Yonkers front yard, I sawed a beanie crotch and a hockey stick out of her tree. She got mad. I don't blame her."

The boys would also keep that football they 'found' in the bushes in good repair.

"It wasn't too kosher but we did it, we'd steal little things like those things you screw on your football. There was a little metal thing that you would screw on top of your valve stem, it would be flush with the football. Well, they'd work loose kickin', passin', bouncin' the football, and you'd lose that thing. Then your valve, like on a bicycle, it was exposed and didn't work too good. So the guys would go to Sears Roebuck or Montgomery Ward, or someplace like that on a Saturday morning when it was fairly crowded, and they'd screw one of those things out of a football and put it in their mouth or put it in their pocket. We'd get outside, 'Did anybody get one?' 'Yeah.' That's all we wanted, we didn't want to rob the place, we just wanted a new valve cover for our football."

Neil's organized sports career got started in 1933 at Vine Junior High, but not without some early trepidation. After attending Lake Street Elementary with many of his neighborhood friends, Neil discovered that his friends would be attending Washington Junior High but he had been assigned to Vine. The railroad tracks behind his house were the dividing line. Only Neil and two girls he knew from the neighborhood went to Vine, because they lived west of the tracks. His friends that lived east of the tracks attended Washington.

Neil reflected, "That was one of the biggest disappointments of my life. I didn't know anybody at Vine. Well, it all worked out."

When Neil started seventh grade at Vine Junior High, he began to focus his talents on the traditional organized team sports; touch football, basketball, and baseball. Kalamazoo had recently started a touch football program at the junior highs and Neil took his playground game prowess to the football field. Neil was just as hard to catch when he was running with a football as he was when he played dart-ass with his Upjohn Park friends.

Throwing all those snowballs; all those rocks; all those footballs and baseballs, constantly throwing something at something, helped Neil separate himself from his peers.

As Neil told it, "As I grew up I could throw better than 70, 80% of the guys and as I got into Junior High School, I would say I had the best arm in my class. Never tested it but from what I could see, you know, just throwing, I could throw better than the rest of the kids."

Neil recalled getting serious about sports, "I think it started about the seventh grade because that's where it's more organized. They had a coach that was hired as a coach. He had the seventh, eighth, and ninth grades. There you had regular teams. If you were good enough to make the school team in the seventh grade, you played. But usually not, most of the players in junior high were ninth graders, but you were on the team and practiced every day. It was organized.

"I got so engrossed, absorbed, by the dawgone games . . . I remember looking out the glass at Vine Junior High School, the whole back of the building is glass, and you can sit there and look out at the playground. We had games on Tuesdays and Fridays and it'd be eleven o'clock in the morning, I'd be looking up at the window [and thinking], 'God, it's gettin' dark. I hope it doesn't rain.' I got mad when it rained.

"Then later on when I played American Legion ball, you played that in the summertime, but you played at night, start out about 5:30, and if it's raining . . . it was a kick in the butt to get rained out. I looked forward [to the games] so much that I started being a weatherman."

By his own admission, Neil wasn't too interested in girls in Junior High, he was too busy playing sports. Then he spotted a girl who was "a cute little dickens," at one of his baseball games. In Junior High, a sporting event was the only place Neil was likely to run into Gloria Lorentzen.

As Neil told it, "I found out that [Gloria] came to as many games as I did. Every time we played she was there and I said, 'gee, that little girl is kinda interested in sports.' She had a good girlfriend that used to come with her. I really met her, kinda broke the ice, by accident. I went for a pop fly foul and she was standing behind third base, or on the outside of third base, and I was just lookin up for the foul ball, and she was lookin up, and I was running as fast as I could go, and I hit her going full tilt. I knocked her six or eight feet. I don't remember if I caught the ball or not, but anyway, I picked her up and that kinda, you know, 'So that's who you are.'"

Some of Neil's neighborhood friends, also good athletes, didn't get the opportunity to play organized sports. They attended the Dutch Christian parochial school and stopped going to school in the eighth or ninth grade so they could go to work. Some also worked before and after school, but Neil was never pressed by his father to work after school, allowing him to play the sports he loved.

"When [Central's football team] went home we'd practice punting, we'd practice passing, imitate this, imitate that [on Upjohn field]. We'd get the football and practice the Jay Berwanger pose, oh geez, guys that were tackles wanted to go out for a pass, and they'd catch it and go . . . (Neil indicates the Berwanger pose)."

Jay Berwanger, the Flying Dutchman of Dubuque, played football for the University of Chicago and was the first recipient of the Heisman Trophy in 1935. The trophy, awarded by New York City's Downtown Athletic Club to recognize the best college football player east of the Mississippi River, was called the DAC Trophy that first year. In 1936 the award was renamed the Heisman Trophy in honor of the club's athletic director who had passed away that year. The Downtown Athletic Club also started considering players from west of the Mississippi for their newly named prize in 1936. Jay Berwanger is the only winner of the DAC/Heisman Trophy to never play professional football.

When he wasn't playing sports himself, watching practices and games was a convenient pastime for Neil, and he held the local stars in high esteem.

"You kind of build up an admiration for the guys who were playing, you know. You could find out that, hey he's a hero in our neighborhood because he played for Central . . . a few of them went on to college, played for Western or Michigan or something like that.

"My biggest star when I was a young kid was a guy named Perk, Lyle Perk. He was the only guy, I'm pretty sure, the only guy that ever played in the ninth grade as a starting football player at Central. And I remember seeing him as a little kid, I thought he was a monster, a big sized guy and one of the first guys to have a butch haircut, really short. A big strong kid and I thought, 'whew,' that's really something to be in the ninth grade and playing on the varsity."

Some of Neil's other early heroes included Herman Everhardus, an All-city End in 1928, and an All-city Halfback in '29. Everhardus, nicknamed the 'Flying Dutchman,' went on to star at Michigan. Herman's brother, Chris Everhardus, was an All-city quarterback in 1932. Paul VanKeuran was an All-city fullback in 1931 and Harold Shank was an All-city center three years in a row, 1931, '32, and '33.

So it was inevitable that Cornelius John Berry, the small but athletically inclined Irish/Dutch boy from the Upjohn Park neighborhood, would play high school football and American Legion baseball. He would excel in both sports and go on to become Kalamazoo's premier prep athlete of the 1930s and one of Southwest Michigan's all-time greats.

They gave me a uniform—the helmet was so big
that if I go like this I'd be looking out the ear hole.

~ Neil Berry

3

A Star is Born

Kalamazoo Central High School

1936 to 1937

By the later part of the 1930s, Kalamazoo was working its way through and out of the depression. Papermaker Sutherland had added a building and started making paper cups in 1935, and KVP (Kalamazoo Vegetable Parchment) brought a new, million-dollar paper mill online in 1938. The Kalamazoo Stove Company remained strong throughout the '30s and was producing 100,000 stoves and employing 2,700 workers in 1937. That same year Kalamazoo paid off its last bond installment and became the only debt-free city of its size in the nation.

The city of Kalamazoo probably didn't have Neil Berry and Upjohn Park's gang of "Tom Sawyers" in mind when they built the juvenile detention home on Gull Road in 1937, by that time Neil was in high school and the only thing he was stealing was local headlines in the sports pages of the Kalamazoo Gazette.

Early on, Neil's sweetheart, Gloria Lorentzen, started clipping those headlines and any article that mentioned Neil Berry, from the sports pages of the Kalamazoo Gazette. After literally running into Gloria at a baseball game in Junior high, Neil and Gloria continued their courtship in High School.

The Franklin Lorentzen family seemed pretty well set in 1921, with 12-year-old Frank Jr. and three girls Genevive, age 13; Doris, age 9; and Helen, age 8. After eight years, Frank and his wife Deane certainly didn't expect to be parents again, but the baby of the family, Gloria, was born August 1, 1921, in Royal Oak, Michigan. Soon after Frank purchased a grocery store on Westnedge Avenue, south of town, and moved his family to Kalamazoo. The Lorentzen family purchased a home on Inkster Avenue, in the Westnedge Hill neighborhood, just down the street from Dr. Homer Stryker and his family.

Neil and Gloria attended kindergarten together, but she wasn't from the Upjohn Park neighborhood so they really didn't meet until Junior High when Neil spotted her at several ball games and realized "that little girl is kinda interested in sports." It was at one of those games that Gloria came between Neil and a foul pop fly. That episode broke the ice but—fortunately—did not break any bones.

Neil reminisced, "Gloria and I went to high school together. And it got to be where I'd see her in school and this and that and the other thing, you know, you get to know each other. We liked the same things, we liked to do the same things, that's the biggest thing."

Frank and Deane Lorentzen liked Neil and approved of Neil and Gloria seeing each other. "[Gloria's] mother, she really liked sports, and she kinda liked me, so she didn't hurt things. She didn't try to keep us apart. So every time we'd play in Muskegon or play in Battle Creek, or Lansing, or anyplace, she was there with [Gloria]. She went to the ball games.

"Gloria was always interested in sports. She was very good in gymnastics, that was her thing. Gymnastics and a lot of dancing.

"I was going with her in the ninth grade, and she would go to a lot of different lessons and stuff, and she told me one day, 'they dropped me last night ya know,' I said 'who dropped ya?' Well she had a dance [with] two big guys, one would grab her, and swing her, and throw her across the [stage] and [the other] guy catches her. And they threw her about 20, 25 feet. They'd throw her from behind the curtain and catch her behind the other curtain, she sailed right across the stage. They were practicing—the guy missed her."

Neil recalled when Gloria and her mother decided to buy a car. "So they get a dandy little Ford coupe with a rumble seat, wire wheels, the neatest little car. Of course, she learned to drive right away, but her mother would take that car and take her to school in the morning. She got that [car] in the ninth grade. In the tenth grade, I was only in school a few months when I got that kidney deal and I couldn't go to school when it rained or anything like that. [Gloria's mother] found that out [and] she'd come over and get me. She'd take Gloria to school and find out I wasn't there, and she'd come over to my house, pick me up and take me to school."

Neil reminisced about summers spent with Gloria and her parents at Gun Lake and related this story about Gloria and fishing. "When I was 15, 16, or so, I got her to go fishing. Her folks, out to Gun Lake, they had a cottage. I stayed with her folks out there, then I'd come into town with her dad for practice every day. [Then] he'd bring me into town to work in the store, then I'd go back out with him. I was fishin' there 'cause I liked to fish since I was a little guy, but she was always scared of worms, so finally she said, 'boy I wish I could go fishin'. I said, 'well get in here, bait your hook, you can go.' By gosh she found an old stiff paint glove, she put that thing on, [and] got it workin' a little bit. She could feel the big angleworm, but she couldn't feel it with her fingers, but she could hold onto it through the painted glove. I said, 'ok, you just hold him and you take the hook and go like this.' She said, 'that's not too bad,' so we went fishin'. [We] did that a few times and she got to where she could do that pretty good. Finally, she tried it without the glove and she could put a worm on by herself.

"One morning I got up, got ready to go to work, and where's Gloria? She's out fishing all by herself. So there she was out there [in the boat] so I walked out to the end of the dock, and all of a sudden here she comes [rowing] in. I'm standing on the dock waiting, I look, [and think], 'cripes sake, she knows how to row a boat,' but she's not making any headway and she's just rowin her little butt off, and finally she gets up to where I'm standin' on the dock, and she gets alongside and I look and I said, 'oh my God, Gloria, you rowed all the way in with the anchor down. What happened?' She could hardly breathe. She had caught six or eight small bluegills or perch and she put them on her stringer. Well, Gun Lake is full of big muskies. There she is sitting all calm in the boat and all of a sudden there comes this muskie with a mouth like this and gets her little fish on the stringer, and she looks down—scared the livin'—she thought she was bein' attacked by a monster. She just rowed all the way in [with the anchor down].

"From then on we fished, that was one of our favorite dates you might say, we would go out and rent a boat, go fishin'."

FOOTBALL - SOPHOMORE YEAR 1936

Neil Berry had demonstrated his athletic ability in the seventh, eighth, and ninth grades at Vine Junior High, but was the elusive, skinny kid big enough to play high school football?

As Neil told it, "Fred Zuidema was my gym teacher at Vine and he kind of liked me. When I was leaving the ninth grade he asked me if I was going out for football the next year at Central. I said 'sure' and he said, 'Well try to put some weight on.' I barely weighed 100 lbs. in the ninth grade so I put on about 20 lbs.

"So my junior high school teacher—he was the assistant coach, coach of the reserve team at Central, you couldn't go out for the varsity in the tenth grade, you had to go out for the reserve team—he said to me, 'I might see you out next year.' We had some pretty good teams in Junior high, 'I might see you out there,' he said. [I said] 'Ok.' Mr. Zuidema his name was, he was a Dutchman too."

Coach Fred "Dutch" Zuidema did see Neil out there, trying out for the reserve football squad, when school started in 1936. He must have liked what he saw in the 14-year-old Berry who had added 20 lbs to his small frame over the summer. Early on Coach Zuidema had Neil slated to be his starting left halfback. In the single-wing offense the left halfback carried or passed the football, and Neil Berry was very good at both.

While Coach Zuidema was putting together the junior varsity squad with the incoming sophomores, Coach Gene Thomas was busy assembling the varsity team for the 1936 season when he realized he had a problem. Coach Thomas had two senior left halfbacks but both had quit school as freshmen, then returned to school the following year. The short time they were freshmen before quitting, cost each of them a year of their four-year sports eligibility. Both of Coach Thomas' senior left halfbacks were ineligible, but there was a sophomore left halfback on the Junior Varsity team, and he was looking pretty good.

About a week and a half into the school year Neil Berry was minding his own business in Miss Milham's large study hall class when he was summoned to the office.

Neil remembered that day, "I was called to the office one

day and I thought, 'now what did I do,' you don't just get called into the office, but I got called into the office and the principal [told me] 'Mr. Thomas would like to see you in his office.' [It was] the little one, so I go in there and he said, 'Do you think you can play on the varsity?' I didn't think I was being boisterous or anything, I just said, 'well sure, yeah.' I'd been watching them practice ever since I was big enough to know a football from a baseball because they practiced right in my front yard.

"Coach Thomas gave me a stack of those recipe cards and told me to take them home and learn those plays. And that's when I kind of floored him, I said 'Mr. Thomas, I know all the plays,' and he looked at me like, well you smart little so and so, why are you talking like that, and I said, 'I know all the plays, I've been watching Central practice forever, I know 'em.' Well he said, 'let's see if you know 'em,' and he gave me the deck and he said, 'tell me what they are.' So I did."

Coach Thomas had himself a left halfback, at least for Central's opener against Grand Rapids Davis Tech on Saturday.

Neil continued, "But God they gave me a uniform—the helmet was so big that if I go like this (Neil demonstrates a twisting motion), I'd be looking out the ear hole. I mean it was big, everything was big, my pants hung down over my shoes and my sweatshirt hung below my hands."

Kalamazoo Central defeated Grand Rapids Davis Tech 20 to 6. Neil didn't start but he did play in that first game of the 1936 season at Upjohn Park. Game coverage in the *Kalamazoo Gazette* noted, "Young Dale[sic] Berry, who was promoted to the varsity squad only Friday night, showed considerable promise in his ball-carrying efforts and in his ability to pass." This was the first and only time that the *Gazette*, and followers of Kalamazoo high school sports, didn't know who Neil Berry was.

In a subsequent article about the game, the paper reported

Davis Tech scored the game's first touchdown in the second quarter, then "Neil Berry, swivel-hipped sophomore, was rushed into the game at this point, and furthered Coach Thomas' confidence in him by slashing off-tackle time after time and twisting and blasting his way to gain after gain."

Neil remembered that first game, "I knew darned well when I was standing down there at the goal line the ball was going to come right to me and it did. And like the guy [once] said, 'just run where the corn is the thinnest and don't let 'em catch ya.' I could run real good, I'd been playing a game that we used to call dart-ass and I could do that pretty good.

"I had a pretty good game and I found out when I looked over that there's my dad, who wasn't too interested in sports, he's over there watchin' every move and he became interested."

Coach Thomas must have seen enough to convince him that the smallish sophomore could indeed play varsity. The following Monday, Coach Thomas took Neil to Miller Boerman Sporting Goods, in downtown Kalamazoo, and bought him a proper fitting uniform and new shoes.

Neil recalled, "I was very proud of those shoes. The shoes, which were purchased by the school, were the ones in the display window and were endorsed by an All-American college football star. Size six."

Neil Berry wore number 11 on his proper fitting uniform for Kalamazoo Central's 1936 football campaign.

"My old Grandfather, who was living with us, thought that practicing football was the dumbest thing, 'If you worked that hard [at something else] you'd be a millionaire by the time you're 20.'

"He said that's terrible because he'd set on the front porch in that rocker and we'd be practicing right across the street, us kids gruntin' and groanin', and smakin' each other, bleedin', and every other thing, and he'd just shake his head and smoke his pipe. Well, before I graduated he was also

Top row, left to right: Bockleman, Trimm, Pennels, Van Keuren, Vander Kolk, and Goodner.

Middle row, left to right: Coach Thomas, Strong, Maartens, McKinney, Shanahan, Trainer Skalski, and Assitant Coach Murdock.

Front row, left to right: Berry, Lemmer, Hord, Watson, Boguta, Schindler, and Manager Lenderink.

Kalamazoo Gazette Photo from Neil Berry's scrapbook

[watching] against the fence over there [and telling me], 'by golly you did good, you did good . . . '"

Central lost their second game of the season to a tough Muskegon Heights squad 14-0 at Upjohn field. Neil started and played the entire game but threw two interceptions and lost a fumble in the contest.

Kalamazoo rebounded the following week, defeating the Holland Dutchmen on their rain-soaked, Riverside Park field, 13-0. Neil passed for two long gains and a touchdown in the game. The *Kalamazoo Gazette* reported that Coach Thomas "seems to have found a capable passer in Neil Berry, sophomore halfback, who before this time has excelled only in his broken field running."

Following the victory over Holland, Kalamazoo lost two Southwestern Michigan Conference contests on their home field; a one point defeat at the hands of Grand Haven, and a 21-6 drubbing by Muskegon. In non-conference play the Maroon Giants suffered two more setbacks on Upjohn field; another one point loss, with Jackson coming out on top, 7-6, and 21-0 thumping by Lansing Eastern.

Kalamazoo then traveled to the Cereal City for a non-conference tilt against traditional rival Battle Creek Central. At stake was the symbolic totem pole, a brightly painted, six-foot-tall trophy that the winning team held—along with bragging rights—until next year's game. Kalamazoo bested the Battle Creek eleven, 14-13, and reclaimed the totem pole after a two year absence.

The season finale was played at Benton Harbor's Filstrup Field. Central overcame an early Tiger touchdown with touchdowns of their own in the second, third, and fourth quarters. The third quarter score was a Berry touchdown pass to Left End, Shanahan. The three touchdowns, with only one successful extra point, gave the Maroons a 19-7 lead with less than ten minutes remaining in the game, but Benton Harbor wasn't done. On their next possession, the Tigers hit on a seventy yard touchdown pass with the last thirty yards coming after the catch. The extra point was wide but Benton Harbor was back in the ball game, trailing by six points. Kalamazoo thwarted Benton Harbor's next drive with an interception at the one yard line, but after a punt and penalty, the Tigers had the ball on Central's 24 yard line. A five yard pass and a nineteen yard scamper after the catch scored the touchdown that tied the game at 20. Benton Harbor then faked a place kick and ran the ball in for the winning extra point, handing Kalamazoo it's third one point loss of the season.

The 1936 Kalamazoo Central football campaign only produced three victories against six defeats. This was Central's worst record since Coach Thomas took over the coaching reigns in 1928, and the first time Kalamazoo finished in last place since joining the Southwestern Michigan Conference in 1930.

The down year for Central was a learning year for their sophomore left halfback, both on and off the football field.

Neil remembered, "Our varsity coach, Gene Thomas, he said, 'Look, you have to stay eligible.' We used to have little cards, the size of a credit card, it was called the eligibility card. You had to take that around, like for football, all our games were played Saturday afternoons, and you had to take that around Friday afternoon to all your teachers, and if they didn't sign it, you didn't play.

"He made a statement, got us all in a big circle down in front of my house, Upjohn Park, he said, 'I always thought this, if you're too dumb to get your schoolwork, you're too dumb to play for me.' That kinda sunk in.

"He was the kind of guy he never yelled, he wasn't a very big guy, but he never raised his voice, never chewed anybody out, never swore at anybody, never did anything like that. He was pretty calm and even. I think that helped too, not just me, everybody."

Neil Berry's speed, and the elusive open-field maneuvers he demonstrated during his sophomore season—along with his Dutch heritage—led the press to bestow upon him the "Flying Dutchman" moniker.

" (That) caused a lot of people to go, 'You Dutch?' 'Where'd you get the name Berry?' I told 'em well, my mother's Dutch and my dad isn't, but my mother is predominant.

"[Playing football] I had a reputation that they couldn't catch me, they called me the 'Flying Dutchman.' I was the second one in Kalamazoo because there was a kid from Kalamazoo [Central] that went to Michigan, that was the original 'Flying Dutchman.' His name was Everhardus, not the second Everhardus, the first one, Herman. I'm almost positive they were comparing me to him."

Comparisons to Herman Everhardus were not carelessly bandied about. Everhardus, the first "Flying Dutchman," ran, kicked, and piled up touchdowns for Kalamazoo Central during their successful 1928 and 1929 campaigns. Everhardus was the honorary captain of the all-state team in 1929 before taking his football repertoire to the University of Michigan where he played halfback. There Everhardus and notable teammates—future president Gerald Ford, and Willis Ward, the first African-American to play for Michigan in forty years—led the Wolverines to back-to-back undefeated seasons and national championships in 1932 and 1933. Everhardus was All-Big Ten and led the conference in scoring in 1933.

BASKETBALL - SOPHOMORE YEAR 1936/37

After the 1936 football season, Neil moved on to junior varsity basketball. It wasn't his best sport but he made the team.

"I played every [sport] you could play and not hurt the other one. In other words, in high school, I could run pretty good, and I could jump. So they would like to have me on the track team but you couldn't go out for track if you went out for baseball. [It was] football, basketball, and baseball, year after year, it was the same thing. I don't think I went home from school, my three years in high school, I don't think I went home a dozen times, [straight] from school to home. There was always a practice."

Neil was able to get home for lunch, "I had two hours [for lunch] because when you play sports in high school at Central, you get an extra hour because you don't have to take gym, so you get an extra hour study period. I had it worked out with my homeroom teacher that I had from eleven to one, double lunch we used to call it. One hour because I didn't have to take gym, and the other was my regular lunch period. So I put them both together so I could go home. I used to get out at 11 o'clock, put my books in my locker, and go right out the side door to Vine Street and run all the way home, down to Upjohn Park, run the whole way, eat, and run the whole way back, every day, and think nothing of it. It was a little over a mile, something like that, and that was good for me."

In basketball, Neil was known for coming up with the loose ball. His football instincts would take over and he wasn't afraid to dive on the hardwood floor to beat the opposition to the ball. That style of play came back to haunt Neil when he ended up with a severe floor burn that would soon threaten his athletic career, and nearly cost him his life.

The improperly treated floor burn became seriously infected and resulted in Bright's disease, a historical classification for kidney disease. The seriousness of the situation came to light when Neil had a seizure at his home and was rushed to the hospital. He was unable to urinate or pass a bowel movement for eight days. Just before his doctors were going to catheterize Neil, he was able to pass the obstruction but he remained in the hospital for several weeks and missed two and a half months of his sophomore year.

Neil recalled, "When I was in the hospital I went down to 87 lbs. in just a couple of weeks. A kid who lived down the street from my family had heard a rumor in school and ran all the way home and told his mother that I had died. They even took up a collection at school for flowers. Finally, I came out of it but the doctor said he didn't think I would ever play sports again.

"When I went outside for the first time since becoming ill, I was only outside for about 15 minutes and when I came in my nose and my eyes [were] swelled up. I looked like a dog who ran into a porcupine."

Neil did, of course, play sports again. In the spring of 1937, he picked up right where he left off on the baseball field, playing shortstop for the American Legion Maroons.

FOOTBALL - JUNIOR YEAR 1937

After a disappointing three win season in 1936, Coach Gene Thomas was looking to his returning letter winners and players from last year's top-notch reserve team to right the ship. During fall practice, Coach Thomas introduced a shift to complement the standard double and single-wing formations in hopes of creating more offense from a larger line in 1937.

"Just who are the boys who will carry the Maroon and White colors into the gridiron wars each Saturday?" asks an unidentified newspaper clipping from the Berry scrapbook. Then answers, "Bob Jones, a senior, at left end . . . his teammates call him 'Sleepy.' He stands six feet and weighs 160.

"Johnny Maartens at the opposite flank is called 'Dutch' or 'Crooked Arm,' the latter because he is left handed, the former because of his nationality. John is over six feet and weighs 165.

"Bruce Warren, left tackle . . . he is called 'Pinky' or 'Windy,' both of which he detests. He is a junior, stands six feet, and weighs 180. Bill Howland, another junior, on the other side of the line, is six feet and weighs 190.

"Bob Schindler, senior, is five-eleven and weighs 160. He does the most work and gets the least credit of any boy on the squad. Gerald Gilman, senior right guard, weighs 160 but towers up six feet three. At center is John 'Red' Watson, the Mighty Might with Titian-tinted hair. He weighs 150 soaking wet and stands five-five.

"Little need be said of left halfback Neil Berry, the Flying Dutchman. He is an inch or two below six feet and weighs 145.

"Captain Will McKinley, the blocking back, stands five-seven and weighs in at 150.

"Right halfback, Jack Bockelman, stands six feet and weighs around 160. Fullback Hale Helmer is handsome, rugged and dependable, Weighs 170 and stands about five-nine."

Jack Sherman, reporting for the *Kalamazoo Gazette* observed, "Neil Berry, triple threat halfback, who is counted upon to uphold the greater part of the offensive burden this year, received special attention with his punting. The tow-head is coming along at a fast clip and looks better every night. Several of his kicks traveled sixty yards Tuesday. He is already an accomplished broken field runner and passer and needs only experience and practice with his booting to make him one of the Southwestern Michigan Conference's finest backs."

Kalamazoo Central's 1937 Football Schedule:

Sept. 25 . . . Grand Rapids Davis Tech . . Here

Oct. 2 . . . . . Muskegon Heights . . There

Oct. 9 . . . . . Holland . . Here

Oct. 16 . . . . Grand Haven . . There

Oct. 23 . . . . Muskegon . . There

Oct. 30 . . . . Jackson . . Here

Nov. 6 . . . . . Lansing Eastern . . There

Nov. 13 . . . . Battle Creek . . Here

Nov. 20 . . . . Benton Harbor . . Here

Sept. 25 versus Grand Rapids Davis Tech - Kalamazoo continued its dominance over Davis Tech. After a scoreless first half, Central's first points of the season came on a third quarter safety. A blocked punt in the fourth quarter gave Central the ball on Tech's 40 yard line. Then, as reported in the *Kalamazoo Gazette*, "the fast shifty Berry broke away for a 22-yard gain." The longest run of the game took the ball to the Grand Rapids 18 but Central turned the ball over on downs at the nine yard line four plays later. "Tech hadn't smartened up and waited until fourth down to punt again" the *Gazette* reported. The punt was blocked and Johnny Maartens took it into the end zone with a Tech player along for a ride. The point-after kick was wide.

Kalamazoo Central 8 - Grand Rapids Davis Tech 0

Oct. 2 at Muskegon Heights - The first Southwestern Michigan Conference game of the year for both schools was played at Phillips Field in Muskegon Heights. With little success running the ball against the larger Height's line Central's Neil Berry took to the air to pick up yardage. He tossed a 12 yard pass to Clair Soules for a touchdown in the second quarter and hit Johnny Maartens with a nine yard touchdown in the fourth quarter. Both point-after kicks were blocked.

Kalamazoo Central 12 - Muskegon Heights 0

Oct. 9 versus Holland - After an early punting duel, Neil Berry got Central on the board first with a drive that started on Central's 40 yard line. Berry ran and passed to get to the Holland 31 before he ran around the right end for a touchdown. The kick was blocked but Central was up 6-0. In the second quarter, the Dutchmen showed off their passing game to get to Central's two yard line before running the ball in for a touchdown. Holland kicked the extra point for a 7-6 lead. Later in the quarter Berry fielded a short punt at the Holland 35, and beat the Dutch defense with a touchdown pass to John Maartens on the very next play. Will McKinley passed to Maartens for the extra point giving Central a 13-7 halftime lead. At the end of the third quarter, Holland returned a punt to midfield. On the first play of the fourth quarter, a 20 yard Holland pass was nearly intercepted by Central but was instead deflected to one of the Dutchmen receivers who raced 25 yards for a touchdown. Maartens kept the score tied when he broke through and blocked the point-after kick.

Kalamazoo Central 13 - Holland 13

Oct. 16 at Grand Haven - After running for a touchdown and throwing for two more in the first half, Neil recalled his coach's reaction, "Gene Thomas never raised his voice, never hollered at us once. He never embarrassed us as some coaches do. One time he showed a little bit of anger. We were ahead 19-0 at the half, we were playing Grand Haven at Grand Haven. We went down into the boiler room and man he really chewed us out for playin' the way we did. He said, 'You're runnin' all your pass plays, you're runnin' every play you got . . . why?' He chewed us out for exploiting the other team, I guess that was it."

The Maroon Giants added touchdowns in the third and fourth quarters. Grand Haven got on the scoreboard after taking advantage of 50 yard penalty assessed against Central for fighting.

Kalamazoo Central 32 - Grand Haven 6

Oct. 23 at Muskegon - The *Kalamazoo Gazette* opined, "Seldom in Southwestern Michigan high school football has a dual between two great halfbacks been so much in evidence. Kalenic[*sic*] and Berry accounted for nearly all their respective team's points. Kolnic's[*sic*] 72 yard broken field jaunt to a touchdown in the first two minutes of play was the finest and most thrilling play of the game. Berry's 60 yard dash to the Muskegon 12 was the next best of the day."

Muskegon's Rudy Kolenic returned a punt 72 yards for a touchdown early in the first quarter and kicked the extra point for a 7-0 Muskegon lead. Central's Neil Berry answered with a two yard touchdown plunge in the second quarter. The extra point kick knotted the score at 7-7. The third quarter was a punting duel between Kolenic and Berry. On the opening play of the fourth quarter Berry fielded a punt on his own 28 yard line and in what was, according to the *Kalamazoo Gazette*, "the finest bit of open field running of the game," Berry "eluded six tacklers before being brought down by Kolenick[*sic*] who caught him from behind." Berry's touchdown pass to McKinley—followed by a missed extra point—put Kalamazoo in the lead, 13-7. Muskegon countered with a long touchdown drive that left the game tied at 13 after they also missed on their extra point try. The score remained tied until the final seconds.

As Neil told it, "Muskegon was always our rival at Central. We lost at Muskegon in a snowstorm with 20 seconds to go. They had possibly a better team than we had but we battled the hell out of 'em. With 20 seconds to go a guy kicked a field goal. You didn't kick field goals in those days . . . in a snowstorm. He kicked one field goal all year and that was it. They beat us."

Kalamazoo Central 13 - Muskegon 16

Oct. 30 versus Jackson - Jack Sherman reported for the *Kalamazoo Gazette*, "Central high's Flying Dutchman, tow-headed Neil Berry, again led the Maroon Giants to victory Saturday. The speedy halfback ran wild against Jackson's Vikings at Upjohn field . . .

"Berry ran 18 yards around his right end for the first counter and swept 45 yards through a broken field for the second. The local star's unfaltering hand also held the ball for the two points after touchdown which Jack Brockelman converted from placement.

"The tow-head sustained an ankle injury as the half ended and was unable to return to the fray. His point making had put the Maroons well in the lead, however, and they needed no more to win."

Kalamazoo Central 14 - Jackson 0

Nov. 6 at Lansing Eastern - Next up was a Friday night road game against the Lansing Eastern Quakers, under the lights at Pattengill field. The Lansing squad, undefeated in their six contests, were averaging over 30 points per game.

Lansing Eastern was surprised by Kalamazoo's stingy defense, scoring only nine points in the game, but the closest

Kalamazoo came to scoring was on Neil Berry's return of the opening kickoff. He was tripped up at midfield by the last man that had a chance to stop him. Central would get no closer to the goal. Berry's punting helped keep the Quakers away from the Central goal line, with several kicks covering 50 plus yards.

Kalamazoo Central 0 - Lansing Eastern 9

Nov. 13 versus Battle Creek - It was color week at Kalamazoo Central leading up to the homecoming game against Battle Creek. The annual, non-conference, rivalry game would be the 34th consecutive contest, and the ninth time the teams played for the totem pole trophy. Last year's Maroon Giant win over the Bearcats brought the totem pole back to Kalamazoo and this year's team intended to keep it.

An overflow crowd of 3,000 converged on Upjohn field for the afternoon homecoming contest. They weren't disappointed. In a second quarter drive, Neil Berry completed three passes with the last going to John Maartens in the end zone for the game's first score. The kick failed "when the entire Bearcat line surged through and blocked Bockelman's attempted point after touchdown" the *Kalamazoo Gazette* reported. Later in the second quarter, Berry had to leave the game with a leg injury. Late in the third quarter, a Kalamazoo drive got the ball to the Bearcat 5 yard line. Will McKinley made four yards on a reverse to the one yard line as the quarter ended. Berry then returned to the game and made the one yard plunge for the score. The point-after kick was wide but Central's defense was too tough for Battle Creek to penetrate. The totem pole would remain in Kalamazoo for at least another year.

Kalamazoo Central 12 - Battle Creek 0

Nov. 20 versus Benton Harbor - In the second quarter, Neil Berry scored on a dive over tackle, then for good measure, the Flying Dutchman caught a pass from Jack Bockelman for the extra point. In the fourth quarter, a

Berry punt pinned Benton Harbor on their own two yard line. The Kalamazoo defense then broke through to tackle the Tiger punter for a safety. The Tigers never got the ball past midfield against the Maroon Giant defense.

Kalamazoo Central 9 - Benton Harbor 0

Kalamazoo Central's final contest of the 1937 season against the Benton Harbor Tigers was also the final high school game for seven varsity performers. Coach Thomas lost to graduation; ends, John Maartens and Bob Jones; guards, Bob Schindler and Gerald Gilman; backs, Jack Bockelman and Captain Will McKinley; and center, John Watson.

Kalamazoo Central's 1937, six-win, football campaign was Central's best since their undefeated seven-win, one tie season in 1932 when they were Southwestern Michigan Conference champs. The defense was stellar with shutouts in five of the six wins. The offense was Neil Berry and he would be back next year.

Central landed four players on the All-City eleven; Senior Left End, John Maartens; Senior Left Guard, Bob Schindler; Senior Center, John Watson; and Junior Left Halfback Neil Berry. Berry and Fullback Chet Jurwiak of St. Augustine, were the only Juniors on the All-City squad. The 15-year old Berry was the youngest.

BASKETBALL - JUNIOR YEAR 1937/38

Next up was varsity basketball with Gene Thomas coaching. Neil, along with several of his football teammates, made the squad.

The Kalamazoo Maroon Giants had an outstanding basketball team that year with a starting five consisting of forwards, John Maartens and Dallas Roe, center Bruce Warren, and guards, Jack Reeves and Dick Hubert. Neil was a sub who could play guard or forward. He made his basketball debut on Central's home court in the fourth game of a fourteen game schedule, subbing in at guard, against Muskegon Heights. After getting in the game in the third quarter, Neil "intercepted a pass and scored on a dog shot," according to the unidentified newspaper clipping in the Berry scrapbook.

A week later at Muskegon Neil came off the bench with a minute play in a tight, back and forth contest. He missed a long shot that would have tied the game and Muskegon tried to freeze the ball and run the clock out. With seconds left a Muskegon player saw an open lane to a layup but missed and Muskegon lost the ball out of bounds. Neil Berry took the inbounds pass, and the *Kalamazoo Gazette* reported what happened next "[Berry] raced down the floor and without stopping to aim, threw the ball in the direction of the Muskegon goal. It found the netting and the game went into overtime."

Central lost the Muskegon game in overtime 31-30 but would go on to win their conference. In the State tournament Central beat Grand Rapids Union, 39-31, in the first round; defeated Saginaw Eastern, 30-15, in the semifinals; and brought home the State Basketball Championship by besting Saginaw Arthur Hill, 29-27.

Baseball - Junior Year 1938

Kalamazoo Gazette clipping from the Berry scrapbook:

Central To Support Baseball This Spring

"Official corroboration of the rumor that Central High would have a baseball team this spring was made last week by Robert Dewey, athletic manager.

"The diamond team, which will be coached by Donald Scott, is the first one to represent Central high in 15 years. New equipment has been ordered and an all class A seven-game schedule tentatively arranged . . .

"A meeting of interested baseball candidates was held a short time ago and nearly 50 boys were on hand. This group included few of the athletes now playing basketball who will make strong bids for various positions.

"Among the basketballers who undoubtedly will fit in someplace are John Maartens, Dallas Roe, Neil Berry, Dick Hubert, Stan Feidorek, Al Taborn, Jack Reeves, Kurt Groggel, and Bill Lines. Others who are primarily interested in the diamond sport are Harold Fleckenstein, Paul Elliott, Reeves Comfort, and Thaxton Terpening.

"Scott reports that he will start baseball practice in the gyms at Central immediately after the basketball season is terminated and will then wait for the first break in the weather for outside work . . . "

Kalamazoo Central had not fielded a baseball team for 15 years, from 1922 to 1937, but many of their athletes had been competing in American Legion ball. In fact, the entire starting infield was made up of Legion Junior stars, including John Maartens at first, Dallas Roe at second, Neil Berry at short, and Bill McLain, Harold Fleckenstein, and Francis (Piff) Thompson vying for third base.

Central started well, beating Grand Rapids Union, 8-1, followed by a 12-0 victory over Grand Rapids South, snapping South's 30 game victory streak. Three straight losses followed with Battle Creek beating the Maroons twice and Jackson once. Home and away wins over Grand Rapids Ottawa Hills were sandwiched around a loss to Lansing, leaving the new Central team with a 4 win, 4 loss season (4-0 against Grand Rapids teams).

Neil Berry – The Shortstop from Kalamazoo
Photo courtesy of Linda Spann

We played games where we had to catch each other.
Constantly. You learn how to zig and zag, zig and
zag. You'd zig and zag in your mind.

~ Neil Berry

4

Football Champions

Kalamazoo Central High School

1938

Kalamazoo Central's first football practice of 1938 took place on Upjohn field, on Thursday, September 1st, at 9:30 a.m. Neil Berry didn't even have to get out of bed early to cross the street and start his final year of high school football.

With only six returning lettermen the *Kalamazoo Gazette* lamented the loss of the graduated players, and proclaimed "prospects are not too bright." The *Gazette* did recognize that Neil Berry, "ace back of last season's team," was one of the returning letter winners.

The *Gazette* also announced the 1938 schedule that included all the usual foes except Lansing Eastern and added an away game with newcomer Bay City.

Kalamazoo Central's 1938 Football Schedule:

Sept. 24 . . . Grand Rapids Davis Tech . . . Here

Oct. 1 . . . . . Benton Harbor . . . Here

Oct. 8 . . . . . Bay City . . . There

Oct. 15 . . . . Grand Haven . . . Here

Oct. 22 . . . . Muskegon Heights . . . Here

Oct. 29 . . . . Jackson . . . There

Nov. 5 . . . . . Holland . . . There

Nov. 12 . . . . Muskegon . . . Here

Nov. 19 . . . . Battle Creek . . . There

The Central team played a tune-up game at Upjohn Park on September 17th with the first team easily defeating the second string 27-0. Neil Berry ran for two touchdowns and completed passes for the other two while he was in the game.

The *Kalamazoo Gazette* was now reporting that Coach Thomas "boasts the best forward wall in history," and "if present indications run true, he should have one of the top elevens in the state."

Neil was slated to be the team's primary runner, passer and punter from his left halfback position. The triple threat star would also serve as the holder for extra-point tries. The *Gazette* predicted that Berry "will probably experience his best year" and went on to report that "Berry, according to Coach Thomas, is as great a back now as was Herm Everhardus." Herman Everhardus, the first "Flying Dutchman," ran, kicked, and piled up touchdowns for Central's Maroons during their successful 1928 and 1929 campaigns.

Neil Berry's small feet had some big shoes to fill if

he was to live up to Coach Thomas' declaration. His first opportunity would come with the season-opening game against Grand Rapids Davis Tech. The Grand Rapids school had been an early opponent and annual whipping boy on Kalamazoo Central's schedule since 1933. Coach Thomas' Maroons had won the game every year and expected to win again in 1938.

KALAMAZOO CENTRAL
vs.
GRAND RAPIDS DAVIS TECH.
Saturday, Sept. 24, 1938—2:30 P.M.
Upjohn Field
GET ACQUAINTED WITH YOUR TEAM

NO. OF JERSEY	NAME	POSITION	WEIGHT
35	Wood, Wayne	L. T.	156
37	O'Dell, Max	Q. B.	140
38	Sanford, Lowell	L. H.	160
39	Schwoebell, Myron	R. T.	185
40	Berry, Neil	L. H.	145
41	Elliott, Paul	Q. B.	150
42	Jones, Charles	R. E.	137
43	Dexter, Richard	R. H.	137
44	Fiedorek, Stanley	F. B.	161
45	Ward, Kenneth	R. G.	147
46	Wiedmayer, Richard	L. E.	156
47	Marks, Jack	C.	185
48	Comfort, Reeves	F. B.	170
49	Doorenbos, Arent	R. T.	160
50	Warren, Bruce	L. T.	187
51	Parr, DeWitt	R. E.	155
52	Drake, Earl	L. H.	145
53	Helmer, Hale	R. G.	176
54	Hubert, Richard	R. H.	155
55	Somers, Gerald	Q. B.	166
56	Ruess, William	C.	165
57	Ranney, Charles	L. G.	160
58	Howland, William	R. T.	195
60	Kries, Marvin	L. G.	160
61	Taborn, Albert	L. E.	205

GRAND RAPIDS DAVIS TECH.

NO. OF JERSEY	NAME	POSITION	WEIGHT
20	Wm. Jarecki	F. B.	154
21	Carl Jelsema	R. T.	150
22	Ed. Kozdrey	L. T.	162
23	Mike Solow	R. G.	155
24	Robert Cebelak	R. E.	150
25	Ed Wasilewski	L. E.	148
26	John Nawara	L. T.	160
27	Frank Thomas	L. G.	138
28	Edward Stouten	C.	150
29	Ray Masiewicz	R. G.	145
30	Ferd. VanderLaan	R. T.	170
31	Ray Sierachi	R. E.	144
32	Stanley Soltysiak	Q. B.	140
33	Wm. Krajewski	F. B.	155
34	Clarence Barth	R. H.	165
35	Eugene Nelson	L. H.	159
36	Edward Sobvoda	C.	145
37	Bernard Bricker	F. B.	152
38	Jack Slagboom	L. H.	145
39	Joe Cichon	L. H.	155
40	Arthur Mauk	Q. B.	138
41	Arthur Mange	L. G.	135
42	Ned Scott	Q. B.	140
—	Don Pelak	L. E.	147
—	E. Van Dam	R. G.	162
—	James Dernehl	L. G.	160
—	Eugene Smiegel	R. H.	158

OFFICIALS
Referee: John Bromley   Umpire: L. B. Genebach
Head Linesman: E. R. Knutson

COMPLIMENTS OF CENTRAL HIGH SCHOOL ATHLETIC ASSOCIATION

September 24 versus Grand Rapids Davis Tech - Neil Berry scored three touchdowns in the contest against the overmatched visitors from Grand Rapids. The *Kalamazoo Gazette* reported, "Opposing players were unable to stop his elusive off-tackle and end runs." One of those runs was for 40 yards and a touchdown. Berry also held while Dick Hubert kicked all four extra points. A clipping from the Berry scrapbook boasted about Hubert, "Central has not had a place kicker like him since grandpa was a boy."

Kalamazoo Central 28 - Grand Rapids Davis Tech 0

Back row, left to right: Dick Hubert, Gerald Sommers, Reeves Comfort, Neil Berry.
Front row: Chuck Jones, Bill Howland, Hale Helmer, Jack Marks, Charles Ranney, Bruce Warren, Al Taborn.
Photo courtesy of Linda Spann

Central's second game opened the Class A, Southwestern Michigan Conference schedule. The contest was played on Upjohn field against perennial conference foe Benton Harbor. The Tigers, who also recorded a 28-0 shutout in their first game, were looking to avenge last year's defeat at the hands of the Maroons.

October 1 versus Benton Harbor - Benton Harbor proved to be a tough adversary, scoring twice in the first quarter. Their first score came when Central's Neil Berry had his punt blocked. Berry prevented a touchdown when he recovered the loose ball in the end zone for a Benton Harbor safety. Later in the quarter, the Tigers added a touchdown on a 20 yard scamper around the right end. Down 9-0, Central woke up in the second quarter with runs by Berry and right halfback Dick Hubert, getting the ball to the two yard line before Berry carried it over. Hubert kicked the point after to bring Central to within two, 7-9. In the third quarter, Central recovered a Benton Harbor fumble at the Tiger's 17 yard line, before Berry found Hubert open and hit him in stride with a well-thrown spiral. Hubert carried the ball untouched into the end zone, scoring what turned out to be the final points of the game when his point-after kick was blocked.

Kalamazoo Central 13 - Benton Harbor 9

A small clipping from an unidentified source in the Berry scrapbook relates that "a Benton Harbor fan in the stands remarked, 'Yes, I played football for Benton Harbor last fall but I never got much closer to that Berry guy than I am right now.'"

Kalamazoo's first away game of the season was a non-conference tilt with the Bay City Central Bees, 190 miles from Upjohn Park. The game was the first-ever played between the schools and promised to be an exciting game, featuring the anticipated matchup between the team's star backs, Kalamazoo's Neil Berry, and Bay City's Ray Sowers.

October 8 at Bay City - Late in a scoreless first quarter, Berry, Kalamazoo's triple-threat back, was stung by the swarming Bees with a kick in the jaw, when he was tackled during a pass attempt. The dazed Berry was unable to return to the game. Both teams scored touchdowns in the second quarter after recovering the opposition's fumble and getting a short field. Kalamazoo recovered a fumble by Sowers, 28 yards out, and the Berry-less offense reached the three yard line before Al Taborn hauled in a short pass from Berry's backup, Earl Drake. Hubert kicked the point for the short-lived, 7-0, lead.

It was Bay City's turn when the Bees fell on Drake's muffed punt on the Maroons 18 yard line. After a Central penalty and several running plays, Bay City's Sower punched it in from the two yard line. The kick-for-point was good for a 7-7 halftime tie. The teams traded punts throughout the third quarter with neither team presenting a serious scoring threat. Kalamazoo dominated the fourth quarter with deep drives into enemy territory and their final effort resulted in a field goal attempt by Dick Hubert. A clipping from the Berry scrapbook observed, "Local rooters at the game (all ten of them) had near heart failure when Dick Hubert missed a field goal by mere inches with three minutes left before the final gun." His angled attempt just missed and left the score tied.

Kalamazoo Central 7 - Bay City Central 7

In his *Kalamazoo Gazette*, "High Spots of Sport" column, Jerry Hagan opined, "When Bay City Central surprised Kalamazoo Central last Saturday at Bay City, the tie could be traced directly to the fact that Berry was hurt in the first quarter and couldn't get back in the lineup the rest of the game."

Back home, after the humbling tie with Bay City's Bees, Kalamazoo Central prepared to face a Grand Haven squad that was thought to be much improved from the team that Central had easily defeated in 1937.

The *Kalamazoo Gazette* headline proclaimed, "Bruised and Battered Maroons Prepare for Grand Haven Game." Jerry Hagan's article did point out that "the boys came through it all O.K., with the exception of Earl Drake who hasn't even been to school since the game. Neil Berry, who was forced out before the first quarter ended, and the others are busy getting ready" for Grand Haven with "nothing but light practice all this week as the boys recuperate." The same preview went on to say Central's Coach Thomas "figures he'll have trouble scoring" against Grand Haven, "even with Berry back in the lineup" and that "Dick Hubert's educated toe may figure in the final result."

October 15 versus Grand Haven - Grand Haven kicked off to open the game and Berry waited for the ball at the ten-yard line. Neil Berry saw a football field full of teammates and opposing players pretty much the same way he saw his playground friends when they played "hunt the gray," or "dart-ass," and the same mantra applied, "just run where the corn is the thinnest."

As Neil told it, "We played games where we had to catch each other. Constantly. You learn how to zig and zag, zig and zag. You'd zig and zag in your mind [when you weren't

Neil makes a defender miss at Upjohn Field.
Photo courtesy of Linda Spann

playing]. You learned by being chased and caught and chasing somebody else [that] when I'm running here, I can see you over there, and if you step out with your right foot, you're a dead duck. I stop and go this way—you can't stop—I go behind you."

So when Neil gathered in that opening kickoff he took off for the thinnest corn on the field in front of him. The *Kalamazoo Gazette's* Jerry Hagan described what happened next. "Baldus, Grand Haven's star left end, played wide so his end would not be turned and Berry, at break-neck pace, cut inside him" and sprinted all the way to the goal line, scoring a touchdown on the game's first play. Dick Hubert missed the extra point.

On the ensuing kickoff, Grand Haven fumbled and Central recovered on the opposition's 23 yard line. Two plays later "Berry passed 20 yards to Al Taborn, Negro end, who was alone in the corner of the field and Central had a 12-0 lead with less than two minutes gone." Hubert missed another extra point but after Bruce "Pinky" Warren blocked a punt leading to a Chuck Jones scoop and score, the rout was on. Hubert's extra point made it 19-0 at the half.

The third quarter featured another Grand Haven fumble, this one at their own 34, and another Berry score. First Neil picked up 20 yards on a pass to Taborn then he "raced off right tackle, cut back sharply and snake-hipped his way through the Grand Haven secondary" (no doubt where the corn was the thinnest) "in the niftiest bit of shifty running seen in Kalamazoo in many a day," according to Hagan's description in the *Gazette*. Hubert's kick was successful. The second string scored the final touchdown in the fourth quarter.

Kalamazoo Central 33 - Grand Haven 0

Author's note: It was commonplace at the time for sports journalists to reference a player's ethnicity, and/or nickname in their stories.

Kalamazoo Central's undefeated Maroon's next opponent was the undefeated team from Muskegon Heights with the Southwestern Michigan conference lead on the line. The winner would be in the conference driver's seat and the loser likely out of contention. The *Kalamazoo Gazette* expected the game to "be primarily a game of punting, according to those who are familiar with Muskegon Heights great fullback, Anderson, and his ability to boot the oval. Coach Thomas expects Neil Berry, Central ace, to hold his own in that department."

October 22 versus Muskegon Heights - The Saturday afternoon game at Upjohn Park lived up to expectations with both teams playing the punting game while waiting for the opponent to make a mistake. The *Kalamazoo Gazette* reported, "both Anderson of Heights and Berry of the locals were kicking on first down, waiting for the breaks." Central got the break and the field position in the second quarter when DeWitt Par fell on a Muskegon Heights fumble on their 40 yard line. Neil Berry and his Central teammates then went to work. Berry gained five yards on an off-tackle run. A pass from Berry to Dick Hubert gave the Maroons a first down on the opponent's 26 yard line. Then, as the *Kalamazoo Gazette* told it; "Berry dropped back and heaved one of his long specialties to Parr who was waiting down the side-lines six yards short of the goal. Parr gathered in the oval" and crossed the goal line untouched. Hubert's kick put Central in the lead, 7-0. After a scoreless third quarter, Muskegon Heights put on a frantic fourth quarter rally in an attempt to tie the contest. Heights partially blocked a Berry punt and recovered the ball at the 50 yard line. An Anderson pass was nearly foiled but was instead deflected off a Central player's hands into the hands of the Muskegon Heights receiver at Central's five yard line. Three running plays each picked up small gains but left the opposing eleven short of the goal with fourth down and their last chance. With what the *Gazette* called "one of the most brilliant defensive exhibitions ever seen in Kalamazoo," Central

Neil Berry, No. 40, breaks loose for a five-yard gain that sets the stage for Central's winning touchdown against Muskegon Heights. No. 47 is Marks of Central and No. 52 is Krepps of Muskegan Heights.

Kalamazoo Gazette Photo from Neil Berry's scrapbook

stopped Muskegon Heights with "the ball so close to the Kalamazoo goal that the end of the oval almost touched the goal line." Central had the ball on downs and when Berry safely punted the ball away, victory was assured.

Kalamazoo Central 7 - Muskegon Heights 0

"Jackson Must Stop Berry To Defeat Kalamazoo Tonight" read the headline on the newspaper clipping in the Berry scrapbook. The accompanying article added that "the not too enviable task of bottling up a one-man hurricane is the task of Jackson High school's football team tonight . . . The one-man hurricane is Neil Berry."

October 29 at Jackson - The *Kalamazoo Gazette* reported, "Central looked like state champions as it scored a lopsided victory over Jackson at the Prison City.

"Neil Berry, who is in the running for all-state honors, led his Maroon teammates to victory scoring twice himself and setting up the other two scoring chances. Berry was as slippery as an eel as he ran and passed all over the gridiron."

Kalamazoo Central 23 - Jackson 7

The Holland Dutchmen were up next and by now the strategy to beat Kalamazoo Central was obvious. The Berry scrapbook clipping reported, "The war cry around the Holland camp this week is 'Block, tackle and stop Berry.'" It was also reported that the Hollanders would "use some new aerial plays developed by Coach Breen for this game," and that "a new passer has been developed," but is being "kept under cover until the need for him is shown in the contest."

November 5 at Holland - Kalamazoo brought their undefeated Maroon Giant football team to Riverside Park in Holland for a conference tilt with the Dutchmen. Jerry Hagan covered the action for the *Kalamazoo Gazette*, "Berry Does It Again - Neal[*sic*] Berry, Central's all-state halfback, romped away for all three touchdowns . . . He went six, 48, and 12 yards for scores on sharp cutbacks through tackle. Twice he fumbled near Holland's goal line or the score would have been larger."

Apparently only Neil Berry could stop Neil Berry. The Holland eleven couldn't. Neither could the Dutchmen get the ball past the Maroon Giant's 49 yard line.

Kalamazoo Central 20 - Holland 0

Now only the formidable and undefeated Muskegon Big Reds stood in the way of Kalamazoo's bid for the Class A, Southwestern Michigan conference title and mythical state high school football championship. Muskegon had not been defeated since 1935 and was riding a 26 game unbeaten streak into Upjohn Park for the showdown game.

November 12 verses Muskegon - A crowd of 5,000 was on hand at Upjohn Park for the clash between the Kalamazoo Maroon Giants and the Muskegon Big Reds, two of Michigan's best Class A high school teams in 1938.

Kalamazoo took the opening kickoff but couldn't gain enough ground to keep the ball so Neil Berry punted. Muskegon started their first drive at their own 20 yard line and moved the ball on power runs to the 38. Then on first down the Reds surprised Central's Maroons with a quick kick that was mishandled by Berry and recovered by Muskegon on Central's 17 yard line. It took Muskegon three running plays to reach the goal and they were up 6-0 after the extra point kick was blocked. Later in the first quarter, Central's Bill Howland blocked a Muskegon punt giving the Maroon Giants the ball at the eleven yard line. Berry picked up six yards on two running plays but third and fourth down plays were thwarted and Muskegon took over on downs at the start of the second quarter.

When Muskegon attempted to punt out of the end zone, both DeWitt Parr and Bruce Warren broke through the line and blocked the kick. Warren recovered in the end zone for a touchdown. Dick Hubert's kick made it, 7-6, in favor of Kalamazoo. Soon after that Stan Fiedorek intercepted a Muskegon pass at the 11 but Central couldn't punch it in and settled for a Hubert field goal, extending their lead to 10-6. At that point, Muskegon started completing their passes and picked up chunks of 17, six, and 12 yards to reach Kalamazoo's 30 yard line. After mixing in two running plays another pass was completed to the four-yard line. Three running plays put the ball in the end zone for the Reds. The extra point was good and Muskegon had regained the lead 13-10.

At halftime Central coach, Gene Thomas had a simple message for his team.

Neil Berry—the Flying Dutchman
Senior Year 1938

Photo courtesy of Linda Spann

Neil remembered, "We were undefeated and we were playing Muskegon and they had us 13-10 at the half at Upjohn Park. We went into the half and Gene Thomas didn't show up [in the locker room]. Finally, the referee stuck his head in the door and said we had five minutes. We all looked around and said where is Coach Thomas? He stuck his head in the door and said, 'If you guys think you can take it for another half, let's go.' That was all we needed, it was like someone had touched us with a blowtorch."

Jack Sherman, writing for the *Kalamazoo Gazette* reported, "With the start of the second half, Central was a new team." Multiple punt exchanges dominated the third quarter and neither team scored. With Muskegon nursing a three point lead, yet another punt gave Central's Maroon Giants the ball on their own 20 yard line. They moved the ball to the Muskegon 19 with Berry, Hubert, and Reeves Comfort all carrying the ball. At that point, an off-tackle run by Berry gained ten yards to the opponents nine yard line but three successive Berry runs left Central three yards short of the goal. Hubert was then called upon to attempt the tying field goal. He missed the kick but an offside penalty on Muskegon gave Central another down with the ball on the one yard line. Central went for the touchdown and got it with a Berry plunge. Hubert converted the kick and Central was back on top 17-13. Later in the quarter, Berry got the better of the punting battle when he nailed a coffin corner kick to give Muskegon the ball at their own one yard line. When Muskegon couldn't get off their own goal line they punted to Berry whose return run gave Central the ball at the Muskegon 25. Berry gained 13 yards on the next play, two Berry runs later it was first and goal on the one yard line. Berry scored the touchdown on his second attempt. Hubert kicked the game's final point.

Kalamazoo Central 24 - Muskegon 13

Kalamazoo Central had done it. They ended Muskegon's 26 game winning streak, won the Southwestern Michigan conference, and laid claim to the title of Class A State Champions for 1938.

Neil Berry and his high school accomplishments were praised by Joe Vanderhoff in this *Kalamazoo Gazette* story:

"Neil Berry's Great High School Grid Career Ends Friday Night

"All good things must come to an end, and so the curtain descends Friday night on Neil Berry, brilliant Central high school star as he ends his distinguished football career with the Maroon and White. This year's playing makes Berry's third as a Central regular.

"Berry, tow-headed, 17 year old senior who weighs but 150 pounds, is slated to make the all-state football team this season.

"Coach Eugene Thomas describes Berry as a 'natural' that comes along once in ten years. Berry is a good sportsman and gives credit for the fine blocking that his fellow team members gave him during the games, blocking that made his touchdown runs possible.

"During the regular season, all of Central's opponents feared the Maroon and White flash, and built their defense to try to stop this great player.

"Berry's specialty was off-tackle smashes but he was rated a triple threat man. His punting, passing, and running were as good as any coach could ask. His ability to play the safety position and his marvelous run backs of punts kept Central's opponents on their toes every minute of the classic. "The present Central ace got his knowledge of football at Vine during the gym classes. When he reached junior high, the city junior high schools started to play touch football and through careful development by Fred Zuidema, a great player blossomed out in the touch football leagues.

"Thomas startled the football experts when he took Berry

off the reserve football grid team in his first year at Central and made him a regular half-back on his varsity team. Although Berry did not play much in his first year on account of injuries, he showed enough zip, and colorful playing to let himself be a marked man in future competition.

"In his junior year at Kalamazoo Central, Neil played most of the time, although he was handicapped with an injured ankle. Except for one touchdown last year, Berry had a hand in all of them. He scored half of the team's markers and passed for the rest of the touchdowns. He was chosen on the all-Southwestern Michigan conference team.

"In his last season for the Maroon Giants, Captain Berry has led his great gridiron team to a Southwestern Michigan championship. Throughout the eight games that the local grids team has played, it has won seven and tied one. During the year, Berry has made 12 touchdowns and heaved four passes that were good for other tallies."

Neil Berry would end his prep football career with one last game against Central's traditional rival, the Battle Creek Bearcats, a team that had won only one game all year. At stake were Kalamazoo Central's undefeated season and a totem pole that the winning team held until next year's game.

He didn't know it beforehand, but Neil's potential selection to the all-state squad was also at stake. Referee Dick Remington would be working the game and seeing Kalamazoo's "Flying Dutchman" perform for the first time this season.

The Michigan all-state team was chosen annually by Remington. A Jerry Hagan piece in the *Kalamazoo Gazette* explained; "Remington goes not alone by what he sees during the fall grid campaign. A well-knit organization of officials, coaches and sportswriters work with Remington each year in the final all-state selections and the full season's play of a candidate is considered."

November 19 at Battle Creek - Perhaps the footballers from Kalamazoo had a let down after their thrilling victory over Muskegon the previous week, or perhaps Battle Creek rose to meet the challenge in an attempt to salvage their dismal season with a win over their state champion rival. In any case, the game was much closer than anyone would have guessed. With the game still scoreless in the final minutes of play, a Berry punt pinned the Bearcats deep in their own territory. They couldn't move the ball and Central's Bruce Warren blocked their punt, with the loose ball going through the end zone for a safety, and the only points of the game.

Kalamazoo Central 2 - Battle Creek 0

Prior to the game-winning safety, referee Dick Remington witnessed Neil Berry fumble a punt in the first quarter and fumble the ball away in the fourth quarter, giving Battle Creek its only scoring chance. In between Central was stopped when Berry, according to the *Kalamazoo Gazette*, "fumbled on Battle Creek's six-inch line . . . or had the ball stolen from him" in the goal line pile up. Neil did lose the ball in the pile, but he has never wavered in his belief that he had scored a touchdown before the ball was yanked from his possession. Unfortunately, referee Remington didn't see it that way. It was not a stellar Neil Berry performance in front of the man who would soon be choosing the best football players in the state for 1938.

In 1993, fifty-five years after that game, Neil Berry was interviewed for a story that appeared in the Kalamazoo Central publication, "The First 100 Years - An Historical Look at Central Football." An excerpt from that article:

"As for the Battle Creek/Kalamazoo Central High School rivalry, Berry distinctly remembers one particular game in 1938. During that game, one of the referees, the same one to pick members of the All-State Teams, was on the field to make calls. In one play, Berry scrambled through the opponents, hurdled his way toward the goal post, plunged through colors of blue and gold and crawled to make a touchdown.

"The dastardly referee sourly over-ruled what Neil Berry certainly considered was a touchdown. The Giants did go on to win the game 2-0, but to this date, Berry still believes he made that touchdown."

Author's note: Neil still knew for certain that he scored that touchdown when he told me the story in 2015. He passed away with this knowledge and has likely brought it to the attention of the appropriate complaint department in the hereafter.

When Richard E. Remington's twelve-member, all-state team was announced Halfback Neil Berry did indeed make the top squad as did St. Augustine's star Fullback, Chester Jurwiak, and Three Rivers Guard, Willard Cross. Remington chose Bay City Quarterback, Ray Sowers, as the team's honorary Captain.

Kalamazoo Central Left Tackle, Bruce Warren, was chosen as Captain of the second team All-Staters, and Guard Helmer made the third team eleven.

In the newspaper article announcing the selections, Richard E. Remington described the attributes of each of his first team selections. He had this to say about the state's best players from Kalamazoo;

"Neil Berry - Punter, Passer, Runner. Three little words but what strength of meaning. The best punter since the days of Bowles when he came down from Muskegon - the best passer since the days of Friedman or Renner at Michigan, and the best runner since Carp Julian's days at Michigan Agricultural College (at present Michigan State), and those who were lucky enough to have seen Carp run, really saw a football player.

"Chester Jurwiak - Although an all around player, plunger, punter, runner and passer and in all departments surpasses most boys. He is not quite as 'nifty' as Berry in 'picking' his way through but just as valuable and of course has more physique than Berry.

"In one game that I officiated, he had runs of 87, 67, and 43 yards for touchdowns, and in another championship game, he carried the ball 11 out of 12 times, practically the full length of the field for the only touchdown."

Although Remington's all-state team was considered "official" in some quarters, his wasn't the only all-state team selected. *Detroit News* sportswriter George Maskin also selected an all-state eleven. Maskin's team included only four players selected by Remington, including Three Rivers' Cross, Bay City's Sowers, and Kalamazoo's Berry. At the Center position, Maskin recognized Detroit Catholic Central's John McHale, a future teammate of Neil Berry in the Detroit Tiger organization.

The *Detroit Free Press* coaches poll also selected the best eleven players in the state and identified second and third team honorees. The *Free Press* article announcing the team proclaimed, "Michigan's best high school football players of 1938 . . . are placed on the official Free Press All-State team selected on the voting of 302 coaches and a host of outstanding officials," and went on to say that the coaches "considered 383 players in their voting before the first team was selected. It is because of this exhaustive study of the records of each player that the Free Press team is recognized as official."

The *Detroit Free Press* named Kalamazoo Central halfback, Neil Berry, Captain of the first team All-State squad for 1938. St. Augustine's Chester Jurwiak was a second-team selection and Willard Cross from Three Rivers garnered third team honors.

Of the three major all-state football teams honored, six state players were selected on two of them, only Neil Berry and Bay City's Raymond Sowers were named on all three.

Neil was also selected to the *Kalamazoo Gazette's* All-Southwest Michigan team as were teammates Hale Helmer, and Bruce Warren. The three were joined on the All-City team by Al Taborn, Bill Howland, and Reeves Comfort giving the Maroon Giants six of the eleven All-City selections. Neil and Chet Jurwiak were named the honorary co-Captains of the city squad.

Neil Berry, the fleet-footed "Flying Dutchman," equaled the high school achievement of the original Flying Dutchman, Herman Everhardus, when he was named captain of the *Detroit Free Press* all-state team in 1938. Following Central's undefeated campaign Coach Gene Thomas described Neil as "a natural that comes along once in ten years."

Comparing the prep careers of these standout performers Thomas, who had coached both boys, declared that Neil Berry "is a greater back right now than Herman Everhardus ever was."

After eleven years of coaching varsity football at Kalamazoo Central, with two Southwestern Michigan Conference and state championships to his credit, Coach Gene Thomas handed the coaching reins over to Fred "Dutch" Zuidema.

The *Kalamazoo Gazette* carried the story:

"One of Michigan's most successful coaches will drop out of football when school opens one month hence.

"Gene Thomas, former four-sport star at the University of Indiana and coach of an unbeaten Class A football eleven at Kalamazoo Central high school last fall, next month will become principal of Kalamazoo's Vine street junior high school. Kalamazoo reserve team coach, Fred (Dutch) Zuidema, a former Western State Teachers College star, will take over in football."

Kalamazoo Central's basketball and baseball teams didn't find the same level of success that the championship football team enjoyed. Neil made the starting lineup for the basketball team that only won four games—beating Benton Harbor three times.

Varsity Basketball starting lineup (from left to right) Neil Berry, Dick Hubert, Kurt Groggle, Bill Howland, and Dick Wiedmayer.

Photo courtesy of Linda Spann

Front row left to right: H. Nap, M. Kindle, H. Segee, Coach Donald Scott, W. Blanchard, T. Moffet, D. Rayman
Middle row: P. Elliot, A. Meyers, W. Lines, Mgr. L. Weissner, N. Berry, H. Otis, W. Vanden Berg;
Top row: Mgr. A. Weenink, K. Groggle, S. Fiedorek, N. Burnworth, R. Hubert, J. Marks, L. Bullard, Mgr. W. Baker.

Photo courtesy of Linda Spann

Neil batted .428 for Central's 1939 baseball team but the team only managed to win two games.

If someone asked me who helped me the most with the fundamentals of baseball . . . I'd say that coach would be Harold McKee.

~ Neil Berry

5

The Legion Maroons

American Legion Baseball

1936 to 1939

In the days before Little League, organized baseball for boys was provided by American Legion posts. American Legion baseball was a serious business with the top teams vying for district and state championships each year.

Kalamazoo's premier American Legion team, the Maroons, was started by a former Michigan ballplayer who had pitched the Michigan Wolverines to a Big Ten title in 1923, beating Minnesota in the championship game. Nicknamed 'Strike' by his Michigan teammates, his baseball stardom for Michigan impressed the local would-be Legion ballplayers—much more so than the fact that he was a doctor.

Dr. Homer 'Strike' Stryker moved to Kalamazoo with his wife Mary Jane in the summer of 1928 and not long after that he started the Maroons through the Joseph B. Westnedge American Legion Post. Dr. Stryker coached the Maroons from 1930 to 1936 leading the team to the American Legion state tournament every year except 1934 when they lost to Battle Creek in the district tournament.

Dr. Stryker often bore the entire cost of transporting and feeding his Legion Maroon teams during the depression era, and when they made their annual trip to the state tournament, he would also pay for the hotel rooms.

Dr. Stryker kept track of the Maroons expenses in a small notebook and years later he would produce it at events honoring team achievements and share what it took to keep the Maroons going in the early days.

Sports Editor Jerry Hagen reported on one such event in an August 1949 article in the *Kalamazoo Gazette*:

"As the Kiwanis club paid honors . . . to the Kalamazoo Junior Legion baseball squad which again won the district and zone championships, one of the luncheon guests was Dr. Homer Stryker, organizer of the Legion Juniors back in the twenties. Dr. Stryker made everyone drool by bringing along his little black book showing expense accounts on trips taken by the first Legion Junior clubs.

". . . A group of 20 or more business concerns contributed enough to get the program started—Partial uniforms and equipment. (Guess who footed the rest of the bills?) There was one item—Squad meals, game at Athens, $5.25, and there was another notation: 'Meals, three-day trip to State finals at Detroit, for squad, $58.' The squad, as now, included 16 to 18 boys . . ."

Players aspiring to play for the Maroons started out playing for the Legion Blues team until they were good enough to play for Dr. Stryker's competitive Legion Maroons team. In 1936, at the age of 14, Neil Berry was good enough to make the Legion Maroons team that lost in the semi-finals of the

The 1936 American Legion Junior team from Kalamazoo.
The team finished 3rd in the State Tournament
Top row, left to right: Moerman, Ross, McLean, Moffet,
Knapp, Groggle, Car, and Martin.
Middle Row: Reeves, Blanchard, Arnold, Pawloski, George,
Schumm, Maartens, and Travis
Front row: Soules, Webster, Coleman, Dr. H. H. Stryker,
coach, and Mascot Lee Stryker, Roe, Wielenga, and Berry.

Kalamazoo Gazette photo from the Berry scrapbook

state tournament.

In the fall of 1936, Dr. Stryker decided to return to University Hospital in Ann Arbor to study orthopedic surgery. He handed over the Maroons coaching duties to his assistant coach, Harold McKee, and while Dr. Stryker was inventing his Turning Frame hospital bed, McKee was coaching the Maroons to the finals of the 1937 state tournament.

McKee, who was also a coach and teacher for the Kalamazoo Public schools, guided the Maroons to 23 consecutive district titles, and a state championship in 1948.

As Neil told it, "Harold McKee helped me more than anybody because he was my American Legion coach. If someone asked me who helped me the most with the fundamentals of baseball and hit me a million ground balls—even though I could catch ground balls . . . what do you do with it after you catch it, where do you throw it?—I'd say that coach would be Harold McKee. I played for him for a long time. He would come early and bat me ground balls; get me out of bed in the morning to hit me ground balls, and after all the kids went home he'd hit me ground balls."

McKee spent that time because he recognized Neil's talent for baseball. A 1941 *Kalamazoo Gazette* article about Harold (Mac) McKee, declared that McKee "thrills at the idea of seeing one of his youngsters perform in advanced fields and he has plenty of opportunity because he has kept a mental list of his outstanding stars who 'had a natural ability for baseball' as McKee explains it.

"According to McKee, Neil Berry, all state footballer from Central and now playing short for the Sutherlands, was the best athlete he has worked with."

This after McKee had been at the helm of the Legion Juniors for five years. The early work on fundamentals with McKee was important. Neil explained, "As you grow up, even in college, the higher you go, the least amount of teaching you get. When you get to the big leagues the coaches look at it this way, 'God damn it–you're here, you should know this. We're not going to spend our time on fundamentals.'"

AMERICAN LEGION MAROONS BASEBALL – 1937

In 1937, Neil Berry was the starting shortstop and leadoff hitter for the Kalamazoo American Legion Maroons. The district tournament was held in Battle Creek where the winner earned the right to represent Southwestern Michigan in the American Legion state tournament in Detroit.

In 1934 the Battle Creek squad broke a string of four straight district wins by Coach Stryker's Legion Juniors but Dr. Stryker had his boys back on top in 1935 and '36. Now

Coach Harold McKee was looking to start a winning streak of his own. The district and state tournaments were double-elimination formats with seven-inning games.

Kalamazoo's Legion Juniors shutout Battle Creek, 9-0, in the first round behind the two-hit pitching of Bob Coleman and the team's 12 hit performance against the Battle Creek hurler.

After scoring a 4-2 victory over Marshall and dispensing with Union City, 4-1, a rematch with once-beaten Battle Creek loomed.

The *Kalamazoo Gazette* reported that the Kalamazoo club "started the scoring in the first as Berry lined a single into right field, went to second on a perfect bunt by Sweetland, and then raced home with the run when Pawloski singled to left."

Battle Creek tied the score at one apiece in the second before Bob Coleman batted home Sweetland, who had reached on an error, for a 2-1 Kalamazoo advantage. Battle Creek fought back to tie the score in the fourth and again in the sixth, knotting the score at 3-3, where it remained until the end of regulation (seven innings). Ken Johnson who had relieved Kurt Groggel in the sixth inning, drove in the go ahead run in the top of the eighth inning for a 4-3 Kalamazoo lead. In the bottom of the inning two singles put men on first and second for Battle Creek with nobody out. Johnson got the next two hitters out without allowing the runners to move up but with one strike on the next batter, the Battle Creek baserunners pulled off a double steal putting the tying and winning runs in scoring position with two outs. Fortunately, Johnson was able to get two more strikes by the batter to win the game and send Kalamazoo to the state tournament for the third year in a row.

For the tournament, Neil Berry collected nine hits in 16 at-bats for a stellar .563 batting average. He scored five of his team's 21 runs and played error-free defense at shortstop. Neil and the Kalamazoo Legion Junior Maroons team were ready for state tournament competition.

The *Kalamazoo Gazette* proclaimed:

LEGION JUNIORS GO TO DETROIT

Squad Leaves Tomorrow to Battle for State Baseball Title

"Coach Harold McKee and the Kalamazoo Legion Junior baseball squad will leave Thursday for Detroit where they will seek the state American Legion tournament championship this weekend in the annual meet at Northwestern field diamonds. Kalamazoo was beaten in the finals in 1935 and in the semi-finals in 1936.

Kalamazoo won the district title last weekend in a five-team elimination tournament at Battle Creek, being the only undefeated club in a tourney which saw every other participant beaten twice . . ."

Major League scouts, looking to stock their team's minor leagues with potential major leaguers, seldom missed state championship tournaments. Detroit scout Wish Egan was no exception.

Aloysius Jerome "Wish" Egan was a pitcher who started three games for the Tigers in September 1902. Two of the three were complete games but he ended up with an 0-2 record and a respectable 2.86 ERA (earned run average). Egan didn't stick with the Tigers but in 1905 he compiled a 6-15 record, with 19 complete games, as a starter for the St. Louis Cardinals. Shortly thereafter an arm injury spelled the end of his playing days. Wish Egan, who joined the Detroit Tiger organization as a scout in 1910, was a fixture at the Michigan American Legion state tournaments over the decades.

Egan, by then the Detroit Tiger's head scout, was looking for new talent at the tournament in 1937, but he was also there to keep his eye on a local pitcher he had been mentoring since 1935, a 16-year-old lefty named Hal Newhauser.

McKee's Kalamazoo squad started well in Detroit. With outstanding pitching from the arms of Bob Coleman, Kenny Johnson, Neil Webster, and Bill Blanchard the Maroons won their first four games.

Neil's girlfriend, Gloria followed the action and clipped these *Kalamazoo Gazette* stories for the Neil Berry scrapbook:

Kalamazoo Legion Juniors Defeat Saginaw, 7-5, In Detroit Tournament

"In the big Kalamazoo fourth, Travis singled and went to second on a sacrifice while Tanner received first base on an error. Two straight walks then forced one run in. Sweetland and Tanner then scored on another error by the second baseman. Pawloski completed the surge by singling in Berry with the winning run after the latter had reached first base on a hit."

Legion Juniors Blank Royal Oak, 7-0, for Second Tournament Win

". . . Lanky Neil Webster allowed only four hits during the seven inning contest with Royal Oak. He fanned 10 men while Wish Egan, the Detroit Tiger scout, was looking at him.

"Bob Travis led the hitting power for the Kalamazoo team as he connected for two hits in three times at the plate . . ."

Bob Coleman Wins Game by 3-to-1 Score

"Allowing only two singles in seven innings of play Bob Coleman, ace hurler of the Kalamazoo Legion Junior baseball team, pitched his team into the semi-finals of the state American Legion baseball tournament here, Saturday afternoon, with a thrilling 3-1 triumph over the Detroit Pittenger Post team.

"Kalamazoo jumped into a lead in the fifth inning by counting on a timely home run by Blanchard. A Detroit base hit, a fielder's choice, and a walk put two men on for the losers in the sixth. With the infield drawn in a slow grounder to Berry allowed a Detroit player to reach third base. Berry's throw to first in an attempt to catch the runner gave the Detroiter time to race to the plate for the losers' only run.

"Tanner beat out an infield hit past the pitcher to start the winning Kalamazoo sixth. Sweetland sacrificed and then Pawloski pulled a squeeze play to score Tanner. Coleman's single with Berry on base accounted for the third and final Kalamazoo tally."

The Berry scrapbook also contained this from the *Detroit Times*:

J. Westnedge Post Upsets Detroit Team

Kalamazoo, Vanker Only Undefeated Teams in Tourney

"Surprising even its most loyal followers, Joseph Westnedge Post of Kalamazoo stamped itself as a chief contender for The Detroit Times-State American Legion Junior Baseball Champion, Saturday, by winning twice to run its string of consecutive victories in the meet to four.

"After eking out a 3-0 victory over Channing in the forenoon, the Westerners came back to eliminate Pittenger Post of Detroit, five-time former state champions, in the nightcap, 3-1, in another pitchers' duel.

"Kalamazoo and Roose Vanker, Wayne County champions, are the only undefeated teams remaining in the race for the title. Vanker, after winning three in a row, drew the fourth round bye, and is paired with Kalamazoo Sunday at Northwestern Field at 10 o'clock."

Rain caused the postponement of Sunday's game pushing it to Monday morning. That Monday morning the boys from Kalamazoo ran into a buzz saw on the mound and an obstacle behind it. The buzz saw played for the Detroit Roose-Vanker Post and his name was Harold Newhauser.

This *Kalamazoo Gazette* clipping from the Berry scrapbook tells the story.

Lefty Newhauser Hurls No-Hitter for Detroit Nine

"NORTHWESTERN FIELD, DETROIT - The Detroit Roose-Vanker post baseball team defeated the Kalamazoo Legion Juniors, 1 to 0 here, Monday, in a fifth round game of the state legion junior baseball finals. The game had been rained off Sunday.

Detroit won in eight innings on a freak happening that resulted in the only tally of the contest. Harold (Lefty) Newhauser, Detroit ace, turned in a no-hit-no-run game against Kalamazoo to beat Neil Webster who allowed only three singles.

". . . Webster and Newhauser put on a dual worthy of teams which had been undefeated in play since last Friday morning. Newhauser's southpaw hooks were more than the Kalamazoo batters could fathom and he turned in a no-run, no-hit classic. Webster was going along in fine style too, and had allowed only two singles as the scoreless game went into the eighth inning.

"Bizecinski, first up for Detroit in the eighth, singled to left, Newhauser sacrificed and Okarski was passed to make possible a play at any base. Bizecinski stole third and Okarski later stole second with daring base running. Rabe was passed to fill the bases. Morgan hit a looper that Webster deflected to Sweetland at second base. Sweetland's hurried throw to prevent a run at the plate hit Base Umpire Hall in the head and the winning run scored. Hall was standing behind the pitcher's box."

Detroit Roose-Vanker wasn't done Monday and neither was Hal Newhauser. The Vanker squad drew an afternoon game with the once defeated Jackson team, winner of the morning game against Port Huron, knocking them out of the tournament.

The Detroit team handled Jackson, 9-3, but not before calling on "Lefty" Newhauser for some relief work.

Still not done for the day Detroit Roose-Vanker was slated for a rematch with Kalamazoo in the Monday night matchup. A Detroit win would crown them American Legion Junior champions for 1937. A Kalamazoo win would mean a Tuesday showdown for the championship.

With no Newhauser curveballs to contend with and no umpire's head to avoid, Kalamazoo starting pitcher Ken Johnson tamed the Detroit nine giving up three hits in a 3-0 shutout. Johnson also tallied two of Kalamazoo's eight hits against the previously unbeaten Vanker squad.

Kalamazoo started the scoring off in the very first inning when singles by Sweetland, Coleman, and Matevia resulted in a run for the victors.

In the third Johnson scored after his double was followed by a pinch-hit single by Pawloski. The third and final run of the contest was scored when Matevia tripled to deep center and then scored when the Detroit shortstop threw the ball away attempting to get him at third.

The game to decide the 1937 American Legion Junior championship was set for Tuesday. The Joseph B. Westnedge Post from Kalamazoo versus Detroit's Roose-Vanker post and their ace, Harold Newhauser.

This *Kalamazoo Gazette* article from the Berry scrapbook describes the action:

"In the title contest, Kalamazoo scored first in the opening inning when Sweetland beat out an infield hit, advanced on an error and scored after two were out when Matevia's fly ball fell out of McDonald's hands in right field. Saroli's home run for Detroit tied the score at 1-1 in the second but Kalamazoo went ahead again, 2-1, in the fourth when Coleman was safe on Okarski's error, stole second, went to third on a passed ball and scored on Blanchard's squeeze bunt.

"Detroit then scored four runs on two hits in the fifth inning . . . Saroli singled and Bizecinski walked. Newhauser bunted to move the runners along and all were safe when Coleman's throw to third was too late to get Saroli. Webster replaced Coleman and forced in the tying run when Okarski was hit by a pitched ball. The Kalamazoo outfielders moved in a little for a throw home after a fly ball. Then Rabe hit one over Stillwell's head in left field for a triple that cleaned the sacks . . . Webster fanned the next three and was invincible the rest of the contest. But so was Newhauser . . ."

Hal Newhauser followed up his no-hit shutout on Monday with a two-hitter Tuesday leading his Detroit Roose-Vanker post to a 5-2 victory over Kalamazoo and the 1937 American Legion Junior championship. Harold Newhauser received the Kiki Cuyler Award as the tournament's best player. If the word wasn't already out, everyone now knew about Harold Newhauser, the left-handed whiz kid that was coveted by Detroit Tiger scout Wish Egan.

Author's note: Newhauser *was considered the correct spelling at the time. His name would be spelled* Newhouser *during his hall-of-fame career with the Detroit Tigers.*

Neil Berry got one of the two hits off Newhauser that day. His four tournament hits resulted in a paltry .167 batting average, but after making two errors in the first game, the 15-year-old shortstop from Kalamazoo settled down and didn't commit another error in the tournament. His seven game total of 11 putouts and 20 assists was impressive and didn't escape the trained eye of Detroit scout Wish Egan.

As Neil told it, "The scout for the Tigers, he was their head scout, and he probably had 20 guys working for him, his name was Wish Egan, an old Irishman. I'd been playin' ball in Detroit since I was eleven/twelve years old for the American Legion. Every year at the end of summer they had a tournament, an elimination tournament. We had to go to Battle Creek and beat somebody from around here, like Marshall, Coldwater, or Battle Creek itself, [before we could] go to Detroit and play in the state tournament. So we finally get to Detroit, that's where he looked at a lotta kids, Wish Egan, the scout. He started talking to me when I was thirteen, fourteen."

AMERICAN LEGION MAROONS BASEBALL – 1938

Tryouts for the 1938 American Legion baseball team were announced in the *Kalamazoo Gazette*:

"Legion Juniors Report Monday - McKee Calls Out Boys Who Seek Places

"Comes another baseball season and another opportunity for young diamond enthusiasts to show their talent. Coach Harold McKee announces the first American Legion baseball practice will be held next Monday at 6 p.m. at Upjohn field.

"After a regional elimination meet between Battle Creek-Kalamazoo area teams, the winner represents the district at the state tournament at Detroit. A banquet is held at the end of the year by the sponsors, the Joseph B. Westnedge Post of the American Legion.

"For many years Kalamazoo Legion teams have been at the tops among state contestants. Last year the Juniors, rated the greatest in Kalamazoo history by Coach McKee, won the Celery City League and Independent league titles of Kalamazoo, the district championship, and played in the finals in Detroit, losing only to the Detroit Roose-Vanker Post.

"Another great year is in prospect. A few veterans return but all positions are wide open and any youthful stars are invited to come out for the team.

"Among members coming back for the second year of play are Neil Berry, Bill McLain, and Bill Vanderberg, infielders; Kurt Groggel and Bill Blanchard, pitchers; and Ken Stillwell, an outfielder. Needed especially are first baseman, outfielders and batterymen.

"Candidates will be given an opportunity to try out for any position they desire, however.

"In the event that weather is bad Monday, the practice will be postponed and further notice of Legion Junior activities will be found in the Gazette."

Coach McKee found the players he needed to make another run for district and state honors. Among those joining the "veterans" from the 1937 team were infielders Ernst, Strobel, and Nap; outfielder Stan Fiedorek; catchers Reeves Comfort and Dietrich; and pitchers Rice and Harlun Tiefenthal.

When the 1938 American Legion District tournament rolled around, Mckee's Maroon Juniors and their star shortstop were ready. The '38 districts were a six-team affair with Battle Creek, Charlotte, Marshall, Reading, and Union City all hoping to upend defending champion Kalamazoo. American Legion tournaments were a double-elimination format with seven-inning games. If necessary extra innings were played to determine the winner.

Neil Berry's scrapbook contained only partial coverage of the tournament. The following excerpts are from Jack Sherman's articles from the *Kalamazoo Gazette*:

Kalamazoo Legion Juniors Beat Charlotte in District Tournament Tilt

Win, 14 to 12, In Tenth at Battle Creek

Berry Stars at Bat with Five Hits in Six Trips.

"BAILEY FIELD, Battle Creek - The Kalamazoo Legion Juniors outlasted the Charlotte nine here Friday morning to win their first round district tourney game, 14 to 12, in 10 innings of play. Starring for the winners at the plate was Neil Berry who collected five for six and scored three runs himself . . ."

Kalamazoo Team Leads Legion

Beats Union City, 1 to 0, In Fast Game

"BATTLE CREEK - Kalamazoo's American Legion Juniors play in the finals of the district baseball tournament here Sunday afternoon at 2, meeting the winner of the Charlotte - Union City game which is scheduled for 10 in the morning.

"Saturday morning the legionnaires resumed relations with Readings[sic] after rain had postponed a game Friday and won, 11-3. Saturday afternoon, Harold McKee's Kalamazoo aggregation defeated Union City, the tourney darkhorse, 1-0, in the best game of the series.

"Kurt Groggel shut out the Union City aggregation . . . with men on base Groggel was the master and with his curveball and high hard one working perfectly, and errorless support behind him, it wasn't such a difficult job.

"Neil Berry continued his marvelous stickwork and got three for four in the morning and one for three in the afternoon to run his average to .750 with nine hits in 12 trips to the platter."

McKee's Kalamazoo Legion Maroons made it through the weekend undefeated and then beat the once defeated

Charlotte/Union City winner Monday morning to win their fourth consecutive American Legion district tournament.

In the 1938 American Legion State tournament Kalamazoo dropped their first contest on Friday morning, a 4-3 loss to Royal Oak. After the Maroons scored two runs in the second and another in the fourth, the Royal Oak hitters got to Kalamazoo hurler Kurt Groggel, pushing single runs home in the fourth, fifth, sixth, and seventh innings to take the game. Starting the tournament in the losers bracket meant the Kalamazoo team would be playing more baseball that Friday. With elimination games looming Harold McKee called on Harlun Tiefenthal to take the mound against Ann Arbor. It didn't start well with the Ann Arbor nine touching Tiefenthal for a run in the first and three more in the second, but Kalamazoo tied it up with four runs of their own in the top of the third and scored five more times before Ann Arbor pushed across another run. Tiefenthal went the distance for a 10-6 Kalamazoo win. Next up was Sturgis.

McKee had already used his best two pitchers and he still had to get his Maroons past Sturgis to set up a matchup with Detroit-Algers the next morning. So Harold McKee, short on starting pitchers, rolled the dice and went with the best arm on the team. He brought Neil Berry in from shortstop to pitch against Sturgis.

A clipping from an unidentified newspaper in the Berry scrapbook told the story.

"The top pitching performance of the day was registered by Neil Berry, of Kalamazoo, in a third round game. Berry gave [up] just one single as Kalamazoo eliminated Sturgis, 9-0. Howard Perucki singled to right in the fourth with two out. Berry also hit a home run."

Neil's teammates supported his brilliant pitching with an 11 hit, nine run, attack scoring in every inning except the fifth.

The Maroons staved off elimination that Friday but lost to Detroit-Algers in the Saturday morning game. The Detroit Roose-Vanker post, with Hal Newhauser pitching in his last American Legion State tournament, easily defended their crown and won the 1938 state championship.

With the secret out about Hal Newhauser's powerful left arm and his Legion ball pitching dominance, major league teams – most notably the Detroit Tigers and Cleveland Indians – couldn't wait to sign the 17-year-old. Detroit's Wish Egan, who had previously signed Newhauser's older brother, Dick, had the inside track and closed the deal on the evening of August 6, 1938, right after the American Legion tournament. Egan got Newhauser's signature on a Detroit contract for a $500 cash bonus.

Shortly after Newhauser signed the contract, Indians' head scout, Cy Slapnicka, pulled up in a shiny new car. He offered Hal a $15,000 bonus and the new car, but it was too late, Hal Newhauser was the property of the Detroit Tigers. Slapnicka had missed the boat while picking up the car.

AMERICAN LEGION MAROONS BASEBALL – 1939

This was the last season that the then 17-year old Neil Berry was eligible to play with coach Harold McKee's American Legion Junior Maroons. He would make the best of it, showcasing his talent locally, then on the bigger stage of the American Legion district and state tournaments.

The 1939 district tournament was a three team affair between Kalamazoo, Battle Creek, and Marshall.

Kalamazoo had no trouble beating Marshall, 13-1, in their opening game Friday morning but Ken Stillwell couldn't find the strike zone against Battle Creek in the afternoon game, issuing four walks and a wild pitch. Combined with two passed balls by Jack Marks, the Maroons gifted Battle Creek with three runs in the second inning. BC added three more runs in the third, aided by a Kalamazoo error. Rice took over for Stillwell but the damage was done. Kalamazoo could only muster five hits and a fourth inning run, losing 6-1 for their first loss in the district tournament.

On Saturday morning Battle Creek eliminated Marshall, 6-2, setting up their chance for a district win if they could beat Kalamazoo on Saturday afternoon. The Kalamazoo squad was looking to avenge their earlier loss and force a final game on Sunday.

The Berry scrapbook includes these clippings from the *Kalamazoo Gazette*:

Legion Whips Battle Creek

Kalamazoo Wins, 10-2; Plays Again Today

"BAILEY FIELD, BATTLE CREEK-Kalamazoo American Legion Juniors walloped Battle Creek, 10-2, Saturday afternoon, in a district tournament game, avenging a 6-1 defeat of the day before.

"Neil Berry, Central high school's all-state halfback and star shortstop, took the mound for the Kalamazoo team today and turned in a three-hit performance. He fanned 11 batters and had the game in hand all the way.

"Bush and Berry led the attack on three Battle Creek hurlers, each getting three hits."

Kalamazoo Legion Juniors Win

Defeat Battle Creek, 1-0 in Title Contest

Kelly Hurls three-Hitter Against Food City Ball Club.

"BATTLE CREEK - Kalamazoo American Legion Junior baseball team today held the district championship and the right to compete in the annual Legion state tournament at Detroit on August 4, 5, and 6 by virtue of its thrilling 1-0 victory over Battle Creek here yesterday.

"Kalamazoo won the contest, its second in two days from the home town squad, in the seventh frame on two hits and a wild pitch. Gerald Kelley hurled three hit ball for the winners.

"Stan Fiedorek's double started Kalamazoo's victory spree in the seventh. He went to third on a wild pitch and scored on Strobel's timely single. No men were out when the winning run scored. The winners obtained only three hits up to this time.

"A double play, which nipped Westcott at the plate in the seventh, staved off a possible Battle Creek run."

In a sidebar to the above article the *Gazette* reported:

Kalamazoo May Not Go to Finals

"Unless some sports fan or legion post comes to the rescue, Kalamazoo's American Legion Juniors may not play in the state finals at Detroit Aug 4 to 6. An individual paid the way through the district meet which Kalamazoo won yesterday at Battle Creek."

The individual who paid the expenses for the district tournament is not known, but it is known that Dr. Homer Stryker was still a big fan of the American Legion Maroons team that he started a decade earlier. It is unlikely that Dr. Stryker would allow his Legion Maroons to miss the state tournament.

The 1939 Legion Juniors state tournament would be Neil Berry's last chance to impress pro scouts and college recruiters on the biggest baseball stage in the state for up and coming teenagers. He didn't disappoint.

The following excerpts are from newspaper articles in the Berry scrapbook:

Kalamazoo Legion Juniors Win Twice in Detroit Meet

"Neil Berry all-state football player from Kalamazoo Central, tossed air-tight relief ball to save Kalamazoo a 2-0 win over Clawson yesterday morning. Berry came into the game in the seventh frame with two men on base with nobody out. He struck out the next three batters, Ken Stillwell's home run won the contest for the Kalamazoo team.

"In the second round Kalamazoo nipped Flint, 3-2. Kelley pitched all the way for the winners. The undefeated Maroons obtained only five hits but bunched them to score twice in the seventh.

"Best pitching performance of the day was by Harlan Tiefenthal, of Kalamazoo, in the first game. He held them to one hit during the six innings he hurled."

Legion Juniors Reach Semi-Finals of State Tournament

"DETROIT – Kalamazoo's surprising Legion Junior baseball club, with members of an unbeaten State high and strong Central high squads in its lineup, won its way to the fifth round of the annual American Legion Junior baseball tournament here yesterday afternoon by nosing out Faust, of Detroit, 4-3.

"Kalamazoo lost its first game Saturday morning when a heavy-hitting Century nine eked out a close 4-3 win over the invading Maroons . . .

"Century rallied with three runs in the sixth inning to nip Kalamazoo at the finish of the first contest on Saturday. Neil Berry, Kalamazoo's all-state football player and Friday's pitching hero, was the victim as Century bunched four singles and a double in the big inning to win. The final run was scored by George Lapay who slid under catcher Jack Marks, holding the ball. Berry starred for Kalamazoo at bat with three singles and a home run."

The loss to Detroit Century on Saturday morning left

the Kalamazoo Legion Juniors with one loss in the double-elimination tournament.

The Kalamazoo boys—hoping to avoid elimination—played the Detroit Pittenger Post team on Sunday morning. It didn't go well. The Pittenger nine need only two hits to take advantage of three errors and score six first inning runs.

Pittenger counted four more tallies in the third inning and Kalamazoo scored four of their own in the bottom half. The Detroit team could only push a single run across the plate in the remaining four innings but their lead was too much for the Legion Juniors to overcome. Final score Pittenger 11, Kalamazoo 7.

The Detroit Roose-Vanker post again defended its title defeating the Detroit Century post.

Kalamazoo settled for a third place tie with Sturgis, but could boast the tournament's best player when Neil Berry was selected to receive the Kiki Cuyler trophy.

Kiki (rhymes with eye-eye) Cuyler was born in Sturgeon Point, Michigan and was an outfielder in the National League for 18 seasons. Many of those seasons were spent with the Chicago Cubs (1928 - 1935) while Neil followed the team on the family radio. Cuyler had an impressive .321 career batting average and was elected to the Hall of Fame by the Veteran's Committee in 1968. The award was created in 1929 to honor Cuyler for his professional baseball career as an outstanding outfielder and hitter.

A clipping from an unnamed newspaper in the Berry scrapbook told the story.

Neil Berry Voted Trophy as Best Player in State Legion Tourney

"Berry, an all-state football player with Kalamazoo Central's undefeated team last fall, and a star on the basketball court, was given the Ki-Ki [Cuyler] trophy awarded annually to the Legion player voted tops by umpires, scorers, officials and newspapermen.

"To win the honor he hit .530 with nine safeties in 17 attempts. He played brilliantly at shortstop and turned in two neat pitching jobs, one a relief stint that saved a game for Kalamazoo."

Neil Berry's American Legion baseball career was over and Wish Egan was there with a Detroit contract.

As Neil told it, "[Detroit Tiger scout, Wish Egan] asked me if I thought about playin' ball, and I told him I was gonna go to college. He said, 'ya know Charlie Maher and I are good friends,' [they had] kinda an unwritten agreement, 'if he has any good kids at Western, he gives me a call and I go look at 'em.' To sign [them] with Detroit, and he signed up a few. So he said, 'if you go to Western that's fine. Do you want to go to Western?' I said, yeah. My heart was set on Western, for one thing, Western had as good a baseball team as anybody. I wanted to go to school to play baseball, and if I could, get a degree. Then I don't know what'll happen, you never know, I'd like to coach someplace, [and] teach. I liked history.

"I had offers, very good offers, for scholarships, by letter and in person, people from the schools. Michigan had a good offer but they wanted too much out of me for what they gave me. My whole theory at that time in my life, I wanted to play [baseball]. So North Carolina State, Purdue, Michigan State, four or five other schools, and Western offered me this, that, and the other thing. I wanted to play ball so I took that into consideration. I was dumb then because Western is very limited on how long you can play baseball [because of the weather]. Down south they didn't have to worry about the weather. In Kalamazoo, in your teenage years, you have a schedule of 18 games and you get snowed out of four or five of 'em, get rained out of a few of 'em, so you play eight or nine games [in a summer season].

"I had other offers, so all my chips weren't in one pot, you might say. I had a guy, Senator Wadsworth, who would give me an appointment to West Point. But I didn't want that, that'd be too much pressure to play ball for West Point. Just to play ball, that's a pretty tough school, academic wise.

"In the meantime, the vice president of the St. Louis Cardinals just showed up here one day, Kalamazoo, in a big long Cadillac. He asked me what I was gonna do, and I said as of right now I'm going to college. He said, 'How would you like to come down to St. Louis and work out with the Cardinals? Let us have a look at ya.' I think I was sixteen/seventeen, and I said well I'll tell ya what, I made a promise to my high school coach, that before I would do anything like that, I would talk to him, and have him talk to you. He said, Well, let's go talk to your coach. I said he's not in Kalamazoo right now he's in Ann Arbor working on his masters or doctorate.

"He said, 'Well, let's go.' [The next day] I packed my bag just like I was gonna go places and we went over to Ann Arbor. We found him real easy. Went up to his room and we told him what the scoop was, and he said, 'now listen, I know a little about the rules, he can't [play in a game]. If he goes down there, works out, fine.'

"I can field all the ground balls, catch all the fly balls, take all the batting practice, as long as I don't get into a game with the other guys, I can keep my amateur status.

"He said, 'now don't go goofing him up so when he comes back he better sign with us because he's not eligible for college anymore because he pinch-hit, or did this, or did that. Don't give me that stuff.'

"He promised he wouldn't do that. So we left and got down around Toledo, and he said, 'you know, I just thought of something, the Cardinals are in the east, on an eastern road trip, but we can go to Columbus,' which was the Cardinals

*The Upjohn Park Team that Won the Lions Club
Tournament
Left to Right, seated: George Georgion, Neil Berry, Neil
Schrier, Tom Molenaar, Bill Moerman, and George
Moerman
Back row, left to right: Clarence Pool, Bob Travis, Hubert
Wolthuis, Andy Vander Molen, Herman Zichterman, and
Richard Durian*

Kalamazoo Gazette photo from the Berry scrapbook

number one minor league team, 'we can go there.' I know
he knew what the scoop was because nobody that's a vice
president doesn't know where their team is, but I didn't care,
me being a sixteen/seventeen-year-old kid and Columbus a
step below the big leagues, 'sure I'll go there.' So we went
to Columbus and I worked out for a week there. He never
asked me if I wanted to hit or anything, I just fielded ground
balls, and threw, and this and that. I met a lot of guys there
that later on, when I signed, years later, these guys were

all big league big wheels. Two or three of 'em became big league managers. I played with one of 'em at Buffalo when he was going down, I was going up. So I met a lot of good ballplayers there.

"So my deal at that time . . . I wanted to play ball. Western had the good reputation and I had three or four teachers in school who vouched for me, my coaches of course, and a couple of academic teachers. But when it got down to the nitty-gritty, [my] marks were fine, good, but [I was] lacking a half year of science. [They told me] you have to take a half year of either chemistry or physics."

Neil was a year younger than most of his 1938 classmates due to starting kindergarten at the age of four. He had also missed considerable time from school in his Sophomore year due to his illness, so in the fall of 1939, Neil went back to Kalamazoo Central for a semester of morning classes, to get his missing science credit. He took chemistry with Mr. Mesick, and also took history and math. Neil remembered, "I didn't mind math 'cause I liked the math teacher. He used to come out and umpire our baseball games. I liked him, his name was Radabal."

That fall Neil got the Upjohn Park gang back together to play in the Lions Club softball tournament. They didn't have uniforms and hadn't played organized ball together but they had always been good friends and good athletes. They won the tournament.

Later that fall tragedy struck the Lorentzen family when on October 28, 1939, Deane Lorentzen, Gloria's mother, died of a heart attack at the age of 52. At the time Gloria was the only child still living at home. Gloria and her father Frank Lorentzen and later the Berry family would occupy the family home on Inkster Ave. for the next seven decades.

As the decade of the '30s came to a close, the economic outlook in Kalamazoo was looking better. Eighteen new industries had been established and employment in Kalamazoo increased by almost 3,000 from 1935 to 1939.

After losing in 1934, the Detroit Tigers won their first World Series title in 1935, beating the Chicago Cubs four games to two. Detroit owner Frank Navin died of a heart attack a few weeks after his Tigers brought home the championship for Detroit. Navin's silent partner, Walter O. Briggs, bought Navin's share from his widow and became the sole owner of the Detroit franchise. In 1938, after expanding capacity and remodeling Navin Field, Briggs renamed the Tiger's home park Briggs Stadium.

Detroit first baseman, Hank Greenberg, won his first Most Valuable Player Award in 1935; he won his second as an outfielder in 1940. The Tigers keystone combination of shortstop Billy Rogell and second baseman Charlie Gehringer played together for seven seasons from 1932 through 1938. They led the league in double plays in 1933 (they were second in '35 and '38), and Gehringer won the American League batting title (.371) and the Most Valuable Player Award in 1937.

On the world stage, the second half of the decade saw Adolf Hitler and the Nazi party's tumultuous rise to power in Germany. The successes of two African-American athletes played key roles in debunking Hitler's proclamations of Aryan racial superiority.

In August 1936, Jesse Owens and his United States teammates traveled to Berlin, Germany to compete in the Summer Olympics. Hitler, who was using the Olympics to show off a resurgent Nazi Germany, had high hopes that German athletes would dominate the games, but Owens almost single-handily dashed those hopes with his four gold medal performance. Owens won the 100-meter dash, long jump, and the 200-meter sprint. He was also part of the winning 4 × 100 meter sprint relay team when two Jewish-American teammates weren't allowed to compete for political reasons.

The 1938 boxing rematch between Joe Louis and Germany's Max Schmeling would be remembered as one of the most famous fights and major sporting events of the 20th century. After knocking out Louis in 12 rounds in 1936, Schmeling became a national hero and the Nazi regime declared that his victory over an African-American was proof of Aryan superiority. Prior to the rematch, a Nazi publicist declared that when Schmeling won, his prize money would be used to build German tanks. This time Joe Louis settled the matter quickly, beating Max Schmeling in two minutes and four seconds. Germany built the tanks anyway, and Adolf Hilter was selected as Time magazine's 1938 Man of the Year for not using them.

The question came up, 'Are you going to be able to play on Sunday?' The Dutch deal came up.

~Neil Berry

6

Sutherland Paper Co.

Kalamazoo City League Baseball

1940

The dawning of the fifth decade of the twentieth century found the city of Kalamazoo debt-free and recovered from the great depression. It also found a city population that wasn't growing for the first time in history. While Kalamazoo Township's population increased 5%, and the County's 10%, from 1930 to 1940, the city's population dropped by 689 (1.3%). This was the first time that the city lost population between the federal censuses, but the citizens of Kalamazoo, and the entire nation, were focused on a much larger issue. The axis powers in Europe and Asia were waging war overseas and details of their triumphs were reported daily in newspapers and on the radio. For many residents, baseball provided a needed break from everyday worries and concern over the ever-increasing likelihood of American involvement in the war.

The Detroit Tigers inserted their prized lefthander, 19-year-old Hal Newhouser, into their 1940 rotation after a single season in the minors. The best player Wish Egan ever signed was good enough to perfect his craft against major league batsmen.

The local baseball scene in 1940 was robust with independent recreational leagues for various skill levels; competitive Industrial leagues for company sponsored teams; and semi-pro baseball at Ramona Park. The independent league teams were sponsored by churches, fraternal orders, law enforcement agencies, or small businesses and the players did not have to be employed or otherwise affiliated with the sponsor. To play for an Industrial league squad a player had to be employed by the sponsoring company. Semi-pro sponsors could actually pay their players, but, according to Neil, "the guys got paid once in a while" when they " took up a collection for the tavern right next to the ballpark. They'd all go over there after the game and drink four of five beers and get a little giddy."

The seven-inning, city league games were played at ballparks all over the city and surrounding area. Many of the ballparks were owned by companies sponsoring teams including KP Park, Stationery Park, Hospital Field, Fuller's Field, and Kindleberger Park, home to the strong KVP (Kalamazoo Vegetable Parchment) team. KVP drew more than 8,000 fans during its championship years in the 1930s.

Other ballparks hosting city league games during the early forties were VerSluis Park, a new ballpark on Douglas Avenue in Kalamazoo's Northside neighborhood; Riverview Park (home of today's Homer Stryker field), along the banks of the Kalamazoo River; and Upjohn Park, in Neil Berry's front yard.

An annual season-ending tournament determined the city Independent and Industrial league champions and those champions played for the overall city championship. The top tournament games and the city championship game were played at Hyames Field and would typically draw thousands of fans. Hyames Field at Western State Teachers College opened in 1939 and was part of an athletic field renovation project that included the construction of Waldo Stadium.

In 1940 the top Independent leagues were Valley City, won by the Legion Blues; Celery City, with Louie's Restaurant taking top honors; and Paper City with the Sheriff's Dept. team coming out on top. Other teams that competed in the Independent leagues included De Molay (a fraternal organization), Fiedorek Service Station, Gilmore Bros., Legion Maroons, Mohawk Cleaners, Quality Bakers, Quality Dairy, Shepard Sales, St. Mary's, and The Upjohn Co.

The city's two Industrial leagues—the American and National—crowned first and second half champs and those teams played to determine an overall league winner. KVP (Parchment) was the first half champ of the American Industrial League and Checker Cab took first-half honors in the National Industrial circuit. Also fielding teams in the city Industrial leagues were Allied Paper, Bryant Paper, Fuller Manufacturing Co., and Sutherland Paper Company in the American; and Atlas Press, General Gas, Kalamazoo Stationery, Master-Craft, and Michigan State Employees in the National circuit. The talent level of the top Kalamazoo leagues was first-rate with industrial league teams recruiting and hiring top baseball players based solely on their baseball talent.

Many of the area's top players were also recruited to play semi-pro ball for Columbia Cleaners at Ramona park, on Long Lake. With most of the nine-inning semi-pro games being played on weekends, Columbia Cleaners was able to recruit top city league players for their roster, including manager Punk Smathers, Dave Ross, and Bob Coleman, Sutherland Paper's outfield. Sutherland second sacker Herb Burris also played for the Cleaners. Sutherland's top industrial league rival, Parchment, supplied power-hitting first baseman, Big Bill Kean, and catcher Wally Koch to the Cleaners' lineup. Other top city league ballplayers that also played for Columbia Cleaners included Louie's Restaurant infielders Augie Klosterman and Bob Metzger; Al Karchunas, infielder, Allied Paper; and Dana DeHammer, infielder, Bryant Paper. The Cleaner's pitching staff included city league stars, Miles Crowe, Sutherland; Bob Lester, Bryant; Ken Cavanaugh, Louie's; and Ray Hiatt, Fuller Manufacturing.

The Cleaner's lineup also included the now 18-year-old Neil Berry. Neil had already been playing with the Cleaners during their Ramona park, home games.

As Neil told it, "The question came up, 'Are you going to be able to play on Sunday?' The Dutch deal came up. Even semi-pro ball you gotta play on Sunday. Well, that came to the [forefront] and the guy who was the manager of a team out at Long Lake—he also managed the paper company team—name was Smathers, Punk Smathers. He worked near my dad, they knew each other, and he came over to the house and he talked to my mother. [He] asked [her] if I could play on Sunday. I was only 15, 16 [years old] and you're not supposed to really play [semi-pro ball at that age] at Ramona Park. They had a team that was owned and run by a guy who had a cleaners in Battle Creek called Columbia Cleaners. His name was Norm Grimes and they got the best ballplayers in Kalamazoo . . . and it was like a semi-pro team. [We were] supposed to get paid, [but] we didn't get paid nothin'. But anyway, I wasn't supposed to play with those guys, but I did. [Punk Smathers] talked to my dad, of course my dad, he didn't care [if I played on Sunday], but my mother was brought up in the church, and so was I. My mother, she probably thought you're going to do it anyway . . . after you're 18, so she said, 'well, ok.' Actually, instead of playing in the yard, I played out there."

The stars playing for Columbia Cleaners and/or city league teams were household names among Kalamazoo area sports fans including hurlers Sum Sleep (Parchment), and Vern Balch (Master-Craft); catchers Ray Fitzgerald (Louie's), and Emko Slater (Sutherland); outfielders Jim Kline and Bill Hill (Parchment); infielders John Maartens (Sutherland), Mike Bass (Quality Bakers), Red Van Lente (Checker Cab), and Neil Berry, the young, slick-fielding shortstop. Neil's speed, rifle arm, and range at shortstop, along with his baby-faced good looks, made him a fan favorite. And he could also pitch.

Neil Berry's high school graduation photo.

Photo courtesy of Linda Spann

In the spring of 1940, Neil was finishing up his high school credits at Kalamazoo Central and was playing shortstop for the Columbia Cleaners semi-pro squad at Ramona Park. Neil was also pitching and playing shortstop for Fiedorek's Service Station of the Celery City Independent League. After his American Legion tournament heroics and a hot start to the baseball season, the Sutherland Paper Company took notice.

A May 29, 1940, *Kalamazoo Gazette* clipping from the Berry scrapbook documented Sutherland Paper Company's interest:

"Neil Berry, who has been playing recreational league baseball with Fiedorek's Service, has been sized up by Sutherland Paper Co's scouts . . . As soon as school is out in June, Neil will be in the line-up with the carton makers. He is still planning a college career at WSTC this fall however."

While playing for Fiedorek, Neil helped the team to a record of three wins, one loss, and two ties (ties were declared due to darkness or time constraints). Along the way, he pitched a two-hit shutout against eventual Celery City League winner, Louie's.

When school was out in June, Neil went to work for the Sutherland Paper Company. It's not clear what his responsibilities were at work, but it didn't really matter, Neil Berry was hired to do what he does best, play baseball. Sutherland was one of the top Industrial league teams in Kalamazoo, taking over from the Parchment club that had won without serious challenge for several years before Sutherland won the city crown in 1939. No doubt Neil's father, Hazen, long a Sutherland Paper Company employee, enjoyed some bragging rights when Neil started playing for the defending city champions. Neil joined Sutherland for the season's second half after the Parchment squad, anxious to regain their dominance, had won the 1940 American Industrial League first-half crown without a loss.

June 1940, was also the month that France fell to Nazi Germany and there was a growing feeling that America would not escape involvement in World War II. While America and Kalamazoo prepared for war, local baseball continued to provide an entertaining diversion.

The *Kalamazoo Gazette* coverage by Everett Clarke—saved for the Berry scrapbook by Neil's biggest fan, Gloria Lorentzen—tells the story of the second half race in Kalamazoo's top league:

City Champions Handed Initial Defeat of Half

"Inspired Bryant Paper Company, a baseball team that forfeited its last contest because only eight men showed up, handed the defending city champion Sutherland Company its lone defeat of the second half race in the American Industrial league race, 5-4, last night at Upjohn Park.

"Sutherland had already won from the strong Parchment, first-half champion ball club, and was all set to capture the second division of play. Defeat puts the losers last night in a tie for first with Parchment and Checker Cabs.

"A fluke home run by Bob Lester in the first inning decided the victory in favor of Bryant. Lester, a pitcher who was playing first base in a makeshift Bryant lineup, smashed a clean 'single' to left. The ball hit a rough spot in the outfield and bounced away from Dave Ross's hands and went for a home run. This hit scored three runs for Bryant and tied the count. "Sutherland started strong with a five hit barrage in the opening period which netted three runs."

Punk Smathers Hero of Hectic City Loop Game

"The bat of La Salle (Punk) Smathers, silent for more than a month, spoke last evening at Kindelberger [*sic*] park and so the defending city champion Sutherland baseball team was lifted from the depths of defeat to a tie for first place in the American Industrial League.

"The Sutherlands outslugged a good Checker Cab

Company nine for a 9-7 victory in do-or-die attempt to stay in the race, already in its last stages. It was the champions third win against one defeat in second half play and the triumph was really well earned.

"It was none other than popular Punk Smathers three hits that enabled the Sutherland team to win. His mighty triple to the road in right field in the sixth scored the tying run and then he scored himself after a bad play at third with what proved to be the winning tally.

"Sutherland will meet Parchment next week Wednesday at Kindleberger in a game which will probably decide the second half race."

Marks Hits with Coleman on Base in Final Inning

"City champion Sutherland Paper Company baseball team waited until the seventh inning at Upjohn park last evening and then handed Parchment its first city league defeat of the season, 3-2.

"It was dependable Clair Marks' single with Bob Coleman on second base which turned the tide of a real battle . . . typical of those put on by the city league rivals of past seasons. One man was out when Marks pushed Coleman across the plate with the telling tally. The Sutherland third sacker had been forced to second when Punk Smathers was walked intentionally.

"Sutherland and Parchment both presented strengthened lineups for a capacity crowd last night. The winners have a 'youngster' infield for the second half race and it is a fast one indeed. John Maartens is on first, Bob Coleman on third, and Neil Berry is at short. Burris, a newcomer, started at second last night. Dave Ross, formerly of Western, is in right. Parchment has veteran Tris Kline in center and Bill Hill, Western State first baseman, in left. Ken Johnson has been added to the pitching staff. He was on Western's team this year.

"The revived Sutherland nine started off at full steam last night and grabbed two runs and two hits in the first frame. Dave Ross led off by walking. Berry then beat out a bunt to first base. Coleman's first hit pushed the runners around, Ross scoring a moment later on Webster's bad throw to first after a grounder, and Berry counting on a fielder's choice.

Sutherlands Down Checker Cab Nine, 2-0

"Sutherland Paper Company took advantage of two lapses in defense by Checker Cab Company's baseball team last evening at Kindleberger park to win its second tilt of the second half race by the score of 2-0.

"Neil Berry, Sutherland's new shortstop, hit a home run for the winners' second run. Moerman, Checker Cab left fielder, misjudged Berry's hit and the ball sailed over his head and bounded far out of reach, Berry circling the sacks for the homer."

Sutherland Beats KVP Nine Before 2,000 in City League Tilt

"Two thousand baseball fans watched a Kalamazoo Vegetable Parchment team, with members of many a city championship squad in its lineup, fall apart at Kindleberger park last evening and lose to Sutherland Paper Company, 5 to 1.

"The defending city champion Sutherland club played its best form of the season to all but capture the second half honors of the American industrial league race.

"For the second time of the second half it was Miles (Jim) Crowe, Sutherland righthand hurler, who turned in a fine pitching performance against the tough Parchments. Crowe limited the opposition to three scattered hits during the full seven innings. Sum Sleep, veteran Parchment hurler, was not right although he allowed only five hits.

"Three straight errors by Runt Galer, Parchment second sacker, really proved the downfall for the former city champion Parchments. The misplays all led to vital runs and were committed in the third inning. Only two of the winner's runs were earned."

The victorious Sutherland Paper Company baseball team was now expected to win the second-half championship of the American industrial league. Sutherland was in the driver's seat with a 4-1 record and two second half victories in hand against first-half winner Parchment, now 3-2. Sutherland simply had to beat the less talented squads from Allied Papers and Fuller Manufacturing in the final contests of the regular season to claim their second-half crown.

After their second win over Parchment, Everett Clarke, of the *Kalamazoo Gazette*, reported that with Sutherland's win "playoff plans . . . are already being considered by city recreation officials" between Parchment and Sutherland, "apparent . . . second half champions."

Taking a break from city league action the Parchment team was scheduled to take on the Chicago American Giants from the Negro American League at Kindleberger Park. The Parchment team had lost exhibition games against the House of David and Grand Rapids Dutch Krafts team earlier in the season, so they decided to bring in some help from their city league rivals.

Portions of Everett Clarke's report about the upcoming game for the *Kalamazoo Gazette* follow:

Year's Biggest Attraction Set For 5:30 Friday

"The two teams will meet at 5:30 Friday afternoon in the summer's outstanding semi-pro contest in Kalamazoo. The tilt is expected to outdraw the House of David-Parchment affair several weeks ago.

"The Parchment club has added two of city champion Sutherland team's outstanding players, Neil Berry and LaSalle (Punk) Smathers, for the game for more offensive strength.

"The American Giants are too tough for local clubs but their games here in past years are remembered as outstanding semi-pro attractions.

"Advance sale tickets are offered at 25 cents and will be 40 cents at the gate . . ."

Jerry Hagan covered the game for the *Kalamazoo Gazette*:

Kalamazooans Outhit Negroes But Cannot Win

"The Parchment-Sutherland semi-pro stars got the hits but the Chicago American Giants got the runs, at Kindleberger Park last night as the Negro American league stars chalked up an easy 7-3 victory.

"The Kalamazooans collected 12 hits to seven hung up by the visitors. But fast double plays nipped local rallies and tight defensive work with men on left 11 local base runners stranded.

"Darkness halted the contest after eight innings, the game starting nearly an hour late because of the late arrival of the Chicagoans. Two thousand fans saw the game.

"Addition of Punk Smathers and Neil Berry to the Parchment semi-pro lineup from the Sutherland Paper City league squad gave the Kalamazoo club more power but it still wasn't enough to keep the team in the game against the Negro American league leaders. Smathers got three for four and Berry two for three and both played good ball in the field.

"The American Giants climbed out of the bus, hustled into their uniforms and started playing. But they stepped out and got two runs in the first inning on a single, double and error. The Parchments got one back when Graham doubled in the first and scored on Smather's single.

"The Chicagoans got two more in the third when Big Jim Reeves tripled to right field. The Parchments picked up one more in their half with the help of an error and singles by Koch and Galer.

"Kalamazoo used three pitchers. Big Joe Pivonka took over for Sum Sleep in the fourth and gave up two runs. In the sixth, Ken Johnson went in. He allowed only three hits in three frames, making the best showing of the local trio. But the visitors got another run with the help of an error and wild pitch. The [sic] Parchment got another, too, when Berry singled and Smathers doubled to deep right center in the seventh.

"As always, the Negro nine's fast double plays erased Kalamazoo rallies and the visitors' speed on the bases kept the local squad in trouble.

"Joe Pivonka hit the longest single ever seen in Kalamazoo, failing to make second in the fourth after clouting a drive over the center fielder's head. Kalamazoo's fielding gem was turned in by Walt Koch. Playing atop the right field hill when Reeves came to bat in the fifth, he robbed the big Negro of a triple or homer. Koch raced into the road to snag a tremendous drive down the right foul line."

After playing with their Parchment rivals in the exhibition game, Neil Berry and Punk Smathers were back with their Sutherland Paper teammates. After defeating Allied Papers Sutherland needed to beat Fuller Manufacturing to win the American Industrial League second-half title. They were then slated to play a best two-out-of-three series against Parchment to decide the overall 1940 champion, but it wasn't that easy as Everett Clarke reported in the *Kalamazoo Gazette*:

Losers Play KVP Monday for City League Honors

"Fuller Manufacturing Company plunged Sutherland's defending city championship baseball team into a tie with Parchment for the American industrial loop second half title by winning from the papermakers, 2-1, last evening at Upjohn field.

"With the second-half championship in its grasp and a play-off series for the season title in view, Sutherland let victory slip through its fingers and now must meet Parchment, winner of the first half, in a single game to determine the second half championship.

"The superlative pitching of Ray Hiatt, veteran Fuller righthander, who has experienced an off year this season, and the fact that the city champs were playing with a make-shift lineup, combined to provide the surprise Fuller victory last evening.

"The Sutherlands were handicapped by the absence of Clair Marks, centerfielder, who suffered a cut on his hand yesterday, and Emko Slater, regular catcher, who was un-able to play because of a death in the family."

Champs Win Second Half Race

"Thirty-five hundred howling fans watched at Hyames field, Western State, last evening as the defending city champion Sutherland nine defeated Parchment, 4-2, for the third straight time . . . and when the chips were down . . . thereby winning the second half honors.

"It was the third consecutive time Miles Crowe had pitched victory for Sutherland over his team's foremost baseball rivals.

"It was dependable Clair Marks, veteran Sutherland out-fielder, who turned the trick for the Sutherlands last night. With the score tied and the game already called for seven full innings because of approaching darkness, Marks hit a timely double to left field with the bases loaded for the winning margin in the seventh frame. Marks' vital hit was preceded by two fielder's choice plays, two errors, and Emko Slater's single."

With the Sutherland victory, the best two-out-of-three se-ries against Parchment to decide the overall 1940 American Industrial league champion was on.

From Everett Clarke, as reported in the *Kalamazoo Gazette*:

Baseball Game Ends, 3-3, Before Crowd of 4,000

"One of Kalamazoo's bitterest baseball battles will be continued this evening when the Sutherland and Parchment nines meet again at Hyames field to playoff yesterday's 3-3 tie in the opener of the series for the American Industrial championship. The defending city champion Sutherland team scored two runs after two were out in the seventh inning to force the contest into a deadlock before a record city league crowd of 4,000 rabid fans, the largest ever to jam the new Western State baseball plant.

Sum Sleep in Good Form as Mates Hit Ball

"The Kalamazoo Vegetable Parchment baseball aggregation stood one-up on Sutherland today in the two-out-of-three game series for the American industrial league championship by virtue of a 5-1 victory last evening before approximately 3,000 fans at Hyames field.

". . . it was too much Sum Sleep for the Sutherlands last night. The pint-sized right hander turned in one of his best jobs of the season in allowing the defending city champs only four hits in seven frames.

"Parchment really hit the ball last night, obtaining nine hits off two Sutherland flingers. The winners slapped Crowe for five hits in the fourth to score four runs before Art Stoops was called in. Stoops allowed but one hit in two and one third innings.

"Hits by Art Gilman, Graham, Runt Galer, Bill Hill, and Jim Kline with Neil Berry's error mixed in scored the four runs for Parchment in the fourth and placed the game on ice."

Sutherland & KVP Decide Title Tonight

"Last Monday Sutherland squared the series with a 6-1 triumph as former WSTC righthander George Timmerman stopped KVP with three singles. Miles Crowe was given a rest. The largest crowd to appear at Hyames field (5,000) was on hand, the largest crowd, too, at a recreational game this year.

"In the third inning Timmerman singled, Berry walked, and Ross tripled, scoring a minute later on a fielder's choice. The final three runs were added in the sixth frame. With the bases loaded, Ken Johnson's spikes caught in the pitching rubber and the consequent wild pitch let Ross and Smathers home. Burris' hit scored Coleman a minute later."

Sutherland Beats Parchment By 7-3 Score in Deciding Game

"The Sutherland Paper Company nine is the team to beat for the Kalamazoo city baseball championship.

"The defending city title holders stepped into the role of the favorite in the impending round robin series by crushing Parchment last evening at Hyames field, 7-3, for the American industrial league championship in the rubber game of a two-out-of-three series.

"The largest crowd ever to witness a city league ball game, playoff or otherwise, was present. Approximately 7,000 fans filled the stands, packed the embankments on either side of the diamond, and watched from points of vantage on trees, cars, and fences. A total of 16,000 fans saw the three-game series.

"The winners outclassed Parchment completely last evening, this fact being particularly true in the pitching department. Miles Crowe bested three Parchment hurlers in allowing but two safe hits during the seven innings. It was Crowe's fourth victory in five starts against Parchment in the second half of the season.

"Big Bill Kean, Parchment first sacker, was a hero even in defeat. He came to the plate with two out in the final inning and smashed the longest home run ever seen at Hyames field. Kean hit the ball far over the left field wire fence, the US-12 highway and into the railroad tracks. His clout scored two of the three runs made by Parchment in the seventh frame.

"Emko Slater led hitters on both sides last evening with three singles in three times at bat. Neil Berry and John Maartens, part of the infield that took many a base hit away from Parchment, each obtained three safeties in four times at the plate."

After their season-long battle with the strong Kalamazoo Vegetable Parchment team, the triumphant Sutherland Paper Company team won the 1940 overall city championship taking the round-robin tournament with 4 wins and no losses. Sutherland beat all three Independent league winners, the Sheriff's Department, Legion Blues, and Louie's Restaurant, before sealing the championship on August 28, by defeating Checker Cab, the National Industrial League winner.

Two days after winning the overall Kalamazoo city championship, Sutherland was playing in the state tournament in Battle Creek. The champs picked up three pitchers from Industrial league rivals for the double-elimination state meet, Ray Hiatt, Fuller Manufacturing Company; Sum Sleep, Parchment; and Dale Hughes, Checker Cab. Both Hiatt and Sleep beat the champions during the course of the season, and Hughes had pitched a three-hit, two run game against Sutherland in a losing effort.

Sutherland's first game was against the Detroit champion, Detroit Sam's, on Friday, August 30. Sutherland literally threw away a slim 2-1 lead when neither shortstop, Neil Berry, or second baseman, Herb Burris, covered second base on a double steal with Detroit men on first and third. Catcher Emko Slater got the tough-luck error when his throw sailed directly over second base into center field allowing the tying run to score and the eventual winning run to advance to third base.

Already down a game and facing elimination on Saturday morning, Sutherland was down 3-0, in the bottom of the ninth to Ann Arbor, identified in the *Kalamazoo Gazette* as "an all Negro aggregation." Neil Berry singled and Dave Ross walked between the first and second outs in the Sutherland ninth, bringing Bob Coleman to the plate. Coleman ripped a triple to center to score both Berry and Ross. An infield single by Herb Burris brought Coleman home with the tying run. Sutherland won the game in the eleventh when Colemen singled, moved to second on Burris' sacrifice, and raced home on Emko Slater's single to right.

After their 4-3 nailbiter eliminated Ann Arbor Saturday morning, Battle Creek Steel and Wire was the opponent for the afternoon game. In the opening inning a walk to Dave Ross was followed by a Punk Smathers triple, and Herb Burris single giving Sutherland a 2-0 early lead. Battle Creek pushed across a run in the fourth, but Sutherland's pitching and defense put the clamps on Battle Creek's metal men the rest of the way. The 2-1 win setup Sunday's showdowns with the Dearborn and Flint teams.

The Sutherland Paper nine showed up with their hitting shoes on Sunday morning scoring six first-inning runs against Dearborn on their way to an 11-2 victory. They continued the hitting barrage with four runs in the first, and four more in the fifth, in an 8-1 win over Flint.

After surviving four elimination games in two days, Sutherland Paper had another shot at the undefeated Detroit Sam's. Two Sutherland wins would be necessary to bring the state title home to Kalamazoo.

Everett Clarke covered Sutherland's final game of the 1940 season for the *Kalamazoo Gazette*:

Detroit Sam's Win, 6 to 0, in Title Contest - Strain of Six Games in Four Days Too Much for Sutherlands.

"BATTLE CREEK - The Kalamazoo Sutherland Paper Company team fell short of a Michigan State baseball championship here yesterday afternoon when an undefeated Detroit Sam's nine rose to heights to blank the papermakers, 6-0, at Postum park.

"Detroit hit both Miles Crowe, Sutherland's starting

pitcher, and Dale Hughes hard, although the latter hurler scattered his hits and pitched well enough had his mates obtained runs for him. Crowe was relieved by Hughes in one and two-thirds innings after allowing three runs and five hits.

"Sutherland's team should have scored in two different innings of the ball game. In the fifth, with nobody out, both Maartens and Slater singled. The next three men, Hughes, Marks, and Berry, went out on fly balls, however, and the threat failed. In the seventh frame, Burris was given a walk to open activities and was called out at third base when Slater, obtaining his second hit, smashed a safety to right. The right fielder made a perfect throw in catching the Sutherland second baseman.

"Even if defeated yesterday, Sutherland made an excellent showing in the Michigan state tourney . . . Each Sutherland player starred at his position and played championship ball until defeat yesterday."

The Sutherland Paper Company (and successor companies) continued to sponsor teams in the Kalamazoo City League through the 1955 season. During that run, Sutherland teams claimed 18 Kalamazoo City League championships and won seven state championships starting in 1946.

Punk Smathers took over as field manager in the late 40s and ultimately led the Sutherland team to a pair of Amateur Baseball Congress national titles in 1949 and 1951.

Along with Smathers, a core group of star players from the 1940 squad were part of the state and national championship teams, including Dave Kribs, Herb Burris, John Maartens, Dave Ross, and Bob Coleman. A bat, engraved with all of the names from the 1951 team, is in the Baseball Hall of Fame in Cooperstown, N.Y.

Riverview Park was renamed Sutherland Park in 1951 to honor Louis W. Sutherland, founder of the Sutherland Paper Company, and a staunch supporter of local baseball.

Relying on a lineup rich in players from Sutherland Paper, Columbia Cleaners compiled a record of 17 wins and two losses for the 1940 season. Their only losses were to a strong Grand Haven team early in the season and a late-season tilt against the Battle Creek Postums in Battle Creek. Fourteen consecutive victories were recorded by the Cleaners between those losses.

While the season-ending city championship tournament was underway, the fans were busy voting for their favorite players to determine the 1940 all-star team. The voting would not be a purely academic exercise to identify a theoretical team. The squad of 20 all-stars had already been scheduled to play a September 7 exhibition game against the original House of David team at Western State's Hyames field. The top vote-getters at each position would comprise the starting lineup. After a week of voting the 1940 all-star team was announced by Jerry Hagan in the *Kalamazoo Gazette*:

Ballots Show Berry and Ross As Co-captains

"Kalamazoo's 20 best baseball players—as selected by the vote of 10,000 fans—today became the 1940 all-city baseball squad.

"Chosen from 113 candidates, the honored stars . . . represent eight different local league clubs.

"High in the balloting were two stars of the city championship Sutherland Paper team and these boys—Shortstop Neil Berry and Outfielder Dave Ross—will be honorary co-captains.

"Three players got more than 4,000 votes. Ross led. He was the choice of 4,737 fans. Berry had 4,683 votes while LaSalle (Punk) Smathers was the choice of 4,237 fans.

"On the squad of 20—all of whom are promised a chance to get into the lineup against the popular House of David veterans—are eight Sutherland stars, four from Louie's restaurant team, three from the Kalamazoo Vegetable Parchment Co. nine, and one each from the Fuller Manufacturing Co.,

Master-Craft, Quality Baking, Allied Paper and Checker Cab Co. nines.

"As originally announced, the nine high in the voting will start. The fans choices for starters and subs were as follows:

"The Starters - Pitcher, Miles Crowe, Sutherland. Catcher Ray Fitzgerald, Louie's. First base, Bill Kean, Parchment. Second base, Bob Metzger, Louie's. Shortstop, Neil Berry, Sutherland, captain. Third base, Augie Kloosterman, Louie's. Left field, Punk Smathers, Sutherland. Center field, Dave Ross, Sutherland, captain. Right field, Bob Coleman, Sutherland.

"The Replacements - Pitchers - Ken Cavanaugh, Louie's. Ray Hiatt, Fuller Mfg. Co. Vern Balch, Master-Craft. Catchers - Emko Slater, Sutherland. First base - John Maartens, Sutherland. Second base, Mike Bass, Quality Bakers. Shortstop - Red Van Lente, Checker Cab. Third base, Al Karchunas, Allied Paper. Left field, Bill Hill, Parchment. Center field, Jin Kline, Parchment. Right field - Clair Marks, Sutherland.

"Honorary co-managers for Saturday's big game will be Ivan Forster, pilot of the city champion Sutherland Papers; Everett Clarke, assistant sports editor of The Kalamazoo Gazette who has covered most of this year's city league playoff and Ben Ford, local baseball enthusiast who is business manager of the Columbia Cleaners. The all-city squad, incidentally, includes all but three of the Cleaner players who have won their last 10 starts at the Ramona Park, Long lake diamond.

"The voting quite naturally favored the stars of the city champion Sutherlands, of the independent champion Louie's restaurant team and the runnersup industrial club, the Parchments. But such new stars as Mike Bass of the Quality Bakers and Red VanLente of Checker Cabs made the squad at the expense of highly regarded Sutherland and Parchment stars."

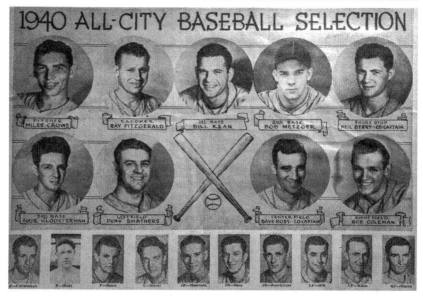

Kalamazoo Gazette photo from Neil Berry's scrapbook.

The fan-voted 1940 all-stars, eight of which were from the Sutherland squad had an upcoming game with the House of David.

The House of David was formed in 1903 in Benton Harbor, Michigan by Benjamin and Mary Purnell. Before long the colony had several hundred members who harvested fruit from a dozen orchards and cultivated grain on the 1,000 acre site. The House of David owned and operated their own electricity plant, providing lighting to the community. They had their own cannery, carpenter shop, coach factory, tailor shop, and a steam laundry. The House of David also had three brass bands, two orchestras, and a baseball team.

Benjamin Purnell was a sports enthusiast and encouraged his members to play sports, especially baseball, to build physical and spiritual discipline. House of David began to play competitive baseball in 1913 and by 1915, they were following a grueling schedule. The House of David baseball team barnstormed throughout rural America from the 1920s through the 1950s, motivated by the need to make money and the opportunity to share their beliefs. The team members wore long hair and beards as they played against Major League, Minor League, independent and Negro League teams. The House of David teams were famous for inventing "pepper" baseball tricks to entertain the crowd.

The House of David continued to sponsor barnstorming teams well into the 1930s and then sponsored weekend semi-professional teams until the 1940s. Mary's City of David (a separate faction headed by Mary Purnell after her husband's death in 1927) sent out barnstorming teams from 1930 until 1940 and then again from 1946 until 1955. Throughout this period, there were numerous teams that wore beards and played under the House of David name.

As the *Kalamazoo Gazette* reported, it was the "original" House of David team coming to Kalamazoo and that the fans "will want to see their favored stars competing in the closing baseball attraction of the season.

"If they didn't they still would come out to see the House of David which for years has been the best drawing card of all ball clubs appearing here.

"And whether they like baseball or not, fans get their money's worth out of the 'pepper game' exhibition which always is presented by Doc Tally, Andy Anderson and Johnny Tucker. Tucker, who turned down big league contracts to stay with the House of David, and his mates have presented their specialty a dozen or more times in Kalamazoo. But they never fail to get a tremendous ovation for the act and the fans never fail to get side-splitting laughs. The trio's belt-length hair is something too."

A limited block of 3,000 advance tickets were made available at 25 cents, and with the gate price of 40 cents, the huge crowd was expected to produce a large gate. The money raised was slated to be spent treating the all-star squad to a Detroit Tiger/Cleveland Indian game at Briggs

Stadium. Money leftover after providing transportation, meals, and choice seats for the Tiger game was promised to the Kalamazoo School Children's Milk Fund.

Punk Smathers went three for three with two triples and three batted in to lead the Kalamazoo all-stars to a 5-3 upset win over the House of David squad. A crowd of 3,000 fans saw all 19 available all-stars play in the game and deliver the first win in five years by a local team over the House of David. Infielder Augie Kloosterman did not participate due to the death of his father, so shortstop Neil Berry was the only player to play the entire game for Kalamazoo. He was hitless in four trips to the plate and was responsible for four putouts, three assists, and an error.

On Sunday, September 22, five carloads of Kalamazoo all-stars and their coaches drove to Detroit for a Detroit Tiger/Cleveland Indian game with pennant implications. The first place Tigers had a two game lead over the second place Indians with six games left to play.

Sitting in the stands at Briggs Stadium, Neil Berry no doubt thought about the day it would be him on the big league diamond, making all the plays at shortstop, and maybe getting a hit or two off Bob Feller. That day would come, but on this day Neil and the contingent of ballplayers from Kalamazoo saw the Cleveland Indians score seven early runs and Bob Feller cruise to a 10-5 triumph over the Detroit Tigers. The Indians knocked Tommy Bridges out of the game after only 1.1 innings and his relief did not do much better. Only rookie lefthander Hal Newhouser could tame the tribe on this day, giving up one hit and no runs in two innings while fanning four. The Kalamazoo contingent was rewarded with a milestone highlight when Tiger left fielder, Hank Greenberg, drove in two runs with his 40th home run of the season off Feller.

The Tigers went on to win the 1940 American League pennant by one game over Cleveland before losing the World Series in seven games to the Cincinnati Reds. A week after the Tigers lost the World Series, Hank Greenberg was among the first American League players to register for the draft.

My class, my freshman class, in 1940, just
before World War II, was probably one of the best
freshman classes that Western ever had. I don't
know why . . . just was.

~ Neil Berry

7

College Freshman

Western State Teachers College

1940 to 1941

Escalating war worries throughout 1940 prompted America to prepare, and on Tuesday, October 15, 1940, Company C, 126th infantry—the Kalamazoo unit of the Michigan National Guard—was called to active duty. The following day, as required by the Selective Service Act, 10,759 Kalamazoo men, between the ages of 21 to 35, registered for the first peacetime draft in history. Across the country, men were enlisting in all branches of the service for the inevitable coming war. Kalamazoo was no exception with 238 local men joining the Navy alone in 1940.

After completing his necessary high school post-graduate requirements at Kalamazoo Central during the 1939/40 school year, and honing his baseball skills playing Kalamazoo

City League and semi-pro ball in the spring and summer, Neil Berry wasn't thinking too much about the war in the fall of 1940. The 18-year-old Berry was likely thinking about Gloria Lorentzen, and definitely thinking about baseball and his freshman year at Western State Teachers College (today's Western Michigan University).

As Neil told it, "I went to school mostly on a baseball scholarship, well Western, they lacked good weather, so what they did every year was have what they called fall baseball. When you start in September there's three or four weeks when it's nice so you practice baseball until the weather gets bad. But I was also on a football scholarship. Well, football starts right away so there was a conflict . . . I'd like to play, loved to play football, but I'm going out for baseball.

"It was just before the war before the army took everybody and there were still enough kids left [to play] and we had a good class. A real great bunch of kids–kids used to come to Western, they didn't have to be recruited, kids from Detroit, kids from Chicago, [Western] had a [good] reputation.

"Well, quick as the last baseball game was over they were

waiting for me, 'hey, when are going to get your butt out here and play football?' I knew the coaches and I said, 'are you serious?'

'Yeah we're waiting, come on.' Well, they hadn't played a game yet, [but] I was thinkin' the [football] guys wouldn't like that too much, I just got done with baseball and I'm gonna come over [to football]. But I said, okay, when? Tomorrow night.

"So I went over and they gave me a uniform and stuff and we practiced twice. Practiced twice at VerSluis Park which was on the north side and all we did, I remember, they used the freshmen as blocking dummies, they're expendable. All we did was try to block field goals and extra points. We did that twice, then the third day they said we were going to play a game.

"The coach of the freshman team, his name was Frank Secory, he was a big star at Western, played fullback on the football team, he got the job as the Freshman coach. And one of his aides was a kid named Dave Kribs, who scored the first touchdown in this new stadium they've got right now, Waldo Stadium. Scored the first one [in 1939], way back when. He was a little guy, but he played three years for Western. He was the backfield coach for our Freshman team. They used the single wing back in those days, no quarterback under center, and they said, 'you're gonna play left halfback.' That's what I did in high school.

"We played Alma's Junior Varsity. We're freshmen, so we play their junior varsity and at the end of the first quarter I think we had 'em beat 40 to nothin.' It was terrible, but we had a pretty good bunch. With University of Detroit and Michigan State, later on, Michigan State had an undefeated team with those same kids, football was over. We won one and lost two. Well, quick as the last game is over we, all, a lot of us, went out for basketball [because] we all played sports. So I was on the basketball team. I was co-captain of the Western freshman basketball team and we played eight games, didn't lose any. So I go out for baseball and we play fifteen games, something like that, and never lost a game."

"I got it all in my yearbook, it's all right in there . . . we went eight games [undefeated] in basketball, and fifteen games, undefeated, in baseball. So out of our whole freshman year, we lost two contests, the two football games, that's all we lost. I would put that freshman class up against any [freshman] class they've ever had up there [at Western]."

The 1941 Western freshman baseball team actually played an eight game schedule and went undefeated. Only one game was played before press time for Western's *Brown and Gold* 1941 yearbook.

From Western's 1941 *Brown and Gold* yearbook:

FRESHMAN FOOTBALL

"The valuable material in this year's Freshmen Football Squad, under the direction of Coach Frank Secory, was able to chart a grid record of 42 points for the Frosh against the 33 points of their opponents.

"Former Kalamazoo High School Stars stood out in the belated first game played at night in the Alma College Field. Neil Berry, former All-Stater, and Ken Stillwell another local star as well as Earl Kelly in the line showed great promise as varsity material for the grids of the future.

"Berry scored four touchdowns, had another called back because of a penalty, and made numerous other runs that pushed the Bronco Colts to the lopsided victory. Stillwell and Bob Mellan scored the other two touchdowns. Western State 40 - Alma 7. Traveling next to Michigan State College at East Lansing to meet the first-year men on their grid field. Michigan State led the game when it was called for darkness. Western State Frosh 0 – Michigan State Frosh 14. In the only home game for the season the yearlings met the University of Detroit Frosh. Western State Frosh 0 – University of Detroit Frosh 12.

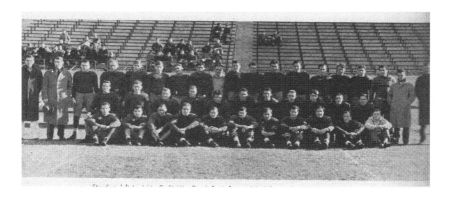

Standing left to right: G. Stukkie, Coach Frank Secory, W. Hillborg, H. Neitzee, R. Hollenbaugh, D. Schroyer, J. Marks, Capt. R. La Blanc, W. Bently, L. Edmonds, E. Kelly, E. Barrett, W. Fitzgerald, H. Boettcher, J. Stenvig, J. Quick, A. Taborn, D. Kribs, W. Cynar.

Second Row left to right: R. Clark, R. Melon, F. Techlun, R. Lillie, D. Firme, M. Persing, J. Skriba, R. Lawson, R. Wells, S. Derby, R. Peacock.

Seated on ground left to right: T. Smith, W. Morris, G. Hogarth, E. Boetcher, K. Stillwell, N. Berry, F. Stevens, F. Waldo, K. Laurent, E. Alexander, D. Pounder (Mgr.)

Photo from Western State Teachers College,

Brown and Gold 1941

"Numerals were presented this year to: Honorary Captain Jack Marks, Neil Berry, Edward Barrett, Walter Bentley, Edward Boetcher, Robert Clark, Walter Cynar, Loren Edmonds, Del Hollenbaugh, Earl Kelly, Herbert Boetcher, Kenneth Laurent, Victor Lawson, Russell Lillie, Robert Mellon, Harold Neitzel, Morris Persing, Fred Stevens, Don Schroyer, Joe Skirba, Kenneth Stillwell, and Gus Techlin. Those winning service awards are: Francis Waldo, John Stenvig, Stanley Derby, Ted Firme, Grant Hogarth, and Walter Morris."

Standing: Coach John Gill, D . Walsh, J. Sherwood, R, Schuessler, H. Bottcher, J. Skriba.
Seated: F. Stevens, H. Gensichen, N. Berry, R. Slater, R. Mellen.

Photo from Western State Teachers College, Brown and Gold 1941

FRESHMAN BASKETBALL

"This year's Freshman Basketball team under Mentor John Gill was out to break the 1939-40 Frosh Team record of eight wins, one loss and a game score of fifty-nine points.

"Playing an eight-game schedule, the Bronco hardwood boys brushed the "W" Club aside in the opener to make room for more sport and tougher games. In the next game, against Valparaiso College frosh, the Western cagers played to an early, easy victory of 73 to 20. Harold Gensichen, All-State star from South Bend, showed his stuff for the first good time in college ball with an individual honor of 19 points; young Dick Walsh followed with 14.

"The Coach Gill Yearlings were out for points and victory

as they trounced Lawrence Tech frosh at Detroit, 66-32. Gensichen scoring 28 points. The greenies were able to defeat the University of Detroit frosh team by a narrow margin of six points, the closest that any team came to Western throughout the entire season. Gensichen scored over half the team's scores, a total of thirty-two points. Western State Frosh, 60 - Detroit 54.

"Back again came Lawrence Tech frosh, this time to be handed another defeat from the powerhouse locals, 63-30.

"Muskegon Junior College came in line next to meet the flash squad. This was a game to set a record in all-high scoring. Western 80 - Junior College 36.

"Valparaiso rested from their first encounter with the undefeated team, came back as the next in line. The all-high scoring record made in the previous game was broken. Western 85 - Valparaiso 25.

"With one game left in the undefeated schedule, the bucket Broncos did not let the University of Detroit boys come as close as they had in their first encounter. To finish off the season with a win - one for good measure - the frosh of Western tripped the Detroit cagers, 74 - 46.

"Needless to say, the 1940-41 Freshman Basketball team surpassed the 1939-40 record by having an average game score of 68 points and by maintaining an undefeated season.

Freshman Baseball

"Coach John Gill, proud possessor of an undefeated Freshman Basketball squad, turned again to find a suitable team in baseball to make this a bang-up year. From all indications he has found this team and is out to produce not only a good working bunch of ball-handlers and club-wavers but to make a bunch of greenies into polished varsity material. Thirty-four turned out for the sport when it was opened for practice. From this squad Gill has made a sizzling, snappy, bunch of yearlings.

Back Row: D. Pounder, J. Mesick, M. Levine, E. Hawks, L. Edmonds, L. Stanley, C. Leutholtz, W. Perrin.
Middle Row: John Gill, R. Wells, R. Walsh, P. Rumps, R. Slater, R. Mellen, N. Berry, H. Leeman, T. Firme, W. Barrett (Mgr.).
Front Row: F. Stevens, J. Weigandt, K. Stillwell, J. Stephenson, R. Dresser, R. Hubert, T. Smith, R. Peacock.

Photo from Western State Teachers College,
Brown and Gold 1941

"In their first game of the season, the only game played before press time, the local frosh pounded the field with a fifteen hit game. The field was literally covered with solid-hit horsehide. But that was not all. In true Western baseball fashion the plugging nine made runs in every inning but the second.

"Dick Slater was the winning pitcher, having allowed only five Calvin College men to tap the ball in the six innings he pitched. Ted Smith, overgrown freshman from Battle Creek, replaced Slater and finished the last three innings allowing only three hits."

An article from the *Kalamazoo Gazette* described Neil's

contribution to the Western freshmen's 17 to 4 drubbing of Calvin College's varsity, at Hyames field: "[Western] exhibited fine defensive ability, in which department the work of Neil Berry, graduate of Kalamazoo Central and last summer selected on the city all-star squad, was unquestionably the best performance of the day."

Neil also had two hits, walked, and stole three bases.

Western's freshman defeated Hope College before a rematch with Calvin resulted in a similar outcome with Western prevailing 15 to 8. Neil was 3 for 6 with a triple and recorded four putouts and six assists.

Muskegon Junior College was the next victim with the Western frosh winning 12 to 5. Neil made two errors in the third inning, contributing to a brief Muskegon lead, but the 10 strikeout pitching of Dick Slater and Western's sixteen hits spelled the difference.

A close game against Grand Rapids Junior College turned into a 19 to 4 route after a thirteen run outburst in the final two frames. Neil and two of his teammates homered in the game. A week later the rematch in Grand Rapids resulted in a closer score but the Broncos rode a four run first inning to their sixth straight victory, 5 to 2.

In between the Grand Rapids games, the Western reserve squad borrowed catcher Joe Stephenson, and shortstop Neil Berry for a game against city champion Sutherland Paper. The reserves beat the city champs 3 to 2. Stephenson had a hit and scored a run. Neil also singled and played an error-free game at short.

Lopsided victories over Muskegon Junior College and Hope completed the undefeated season for Western's 1941 freshmen, a feat also accomplished by John Gill's 1940 freshmen team.

Academically, Neil was getting by and staying eligible after he got his class load reduced, and his schedule changed to one that better accommodated sports and sleeping in. Near the end of his freshman year Neil needed to write a paper for his Rhetoric class (the art of effective or persuasive speaking or writing). He already had a pretty good paper, one he had written in high school with the help of his chemistry teacher, Mr. Mesick.

As Neil told it, "I did it for Chemistry in high school. That's what I wrote that for but when I had to write another one for college, I looked at that thing and thought, 'I got a nice mark on this, if I could just alter this and edit a little bit, I'll turn this baby in.' It's mine, I did it, I handed it in."

The paper about the chemistry of glass production was good. Maybe too good. Neil may have had a little too much help from Mr. Mesick, his high school chemistry teacher.

Neil recounted the last day of Rhetoric class and his last day at Western State, "[Miss Siker] had a big pile of those folders, and I sat right in the front seat, and she said, 'I can't stand people who either steal or buy.' She starts handin' those [folders] out—last day of school—mine was black, had a black cover, and there's [one with] a black cover on the bottom. She gets down there [to mine], that's it. Class dismissed. Right across the hall is the door to her office. I followed her right across the hall and I said, 'Miss Siker, may I have my thesis?' and she said, 'that's not yours.' I said, 'yes it is ma'am and I can prove it.' She put it on her desk, she said, 'I'd like to know where you bought it, who's it is, how much did you pay for it? It's not yours.' Then she said, 'if it is, you're one of the smartest ones we have in class, that's a real fine thesis.' Well, I puffed up a little bit.

"It's mine, I can prove it. I'll just go down and call Mr. Mesick but no, she wouldn't do that. She said, 'No, you're going to get a complete, incomplete—for the year. I knew what that meant, that meant I'd be ineligible for the next year for sports."

That was bad news, not only for Neil Berry but also for Western State's sports teams. Freshman basketball and baseball coach John Gill got with Dean Hoekje to see what could be worked out and the powers that be decided that Neil could go to summer school and write another paper. He wouldn't miss a beat and be eligible again that fall. A good plan and everyone was happy, except Neil.

"I said, 'Mr. Gill, anybody else in class gonna go to summer school?' He said, no. I knew it was mine, that's what made me mad. I said, 'I know that's mine, in fact I've got it.' I took it right off her desk when I walked out. I broke her door. I said, 'I'm not gonna go to summer school [to redo] something that is mine and I don't think you believe me.'

"He said, 'I don't know what to do.' I said, 'I know what I'm gonna do, I'm goin home and gonna get on the telephone and I'm gonna call the Detroit Tigers and tell 'em I'm ready to sign.'

"My coach said, 'Well why don't you just come to summer class, it'll only be a few weeks until you write that paper.' I said, 'Nope, adios,' and I went home and made the call.

"[Western] didn't like what I did. They didn't say anything, but I know that I was never invited for an alumni game even though I did play in the big leagues. A lot of guys that never made the big leagues played up there. They said, well, you didn't finish school. A lot of guys didn't finish school [but] they played at Western. The alumni game was for people that went to school, not because they graduated . . . because they played ball there. Western, every year, I don't know if they still do it or not, they'd get a bunch of guys [from] around, not too far 'cause it'd cost too much money that way, but [guys that] had played for Western [and] that were still in fairly decent shape, younger guys, [and they would] play a game against Western's varsity, an alumni game. The alumni usually won. They'd invite guys, Charlie Maxwell used to go, and the kid [that] pitched for the Yankees, he went to Western just one year, but he pitched for the Yankees and he did a pretty good job, he came back and pitched. And guys I went to school with that didn't finish school because of the war, they were invited back, but they never invited me back, so I never said a word.

"But [they had] that little [bad] taste in their mouths because I did quit school under those circumstances, but I said, hey it's your fault. I had an A, three Bs and a C. I had good marks. The only one I didn't have was the Rhetoric class and she gave me an incomplete. Rhetoric to me was so . . . I mean, I couldn't see any point to it, reading Lorna Doone and things like that. (Neil imitating the Rhetoric teacher) 'A guy walking down the street with a sack of potatoes on his back, what does that mean?' Well, to me, he had a sack of potatoes on his back and he's goin someplace. (Imitating the Rhetoric teacher) 'Oh no, that's not what the author meant at all.' Well, okay [but] I didn't like that."

Neil Berry was done with his collegiate career at Western State, after an outstanding freshman year in sports. His college days ended with the controversy over that alleged stolen paper for his Rhetoric class. Ironic that after getting away with all the tomfoolery and petty capers of his youth, Neil got into that much trouble for something he didn't steal.

While the Western freshmen were in the midst of their undefeated basketball season, 54 young men—the first draftees from Kalamazoo—were sent to Fort Custer for processing in January, 1941.

[We] had just walked into the bowling alley and,
'Attention!' Everybody stopped like the world's
coming to an end—we'd just been bombed at Pearl
Harbor.

~ Neil Berry

8

War Worries

Kalamazoo City League Baseball

1941

War worries were at an all-time high with the draft already claiming young Kalamazoo men for service. Neil recalled that "they started takin' kids outa class [at Western]. You go into a class, sit down, 'where'd that guy go?' He got drafted."

In an April 1941, article in the *Kalamazoo Gazette*, Everett Clarke, reported that there will be "many new faces on city league baseball teams this summer. The draft will take a heavy toll among the city's baseball stars . . ."

After the excitement of the Sutherland/Parchment battles in the race for the American Industrial League crown during the 1940 city league baseball season, the 1941 season promised to be every bit as compelling.

The *Gazette* anticipated a "wide open" first half race in

the American industrial league, the city's top league, but predicted the "second half campaign should narrow down to another battle between Sutherland's defending title holders and Parchment."

The reason given for a potentially tight race in the first half was that the defending city champ, "Sutherland will definitely not be at its full strength until the second half when Neil Berry, Dave Ross, Dave Kribs, John Maartens, and possibly another starting pitcher are made available."

The *Gazette* did report that "Bill Moerman, lefthander, who hurled for Checker Cab's National league title holders last year; George Moerman, young catcher, who backstopped for Fiedorek Service last summer; and Bob Travis, outstanding outfielder from the independent groups," had been added to the Sutherland Paper Company roster.

While Neil Berry was playing for the Western State freshmen, the less-than-full-strength Sutherland squad took the first half of the American Industrial League with a perfect 8-0 record. Nonetheless, their goal was a state championship and to that end, the defending city champs bolstered their roster for the second half. Dave Ross had already joined the team for the last game of the first half and the *Kalamazoo Gazette* reported that the Sutherland team had also added, "Andy Messenger, Western Michigan College sophomore, who won three games and lost none for the Broncos this year; Neil Berry, sensational shortstop of the Bronco Frosh squad; Dave Kribs, former Bronco infielder and Michigan State leaguer; Joe Kelly, elongated Central high right hander; and Leon Phelps, former Western outfielder and catcher," for second half competition.

With their all-star lineup, Sutherland cruised through the second half of the American Industrial League season with seven wins and no losses. Along the way to a stellar 24-3 record, the Sutherland nine defeated the Chicago American Giants of the Negro National League, 7-6, at Hyames field before 3,000 fans, and beat the Dowagiac All-Stars, 10-5, in the team's first-ever night game under the lights, at Dowagiac. The lights didn't affect the team's hitting with a 14 hit, 10 run attack, but the normally reliable keystone combination of Kribs and Berry committed five errors (three by Berry) on the artificially lit infield.

After 19 straight victories (following the tuneup loss to the Western State reserve squad), Sutherland lost an exhibition game to the Birmingham Black Barons, first-half champs of the Negro National League, 10-6. Sutherland outhit the Barons, 14 to 9, but left 13 runners on base.

The Sutherlands then finished off a strong Master-Craft team for the city championship before beating Wyandotte, Battle Creek, Grosse Pointe, and Lansing in the State tournament. Pontiac ended Sutherland's and Kalamazoo's state championship dream with consecutive victories over the papermakers in the final round of the tournament. Pontiac then lost the championship game to the Dearborn Winston Jewelers.

The Columbia Cleaners semi-pro squad with its home base at Ramona Park, Long Lake, also had another successful season playing with the best talent Kalamazoo had to offer, including Neil Berry and several of his Sutherland teammates.

Neil remembered, "In 1941, before the war started, Fort Custer had a team. We played and beat Fort Custer. They had four or five guys that played pro ball, had a catcher that played for the Cubs [and] another kid, a pitcher . . . We tried to get Hank Greenberg, he was at Fort Custer, but he didn't play ball, he was a big wheel."

Hank Greenberg had been classified 4F for "flat feet" by the Detroit draft board and was recommended for light duty, but flat feet didn't prevent Greenberg from patrolling the outfield and clubbing home runs for the Detroit Tigers. Negative publicity and rumors of a bribed draft board led Greenberg to request another examination. On April 18, 1941, he was reclassified as fit for regular military service.

On May 7, he was inducted into the U.S. Army and reported to Fort Custer in Battle Creek, Michigan.

Columbia Cleaners also beat some other loaded ball clubs, including, the Grand Haven Millers, 2-1, sending the Millers to their first defeat of the year; they shutout Fort Custer's Second Infantry club, 2-0, on the two hit pitching of Andy Messenger; they downed a tough Clark Equipment Co., Battle Creek's entry in the upcoming state tournament, 4-3, in thirteen innings; and beat the American Legion team from Grand Rapids that featured future Tiger pitcher Frank (Stub) Overmire.

An early season loss to Clark Equipment and a loss in the second tilt against Grand Haven were the only blemishes on Columbia Cleaners 21-2 record in 1941.

Speaking of his Sutherland and Columbia Cleaner teammates, Neil related that they were "all a fine bunch of guys, good guys. I learned a lot of good baseball, and I played against a lot of good guys."

As the 1941 baseball season in Kalamazoo was nearing an end, the fall semester was about to start at Western State. This clipping from the *Kalamazoo Gazette*, dated September 8, 1941, announced Neil's decision to leave school:

Here's Bad News For Broncos; Berry passes up College

"Here's bad news for Western Michigan College coaches and for Southwestern Michigan sports fans.

"Neil Berry, Kalamazoo all-city baseball star and an all-state halfback in football when at Kalamazoo Central high, will not return to college this fall at Western. Berry won frosh numerals a year ago in football, basketball, and baseball.

"On direct questioning, Berry said today: 'I just don't like college. I'm going to keep on working. Next spring, if the offers are good enough, I might consider professional baseball.'"

The fans again voted for their favorite players for a year-end exhibition game against the House of David. Some of the usual suspects were voted into the starting lineup, Catcher Emko Slater, Sutherland; First baseman Bill Kean, Parchment; Second basemen Dave Kribs, Sutherland; Shortstop Neil Berry, Sutherland; Third baseman Augie Kloosterman, Louie's; and Outfielders Dave Ross and Punk Smathers, Sutherland, and Fred Peifer, State Employees. The top vote-getter and captain, with 6,011 votes, was Master-Craft Pitcher Vern Balch.

The Kalamazoo all-stars, according to the *Gazette*, "handed the House of David team one of the worst defeats it ever suffered" with its 12-2 victory. The victors smashed 14 hits including a Punk Smathers triple and doubles by Smathers, Dave Kribs, Neil Berry, Don Shoup, and two by Bill Kean.

The 1941 city all-stars were treated to a Sunday afternoon Detroit Tiger/Chicago White Sox doubleheader at Comiskey Park in Chicago, on September 21. In the first game, they saw Tommy Bridges go the distance for his ninth win, a 6-3 decision over the White Sox. Pinky Higgins sealed the victory with a two-run homer in the eighth. In the second game, Detroit's Schoolboy Rowe was matched against Chicago's Johnny Rigney. Each team had one tally after nine innings, so Rowe and Rigney kept pitching. After 14 innings the game was declared a tie. Rowe and Rigney ended up with remarkably similar lines; 14 IP, 8 hits, 1 earned run, 3 bases on balls. Rowe struck out six to Rigney's five. It's not known how long the Kalamazoo contingent stuck around.

Kalamazoo baseball was all but over for the 1941 season save for one final exhibition game.

The *Kalamazoo Gazette* reported:

"The 1941 baseball season—greatest year in Kalamazoo's diamond history—will come to a close next Thursday afternoon when the city champion Sutherland Papers play the Kansas City Monarchs at 5 p.m. at Hyames field.

"LeRoy (Satchel) Paige, the Negro Bob Feller, will be the feature attraction in what is Kalamazoo's biggest ball game since Paul Dean and the St. Louis Cardinals played here four years ago."

Jerry Hagan reported on the game for the *Kalamazoo Gazette*:

Kalamazooans Score Twice on Satchel Paige

"The Kansas City Monarchs whipped the Kalamazoo champion Sutherland Papers, 6 to 3, before 2,000 fans at Hyames field last night but it was through no great effort of the highly-publicized Satchel Paige.

"Paige went in with a 5-1 lead and didn't extend himself as he hurled his three innings. He gave up two scratch hits and two unearned runs.

"The gangling, slow-moving Paige was driven up to the park by his chauffeur in a big limousine after the game was under way and after both the Monarchs and the Sutherlands were tearing their hair as to his whereabouts.

"As to Paige's three innings. He fanned none and walked none. Two balls were hit out of the infield off him. But he only rarely threw his great fastball. Instead, his knuckler and change of pace had the Sutherlands popping up and Paige was content to let it go at that. His hesitation delivery probably bothered the local boys as much as anything.

"Kalamazoo got one run off Hilton Smith, the Negro league's No. 1 pitcher in the won-lost column. That came in the first inning after Clair Marks singled, advanced on an infield out, and scored on Dave Ross' single.

"The other Sutherland runs came off Paige in his first inning on the hill. An error started the trouble. Then Timmerman and Berry came through with timely singles. After that, Paige never was in danger."

"... In the filled grandstand was Wish Egan, Detroit Tiger scout who had learned that Neil Berry was not returning to school and who came to Kalamazoo to look over the fast-stepping shortstop.

"Egan should have been interested, too. Berry handled 10 chances without a bobble and got two of Kalamazoo's five hits.

"Two years ago, Egan was one of three major league scouts who wanted to sign up the former Kalamazoo Central athlete. And now that Berry is not going back to college, Egan and the Tigers are interested again."

A couple of days later the *Gazette* published this item:

"Major league baseball scouts should be told that Neil Berry, best Kalamazoo prospect since Fred Spurgeon went up to the Cleveland Indians, is ready to listen to offers.

"Berry carried a .462 batting average and a 1.000 fielding average through the 1941 city major league baseball season. Big league scouts pestered him two years ago after he won the Ki-Ki Cuyler trophy at Detroit as the outstanding performer in the State American Legion tournament. They left him alone when Berry, then only 17, insisted he was going to get a college education before listening to pro ball offers. Berry, a former all-state halfback at Kalamazoo Central, won letters in three frosh sports at Western Michigan College. But he didn't like college and won't return when classes are resumed this fall."

Neil knew he had other options and stuck with his decision to leave school. The chance to play his first professional season close to home, and close to Gloria, helped seal the deal with Wish Egan and the Detroit Tigers.

A November 1941, *Kalamazoo Gazette* article announced, "Neil Berry, Kalamazoo's outstanding city league player, today is the property of the Detroit Tigers.

"Berry confirmed last night that he had signed a contract with the Detroit club through Wish Egan, the veteran scout. He will report next spring, assigned to Muskegon, where he will replace Johnny Lipon, the slugging shortstop who led the state league in hitting this year and who will be moved up to a higher league in 1942. Berry spurned a $500 bonus offer made by the St. Louis Cardinals and although his check for lining up with Detroit was smaller than that, the Kalamazoo star will be able to remain in Michigan for his minor start. Berry is 19 years old, the son of Mr. and Mrs. Hazen Berry, 909 Walter street. He was an all-state footballer for Kalamazoo Central three years ago and last year starred in three sports as a freshman at Western Michigan College. Berry stands five feet 11 and weighs 165 pounds."

Subsequently, the *Gazette* kept the public informed on what Neil was up to that winter when it reported that "Neil Berry, Kalamazoo baseball star recently signed by the Tigers, is keeping in shape this winter by playing basketball." The Gazette also divulged that "Neil Berry, Kalamazoo shortstop signed by the Tigers, is bowling this winter to keep in condition."

As Neil told it, "Me and a couple of other guys used to bowl a lot—just goofin around—we liked to have fun bowlin'.

"A good friend of mine's dad had an automobile fix-it garage right at the base of the hill on East Main. His name was Glen Travis. His son, Bob Travis had just bought himself— or his dad did—a yellow convertible Oldsmobile with red leather upholstery. That was the car we got around in. Bob was a good ball player, a damned good player, an outfielder. Played on the high school team, played on the Legion team.

"Anyway it was Sunday and we had this friend named Hut, Hank Hut, from out there in Portage, and he and I and Bob had just walked into the bowling alley and, 'Attention!' Everybody stopped like the world's coming to an end—we'd just been bombed at Pearl Harbor. That's where we were on December seventh, 1941."

The Detroit Tigers didn't give us a winner but they did give us Berry.

~ *Twin-City Sentinel*

9

Pro Ball

The Winston-Salem Twins

1942

In November 1941, Detroit Tiger Hank Greenberg, while serving as an anti-tank gunner, was promoted to sergeant. On December 5, Congress released men aged 28 years and older from military service, and Greenberg was honorably discharged. Two days later, on December 7, 1941, Japan bombed Pearl Harbor and the United States entered World War II.

In Kalamazoo and across the country local draft boards were required to supply large quotas of men for military service. Rationing of tires, gasoline, and even food was soon instituted. Air-raid wardens were identified and trained due to the possibility of enemy attacks. Industries throughout the country, including many in Kalamazoo, were turning to war production and women were beginning to work on production lines that were previously staffed by men.

In April, women in Kalamazoo formed the first Fort Custer service club to entertain the men training there. The young women first met the troop trains on the way to Fort Custer at the Kalamazoo depot. They served up sandwiches and treats while the new hit, *I've Got a Gal in Kalamazoo*, played on the radio. The song and the young and attractive Kalamazoo women, no doubt gave many a boy soldier the idea that, maybe, they would have "a gal in Kalamazoo" to return to.

I've Got a Gal In Kalamazoo was recorded by Glenn Miller and His Orchestra in 1942 and spent eight weeks as the number one song in the country in September and October.

On September 20, 1942, an article in the *Kalamazoo Gazette* identified Sara Woolley as the "lovely 'Gal in Kalamazoo' made famous by songsters from coast to coast." Miss Woolley was a Junior at Kalamazoo College and a "dazzling dark-eyed beauty" who was elected by the male students as the "girl who would best fit the song." The title of the "Gal in Kalamazoo" made Sara Woolley nationally known, and throughout the war, she appeared at USO programs and defense bond drives.

While World War II was being waged in 1942, Neil Berry was slated to play his first year of professional baseball in Muskegon, Michigan, just 90 miles, and an hour and a half drive from home. Neil was looking forward to playing professional baseball while remaining close to his own "gal in Kalamazoo," the "cute little dickens," Gloria Lorentzen.

Gloria, still living at home with her father in the family home on Inkster Avenue, was also thrilled that Neil would be playing so close to home, but ultimately, staying in Michigan for his first year of professional baseball wasn't to be for Neil and Gloria. The Michigan State League suspended operations for the 1942 season, and Detroit reassigned Muskegon player contracts to the Winston-Salem Twins in the Piedmont League. Along with Neil, ten other Tiger farmhands, and player/manager Jack Tighe (pronounced TYE) were assigned to Winston-Salem.

Piedmont was a bus league that consisted of five teams in North Carolina and three teams in Virginia. The league played a demanding 140 game schedule in 138 days, starting the last week of April and running through the first week in September. The only off days were rainouts with doubleheaders making up for lost games. The teams were scheduled for three or four game series. One way bus travel varied from about two hours (Charlotte and Durham) to nearly six hours (Norfolk and Portsmouth). The exception was nearby Greensboro, just 40 minutes to the east. The Twins and Greensboro Red Sox played home and away games in every series—including day/night doubleheaders on Sundays and holidays—with a game in each city.

The teams that made up the Piedmont League in 1942, and their major league affiliate were (listed in order of the 1941 Piedmont league standings):

Durham (NC) Bulls, Brooklyn Dodgers

Portsmouth (VA) Cubs, Chicago Cubs

Greensboro (NC) Red Sox, Boston Red Sox

Norfolk (VA) Tars, New York Yankees

Richmond (VA) Colts, unaffiliated

Charlotte (NC) Hornets, Washington Senators

Asheville (NC)Tourists, St. Louis Cardinals

Winston-Salem (NC) Twins, Detroit Tigers

The Winston-Salem Twins finished the 1941 season in last place, 39 games behind the champion Durham Bulls. The Twins were no strangers to the basement, having established themselves as the league doormat by finishing in last place every year since rejoining the league in 1937, after a three year absence. The 1937 team lost 105 games and finished a whopping 54.5 games behind the league champs, and 30.5

Ready for the start of the Piedmont League season are Winston-Salem Twins probable starters (front to back) Manager Jack Tighe, catcher: Don Murray, third base; Neil Berry, shortstop; Pete Peterson, right field; John Radulovich, second base; Stewart Williams, center field; John Mueller, left field; George Vico, first base; and Joe Moceri, pitcher.

Twin-City Sentinel photo from Neil Berry's scrapbook

games behind the seventh place team. Manager Jack Tighe was looking for a better result in 1942.

John Thomas (Jack) Tighe was signed by the Tigers as a catcher in 1936 but only made it as far as Class A1—two levels below the major leagues—with the Beaumont Exporters of the Texas League in 1938 and '39. In 1940 Tighe was named player/manager of the Muskegon Clippers, Detroit's farm club in the Michigan State League. He guided the Clippers to a fifth place finish in 1940, and fourth place in 1941;

Neil Berry—the shortstop from Kalamazoo—in uniform
for the Winston-Salem Twins in 1942.

Photo courtesy of Linda Spann

good enough to get a shot at improving the fortunes of the Winston-Salem Twins.

With Neil Berry leading off and playing shortstop, the Winston-Salem Twins, cellar dwellers of the Piedmont circuit for the last five years, opened the 1942 season with their annual exhibition game against Hanes Hosiery, a semi-pro team sponsored by the Winston-Salem based Hanes Company (maker of underwear and socks). The 500 fans in attendance at Southside Park saw Neil Berry drive in three runs with a long triple, and the Twins scored seven runs, in the decisive third inning. They went on to win 13 to 3 over the Hosiery team.

Neil Berry's day—batting 2 for 3, 2 runs scored, 3 RBIs; fielding, 2 putouts, 4 assists, and 0 errors. Although just an exhibition game, it was a pretty good start for the shortstop from Kalamazoo.

On April 22, the Winston-Salem Twins opened the 1942 Piedmont League baseball season against Greensboro's Red Sox at War Memorial Stadium, Greensboro, North Carolina. The sloppy (11 errors), but the high scoring contest wasn't decided until the ninth inning. The top of the ninth saw the Twins tie the score at ten apiece before the Red Sox pushed the winner across in the bottom of the ninth to take the game 11 to 10.

Twin-City Sentinel Sports Editor Nady Cates had this to say about Neil Berry's professional debut: "Playing his first pro game, Shortstop Neil Berry was as jittery as any raw recruit on the firing line, made two costly errors. But the slender young shortstop, who usually handles himself with the grace and precision of a ballet dancer, showed he had guts when he crashed into Catcher Kluk at the plate, knocked the ball out of his hand and scored a run."

After beating the Sox in their home opener, it was back on the bus, and back to Greensboro, for game three of the four game series. The Twins and Red Sox were tied, 6 to 6 when the game was called in the tenth inning due to a blackout warning.

During the war, city lights along the Atlantic coast served to silhouette Allied ships and expose them to German submarine attacks. To help protect the Allied ships, the U.S. Government issued blackout restrictions along the East Coast that were enforced by Civil Defense wardens. It is not known if the blackout that disrupted the game was a drill or due to a potential threat.

The *Winston-Salem Journal* reported, "When the blackout warning sounded, the Twins and Red Sox scampered off the field, the lights were turned out, and the handful of fans remained in their seats in total darkness until the all-clear signal was given 31 minutes later.

"By agreement beforehand, the umpires and rival managers agreed to call the game if the black-out lasted as much as 30 minutes. It was called just before the all-clear signal was given, the postponement receiving a round of boos from the fans who wanted to see the closely-fought game continued."

April 25, Southside Park—The Twins were back home for the final game of the series. Greensboro broke open a close game in the eighth inning with 6 unearned runs, then held off eighth and ninth inning rallies by the Twins, to win the series finale 7 to 5.

From the *Winston-Salem Journal*:

". . . The game was marked by some of the season's finest defensive play. Neil Berry, at shortstop for the Twins, handled eleven chances and several of the stops were beautiful to watch.

". . . Not only did Berry sparkle brightly as the lights above his head but he contributed three of the Twins hits in the attack."

In the April 28 edition of the *Twin-City Sentinel*, Sports Editor Nady Cates, had this to say about the 1942 version of the Winston-Salem Twins, "Second baseman John Radulovich and shortstop Neil Berry, two boys with only meager pro experience, have developed into a surprise combination at the keystone. Neat fielders both, they may belie early predictions and stick."

In an early season game, during infield warm-up at Southside Park, Neil accidentally overthrew first base from his shortstop position. The ball sailed harmlessly into the segregated—black only—right field bleachers, giving a fan there a souvenir. After that first accidental overthrow, Neil continued to *accidentally* do it on purpose, now and then, and the fans loved it. During pregame warm up the fans shouted out, "Misr Berry! Misr Berry!" imploring him to let one loose. The fans scrambled for the souvenir baseball every time Neil sailed one well over the head of the first baseman—and future Detroit Tiger GM—Johnny McHale.

John Joseph McHale was born on September 21, 1921, in Detroit, Michigan. McHale attended St. Agnes Parochial School and Catholic Central High School in Detroit, where he starred in football and baseball. McHale, a first baseman, who threw righty but batted lefty, played American Legion ball and also played in the Detroit Baseball Federation. He graduated high school in 1939, then went to the University of Notre Dame, where he lettered in both football and baseball. McHale was a reserve center and defensive tackle for the Fighting Irish, but on November 2, 1940, with the regular center injured, he got the start against Army, at Yankee Stadium. Notre Dame beat Army, 7 to 0. Years later McHale liked to point out that he was one of the few people to play to a full house at Yankee Stadium in both football and baseball.

In December 1940, Detroit scout "Wish" Egan gave McHale, at the time a sophomore, the chance to sign with his hometown team, the Tigers. McHale signed, but he eventually earned his degree with honors in economics in 1945. Years later McHale was said to have quipped, "Wish later gave me the formula. He said the best time to approach a college boy on a bonus deal is before Christmas—when he needs the money"

In his first pro season in 1941, McHale hit .277 with 14 homers for Muskegon in the Michigan League. He also led the league with 103 strikeouts and 26 errors. McHale and the Tigers were both hoping for better results in 1942.

Following the season opening series loss to Greensboro, the Winston-Salem Twins lost a series at Charlotte (0-3), lost a home series against the Asheville Tourists (1-2), lost road series against Portsmouth (1-2) and Norfolk (1-2), before returning home.

May 11, Southside Park—The Portsmouth Cubs defeated the Twins 5-4 in a fifteen inning marathon, sweeping the three game series. Neil Berry played one of his best professional games to date, going 2 for 5 with a run scored, and added 3 stolen bases to the Twins attack. Defensively he flawlessly handled his nine chances at shortstop.

May 12, Southside Park—The Twins beat the Durham Bulls, 8 to 1, with a 13 hit attack supporting the five-hit pitching of Mike Lake.

Durham took the next game with bad weather claiming the rubber match. Four losses on the road at Richmond followed. With only five wins in their first 24 games, and sporting a team batting average of just .228, Winston-Salem was in their customary position—last place—in the Piedmont League.

The poor start left manager Jack Tighe feeling powerless. Too often his bad back kept the player/manager on the bench when his team needed his help on the field. Tighe started feeling better when Detroit named him a coach for the parent club. Detroit chose 29-year old, Al Unser—also a catcher—as Tighe's replacement.

Before Al Unser and Al Jr. earned their fame at the brickyard, winning the Indianapolis 500 multiple times, Al Unser (no relation) was a major league baseball player.

Albert Bernard Unser—the third of eight children—played baseball on weekends, but otherwise worked on the family farm in Morrisonville, Illinois all through his childhood and high school years. He started his professional career as a pitcher in 1933 but gave it up after he struggled to get outs from the mound. Unser played catcher, third base, and the outfield, in six seasons in the Cardinals chain from 1934 through 1939 and, at age 26, he managed Gastonia of the Tar Heel League. Following the 1939 season, he married Ruth Marten from Farmersville, Illinois. The couple started a family that would eventually include eight children, four girls, and four boys, including Del who went on to have a 15-year major league career.

In 1940 Unser played with Winston-Salem before the team was affiliated with Detroit. He then joined the Detroit Tigers organization in 1941 and was sent to Beaumont of the Texas League.

In 1942 married men with dependents weren't being drafted, and Unser made Detroit's roster as bullpen and third-string catcher, behind Birdie Tebbetts and Dixie Parsons. Before getting into a game, Unser was sent to Winston-Salem to be the player-manager of the Twins, trading places with Jack Tighe.

New Twins player-manager Al Unser debuted on May 19, at Durham. In the lineup at catcher, Unser went 1 for 4, and drove in a run, helping his Twins secure a 5-3 win over the Bulls. Neil Berry had a double and a triple in 4 at-bats, scored twice and drove in a run for his new manager.

The next night the Unser led Twins won again over Durham, 3 to 2, winning back to back games for the first time and winning their first series of the 1942 campaign.

Returning home for a nine game homestand, the Twins announced that Friday night, May 22, would be, "Welcome Al Unser" night when they host the Richmond Colts.

The *Twin-City Sentinel* reported that it "will be Unser's first appearance before the home folks, since 1940, when they had another 'Unser Night' in honor of the most popular player on the club. The now-skipper was the then-outfielder and man-of-all-jobs, who played every position on the team."

Bobby Hogue, the only veteran pitcher on the staff (having pitched for the Twins in 1941), was scheduled to pitch the welcome Unser game.

Robert "Bobby" Hogue was born April 5, 1921, in Miami, Florida. His father, Oakley Hogue, trained boxers and under his tutelage Bobby won 36 of 39 amateur fights before deciding to go with baseball.

In 1940 Hogue signed with an unaffiliated Miami club in the Florida East Coast League and posted an 8-11 record with a 4.15 ERA. The Tigers bought his contract in 1941 and sent him to Winston-Salem. He went 9-8 with a 2.38 ERA, for the last place Twins and also experienced his most embarrassing moment on the field.

Hogue told *Complete Baseball*: "It had rained all morning and muddy Carolina red clay is the slickest stuff in the world. The first man up bunted. I fielded the ball and, honestly, skidded not only off the infield but also into the Asheville dugout. When I finally climbed out, the guy was on third with a triple."

May 23, Southside Park—Bad weather postponed the Friday night game in favor of a Saturday doubleheader against the

Richmond Colts. The now streaking Twins won both games, 1 to 0, behind Bobby Hogue's four-hit pitching, and 9 to 7, with a 6 run fourth inning, and a Johnny McHale home run. In the second game, Richmond's player/manager, Ben Chapman, took out Neil Berry at second base with an out-of-the-baseline, spikes up slide, to break up a double play. With unrelenting boos and insults, the Twins fans let Chapman and the Colts know how they felt about the mistreatment of their favorite player.

From the *Twin-City Sentinel*, Cates' Comment by Nady Cates

Hungry Wolves

"Chauncey Durden, sports editor of the Richmond Times Dispatch, calls Winston-Salem fans the 'worst bleacher wolves' in the Piedmont and complains bitterly at the way the wolves howled at and abused his tender Colts when they were at Southside Park recently.

"'The bleacher wolves are voracious,' says Mr. Durden, using a resounding adjective. Now I ask you Chauncey, wouldn't your 'wolves' be hungry, too, if they had been locked in the cellar for five years with nary a slice, nor even a smell, of the pennant pie?

"Mr. Durden, who so far as I know, has never attended a Winston-Salem game, certainly not in recent years, obviously received second-hand the information on which he bases his tirade against the Twin City fandom.

"Saturday's incident probably was reported by Colt players. But it is inconceivable to my mind, that either the players or their manager Ben Chapman would complain of harsh treatment from our fans. The worst that our fans could have done—if you accept the Richmond version of the incident without so much as a grain of salt—was to threaten to annihilate the said Mr. Chapman for taking out our Shortstop, Neil Berry, with his spikes on an attempted double play and to hit Catcher Don Vettorel in the back with a pop bottle. Those were just love taps compared to the treatment the Colts get everyday from Ben Chapman, a veritable martinet of managers. A season under Chapman, I'm told, would make any player welcome a life sentence in the salt mines of Siberia, a job building straw brick for the task masters of Egypt or a slave's role under Simon Legree. After a couple of months of the Chapman regime, the Colts should have pretty thick pelts."

"The whole story of Southside Park was not told at Richmond. It's true, the fans gave Mr. Chapman a good verbal going over for the cat's-pawing he inflicted upon their shortstop, who is by the way of being the darling of Twin City fans at the moment. Probably some hoodlum—you can't keep them out of ballparks—did toss a bottle at Vettorel.

"But Mr. Chapman was not altogether blameless. Durden reported that Chapman, 'with a baserunners right, took the Twin's shortstop, who was covering second, out into left field.'

"Actually Mr. Chapman exceeded a baserunner's right. He didn't take shortstop Berry out into left field at all. Berry had made the play at second and had stepped out in the direction of right field when Chapman, with spikes flying, slid out of the baseline and mowed down the shortstop in right field. The umpire would have been within his legal right to call Chapman out for interference but he chose to look down his nose and let matters rest.

"The incensed bleacherites, who were closer than the rest of the fans to the play, thought it was dirty baseball.

"I thought Mr. Chapman did a very clever piece of baserunning, if he could get by with it—and he did."

William Benjamin "Ben" Chapman began his career in 1930 with the New York Yankees. He was a teammate of Babe Ruth, Lou Gehrig, Bill Dickey, Red Rolfe, and other

Yankee stars in the early and mid-thirties. Chapman, who batted and threw right-handed, hit .316 in his rookie season and played second and third base. After leading the American League in errors at third base while only playing 91 games there, he moved to the outfield in 1931 to take better advantage of his speed and throwing arm. Chapman led the AL in stolen bases the next three seasons and his 61 swipes in 1931 were the most by any major leaguer between 1921 and 1961. While with the Yankees he batted over .300 and scored 100 runs four times each, twice batted in 100 runs, and in 1934 led the AL in triples. He batted .294 with six runs batted in, helping the Yankees sweep the Chicago Cubs in the 1932 World Series. Ben Chapman played in the first three All-Star games and was the first American League batter in All-Star history when he led off for the Junior Circuit in the 1933 inaugural game.

It was during Chapman's six-plus seasons in New York that he first showed himself to be a bigot when he mocked Jewish fans at Yankee Stadium with Nazi salutes and disparaging monikers. In a 1933 game, he intentionally spiked Washington Senator second baseman Buddy Myer— who he incorrectly believed was Jewish—and triggered a brawl that included 300 fans.

With the arrival of Joe DiMaggio in 1936, Chapman was expendable and was traded to the Washington Senators. He continued to be a productive player for the Senators, the Boston Red Sox, and the Cleveland Indians before finishing his major league career hitting .226 for the Chicago White Sox in 1941.

In 1942 the fiery Chapman was the player/manager of the Richmond Colts in the Piedmont League. His spikes up, out-of-the-baseline, slide that took out Winston-Salem shortstop Neil Berry drew the wrath of the angry Twins fans but his actions five years hence drew the wrath of a nation.

Ben Chapman played and managed one more season in the Piedmont League, 1944, after he was suspended for the 1943 season for punching an umpire. Chapman ended up in the Phillies organization and took over as manager of the major league club in 1945. He was still at the helm in 1947, the year Jackie Robinson broke major league baseball's color barrier with the Brooklyn Dodgers. Being the first black player in the major leagues wasn't an easy task for Robinson with several of his Dodger teammates initially against his inclusion on the team. Other teams, including the Philadelphia Phillies, were also opposed to integration, and during an early-season series at Ebbets Field—Brooklyn's home park—the level of vile verbal abuse directed at Robinson by Phillies manager Ben Chapman and his players reached such outrageous proportions that it made headlines across the nation bringing to light how badly Robinson was being treated. Chapman—in an attempt to explain away his actions—called his verbal abuse of Robinson "bench-jockeying." Baseball bench-jockeying is when a vociferous player, coach, or manager attempts to bait or harass an opposing player—usually from the bench—in order to distract the player into making mistakes or getting him rejected for retaliating. Using his bench-jockeying defense, Chapman explained how he also used ethnic slurs against Italian-American player Joe DiMaggio and Jewish player Hank Greenberg. If anything, Ben Chapman was an equal opportunity racist.

Chapman also instructed his pitchers to hit Robinson—rather than walk him—if the count got to three balls and no strikes. Chapman's unrelenting and racist intimidation of Jackie Robinson ultimately backfired, with the backlash against Chapman so severe that he was asked—more likely told—to pose for a conciliatory photograph with Robinson when the two teams met in Philadelphia in May.

Jackie Robinson agreed to pose for the photograph with Chapman but refused to shake his hand. Chapman and Robinson held opposite ends of a bat for the publicity stunt. Robinson later wrote, "I have to admit that having my picture taken with that man was one of the most difficult things I had to make myself do."

In the end, Ben Chapman's overt bigotry would become his baseball legacy with his shameless racism called out in books and movies about Jackie Robinson's life.

May 25, Southside Park—The Twins shutout the Norfolk Tars 4-0 for their fifth straight win. George Vico and Johnny McHale led the offense, each homering, while manager/catcher Al Unser also delivered an RBI for the Twins' team that had not lost since he took over. But the story of this game was the 5-hit shutout pitching of 17-year old southpaw Ted Gray.

Ted Glenn Gray was a star pitcher and a hot-shot prospect, fresh out of Detroit's Highland Park High School, when he signed with the Tigers in 1942, at the age of 17. In an early season game against the Greensboro Red Sox, Gray was throwing bullets and mowing down the Sox. The Sox' forty-year-old manager, future Hall of Famer (1964) Heinie Manush—a former batting champion with the Tigers—was riding young Ted from the bench, trying to rattle him.

Gray wasn't intimidated by the bench-jockeying, "If you think I'm just a punk busher, why don't you get up there with a bat?" he shouted. Manush accepted the challenge and inserted himself into the lineup as a pinch-hitter. Gray struck him out on three pitches.

"He's one of the best left-handed pitchers I ever saw," Manush later admitted.

May 26, Southside Park—The Winston-Salem Twins won their sixth straight game, 4-3, from Norfolk, but the Twins stayed in the cellar because seventh-place Durham also won.

May 27, Southside Park—It was Ladies Night but that

didn't help the Twins who saw their six-game win streak come to an end as the Norfolk Tars won the series finale, 12-8, in a see-saw battle that wasn't decided until the Tars added three insurance runs in the ninth inning.

May 28, Southside Park—The Twins lost a 12 inning affair to the Greensboro Red Sox, 5-3, before 3,000 fans at Southside Park. Proceeds from the police-sponsored game will be used to buy uniforms for the auxiliary police.

From the *Twin-City Sentinel*:

"Great Fielding - The game was marked by some very fine fielding, especially on the part of Neil Berry, Twins' shortstop. The fleet youngster handled 11 chances flawlessly and several of the pick-ups and throws were nothing short of brilliant."

May 30, Southside Park—In the afternoon home game of the Memorial Day home-away doubleheader Twins southpaw, Tiny Ted Gray, pitched a four-hit gem blanking league-leading Greensboro, 3-0.

Writing for the *Winston-Salem Journal*, Frank Spencer, Journal Sports Editor reported;

". . . Tiny Ted was hotter than the sun that boiled down from above as he toyed with the powerful sluggers of the Red Sox, scattered his four hits in three innings, allowed only two men to reach second base and wrote one-two-three in six of the nine frames.

". . . Neil Berry paced a brilliant defensive style of play that the Twins threw-up behind smooth-working Tiny Ted. He had seven chances and several were the kind that made the fans hold their breath until the play was over."

Greensboro won the night game at their place, 8-3.

May 31, Asheville, NC—The Asheville Tourists handed the Winston-Salem Twins their third extra-inning loss in four days, winning 6-5. Two runs to tie the game in the ninth and snatched the victory from the Twins before the Tourists won it in the tenth. Asheville went on to sweep the three game series.

June 3, Southside Park—It was Ladies Night at Southside Park, and a banged up Twins team lost another one run game, 3 to 2, in the opener of a three game series against the Charlotte Hornets.

First Baseman Johnny McHale (split finger) and Third Baseman Adam Bengoechea (sprained ankle) were out of the line-up. Shortstop Neil Berry suffering from a bruised foot, played. A Pitcher and a Catcher played in the outfield so that two outfielders could man Third and First base. This patchwork lineup committed two errors, left 10 men on base, and couldn't come through to support Ted Gray's stellar pitching.

Another one run set back, 4-3, against the Charlotte Hornets extended the last place Winston-Salem losing streak to six games.

June 5, Southside Park—The 800 fans that turned out for the Twins' series finale against Charlotte were treated to a four-hit, 5-0, shutout by Bobby Hogue. Hogue's heroics, along with the team's timely hitting, and excellent defense, ended the Twins' six game losing streak.

The *Winston-Salem Journal* reported:

". . . The keystone combination of Neil Berry and Johnny Radulovich sparkled brighter than the arc lights above during the game. They were all over the infield, pulling down hard smashes and making long and accurate throws."

June 6, Norfolk, VA—Winston-Salem took the opener of this three game series, 7-2, behind their effective pitcher, Mike Lake, who allowed eight hits but was never in trouble after his teammates staked him to a four run lead with a run in the first and three in the third.

A twin-bill the next day resulted in a split with each team winning 4 to 1. Lefty Teddy Gray was superb in pitching the

Twins to the win in the opener. Robbie Roberts pitched well in his first start for the Twins giving up six hits but was undone by five walks, a hit batsman, and two errors.

From the *Twin-City Sentinel*, June 8, 1942

Cates' Comment by Nady Cates

More About the "Wolfing" Incident

"Now, will Chauncey Durden of the *Richmond Times-Dispatch* please hush! I claim I won a clear-cut decision over him in our little controversy on the "bad, bad wolves" incident at Southside Park.

"Jake Wade of the *Charlotte Observer* has stepped into the argument and—if wishful thinking plays me not falsely—he is unmistakably in my corner. With Durden's kind permission, I hereby appoint Jake as the official referee in this bout.

"'Good, healthy incident,' the *Observer* columnist calls the wolfing episode . . .

"But read his comment for yourself: '. . . The league, it seems, is still alive. Winston-Salem, the Brooklyn of the Piedmont, is down the line as strong as ever in loyalty to its bums. Incidentally, whether the Twin City fans know it or not, the fans all over have been pulling for the Twins to emerge from their cellar home, cheering their recent good work. And Mr. Durden, if he knows what's best for him, had better lay off those Twin City fans. The guy who drew the bead with the pop bottle has been duly dispatched to his proper place in society by Mr. Cates. Let those with only lungs to exercise get a little fun in this madhouse world.'"

June 11, Southside Park—It looked like a strong pitching performance by Portsmouth Cubs Pitcher Lefty Johnson would deny the Twins and keep Winston-Salem in the Piedmont League cellar another day. Johnson gave up only two hits through eight innings, holding the Twins scoreless while the Twins hurler Bobby Hogue allowed 10 scattered hits and two runs. But baseball is a nine inning game and a tiring Johnson still needed three outs to secure a victory for the Cubs. The Twins weren't about to make it easy. Neil Berry started the bottom of the ninth by working Lefty for a walk. Singles by Murray and Radulovich weren't enough to score Berry, but loaded the bases and spelled the end of the night for Lefty Johnson. Cubs skipper Tony Lazzeri brought in Wesley Livengood to put down the rally and save the game. Livengood got Unser to foul out to his catcher on the first pitch he threw. With one out and the bases full of Twins, Unser called on Johnny McHale to bat for Mueller. McHale, still nursing a split finger that had kept him out of the line-up, stepped up to the plate. On a one-one count, Johnny saw a pitch he could hit and drove the ball. If the swing hurt his injured finger he didn't show it, not that anyone would have noticed if he did—they were watching the baseball clear the wall at the 319-foot marker in right field. McHale's heroic grand slam gave the Twins more than a 4-2, come-from-behind victory, it also lifted the team a half-game ahead of the now last place Durham Bulls.

June 12, Southside Park—A battle for seventh place in the Piedmont league was waged between the Winston-Salem Twins and the Durham Bulls. 1500 fans turned out to see if the Twins could stay out of the cellar another day. They couldn't. The Bulls erased an early Twins lead with three runs in the eighth and one in the ninth to win, 5 to 3, and move the Twins back into the cellar.

The *Winston-Salem Journal* noted that "Berry's fielding of everything that came in his direction at shortstop was a high spot of the game . . ."

The following night the teams split a twin bill to set up a battle to determine who will reside in the cellar when the teams conclude the series on Monday night.

June 15, Southside Park—Bobby Hogue scattered 4 hits and shutout the Bulls, 3-0, sending Durham home in the same position they arrived in, last place. Johnny McHale provided the power necessary to secure the victory with a three run homer in the fifth inning scoring Berry (singled) and Radulovich (walk) ahead of him.

June 16, Richmond, VA—The Winston-Salem Twins swept a double-header from the Richmond Colts winning the opener, 3-1, and the nightcap, 3-2. Joe Moceri and Mike Lake notched the victories that, coupled with a Durham loss, moved the Twins a game and a half ahead of the last place Bulls.

June 20, Durham, NC—The Bulls drew first blood in the series that should decide seventh place in the Piedmont League besting the Twins, 4-1, behind the left arm of Lefty Hamill. The Twins made contact for 10 scattered hits off the Bull's lefty but could only push across the single run when Berry drove in Vico in the ninth. Bobby Hogue gave up nine hits but too many were in the sixth inning when the Bulls pushed across three runs.

June 21, Durham, NC—The Twins are once again looking up from the bottom after reclaiming the Piedmont cellar with a pair of shutout losses to the Durham Bulls. The Bulls took the opener, 5-0, when Bull's hurler Moulder gave up six harmless hits.

The Twins only managed three hits against Durham's Nagy in the second game, losing 2-0. The shutout shellacking should not come as a surprise to those who have followed this series as the Twins have now gone seventy-five innings in Durham with only one run to their credit.

June 22, Durham, NC—The Durham Bulls completed the four-game sweep of the Winston-Salem Twins, 3-0, with all the scoring coming in the first inning off Fisher, a newcomer to the Twins staff. The Twins arrived in Durham hoping to extend their game and a half lead on the Bulls but instead limp out of town firmly cemented in the cellar two and a half behind seventh place Durham.

From the *Twin-City Sentinel*, June 23, 1942

Ball-Hawk Berry Class of League

By Nady Cates

"The kid from Kalamazoo is the guy everyone is talking about at Southside Park. When Neil Berry-age 20, previous experience none—reported for spring training, he was tagged as a 'likely looking youngster.' But no one, not even that peer of Detroit scouts, 'Wish' Egan, who picked him up on the sandlots ofd Kalamazoo, Mich., expected him to make the team his first year in professional baseball. The ivory experts had merely written him down in the 'future book' of baseball.

"Today, after two and a half months of the season in which he hasn't been out of the lineup a moment, even when a bruised heel had him walking around on tiptoe, Neil Berry is hailed as the best fielding shortstop seen in the Piedmont since John Pesky cavorted for the Rocky Mount Red Sox, and Phil Rizzuto picked 'em up and put 'em out for the Norfolk Tars."

The "Ball-Hawk Berry" article was accompanied by the first individual photograph of Neil Berry to appear in the *Sentinel*. The photographer must have had a deadline. Instead of a picture of Neil in his Twins uniform, the *Sentinel* photo shows Neil, neatly dressed in an open-collar shirt and sweater vest, with a slight smile, and every hair in place, eating a grapefruit. The *Sentinel* used that photograph, cropping out the grapefruit, four additional times during the season when they ran an article about Neil.

June 23, Southside Park—The Richmond Colts and their brazen manager, Ben Chapman, returned to Southside park for the first time since Chapman, with spikes high and out of the baseline, took out shortstop Neil Berry to break up a double play. The bleacherites reacted to the mistreatment of their favorite player by raining abundant verbal abuse on Chapman. That led sportswriter Chauncey Durden, of the

Richmond Times-Dispatch, to label the Winston-Salem fans the "worst bleacher wolves" in the Piedmont League.

Twin-City Sentinel sports editor Nady Cates responded, pointing out that, "The umpire would have been within his legal right to call Chapman out for interference."

Jake Wade of the Charlotte Observer joined the argument, on what must have been a slow day for sports reporting, apparently agreeing with Cates and pointing out, "The league, it seems, is still alive."

The Twins' fans again let Chapman have it, booing and insulting him at every sighting, but Ben took it in stride displaying a broad grin throughout the contest. It made for a jovial mood as the Twins also treated their fans to a 6-3 victory behind the pitching of Bobby Hogue and five RBIs from Jim Mathews, just back from a six week absence due to a broken hand did manage to induce riotous applause from the bleacher "wolves" when his pinch-hit effort in the ninth resulted in a weak ground out.

June 25, Southside Park—The young Winston-Salem Twins had lost more 1 and 2 run decisions than any team in the Piedmont this year but four Twins hurlers couldn't contain the Richmond Colts on this forgettable day at Southside Park. The Colts tallied 20 hits and scored in six different innings on their way to a 19-0 embarrassment of the Winston-Salem club. Six Twin errors, including three by manager Al Unser, contributed to the inflated Richmond score.

From the *Twin-City Sentinel*:

"'I'm glad we got that out of our system,' breathed Skipper Unser, with a sigh of relief, 'I was as bad as anybody.' The manager was so hoarse from a cold that he could hardly speak above a whisper. The breeze from those Richmond hits didn't give him the cold. He had it before the game."

On June 25, 1942, the *Twin-City Sentinel* reported:

Twins Are Youngest Ball Club in Country

"Winston-Salem has the youngest professional baseball club in the entire country, local officials believe.

"The Twins average is only 19 1/2 years in age, not counting manager Al Unser, who is 26.

"Pitcher Ted Gray, 17, is the youngest. Outfielder Don Murray, 23, the oldest.

"Others range in between as follows:

Age 18 - Pitcher Joe Moceri, Outfielder George Vico, Second Baseman Johnny Radulovich.

Age 19 - Catcher Martin Tabacheck, Pitcher Mike Lake, Pitcher Hubert Roberts.

Age 20 - First Baseman Johnny McHale, Outfielder Jim Mathews, Shortstop Neil Berry, Pitcher Bobby Hogue.

Age 21 - Pitcher Gilbert Elliott.

Age 22 - Outfielder Nick Rhabe."

The youngest team in the country was about to get younger. On July 1, Detroit signed Vic Wertz, a 17-year-old pitcher and outfielder from Reading, Pennsylvania, and assigned him to the Winston-Salem club.

Victor Woodrow Wertz was born on February 9, 1925, in York, Pennsylvania, the youngest of Paul and Manerva Wertz's five children. The family relocated to Reading when Vic was 11 years old. Vic took up baseball in Reading and starred for the American Legion Gregg Post team, and at Reading High School, winning state championships with both in 1941.

Wertz turned down bonus offers and signed for no bonus money with his favorite team, the Detroit Tigers.

Wetz debuted for the Twins when he pinch-hit for Bobby Hogue in the second game of the July 4 holiday doubleheader, at Southside Park. Vic Wertz was 0 for 1 in his first professional game and no one remembers how he

Vic Wertz on the cover of the 1951 Tiger Facts booklet.

From Author's collection

made the out. Twelve years later, playing on baseball's biggest stage, Vic Wertz made an out no one will ever forget.

After a midseason trade to the Cleveland Indians in 1954, Wertz contributed 14 home runs and hit .275 in 295 at-bats, for the Cleveland club that won 111 games and the American League pennant. They faced the National League champion New York Giants in the 1954 World Series.

The series opened in the Polo Grounds, the Giants expansive home park. Vic Wertz was the Indians offense that day with four of their eight hits including a 420-foot triple to right-center, a 400-foot double to left-center, and two line singles. He drove in both of his team's early runs. In the eighth inning, he came to bat for the fifth time with the game tied 2-2, and two runners on base. Wetz crushed the ball with home run distance in any park—any park other than the Polo Grounds—well over the head of any center fielder—any center fielder other than Willie Mays. Mays, sprinting toward the center field bleachers with his back to the plate, caught up to the ball and made an over the shoulder catch 450 feet from home plate. May immediately whirled around and threw it to the cut off man to keep the Indians from scoring.

The Giants won the game in the bottom of the tenth inning with a three run, pinch hit home run by Dusty Rhodes.

Rhodes' home run landed in the first row a few feet inside the right field foul pole a short 270 feet away.

If that game had been played in Cleveland's Municipal Stadium—or most other major league parks—Wertz's drive would have been a home run and Rhodes' drive would have been caught for an out. The Giants went on to sweep the favored Indians and win the 1954 World Series.

Willie Mays' outstanding play will forever be known simply as, "The Catch."

For Mays, "The Catch" became one of the many highlights, in a Hall of Fame career filled with them. Mays' unlikely catch led to a game one win for the Giants, but it also robbed Vic Wertz of the first five-hit game in World Series history. Vic Wertz went 4 for 5, with two RBIs in game one of the 1954 World Series, but in many corners, he will only be remembered as the answer to a sports trivia question.

Nearing the halfway point of the 1942 season the young Twins, after briefly visiting seventh place were back in last place with a 25 and 40 record, two games behind the Norfolk Tars. Defensively the Twins were fourth in the league with .961 fielding percentage, but they had the lowest team batting average in the league at .230. Neil Berry had not missed a game at shortstop and was sporting a .231 batting average.

After managing only four wins against seven losses in the first half of July, the Twins went into Asheville for a three-game series with the Tourists.

On July 16, the *Twin-City Sentinel* reported that "the Twins all but went mad here last night as they unleashed such power as has never been known for a Winston-Salem club to produce in solidly trouncing the Asheville Tourists, 16-7 to pull within one-half game of seventh place and sweep the three-game series . . ."

Winston-Salem, along with Norfolk and Asheville, were in the race—the race to finish out of the Piedmont League basement. The Twins, with 33 wins and 60 games left to play, were also looking to eclipse the previous win total of 54 games, set by the '39 squad, and tied by last year's last place team.

On July 24, the *Twin-City Sentinel* reported:

"Norfolk, Va.—The Winston-Salem Twins swept into a tie for sixth place in the Piedmont League standings on the sound left arm of Teddy Gray by defeating Norfolk here last night by a score of 5 to 2.

"Tiny Ted going the full route in brilliant style, held the Tars to four well scattered hits and gained a deserved triumph over the Tars.

"Norfolk and the Twins are now deadlocked for sixth place in the standings.

"The Twins move across the ferry tonight to open a four-game series against the Portsmouth Cubs."

July 24, Portsmouth, VA—The Twins split a doubleheader with the Cubs, falling 4 to 3, after their seventh inning rally fell a run short of extending the first game. Bobby Hogue won the second game, 3 to 2, effectively scattering the 11 hits he gave up, to earn his thirteenth victory of the season.

Another doubleheader resulted in two close games, but the Twins were on the wrong side of both scores, losing 1 to 0, and 3 to 2.

July 28, Southside Park—The Twins were back within sniffing distance of sixth place after beating the Norfolk Tars, 5 to 4, in the first of a four game series. A ninth inning rally accounted for all the Twins' runs.

Norfolk won, 4 to 0, the next night when Bobby Hogue couldn't shut down the Tars on two days rest and the Twins couldn't score with their six hits.

The results of the third game in the series was reported in the *Winston-Salem Journal*:

"They turned on the lights at Southside Park last night. There is some argument as to what happened after that.

"Norfolk partisans will probably say it was a baseball game. The Tars had their fun at the expense of the Twins in winning a 13-6 victory and pushing their sixth-place lead to two and a half games."

Make that three and a half games between sixth place Norfolk and seventh place Winston-Salem after the Tars won the series finale, 7 to 3.

With a record of 43-57, on August 5, three-quarters of the way through the 1942 season, the Winston-Salem Twins had worked themselves into seventh place, six games ahead of the Asheville Tourists, and only a half-game behind sixth place Norfolk. They got there by playing .500 baseball (38-38) for manager Al Unser after he inherited a Twin's team that had only won 5 of its first 24 games.

Neil Berry had raised his average to .240 while the Twins remained last in hitting with a .230 team average. Neil's defense was drawing favorable comparisons to some of the best ever Piedmont League shortstops, and current major leaguers.

From the *Twin-City Sentinel*, August 7, 1942:

Berry Rates "Tops"

Handles More Chances Than Anybody

By Nady Cates (*Sentinel* Sports Editor)

"Cold figures do not tell the whole story.

"But they do support in commendable fashion what scouts and baseball savants have known all along: that Neil Berry of the Twins is the sweetest fielding shortstop in the league this year - and for a good many years back.

In Top Trio

"Berry is not leading the league in fielding percentages. That honor goes to Roberts, of Charlotte, with Dente, of Greensboro, second and Berry third.

"But no player ever got to the major leagues on his fielding percentages. Any scout will tell you they are deceptive, and not to be trusted in picking men for future service in the majors. A fielder who plays "safe" and never goes after the hard chances can finish the season with a near-thousand percentage, if indeed any club would allow such player to finish the season.

"Berry's fielding record, ranking him among the first three, is quite remarkable when you consider the [20]-year-old [Kalamazoo] kid, playing his first professional ball, covers more territory than any of his brethren and handles chances that no other shortstop would even throw his cap at.

Better Than Pesky, Rizzuto

"Seasoned observers contend that Berry covers more ground, to left and to right and in the near outfield than did either John Pesky when he played with Rocky Mount in 1940 and Phil Rizzuto with Norfolk in 1938. His fielding average of .948 (through August 3rd) was higher than the averages of either of those now major leaguers when they were Piedmont "farm" hands of the Boston Red Sox and the New York Yankees, respectively. Pesky compiled a .940 average to finish third in the league in 1940 and Rizzuto ranked fourth in 1938 with .937.

Berry Leads in Assists

"Berry shines brightest in the figures that really count. No other Piedmont shortstop is within shouting distance of 'Nimble Neil' when it comes to going after the hard ones. He has handled 582 chances—over 100 more than the average of all the shortstops and 78 more than Portsmouth's Smith has handled. Playing in only three games less than Berry, the Cubs shortfielder has handled 504 chances.

"He leads the field, too, in the tell-tale assist column, with 347 to Smith's 310 and stands second in putouts with 205 to 236 for Dente, of Greensboro.

Ballet Dancer Poise

"Berry, who plays short with the grace, precision and poise of a ballet dancer, does not look like an 'iron man.' But the kid is tough and long wearing. He has played every minute of every game this season, never stopping even for a bruised heel which had him walking on tiptoe for a whole week. He has played in 99 games; Kinzer, of Richmond, 97; Smith 96, and the others quite a few less.

"If he keeps up the pace he's set for himself, nothing short of hell, highwater or war can keep the sensational Twins' shortstop out of Detroit Tigers' line-up in 1944."

The *Winston-Salem Journal* covered the Twins' doubleheader loss to the Bulls at Durham on August 9:

"The hopes of the Winston-Salem Twins to overhaul sixth-place Norfolk was all but blasted here this afternoon when they fell twice before the Durham Bulls. The score was 3 to 0 and 2 to 1.

"Nagy, who went the route for the Bulls in the first game, set the Twins back with only one hit and barely missed blanking the invaders without a safety.

"Nagy walked only one man, Berry, who also claimed the lone hit off of him and as a result Berry was the only Twin to reach first base and he was left stranded both times."

The *Journal* report failed to mention that the only hit off Durham Bull's pitcher, Steve Nagy, in the first game was Neil Berry's two-out, ninth-inning bunt.

One of the unwritten rules of the baseball "code," is that you don't break up a no-hitter late in the game with a bunt.

You and your teammates swing away and get a hit, or the pitcher gets his no-no. Decades later when asked about this "code" violation, Neil defended his actions, stating, "the rules are all written down, and we were trying to win a ballgame."

At the time Neil must have had an awareness of the wrath a two-out bunt would incur because he got permission to try it from his manager, Al Unser.

The sports editors around the league had their say. This from the *Winston-Salem Journal*:

Says Berry Did Right In Trying to Spoil No-Hitter

"Wilt Garrison, writing in the *Charlotte Observer*, sides with the Winston-Salem Twins and Neil Berry in the hot battle of words being waged by sports writers and baseball fans.

"He recommends Berry for spoiling Steve Nagy's no-hitter with a bunt in the ninth at Durham last Sunday and predicts the young shortstop will be in the majors when he learns to hit.

"He wrote: 'Just offhand, we should say that Piedmont League baseball is getting very namby-pamby and anemic when sports writers, fans and players complain that breaking up a no-hit ball game is not exactly cricket . . . It happened when Neil Berry, of Winston-Salem, scratched a single with two down in the ninth inning to rob Steve Nagy of his no-hitter. Berry bunted instead of swinging . . . . Whereupon Durham fans booed and E. V. Mitchell of the Herald complained that Berry's act was unorthodox and that he should have cut at the ball to try to keep his team in the game . . . We'll grant that there is that aspect to it, of course . . . But baseball players are paid to play for blood and no team wants the disgrace of a no-hitter being flung at it. Manager Al Unser of the Twins outsmarted the Bulls, that's all, because he wanted that hit. And Berry, a young shortstop who will be in the major leagues when he learns to hit, also wanted it.

. . . Manager Bruno Betzel of the Bulls would have done the same thing under the circumstances and don't tell me he wouldn't; Bruno is of the old school of scrappers. . . . Anything is fair in love and war—and to a fighting ball player' . . ."

This piece appeared in **"Cates' Comment, by Nady Cates"** in the *Twin-City Sentinel,* on August 14, 1942:

Two Guys From Gowanus

"We're playing this game of baseball for keeps, gentlemen. Give no quarter, take none. Any other kind of baseball would not be worthy of the name.

"You'd think men like Branch Rickey Jr., head of the Brooklyn 'farm' system, and Scout Fresco Thompson would realize there are no hand-outs in baseball. None, not even when the distinguished Mr. Rickey and noted Mr. Thompson so far demean themselves as to pass the tin cup.

"We'd expected better things of Branch and Fresco than to act just like ordinary fans, and worse even. We'll recite what happened at Durham Sunday and see if you think what they did was any fitti'n way for a couple of dignified baseball men to act—men who were bred and all but born in the tradition of baseball and should know better. In my opinion they acted just like a couple of 'guys from gowanus.'

"The Durham Bulls were beating the Winston-Salem Twins in the first game of a double-header. Pitcher Steve Nagy was doing himself real proud. In the ninth inning, with two away, he had a no-hitter within his grasp.

"Then Neil Berry stepped to the plate, Laid down a neat bunt and beat it out for a single. It was keen strategy on Berry's part—tough luck for Nagy, whose bid for admission to the hall of fame went a-glimmering.

"Durham fans were highly incensed, naturally. They figured their pitcher had been "cheated" out of a just reward.

"But men of seasoned baseball experience, as a rule, take a different view of these matters. Any good scout would applaud Berry for breaking the hit-drought and putting the Twins in the ball game even at that late moment.

"No so Rickey and Thompson! They acted like a couple of deep-dyed bleacherites from Flatbush.

"As Berry and Unser were leaving the field, they pulled themselves up in high scorn and yelled at Berry: 'Bush!'

"Unser retorted, 'He may be bush but you'd like to have him.'

Sports Scribe Says It's Okay

"It's a pity Rickey and Thompson are not as good sportsmen as one of the Durham sports scribes. Commenting in his column, 'You May Not Agree,' Hugo Germino wrote:

'There are two sides to every question.

'Some fans will argue that Berry displayed poor sportsmanship by employing the bunt method of getting on base.

'Other fans will say that baseball is baseball and Berry was entirely in his rights to reach first any way he saw fit—regardless of whether a no-hit, no-run game was at stake.

'Several fans have requested the author of this column to express himself on the issue. And since a sports scribe often finds himself "on the spot" we don't mind occupying that position right now. Here goes:

'Berry was entirely in his rights to use any method at his disposal to reach first base in this situation. Of course, local fans wouldn't have cared so much if he had knocked out a clean single. The fact that he reached first on a bunt angered local fans.

'Many ball games have been won and lost in the ninth

inning—after two outs. And with Berry on first base the Twins yesterday became a definite threat against Durham's three-run lead.

'Suppose, for example, that the man who followed Berry also reached first base safely. And then suppose the next player had knocked out a home run. Yes, the score would have been tied up. Of course, this didn't happen, but it could have happened.

'Sure, it's tough luck on Nagy's part that his no-hit, no-run game was ruined. But even Nagy, we are sure, would prefer to have a bona fide one-hitter than a no-hitter handed to him on a silver platter.'"

Decades later there is still controversy over this unwritten rule of the baseball "code." Although with the advent of the internet, the code of unwritten rules has now been written, explained, and analyzed for the sole purpose, it seems, of defending or prosecuting the most recent offenders.

The following excerpts are from a story that originally ran on *ESPN.com* in May 2014.

"Baseball's unwritten rules quietly took form in part to reprimand a player for running too slowly around the bases, celebrating as he goes, after a home run in the eighth inning of a 10-1 game, and, in a development of the past 10 years, flipping his bat as he stands at the plate to admire his feat. The unwritten rules were built to penalize a player who stole a base when his team was ahead by 10 runs, or swung as hard as he could at a 3-0 pitch when up by 12, or dropped a bunt in the ninth inning to break up a no-hitter.

"On May 26, 2001, the Padres' Ben Davis, a slow-running catcher, dropped a bunt single in the eighth inning against Arizona that ruined Curt Schilling's bid for a perfect game. The score was 2-0 at the time, but that bunt single set off a firestorm.

"Bob Brenly, the Diamondbacks' manager at the

time, called the Davis bunt 'a chickens–t play.'"
George Will, author of four baseball books including, "Men
at Work" and "Bunts," had this to say about the Davis bunt.
"In the codes, as in law generally, dogmatism can be dumb.
The rule is that late in a no-hitter, the first hit must not be
a bunt. So the Padres' Ben Davis was denounced for his
eighth-inning bunt that broke up Curt Schilling's no-hitter.
But the score was 2-0; the bunt brought to the plate the
potential tying run."

The *ESPN.com* story asked:

"When—if ever—is it acceptable to bunt during a no-hitter?
According to Cubs catcher John Baker, "Most agree that it's
OK to do so early in the game. And most agree that if the
game is close late, it's acceptable for a fast guy, a bona fide
bunter, to lay one down in an effort to get on base."

In 1942—and for many years before and after—Neil Berry
was "a fast guy," and "a bona fide bunter," so, by this code
clarification, Neil was right to bunt according to both the
written rules and the unwritten code. Many agree, but not
all.

The *ESPN.com* story went on to report:

"On July 31, 2011, the Angels' speedy Erick Aybar bunted
on Justin Verlander in the eighth inning of a no-hitter with
the score 3-0. Verlander fielded the bunt and threw it wildly
to first. The play was scored an error, but Verlander yelled
at Aybar from the dugout for bunting so late in the game.
"Verlander eventually lost the no-hitter, but a great debate
raged in the wake of the game about Aybar's at-bat.
"The unwritten rule is this: If you are just trying to break up
a no-hitter, you shouldn't bunt, especially if you are someone
that never bunts,' [Cubs catcher John] Baker says. 'If you
are bunting to try to win the game, you should bunt. The
circumstances are a big thing. If you bunt for a hit in a no-
hitter when the score is 9-0, that's weak. I think 100 percent
of the players would agree with that.'"

The race to stay out of the Piedmont League basement was heating up. From the *Twin-City Sentinel*:

Twins Win Double Bill For "New Papa" Unser

"The Twins celebrated a 'blessed event' in the Unser family last night by winning their second double-header in two successive nights.

"A few hours after Mrs. Unser presented 'Papa' Al with a bouncing baby boy, his teammates presented him with the most sensational win-streak seen in Winston-Salem in six years of Piedmont League baseball. Never before in the recent annals of baseball have the Twins won a double double-header.

"Following up a Two-ply victory over Richmond Thursday night, the Unseremen continued to cash in on superb pitching and defeated the league-leading Portsmouth Cubs twice last night, 2-1, 2-0"

That twin doubleheader win was the highlight of Winston-Salem's attempt to escape the basement of the Piedmont League in 1942. The Twins finished the season like they started it, with only five wins and 24 losses, including a nine game skid that was only halted by the end of the season.

The young and tired Twins finished with a record of 52 wins and 81 losses but they did well in the annual pregame track meet with Greensboro.

From an unidentified newspaper in the Neil Berry scrapbook:

Berry Fastest Around Bases

"Shortstop Neil Berry of the Twins captured the featured

event in a field meet preceding the Twins-Red Sox game at Greensboro last night.

"He out ran the field in circling the bases. His time of 14.2 seconds was fourth[*sic*]-tenths faster than Pete Lewis, Sox outfielder."

Neil Berry's scrapbook also contains these clippings that show how much Neil was appreciated in his one season in Winston-Salem.

From the *Twin-City Sentinel*, on August 14, 1942:

We Still Have Berry

. . . "The fans read their newspapers with considerable apprehension this week. They saw a story out of Detroit announcing the Tigers had called up Catcher Reibe and Shortstop Lipon from the Beaumont club. This could mean that Beaumont, with the Texas league pennant within its grasp, would ask for, and get, Berry to fill in at shortstop, after having already taken the Twins second catcher, Martin Tabacheck.

"Thus far General Manager Jack Zeller has given no indication that Berry will be moved, as Beaumont has already had a pretty fair shortfielder in addition to Lipon.

"It would be a sad blow to baseball in Winston-Salem if Berry should go. Neil is the biggest drawing card at Southside Park. His thrill-a-minute cavortings keeps the fans entertained and coming back, even when the Twins are losing.

"He is the main reason why some of the fans feel the season's been a success.

"The Detroit Tigers didn't give us a winner but they did give us Berry."

From an unidentified Winston-Salem newspaper, September 4:

Berry to Be Honored

"They're going to have a sort of 'Neil Berry Night' at Southside Park, featuring the double-header with Greensboro Saturday. The brilliant [20]-year-old schoolboy has been the one bright spot in a rather drab season for the cellar-dwelling Twins. The fans have enjoyed his sparkling plays in the 'hot field' even when the Twins were losing.

"Neil leads in the popularity poll by such a wide margin that it's hardly conceivable that any of his teammates can overtake him by poll-closing time Saturday.

"So Berry will step to home plate between games and be rewarded with a beautiful Benrus watch, donated by a local jeweler. A token of the fans' esteem that he can carry and remember for many years to come. General Manager Zinn Beck still wears such a watch, given to him by fans 25 years ago."

From an unidentified Winston-Salem newspaper, September 6:

Berry Picked For Piedmont All-Star Club

. . . "For the first time since they entered the league in 1937, the Winston-Salem Twins were represented when Shortstop Neil Berry won his berth in a tight race with Lou Welaj of Durham, his margin of victory being a single vote. Welaj did not join the Bulls until after the close of school and left early to join the navy."

The 1942 Piedmont League baseball season was over, but World War II raged on. For most of the Twins players the reality of the war, and the fact that they would be active participants, had started to set in.

After the season John McHale enlisted in the U.S. Navy's V-7 program at Central Michigan College, and was eventually transferred to Abbott Hall at Northwestern University. Between his Navy assignments he got into a few games with the Tigers in 1943.

In 1944, McHale suffered a perforated stomach ulcer that required surgery and he was hospitalized for three months. He received a medical discharge on August 15 and got into only one game with the Tigers in 1944. All of his 1943 and '44 appearances were as a pinch-hitter. He did not play in the minors in either year. In spring training 1945, the Tigers tried McHale in the outfield but he was ultimately assigned to Buffalo in the International League. It was in Buffalo that McHale switched to a lighter (31 ounce) bat that was faster through the strike zone. It worked. He blossomed as a hitter, with 22 homers, 75 RBIs, a .313 average. He struck out a mere 37 times in 92 games.

McHale was called up to the Detroit club for parts of May, June, and August and got into 19 games as a pinch-hitter. The Tigers kept McHale on the 1945 postseason roster and he made three pinch-hit appearances, all resulting in outs, in the World Series against the Chicago Cubs. The Tigers prevailed, winning the series in seven games, and John McHale got his World Series ring.

McHale hit .270, with 25 home runs, and 94 RBIs for Buffalo in 1946 but—with the return of veteran players from military service—did not get a call up to the major league club.

McHale's production in Buffalo in 1946, and some say, his February, 1947 wedding to Patricia Anne Cameron, niece of Tigers owner Walter O. Briggs Sr., earned him a position on the Tiger's 1947 squad. That season, backing up the new regular first baseman, Roy Cullenbine, accounted for most of his big-league action. He hit .211 with three homers and 11 RBIs in 39 games.

John McHale quit the field for the front office after one plate appearance in 1948. Early on there may have been some truth to the nepotism speculation, but John J. McHale Sr. went on to become a highly esteemed major-league executive over his 40 year career. He worked for the Tiger's organization serving as General Manager from 1957 to 1959, then worked for the Milwaukee and Atlanta Braves, the Commissioner's office, and the Montreal Expos. McHale also received significant support as a possible baseball commissioner.

McHale's manager at Muskegon, Jack Tighe, managed the Tigers in 1957, and part of 1958, when McHale first became Detroit's general manager. Tighe had this to say about McHale, "The best in the business when it comes to analyzing a boy—not just his playing ability—but his character, behavior, and everything that goes into the making of a man."

Bobby Hogue won 17 games for the 1942 Twins before joining many of his Winston-Salem teammates in volunteering for military service, joining the Navy in 1943. After the war, Detroit optioned Hogue to the Dallas Rebels of the Texas League where he pitched very well in 1946 (9-7, 2.43 ERA) and even better in '47 (16-8, 2.31). Along the way he beat Beaumont, 4-0, with a no-hitter. Former Detroit GM, Jack Zeller, was now the chief scout for the Boston Braves, and he convinced Boston to purchase Hogue's contract at the end of the 1947 season.

Bobby Hogue was 27 years old when he broke into the majors with the Braves on April 24, 1948, four days after Neil Berry's debut for the Detroit Tigers. The 5-foot-10, 195-pound Hogue was referred to as "the roly-poly right-hander," but posted an 8-2 record, with two saves and a 3.23 ERA during his rookie year. Hogue pitched primarily in relief, making only one unsuccessful start. He appeared in 40 games and finished 15, often throwing four or more innings, while, at times, bailing out well-known starters, Warren Spahn and Johnny Sain.

Hogue's eighth, and final decision of the season gave

Boston a 2 1/2-game lead in the pennant race just before Boston's two top starters began a run of stellar complete games that led to the famous adage, "Spahn and Sain and Pray for Rain."

Warren Spahn and Johnny Sain are justifiably credited with leading the Boston Braves to the 1948 National League pennant, but stellar relief pitching from rookie right-hander Bobby Hogue and others also helped the Braves get to the World Series that fall.

The Brave's ultimately lost the series in six games, but their American League opponent wasn't determined until the Cleveland Indians won a one game playoff over the Boston Red Sox.

"Tiny" Ted Gray posted a record of 13–14, with a stellar 2.04 ERA for the Twins in 1942. Gray enlisted in the Navy after the 1942 season. He was assigned to the Great Lakes Naval Training Station where he joined Tigers pitchers Schoolboy Rowe and Dizzy Trout, and pitched for the Great Lakes team managed by former Philadelphia and Detroit catcher, and future Hall of Famer (1947), Mickey Cochrane. Gray also pitched while stationed in New Hebrides, in the Pacific Theater, where he was a Ship's Cook, Second Class. He won 12 straight games at one point, and averaged an astounding 17 strikeouts per game in his Navy career.

The Sporting News, in its February 22, 1945 issue, raved: "You can't tell any of the fellows in this war sector that when peace is restored, Ted Gray won't match the records of Grove, Hubbell, Pennock, Newhouser and the other great lefthanders[sic]. He has a world of stuff . . ." Gray never quite lived up to the expectations that were created by his wartime performance, but he did become part of the Tigers starting rotation from 1949 to 1953. In 1949, he won 10 games and had a career-best 3.51 ERA.

Gray then got off to a sensational start in 1950, with 10 wins before the All-Star break while holding opponents to a .229 batting average. He was selected to the American League All-Star team but ended up the losing pitcher after giving up a game-winning home run to Red Schoendienst in the 14th inning at Comiskey Park, in the first-ever televised midsummer classic. Gray failed to win another game for the remainder of the year, finishing with a 10-7 record.

"[Ted Gray is] tough. He's real quick and he has the moxie to throw the ball in there. He throws it and dares you to hit it. I like that in a pitcher. He's one of the toughest for me to hit." - Ted Williams in Baseball Magazine (October 1950).

Gray also gained a degree of notoriety around the league for his uncanny resemblance to actor Alan Ladd, but there would be no Hollywood ending for Ted Gray. He struggled over the next three years to a record of 29-46, with a mediocre 4.25 ERA. After he won only three games for Detroit in 1954, the Tigers traded him to the Chicago White Sox. Gray pitched for the White Sox, the Indians, the Yankees, and the Orioles in 1955, won a single game, and was released by all of them. Gray posted a career record of 59 wins and 74 losses, with a 4.37 ERA, in 222 career games.

Vic Wertz played 63 games for the '42 Twins. The left-hander hit .239 with no home runs. In 1943 he got 18 games under his belt at Buffalo of the International league, before he was drafted into the Army.

During his three years with the 81st Infantry Division, including 22 months in the Pacific, Wertz did not see combat, but did play a lot of baseball. Watching Enos Slaughter hit, convinced Wertz to change his swing and pull the ball.

After the war, playing in Buffalo, Wetz was a bigger, stronger version of himself. In 1946 he hit .301 with 19 home runs, and 91 RBIs in 139 games, and made the Tigers roster in 1947.

Wertz responded by hitting .288 with six home runs in 102 games. He hit for the cycle in a September game at Washington.

In 1948 Neil Berry joined Vic Wertz on the major league club. That year Wertz fell to .248 with seven home runs in a platooning role, but in 1949, with new manage Red Rolfe in place, Wertz had a breakout season with 20 home runs, 133 runs batted in (third in the league), a .304 batting average, and an All-Star Game appearance.

Wertz had several productive years and career highlights with the Tigers. In 1950 Wertz clubbed 27 homers and drove in 133 runs for the contending Tigers. During a five game stretch in late July he hit seven home runs, four doubles, and had six walks while going 13-for-17.

In 1952 Vic Wertz was sent to the St. Louis Browns as part of an eight-player deal on August 14. Wertz finished strong for the Browns who finished one spot ahead of the Tigers. He was the best hitter for the last place Browns in 1953, but started slowly for the St. Louis Browns-turned-Baltimore Orioles in 1954.

Vic Wertz was traded to the Cleveland Indians and that set the stage for his World Series Game one hitting heroics when he went four for five with a double, a triple, and two singles. His lone out found the glove of Wille Mays.

Twins manager Al Unser started the 1943 season with Buffalo of the International League, but was called up to Detroit in mid-June because Dixie Parsons had a sore arm. Unser started 30 games for the Tigers that year. In 1944, Unser played in just 11 games for Detroit and was just 3-for-25 with the bat, but he did have a career highlight when, on May 31, Unser hit his first major league home run—a pinch-hit, walk-off grand slam—against the Yankees. Al Unser's major league career was over after the 1945 season but he remained in baseball playing a few years in the minor leagues, and then serving as a minor-league manager, and later a scout, until the late 1970s.

Of the 23 players who were on the Winston-Salem Twins roster in 1942, 17 joined the military or were drafted following the season. Most of those boys would not play professional baseball again until the 1946 season.

Two members of the '42 Twins squad made the ultimate sacrifice for their country. Joseph T. Moceri, age 20, died June 30, 1944, in Normandy, France. Frank F. Faudem, age 23, died January 12, 1945, in the Philippines.

I was gonna be drafted. So rather than being drafted, I enlisted in the Air Corp, and boom, right down to Texas.

~ Neil Berry

10

The War Years

A Base Without Baseball

1942 to 1946

During the war years a number of major league players were actually recruited by the armed services to play on Army and Navy teams. Most of these players were assigned to the Physical Training Department as physical training instructors. When they weren't playing baseball, they were responsible for leading calisthenics and recreation programs on their assigned base. Whether they enlisted or were drafted into military service, recognized major league talent often ended up on the top service teams. The best of these service teams rivaled any team playing in the major leagues during the war.

The Navy in particular recruited professional ballplayers for teams at the Norfolk, Virginia base, and the Great Lakes

Naval Station near North Chicago, Illinois. Mickey Cochrane coached the Great Lakes squad that included major league stars; Billy Herman, Johnny Mize, Gene Woodling, Walker Cooper, Schoolboy Rowe, and Bob Feller. The team was 163 and 26, a mind boggling .862 winning percentage, from 1942-44.

Many of baseball's star players did not ask for special treatment or assignments that would have allowed them to play ball and keep their skills sharp. Boston's Ted Williams enlisted in the U.S. Navy Reserve and became a Naval aviator. Cleveland's Bob Feller and Detroit's Hank Greenberg both left favorable assignments when they requested, and were granted, combat duty. Feller served as Gun Captain aboard the USS *Alabama* and Greenberg served in the China-Burma-India Theater.

Hal Newhouser intended to join the Army Air Force and had planned on being sworn in on the mound in Briggs Stadium. The plan failed when he was classified 4-F—unfit for duty—due to a heart murmur. Newhouser was unfit for military service, but he could still play baseball if baseball was going to be played during the war.

In January 1942, Baseball Commissioner, Judge Kenesaw Mountain Landis, penned a letter to President Franklin D. Roosevelt asking if major league baseball should be suspended for the duration of the war. "The time is approaching when, in ordinary conditions, our teams would be heading for Spring training camps. However, inasmuch as these are not ordinary times, I venture to ask what you have in mind as to whether professional baseball should continue to operate," Landis wrote. "Of course, my inquiry does not relate at all to individual members of this organization, whose status, in the emergency, is fixed by law operating upon all citizens"

Landis closed his letter: "Health and strength to you—and whatever else it takes to do this job."

Roosevelt answered the letter the next day with what would be labeled the "Green Light" letter.

My dear Judge:

Thank you for yours of January fourteenth. As you will, of course, realize the final decision about the baseball season must rest with you and the Baseball club owners - so what I am going to say is solely a personal and not an official point of view.

I honestly feel that it would be best for the country to keep baseball going. There will be fewer people unemployed and everybody will work longer hours and harder than ever before.

And that means that they ought to have a chance for recreation and for taking their minds off their work even more than before.

Baseball provides a recreation which does not last over two hours or two hours and a half, and which can be got for very little cost. And, incidentally, I hope that night games can be extended because it gives an opportunity to the day shift to see a game occasionally.

As to the players themselves, I know you agree with me that the individual players who are active military or naval age should go, without question, into the services. Even if the actual quality to the teams is lowered by the greater use of older players, this will not dampen the popularity of the sport. Of course, if an individual has some particular aptitude in a trade or profession, he ought to serve the Government. That, however, is a matter which I know you can handle with complete justice.

Here is another way of looking at it - if 300 teams use 5,000 or 6,000 players, these players are a definite recreational asset to at least 20,000,000 of the fellow citizens - and that in my judgment is thoroughly worthwhile.

With every best wish,

Very sincerely yours,

Franklin D. Roosevelt

A number of major league ballplayers enlisted after the 1942 season including star players such as Joe DiMaggio and Ted Williams. Many minor league players also chose to enlist rather than wait to be drafted.

Neil Berry enlisted in the Army Air Forces in October, 1942. "I had an older brother who had just got his lieutenant bars as a fighter pilot so I took an examination, a physical for that, but I was color blind. [They said] forget it, so I did, but I could get into the air corp as just the air corp. That's why I did that and I'm sure glad. That was the best move I've ever made."

After playing a year of professional baseball in the low minors, Private Berry wasn't recognized as a bonafide baseball talent outside of Michigan and the Piedmont League, and was stationed at a new bombardier training base in Midland, Texas. A base that didn't have a baseball team.

"Basic training in the air corp was like boy scout camp. I was surprised, the field we went to was a brand new field. What it was was a bombardier school, they trained bombardiers. Of course they had pilots, copilots, navigators, they had bomb guys that worked in bomb maintenance, and bomb sight, they had a whole big maintenance school to keep those bomb sights, and they had guys in the bomb squadron that made up bombs, whether they were sand filled, 100 pound bombs, or flour filled, or regular bombs, had that. Then they had a regular field, an air base squadron, [with] the guys that worked in headquarters, MPs, the guys that worked in the mess hall, those were the field guys. Then they had the physical training department, and stuff like that. Well that was all brand new.

"After we finished a couple of weeks of just marching around the field, which we [also] did at Western in a class called, Elementary Gymnastics and Games, it was called. It was an hour everyday and during that we learned a lot of teaching games, everything there had a tendency to go

toward teaching, anyway, during that—and I'm really glad—
we learned how to march. We had guys from ROTC teach us
how to march. Flank movements, this and that, squad left,
squad right. We did that at Western so when I got down there
in the Army [it was a] piece of cake. So we'd march around,
and I used to smoke then, we'd march for 45 minutes, then,
'Whoa, rest, smoke 'em if you got 'em.' So I lit up.

"After about three weeks they said, 'hey, tomorrow we're
gonna do something different.' What are we gonna do?
'We're gonna go out to the firing range.' [We] learned how
to fire a carbine, a 45 pistol.

"Then one day we went to chemical warfare; learned how
to put on a gas mask and went through a barracks that was
full of gas, not a real serious gas, but it could burn your eyes;
learned how to put it on, take it off. That was our chemical
warfare training.

"Now you're through with basic training, what do we do
now? 'You go report to the 486th bombardier squadron,
right there.' So we go over there, and there we are, two or
three hundred of us. What do we do? 'Tomorrow morning
at six o'clock you go down to the line where the planes are.'
What're we gonna do? 'They'll tell ya when you get down
there.'

"We get down there, 'Hey you guys there's some barrels
over there with some rags in there, everybody get a rag.'
So I did, and I kinda looked around, these planes aren't big
planes, they're twin engine but they're small, they've got a
bombay; they've got a bomb sight, got a bombardier section,
they're trainers. They've got [room for] a copilot and a pilot,
an instructor, and two cadets. Everyday they'd take off and
bomb all around Texas. So, we get down there and there
were 13 guys, new guys, on a plane with rags, washing the
plane off. I looked around and I thought, 'oh geez.' So the
next morning we get up and go down there, thirteen guys
[per plane] again, [washing planes].

"So, I didn't want to do this but I had to do something, I

got desperate, a little desperate. So our captain, his name was Anderson, he was a boxing instructor at Ohio State in civilian life, a little guy–a tough little fart, about five foot, two or three, little guy–135 pounds. Anyway, I went in the morning, went over to our squadron headquarters, and there was a sergeant there, and I said, can I have permission to speak to the Captain? He said, 'What for?' I told him [and he said] 'I guess so.' If he'd said no, I would've been screwed, but he said ya, you can. So I waited until he gets in because he lives in town of course, the captain. He came and [the sergeant said], 'Captain, private Berry would like to speak to you.'

"'Well sir,' I said, 'about the physical training, all the other squadrons have physical training instructors, for their squadron,' and I said, 'we don't have any.'

"He said, 'Oh, well what would you suggest?'

"I said, 'Well, I'd like to be the physical training instructor.' So he went and got my records out, looked at form 20, I think you call it, seen that I had played a year of ball, and I went to Western and played sports in school. He was familiar with the area because he had gone to Ohio State, he knew where Western was. So he says, 'I'll tell you what,' and I don't know if he had a couple of drinks or not, but he said, 'let's see here, you go down to the line in the morning, and after they finish their early mission' —they go out, bomb, they come back— 'and everybody's off the plane [you do their physical training].' That means they'll be free about 10 o'clock, they start about five, [by ten] they'll be off their first mission. 'After that, you come back to our area, the squadron area, and there will be me and my assistants, and the guys that work in headquarters, and the guys that work in the supply room, there'll be about thirty of us up here, you can give us our physical training. That's at 2 o'clock. Then at 4 o'clock you go back to the line and get all the guys that are gonna go on the night duty, get 'em before they take off. That's 10–2–4,' he said, 'Dr. Pepper isn't it? Dr. Pepper hours.'

1943 - Midland Texas. Army Air Corp Physical Training Instructor Neil Berry.

Photo courtesy of Linda Spann

"I said, Yeah. 'That's it, you're going to be my physical training instructor and if anybody gives you any trouble, you tell 'em to see me. You're my boy.'"

Dr. Pepper, a drink that originated in Waco, Texas, in 1885, used the slogan "Drink a bite to eat at 10, 2 and 4" in the 1920s and 1930s. The slogan and bottle logo were meant to encourage people to drink Dr. Pepper around 10 a.m, 2 p.m., and 4 p.m. as a source of quick energy. Research at the time suggested that people hit an activity lull around those times. During World War II, a syndicated radio program, The 10–2–4 Ranch, aired in Texas and other southern states where Dr Pepper was distributed. The show featured western music (before it was forever linked to country), with hits like "Tumbling Tumbleweeds" by Sons of the Pioneers, a Western singing group that included Roy Rogers.

Maybe Captain Anderson was a Dr. Pepper drinker; maybe he was a fan of the 10–2–4 Ranch radio show; maybe he just knew the Dr. Pepper slogan, or maybe he was aware of the 10, 2, 4, time-of-day research and thought physical training was a better option than a shot of Dr. Pepper. It didn't matter to Neil—ten, two, and four o'clock was an ideal work schedule for a physical training instructor.

Neil and his good friend Walter, also a physical training instructor, soon discovered the extra benefits available to them as physical training instructors. They kept track of who showed up and check marks indicating that a person had participated in physical training became a form of currency for them. They could check a box if you could do something for them—something like breakfast.

On the base there was an opportunity to make up to an additional 50% more than your base pay by working in the officer's mess kitchen. Walter got himself and Neil the job of drying the silverware after it was washed, even though the silverware came out of the dishwasher steaming hot and didn't need to be dried. They soon discovered that a lot of the kitchen guys didn't like physical training.

"Walter was a conniver as far as getting deals and that's the big thing in the service, you make some deals. Walter could make deals, and we had it knocked—in Midland we had it made.

"We'd go there in the morning and sit in the kitchen— they had a picnic table, a wooden picnic table—we would sit down [and] the guys that we were doing this for—the cooks, and the bakers, and the guys in the mess hall—would bring us the Fort Worth paper, the Dallas paper, put 'em on the table and say, what do ya want for breakfast?"

Neil settled in and easily adapted to military life and his cush schedule as a physical training instructor. He was on the base basketball team that flew to their away games at other bases and was soon in the best shape of his life. There was no baseball and something (someone) else was also missing. That someone was Neil's high school sweetheart and his gal in Kalamazoo, Gloria Lorentzen. Many soldiers had their own "gal in Kalamazoo," somewhere. No doubt that gal, wherever she was, came to mind every time the radio played *I've Got a Gal in Kalamazoo* by Glenn Miller & His Orchestra, but how could these lyrics from that famous song be about anyone other than Neil and Gloria?

> . . . *Wait until you see her you'll agree,*
> *My hometown gal's the only one for me.*

> . . . *Don't wanna boast*
> *But I know she's the toast*
> *Of Kalamazoo-zoo-zoo-zoo-zoo*

> . . . *I liked her looks*
> *When I carried her books*
> *In Kalamazoo-zoo-zoo-zoo-zoo*

As Neil told it, "[Gloria] was my girl, that was a known fact. When I went into the service it was kinda a tear jerker for her. I went to Texas and I was there a few months and she decided, 'why can't we get married?' I was there and I had a job there, I mean I was going to stay there, I found that out. I wasn't gonna get shipped out the day she got there. You had to find those things out, and I found out I was going to be there awhile. So by God there she comes, the little fart. She comes down there lock, stock, and barrel. We were gonna plan on doin' this, and doin' that. Well the first thing we've gotta do is get a license in Texas. 'Where?' There's the courthouse, right there, and the Justice of the Peace. 'Well, let's go over.' Okay–I had her all fixed up at the hotel and everything–so we go over there, and I'll never forget, we walked into that place,

'Can I help you folks?'

'Yes, were thinking about getting a marriage license.'

She said, 'Oh, that's nice.' She was a nice old gal. 'Where you from?' Gloria said, 'Kalamazoo.' She said, 'No, let's be serious now.' She didn't believe there was a Kalamazoo. She'd heard of Kalamazoo, but said, 'I thought that was a song.' Anyway she says, 'that's fine, when do you plan on getting married?' Well, we'll have to make arrangements with the field and this and that and the other thing. She says, 'how long you've known this girl?' and I said just to be smart with her, that I went to kindergarten with her, which I did. She said, 'well, you've known her for a long time. What are you waiting for? Why are you waiting?' And I thought what's the matter with this old gal. She said, 'do you mind me buttin' in?' No, go ahead. She got on the phone and said, 'Reverend, I've got a couple over here from Kalamazoo, Michigan that want to get married. They're all set, I've got their license and everything. Is your wife there?' Yes. 'Is so and so there?' Yes. 'And so and so?' Yes. 'Well what if they come over about two o'clock, with those witnesses will you marry them?' Yes. She says, 'there you go.'

"So [Gloria] went back to the hotel to change her clothes–I didn't have to change, I had Uncle Sam's uniform,

I was accepted anyplace. So we go back to the hotel and she changed her clothes. The church was right behind a captured Japanese submarine that was on display. It was a two man suicide sub that they'd captured."

Apparently the prospect of getting married in the shadow of a two person suicide sub did not deter Neil and Gloria and they got hitched without a hitch on January 19, 1943.

An article in the Berry scrapbook from an unidentified newspaper divulged that, "the bride wore a beige suit with matching brown accessories."

Back at the base, Neil told his Captain about his just completed nuptials.

"You did what?"

"I got married."

"Tonight is your wedding night isn't it?"

"Yeah."

"Do you know you're going to play basketball on your wedding night?"

"I am?"

"Yeah, but it'll be over by nine o'clock."

Neil's Captain was referring to the game, not the marriage. Good thing Gloria was a sports fan.

The *Kalamazoo Gazette* reported, "Franklin D. Lorentzen, West Inkster avenue, announces the marriage of his daughter, Gloria Helen, to Pfc. Cornelius J. Berry, Midland Field, Midland, Tex., son of Mr. and Mrs. H. J. Berry, Walter street, Kalamazoo. The couple spoke their marriage vows Jan. 19 in Christ church, Midland, Tex., with the Rev. John E. Pichering[sic] officiating."

Neil Continued, "Walter was a conniver he was, anyway he threw that party for me [and Gloria] and I got drunk. It was the only time in my whole life that I drank something and got a little woozy. I was gonna be a big wheel. In Midland,

Texas, if you bought a bottle of booze, you had to buy a bottle of rum with it, couldn't buy one alone. It was a state law, or a county law—it was the law where we were. How they got that through I don't know, but they did. So we had this party, there were a couple of hundred people there, all the guys on the post that knew him (Walter). They had a nightclub-like [place] in Midland, [it had a] long table and about every five feet they had a bottle of rum and a bottle of booze—bottle of rum, bottle of booze—most of the guys didn't like the rum they'd rather have the booze.

"So Neil's gonna be the good friend of Walter—we're just like this—I'm gonna drink rum and coke. You getta drinkin' rum and coke and pretty soon it's sweet, just like drinkin' candy and pretty soon it was ugh. My wife [told me] you got up to walk across the dance floor—you had to go outside to the bathroom—and she said you walked like, straight as a string [and] everybody looked—oh he's okay.

"Well that air hit me outside that thing and knocked me on my butt. They said my toes were draggin [while they were getting me] in the first sergeant's car. They said your feet were stuck up by the back window and your nose was hangin' [out] the door opening. You were sicker than—they were letting me clean myself out I guess. Now it's after midnight, they gotta take me home and [Gloria] said we gotcha to the house—we had a long driveway goin' up to a veranda and we had to walk underneath that to the back of the house to our apartment. She said you got out of the car and you walked straight as a string up that—I was gonna help—and you says I don't need any help, leave me alone, but I didn't know where the hell I was."

Later Gloria told Neil that he had drunk an entire bottle of rum and part of another one. Neil went to work the next day and claimed he didn't have any after effects, but added, "I haven't drank any rum since then."

Neil thoroughly enjoyed his role as a physical training instructor for the 486th, but his assignment was unusual because he wasn't part of the Physical Training Department for the Midland base.

"[I was a physical training instructor] just for our squadron, the 486th bombardier squadron, and finally someone said 'hey?' and I started to get squeezed out. There was about seven or eight squadrons on the field, there was also a quartermaster squadron, anyway, they all had physical training instructors but they were all under one head, the Physical Training Department. I was the only instructor on the field that had his own squadron, because my captain said so. But after a little while, eleven months or so, I said to my captain—we got to be pretty good friends, he came out for physical training every day, he was pretty good [about it], 'Captain, they're squeezing me out, they want me to join the field physical training department.' He said, 'How do you know?' I said, 'They won't give me any more equipment that comes through special services.' Special Services is where you get your balls, your bats, your gloves, all your equipment, and they wouldn't give me anymore. 'Kinda looks like you're gonna haveta go, doesn't it?' and I said, yeah.

"So I went over to this new department, new squadron, new everything. Left my old squadron, went over to this new squadron and joined the Physical Training Department and I did that for 30 some months. It was nice, good guys. I was so glad to do that because guys were being picked out, going here, going to the infantry, going here, going there, going overseas. So all I did was that department and it was a wonderful bunch of guys. We had our own barracks."

Neil chuckled, "We had four lieutenants and a captain for 13 guys."

Neil's former Winston-Salem manager—and current Detroit catcher, Al Unser, had replied to a letter from Neil. In the letter Unser talked about his first major league home run on May 31, 1944, a grand slam, with two out in the bottom of the ninth, to beat the Yankees 6-2.

This piece in the Berry scrapbook is from an unidentified newspaper, and is dated August 6, 1944.

"Cpl. Neil Berry, who is under contract to the Detroit Tigers, and was a professional baseball player of note before entering the service, keeps in constant touch with what's cooking in the baseball world and especially with his own team. Last week he received the following letter from his old teammate, Al Unser, [catcher] for the Tigers.

Dear Teammate:

The letter I received from you was certainly a welcome gift, as I had asked many where you were, and no one knew. As you know, you are my ideal of a good ball player, and one with a bright future. If we can get this conflict over, and you return to Detroit, I know very well that you will make the grade in the big league baseball world.

You asked where I get the power to hit. Well, I have always had it, but up here seldom get to use it. But I must say that it was a thrill to hit one in that stage of the game. In fact anytime its a thrill, but to pinch hit and connect is much more of a thrill.

You remember Dick Wakefield, well, he returned and should help out our team. We have a fair ball club, but lack a little punch at the right time.

Do you fellows down there get any baseballs to play around with? If not, let me know and I'll send some to you, so you can keep in shape and not lose all your baseball ability. But I don't think you will.

Well, Neil, if you get home sometime before the season ends drop in for a workout or just to say hello. Write and I'll do the same.

Good luck, Al Unser, Detroit Tigers

Neil related, "While I was there, Gloria was down there for all that time, she stayed in Midland. One day I had to tell her I had to take an exam for B-29 gunnery. That was the first of anything that was gonna pluck us out of this soft job, it wasn't soft, but it was a good job, something that I really liked. I played on the basketball team, and we did this, and we ran that. We put on boxing matches, had the golden gloves for the whole area down at our field; we built a big swimming pool, taught swimming; taught kids Red Cross life saving stuff; taught cadets who couldn't swim, a lot of kids from Oklahoma and Nebraska couldn't swim a lick, we had to teach 'em at least to dog paddle. We had a six man life raft we put in the pool and learned the fundamentals of that.

"We'd work as a lifeguard on weekends for a little extra money 'cause people from town, they could bring their wives and kids to the pool. So after it closed for the GIs, on Sunday and stuff, they'd bring their families in, Saturdays and Sundays, but we had to have lifeguards there, so we did that.

"Then we put on demonstrations where you'd dive in the water off the high dive, jump off into a flaming, gas not oil, jump off about 20 feet into flaming water but like I said [it was] gas. You could splash gas out, but you can't do that to oil. Oil will just keep burnin'. So we went to both towns, both Midland and Odessa, and put on a demonstration of how you can do that and how you can swim in the water, push the gas out of your way, and those things. We also taught elementary parachute landing, we did that, [but] I didn't jump [out of a plane].

"They needed B-29 gunners and they wanted guys that were in pretty good shape, certain build, certain height, certain weight, so they raided the physical training department. That's a good spot to get 'em, and out of 13 guys, only three of us passed. A guy was too big, too fat, too thin. They took three of us. I had to go to gunnery school [in Denver]."

"[Gloria] beat me there. The day I was supposed to leave she was already gone. When I got to Denver she already had an upstairs apartment in a nice section [of town]."

During the war Denver's Lowry Field was a United States Army Air Forces (USAAF) training base for B-29 pilot

Gloria and Neil in Denver, Colorado April, 1945

Photo courtesy of Linda Spann

qualification and for B-29 operational crew readiness. After his initial qualification training, Neil was assigned to a B-29 gunnery crew.

"We got orders that we were gonna go to advanced gunnery school, that's where you fly, you didn't fly in Denver. Advanced gunnery school was [in] Fort Myers, Florida, where we actually flew and put all this stuff together as a crew. You flew over the Gulf, did different maneuvers and stuff as a crew—pilot, co-pilot, bombardier, navigator, flight engineer, and the gunners. [We] got to know each other, listen to our voices on the mike. We had one guy from shitsville, Georgia—he couldn't hardly talk—what'd you say? He was tryin to tell us we were being attacked from 3 o'clock, [but] it took him 10 minutes to say [and] and by that time we [would have been] shot down. You had to learn [what he was saying], that's why you practiced together as a crew."

Neil was the right size and had the mental fortitude necessary to become a Central Fire Control gunner (CFC) on the crew's B-29 Superfortress.

Neil explained, "You had five gunners and the bombardier was a gunner too when he's not runnin' his bombs. If they were all firing at a different target, and all released their guns—took their hand off the switch—all the guns went to me. Every gun on the ship I could control."

Neil didn't say why a gunner would take his hand off the switch, he didn't need to.

After completing their training in Fort Myers, the orders that Neil and his crewmates were expecting came in the first week of August, 1945.

"Orders came up one day, 'this Wednesday you guys go pick up all your stuff.' We go to the supply room and guys were all lined up, just like always in the army. We got a wheelbarrow, each guy got jackets, and boots, and hats, and this, that, and the other thing. So much you couldn't carry it. Got back to the barracks, hung it all up. The deal was this—this was on Wednesday—Thursday morning were all gonna take our stuff, get on a truck, then get on a plane and fly to Lincoln, Nebraska. From Fort Myers were gonna fly to Lincoln, Nebraska and pick up a brand new B-29 and fly that, as a crew, to Australia.

"Wednesday was kind of a sad-ass day because we were gonna leave for Lincoln the next morning. And oh boy, Gloria, she's already taken off for home. The next morning we get up—attention, now hear this, now hear this—all flights cancelled. Oh God, what the hell happened?"

That Thursday was August 9, 1945, the day the United States dropped the atomic bomb on the city of Nagasaki, Japan. Three days earlier the American bomber Enola Gay had dropped the first atomic bomb ever used in warfare over Hiroshima. Six days after Nagasaki was destroyed, Japan surrendered and World War II was over.

"The next week, Monday, we was all just hanging around the barracks, a bunch of happy guys. I went out in the yard and there were a bunch of washstands where you wash your clothes outside. I was out washing some stuff, I had a pair of white shorts on—I don't mean dress shorts, I mean undershorts—and I was out there, and I was smoking a cigarette, washing some underclothes, and some kid came up to me, 'Your name Berry?' I said yeah, 'The captain wants to see you.' [I thought] awe shit, I didn't do anything.

"Ok, so I put my cigarette out and I can remember walkin into the Captain's quarters in my shorts, and I had a pair of shower clogs on. 'Berry reporting for duty sir.' He said, 'sit down.'

"I thought, well if he's gonna be that nice, 'Do you have another cigarette sir?' So I sat down with a cigarette [and] he says, 'You know flyin is cancelled.' Yeah. 'Well we gotta have a baseball team. I looked at your file, says here you played pro ball.' Yeah. 'Well your gonna be my manager.' I thought, awe shit. I says, 'sir, I can't do that [but] I'll tell ya what I'll do—after thinking for a few minutes—I'll be the manager on the field, but you have to get somebody else to get the guys together.' I'm not gonna [be able to] round all these guys up [from] three, four hundred guys. He said, 'Okay, I can do that.'

"Well it just happened to be that from here to Westnedge (about two blocks) was a beautiful baseball park, locked, you couldn't get in. It was the Pittsburgh Pirates spring training field at Fort Myers and it was all locked under key [but] they were gonna let us use it for the tournament. What kind of a tournament? Well, we're gonna be the home field so we can have I don't know how many teams, but try to get each squadron to have a team and all the teams in Florida that have fields, fields that have teams I should say, are gonna send their teams because we're gonna have a tournament because flight was cancelled. So there's gonna be about eight teams down there with us. So we finally got a team together. I ended up with all the kids from my barracks. I'd watched these guys, I'd been playing volleyball with 'em, and this with 'em, and that with 'em, I got to know 'em pretty good after so many weeks. We had no [baseball] uniforms, nothing except for gloves, we had gloves and things like that.

"I never looked it up, but I either pitched a one-hitter or a no-hitter in the first game. We won, then we got a bye, and God, we won the tournament. We beat these teams that came down with full uniforms on, we beat 'em, our bunch."

Neil pitched every game of the tournament for his team. "My little buddy from Fort Dodge, Iowa, little Rusty Lowe, was my catcher, with no chest protector. We won, and a couple days later the Captain wants to see me—now what the hell did I do? He says, 'You know, I graduated from West Point, but I've never won anything. I've had teams before as squadron commander but never won anything. You're the first one. How about getting this ball signed and he gave me a ball, you shoulda seen that ball, jeez, like you had it under your front porch for a year, all dirty. I said, come on Captain you can do better than that—I don't know if I used those words—I said Captain go to the supply room and get a new ball. He said, 'can I do that?' Why sure, you're the Captain. Send one of the kids over there and tell 'em you want a new baseball and then we'll get it signed. He wants my players to sign it.

"The next day I got orders—you're shipping out—back to Montgomery, Alabama, where you came from. I got shipped back up to Montgomery, Alabama. I was there for about a month and a half. I got shipped back to Denver, and I got there about a good month before Christmas. The only reason I can remember that is because we wanted to come home on a Christmas furlough, me and a kid from Flint, we were gonna hitchhike home. I know it was around Christmas. So we got that [furlough], we got here, [then] went back to Denver. I got back into the physical training department, but I didn't do too much."

By November, 1945, Lowry Field was a USAAF Separation Base and by the end of 1945, Lowry's separation center was processing about 300 discharges a day. Sergeant Cornelius J. Berry's turn came on February 4, 1946, when he was "Honorably Discharged from the military service of the United States of America," after 39 months of "Honest and Faithful Service" to his country.

I met a lot of nice guys and we had fun. It's a heck of a thing to say about the service, but we had fun.

~ Neil Berry

I played against Jackie in '46 when Jackie Robinson was playing for Montreal. He was a god up there.

~ Neil Berry

11

The Buffalo Bison Years

Back to Baseball

1946 to 1947

After 39 months of stateside service in the Army Air Force and falling just short of joining the action as a Central Fire Control gunner (CFC) on a B-29 Superfortress, Neil Berry was back home in Kalamazoo. He and Gloria were living with Gloria's father on Inkster Ave. Neil was still the property of the Detroit Tigers. He had agreed to a contract for the 1946 season, and after being home from the service for less than two weeks, he received a Western Union Telegram on February 18, 1946 instructing him to report to spring training.

A few days later Neil was at Henley Field in Lakeland, Florida.

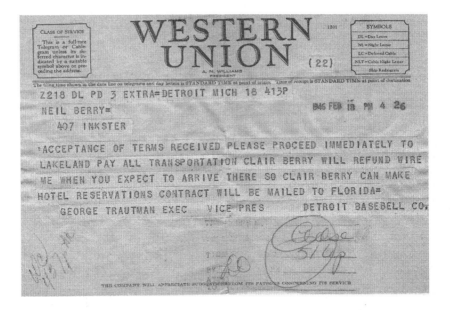

Neil remembered, "I was probably in the best shape I was in, in my whole life. I got out of the service, I went down to Lakeland, Florida, and it just happened to be that Detroit played in the World Series in 1945, this was 1946, so all those guys that were on the team during the World Series [were there], plus, during the war, if you had a job [before the war], the government said that you had 30 days that you had the right to go back to that job, and get your job back. That was the deal. So a lot of guys that didn't want to play ball anymore, they said to themselves, 'look, I've been in the army three or four years now, and I was playing ball before. I can go to spring training down in Florida for 30 days, live like a king, then I can go home and do what I want to.' They were gonna take a vacation on Uncle Sam, so we had guys all over the place down there. But I get down there and, what they did, they sent me a letter when I was in the service, said you have been put on Detroit's roster, on their big league roster. So I belonged to the Tigers, right then. So when I got out of the service and came home, nine days later I was in St. Petersburg playing in a game. I hadn't played for four years and there I was in St. Petersburg, playing shortstop against the Yankees, nine days after I was discharged.

"A couple games in Florida was all I'd played in four years and there was Joe Dimaggio and Yogi Berra, and I thought holy shit what are you doing here. The uniform I had on was big enough for a giant cause I had to get number 56 I think it was, it was Steve O'Neill's, the manager's extra uniform and he was about 5' 10" and weighed 250 pounds and I was 175 at that time, so you know what I looked like—terrible—but I only played three innings.

Neil probably garnered a few laughs—from teammates and opponents alike—while he was wearing O'Neill's oversized uniform, but as Neil told it, "God, the first time I saw [Yogi Berra] we laughed. He was catching batting practice before the game and when he stood up where you could see a front shot of him, both his shin guards were turned to the outside like he had 'em on sideways. And laugh, look at 'em. [When] he got down [to catch] just the tops turned to the outside, how he did it I don't know."

The Yankees sent Yogi to the Newark Bears of the Triple-A International League. Neil Berry and Yogi Berra—both on International League teams—would see a lot of each other in 1946.

"I didn't have much time to get warmed up [after I got to Lakeland], but all the other [shortstops] were 'doing something,' which I didn't know about. My good buddy, Lipon, had a bad arm. Eddie Lake stayed in California, Skeeter Webb—he married the owner's niece—he didn't feel like playin. Anyway, being the first year with the team I volunteered for everything, I was the new guy. There must have been 80 or 100 guys in Spring training."

One of the grizzled veterans in camp that did want a job was 37-year-old third baseman Pinky Higgins. Higgins debuted with the Philadelphia Athletics in 1930 at the age of 21. Since then Higgins has played for Boston ('37 and '38) and Detroit ('39 to '44). He missed the 1945 season after enlisting in the Navy where he spent the year as player-manager for the Great Lakes Naval Station ballclub.

A highlight of Higgins time in Boston came in 1938 when he had 12 hits (with two walks) in 14 plate appearances between June 19 and 21, breaking an AL record set by Cleveland's Tris Speaker in 1920 and tying the major-league mark set by Johnny Kling of the Cubs in 1902.

Neil recalled, "We were playin an exhibition game in 1946. One of the third baseman was an old, rough, mean old fart, big guy, pretty good sized guy from Texas—he shoulda been sittin on a cow somewhere—Pinky Higgins his name was.

"We're playin' a minor league team in Lake Wales—is there a Lake Wales? (there is)—I think it was Lake Wales [Florida] we had a split squad, half of 'em went someplace and we went to Lake Wales to play some triple-A team. He's playin' third and I'm playin' short and it was windier than hell. There was a high pop fly that went up between short and third—it was right above me—and I said, 'I got it.' Then the wind took that sucker and I chased it, and I chased it, I chased it, and Pinky Higgins playin' third—he's just standin' there—and I went right by him into foul territory, way over, and I missed it. I couldn't reach it.

"I don't think I said anything to him but I did make the mistake when that ball went up I said, 'I got it.' and he said to me, 'kid when you say you got it, god damn it, get it!' Otherwise he coulda [got it]. I don't know if he woulda or not, he was a lot closer than me."

This wouldn't be Neil's last lesson on a play that involved a wind-blown pop fly.

Neil attracted a lot of attention in his first spring training with the Tigers.

"Eddie Lake never did show up, and they sent John [Lipon] to Beaumont, I think, where he'd played before. I stayed there, and stayed there, and stayed there, and everybody is gone and right down the road a piece—where they make orange juice, they have a factory there—that's where Buffalo had spring training and that's where they sent me on the last day. In other words they sent me today, tomorrow they're leavin' Lakeland to go back for opening day."

Neil hadn't played baseball at the professional level since his last game with the Winston-Salem Twins at the end of the 1942 season. The 41 month layoff while he was in the service didn't seem to affect his defense, throwing, or speed, but his hitting was another matter.

Spring Training press accounts—pasted into Neil Berry's scrapbook—from various unidentified sources reported:

"CORNELIUS BERRY, Tiger infield recruit, who is described as having one of the best throwing arms in Florida today. He is an exceptionally good fielder and base runner but is weak at the plate."

"Berry, the 24-year-old shortstop from Kalamazoo, was the fielding star, He came up with a pair of nice plays and continued the play that made him the talk of the Tiger camp to date."

"Berry's fielding is amazing, considering his limited experience. He is fast, agile, covers a great deal of ground, gets in front of balls and has a rifle arm. He is weak against curve ball pitching."

"[Detroit manager] Steve O'Neill sat in the dugout, watching Cornelius Berry at bat. Cornelius struck out on three pitches, swinging late at each pitch.

"Now, you would not want a much better fielding shortstop than Berry. He is fast and agile. He covers much ground. He has a good pair of hands and there is not a shortstop in the league who tops him throwing. He gets the ball away quickly, throws fast and accurately. But he can't hit."

"With 60-odd ball players bouncing around the Detroit Tigers' Spring training camp here, it isn't surprising that some of the rookies are known to other players by no more than: 'Hey you.'

"But there's one lad whose name the boys have taken time to learn—that of Neil Berry, 24-year-old Kalamazoo shortstop regaling now in the pleasures of his first big league training camp.

"The last intra-squad game here made the boys take the trouble of finding out who Neil Berry was. He had looked pretty fair at shortstop. But in that tilt, with a couple of men on, Billy Hitchcock drove a wicked grounder. Berry made a diving back-handed grab, righted himself and machine-gunned a throw to first that nailed the ex-major, who is no slowpoke.

"Since then, Neil has been demonstrating that play wasn't a blind stab. No one expects him to make the Detroit club this year, but they think he is a definite long range prospect because of his fielding, throwing, speed, aggressiveness and mental sharpness.

"Neil sometimes has to pinch himself to prove he's awake as he mingles with the stars of the world champion Tigers."

Neil explained, "I knew what the scoop was, they had all these guys back and I hadn't played in the big leagues before, I played in the minors, only one year in Class B ball, but they brought me up, they kept me on their roster. How they did it I don't know, but anyway, I knew I wasn't going to stay with the parent club, with Detroit, in 1946. I knew that. I was so glad to be in spring training, glad but I didn't know where they were gonna send me. Well, they sent me to Triple A which is the best there is. Triple A is just one little step below the big leagues. They sent me to Buffalo."

Joining Neil in Buffalo of the International League, for the start of the 1946 season were some of his teammates from the 1942 Winston-Salem Twins; first baseman John McHale, second baseman John Radulovich, outfielder Vic Wertz, and Catcher Martin Tabacheck.

THE BUFFALO BISONS - 1946

All my best managers were catchers.

~ *Neil Berry*

In 1946 the Buffalo Bisons were managed by "Gabby" Hartnett, a former all-star catcher with the Chicago Cub teams that Neil had listened to on the family's radio as a youngster.

Charles Leo Hartnett caught the attention of major league scouts with this outstanding throwing arm and was signed by the Cubs as a backup catcher in 1922. The shy 21-year-old Hartnett didn't speak to the press and had very little to say to his teammates earning him the ironic, but good natured "Gabby" moniker.

An injury to the Cubs starting catcher in 1924 opened the door for Hartnett who made the most of the opportunity, hitting .299 with 16 home runs in 111 games. He would eventually play 1,728 games at catcher—a record at the time—over 19 seasons with the Cubs. Hartnett was voted the National League Most Valuable Player in 1935 (the year the Cubs lost to the Detroit Tigers in the World Series) and was an All-Star team selection six times from 1933 to 1938.

Gabby Hartnett was behind the plate for Babe Ruth's "called shot" home run off Cubs pitcher Charlie Root in the 1932 World Series. It was the top of the fifth inning of Game Three when Ruth raised his arm and gestured toward the pitcher and the outfield and purportedly called his home run shot but according to biographer William McNeil in his book, *Gabby Hartnett: The Life and Times of the Cubs' Greatest Catcher*, Gabby later said, "I don't want to take anything from the Babe, because he's the reason we made good money, but he didn't call the shot. He held up the index finger of his left hand . . . and said, 'It only takes one to hit.'"

Babe Ruth and the Yankees had been taunting the Cubs

during the series as cheapskates because the Cubs—with Billy Jurges and Billy Herman casting the dissenting votes— denied former Yankee and Ruth's friend Mark Koenig a full series share. Koenig—a shortstop—was picked up as insurance and batted .353 in 33 games for the Cubs.

The Cubs gave it right back to Ruth with taunts of big-belly and balloon-head every time he came up to bat. During the "called shot" at bat, Babe pointed at the Cubs dugout after each pitch, and also pointed at starting pitcher Charlie Root. He was pointing in the direction of Root—or center field—saying he only needed one good pitch, then hit one of the longest home runs in Wrigley Field history on the next pitch. This dubious tale of the called shot will forever be part of baseball lore and the Babe's legendary career.

Hartnett was also behind the plate in the 1934 All-Star Game when New York Giants pitcher Carl Hubbell struck out five consecutive American League All-Stars and future Hall of Fame hitters. The battery of Hubbell and Hartnett fanned Babe Ruth, Lou Gehrig, Jimmie Foxx, Al Simmons, and Joe Cronin.

Perhaps the greatest moment of Gabby Hartnett's career came during the closing days of the 1938 season with the Cubs chasing the Pittsburgh Pirates for the pennant. On July 20, 1938 Cub's owner Philip Wrigley replaced his experienced manager with Hartnett and Gabby had the Cubs in second place—a game and a half behind the first place Pirates—with seven to play; three against the Pirates at Wrigley Field, and four at St. Louis to close out the 1938 regular season.

The Cubs won the first game to pull within a half-game of the lead. The teams met again the next day and with the score tied at 5-5 after eight innings, darkness threatened to end the game before the players could. The umpires determined that the ninth inning would be the last of the day. With two out in the bottom of the ninth, Hartnett came to the plate to face the Pirates' standout relief pitcher,

Mace Brown. Brown got two quick strikes on Gabby with his fastball, then Brown made a mistake and tried to trick Hartnett with a curve ball. The pitch stayed up in the strike zone and Hertnett didn't miss it.

From the book, *The Golden Era Cubs: 1876-1940*, by Eddie Gold and Art Ahrens,

"Hartnett said, 'I swung with everything I had, and then I got that feeling, the kind of feeling you get when the blood rushes out of your head and you get dizzy. A lot of people have told me they didn't know the ball was in the bleachers. Well, I did. Maybe I was the only one in the park who did. I knew the moment I hit it … I don't think I saw third base … and I don't think I walked a step to the plate—I was carried in.'"

Called the "Homer in the Gloamin'," it remains one of the signature walk-off home runs of all time. The Cubs swept the series the next day, and then swept their remaining games with St. Louis to win the 1938 pennant by two games over the Pirates. They didn't fare as well in the World Series where they were swept by the Yankees.

Hartnett managed the Cubs for two more seasons before he was fired. He played one more year as a player-coach with the New York Giants in 1941 and hit .300 in 64 games.

Hartnett then managed five seasons in the minors. He managed Indianapolis of the American Association in 1942, and skippered Jersey City of the International League from 1943 through 1945.

With Gabby Hartnett as Manager and Bucky Harris as General Manager, the first post-war Buffalo Bison team was being run by a pair of future Hall of Famers.

Neil Berry reported to the Buffalo Bisons training camp in Winter Haven, Florida on March 28, in time to suit up and play in an exhibition game against the Washington Senators. Neil batted leadoff and played shortstop. He had three hits and played stellar defense in his first game with the Bison "herd."

Neil cemented his position at shortstop and leadoff batter in Buffalo's remaining spring games and was ready for International League opening day on April 18, 1946. Neil got two hits that day in a Bison win over the Bears in Newark, NJ. The Bisons were playing the third game of their season's first series against the Bears when Neil was injured while tagging out Hal Douglas sliding into second base.

"We were playin' in Newark. Newark had a good team, it was the Yankees triple A farm club. Vic Wertz was playin' right field for us and I was playin' shortstop and the guy hit a ball a little toward center field from the right fielder. Wertz went over [to get] the ball. The kid who hit the ball—name was Douglas—was a small outfielder that could run like hell. Wertz went to get the ball so I knew I had to cover second base. So on his throw in, by god here he comes from first base. He had rounded first and saw that Wertz had to go toward center so he ran. I'm over on second base and saw the ball coming. It wasn't right on second base, it wasn't on target. I had to go get it then I had to dive back to tag the guy. When I dove back, my hands, my arms, went down between his legs. Well, instead of stickin [his slide] in the dirt he stuck into me and I heard an umph like a bass drum. He was out and I held onto the ball. Then I felt my arm and there was nothin' there. I kept goin' and [my elbow] was over there. It hurt."

Suffice to say that Neil's elbow wasn't where it belonged.

The *Buffalo Courier-Express* reported that, "Berry suffered his injury in tagging Douglas out at second in the third inning and after the local club doctor yanked a dislocated left elbow into place he was removed in a taxicab to St. James Hospital for X-rays. The doctor expressed fear Berry may have a chipped bone in the arm."

On April 22, the *Buffalo Courier-Express* reported, "Berry, injured in a collision during Saturday's game, returned from a visit to a Newark hospital to report that X-rays revealed no fracture in his left arm. However, physicians advised complete rest and constant treatment for a week and recommended that another picture be taken at the end of that period.

"General manager Bucky Harris indicated that he would send Berry to his Detroit home to receive treatment at the Ford Hospital where the parent Tiger organization cares for all injured players owned by the club."

The next day, Harris decided to take Berry along on the team's trip to Baltimore to get a further diagnosis of his arm injury at John Hopkins Hospital.

Initially, 33 year-old journeyman Packy Rogers took over at shortstop but was supplanted by Ray Hamrick after six games. Rogers was released leaving Hamrick and an injured Neal Berry as the only shortstops on the Buffalo roster. Hamrick was handling the position well enough to cause speculation that a competition for the position would ensue when Neil had healed enough to return.

On May 15, with Neil still nursing his arm injury, Hamrick was penciled in the lineup at shortstop but during batting practice Hamrick was hit on the elbow by a Zeb Eaton pitch and was knocked out of the game before it started. An unnamed newspaper in the Berry scrapbook stated, "With Ray Hamrick disabled in batting practice, Neil Berry unwrapped the bandages from his left elbow and did a courageous job at shortstop Wednesday night.

"Berry couldn't swing a bat but he tried despite the fact that he winced with pain. His double in the seventh was hit with one hand down the right-field line. When he pulled up at second, he turned his face to centerfield and stood on the bag with his back to the crowd."

Neil recalled, "I didn't know how many weeks it was that I

didn't use [my left arm] then I finally used it one day because the guy we got to take my place got hit in the arm. I swung the bat like this and I hit a double over the first baseman's head—a George Kell job—and Gabby told me I was a better hitter with one hand than I was with two."

Neil Berry could field, throw, and run but he wasn't healed enough to hit on a regular basis so Ray Hamrick was back in the lineup the next night for the start of a three-game series at Rochester. Hamrick was still starting at shortstop when the Herd returned home for a historic Sunday double-header against the Montreal Royals and Jackie Robinson.

Brooklyn Dodgers GM Branch Rickey signed Jack Roosevelt Robinson in August of 1945 expecting that the talented second baseman would break the major league color barrier. But before making history in the National League in 1947, Jackie Robinson had to break the color barrier in the International League while playing for the Montreal Royals. Believing it was crucial for Robinson to have a black teammate, Branch Rickey also signed Pitcher John Wright and—after Wright was demoted—Pitcher Roy Partlow to the Montreal roster.

On April 18, 1946 when the Jersey City Giants hosted the Montreal Royals in an Opening Day contest at Roosevelt Stadium, Jackie Robinson became the first black player to appear in white organized baseball in the 20th century. He did well going 4-for-5 with a home run, four runs scored, and two stolen bases in a 14 - 1 Royals victory.

Thanks in part to Robinson and a powerhouse offense that included (with 1946 season stats) first baseman Lester Burge (.285, 15 HR, 101 RBI,) right fielder Red Durrett (.256, 17 HR, 97 RBI,) catcher Herman Franks (.280, 14 HR, 67 RBI,) and third baseman Lew Riggs (.303, 15 HR, 73 RBI,) the Royals were in first place when they visited Buffalo's Offermann Stadium for a Sunday doubleheader on May 19. The Royals came in with a 17-8 record, two and a half-games ahead of Syracuse, and four games ahead of the third place Bisons.

A crowd of 12,243 turned out for the historic twin bill. In the first game Bisons left-hander Billy Pierce threw a complete game for Buffalo in a 7 -3 comeback win, giving up two runs on six hits and nine walks. Four of those walks were granted to Jackie Robinson who scored from first base on a double in the first inning. Five runs in the final two innings won it for the Herd. Zeb Eaton pinch hit for shortstop Ray Hamrick in the seventh inning and in a bit of baseball irony, Eaton— who had hit Hamrick during batting practice—was hit by a pitch. Eaton was replaced by Neil Berry who failed to hit safely in his only at bat of the game.

W. S. Coughlin, reporting for the *Buffalo Courier-Express*, described the between game ceremonies to honor Jackie Robinson and Roy Partlow.

"Nothing was left undone by Chairman Harold G. Robinson's citizen's committee in the way of honors for the visiting Negro athletes as Kneeland B. Wilkes president of the City Council, acting on behalf of Mayor Bernard Doud, presented them with a various assortment of gifts, including cash, wallets, wrist watches and traveling bags.

"Assistant District Attorney Robert A. Burrell took over the microphone to act as master of ceremonies while a platoon of photographers took a pictorial record of the proceedings."

In the second game of the twin bill, scheduled to go seven innings, Right Fielder Chester Wieczorek won it, 5-4, for Buffalo with a walk-off home run in the bottom of the seventh. Robinson was one for three after legging out an infield hit but was thrown out trying to steal second base by catcher Martin Tabacheck on a pitchout.

Five days later, after two losses and a tie in Toronto, the Buffalo Bisons were in Montreal for a double header. Gabby Hartnett penciled Neil Berry into the starting lineup, leading off and playing shortstop, for the first time since his

elbow injury. The Herd lost both games.

Neil was three for five with two singles, a double and an RBI the following day but the Bisons lost again to go winless on their Canadian road trip.

Neil reasserted his claim to the starting shortstop position with his stellar play and by "covering more ground than a circus tent" according to a newspaper clipping from his scrapbook. He was also hitting .316 in the leadoff position by July 21. Among his best games after reclaiming his starting role was his performance in a Fourth of July double header against the Montreal Royals.

A crowd of 10,159 turned out for the doubleheader at Buffalo's Offermann Stadium. They came to cheer their Bisons and they came to see Jackie Robinson play, but it was Neil Berry who paved the way to victory in the first game.

After Ted Gray gave up three runs in the top of the first inning the Bisons responded with four runs of their own in the bottom half. Buffalo won the game 11-7. Both teams would eventually get 13 hits with Jackie Robinson getting hits in three consecutive at bats. Neil Berry set the table for his teammates with four hits in four at bats including a double. He also stole a base and scored three runs. Neil led off game two with a double for his fifth straight hit and later added a single, going six for eight on Independence day. Jackie Robinson was given the second game off but the Royals knocked around Art Houtteman and his relief for a 10-4 Montreal win.

Montreal went on to win 100 games against 54 losses, winning the International League title by 18.5 games over second place Syracuse. Their offensive numbers for the season were staggering. They led the league in hitting at .288 (Buffalo was second at .272) and in runs scored with 1019, an astonishing 217 runs ahead of Buffalo. They stole 189 bases, 105 better than any other team.

The Royals defeated the Newark Bears four games to two in the first round of the International League playoffs, then beat Syracuse four games to one in the Governors' Cup finals. They went on to beat the Louisville Colonels— champions of the American Association—in six games to win the Junior World Series. The '46 Montreal Royals are ranked as one of the greatest teams in the history of Minor League Baseball.

Jackie Robinson led the International League in hitting in

1946. His .349 average was a new Montreal team record. He also topped the league in runs scored with 113, and was second in stolen bases with 40. Jackie Robinson's 1946 AAA season proved that he was ready for the major leagues and on April 15, 1947, he broke the major league color barrier, when he started at first baseman for the Brooklyn Dodgers at Ebbets Field against the Boston Braves.

In spite of the "bench-jockeying" antics of Ben Chapman and others, Robinson hit .297, scored 125 runs, and stole a National League leading 29 bases, while helping Brooklyn win the 1947 National League pennant. Robinson also led the league's second baseman in fielding (.985). For his outstanding play in his rookie season he was honored with the first ever Rookie of the Year Award from the Baseball Writers' Association of America.

During his 10-year MLB career, Robinson won the National League Most Valuable Player Award in 1949 and was an All-Star for six consecutive seasons from 1949 through 1954. He played in six World Series and contributed to the Dodgers' 1955 World Series championship. Robinson was inducted into the Baseball Hall of Fame in 1962. In 1997, MLB retired his uniform number 42 across all major league teams; he was the first professional athlete in any sport to be so honored.

The Buffalo Bisons finished fifth in the league with a 78-75 record, 21.5 games out of first place but only three games behind Syracuse in a tight race for second place. They missed the playoffs by finishing 1.5 games behind fourth place Newark. With credit to the end of the war and the draw of Jackie Robinson, 293,813 fans attended games at Offermann Stadium. Buffalo's highest attendance in 43 years.

Gabby Hartnett never had a fixed lineup to work with in

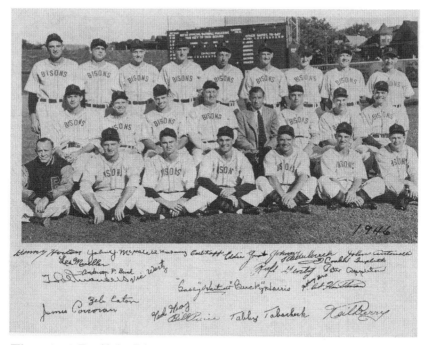

The 1946 Buffalo Bisons

Photo courtesy of Linda Spann

Buffalo with 42 players coming and going. John McHale, at first base, hit 24 home runs and had 94 RBIs. Tiger farmhand Vic Wertz, playing right field, impressed with a .301 average, 19 home runs and 91 RBIs. The most successful of a troupe of 16 pitchers was Art Houtteman (16-13).

Neil Berry started 134 games for Buffalo after missing 17 games due to his early season elbow injury. Shortly after his return to the lineup Gabby Hartnett was quoted in an unnamed newspaper clipping from the Berry scrapbook, saying "Berry is the league's best leadoff man. He has been playing under a severe handicap, because of a dislocated elbow suffered early in the year, he's hitting and improving in the field. But he's not the shortstop he will be when his left arm straightens out."

After his return to the lineup on May 24, Neil Berry started at shortstop and hit leadoff for the remainder of the season, including both games when the team played a doubleheader. Neil's batting average was above .300 for a good part of the year but he slumped a bit down the stretch. An unidentified newspaper clipping from the Berry scrapbook stated, "We knew all along that Neil Berry, the Kalamazoo boy, was an excellent fielder. He has fine range and a strong arm. But his hitting has surprised us. He was near the .300 mark for Buffalo all season until the club ran into four straight double-headers. He looked tired then and didn't hit."

Neil Berry's 1946 stats: .286 Batting Average, 556 AB (At Bats), 159 hits (including 21 doubles and 8 triples), 93 runs, 36 RBI, 8 Stolen Bases.

Numbers good enough to get Neil invited to Detroit's spring training camp in 1947. Neil looked good in March but with Eddie Lake pegged to play shortstop, the Tiger brass wanted Neil to play, not sit, and sent him back to Buffalo.

The Tigers also released Catcher Paul Richards so he could manage the 1947 Buffalo Bisons.

THE BUFFALO BISONS - 1947

Paul Richards is the only guy that ever told me to hit the ball to the opposite field.

~ Neil Berry

Gabby Hartnett retired after the 1946 season and Bucky Harris took over the managerial reigns of the New York Yankees. Paul Richards was called on to replace both.

The contrast between Hartnett and Richards was night and day. Hartnett had been a major league star; he was rotund, approachable, and lived up to his gabby nickname. Richards had never been an outstanding player; he was lean, serious, and somewhat reticent.

Paul Rapier Richards was a backup Catcher in the early 1930s for Brooklyn and New York in the National League and Philadelphia in the American League.

In 1933 New York Giant lefthander Carl Hubbell was the National League MVP. Hubbell posted a 1.66 ERA, the lowest since the Deadball era and pitched a league record 45 consecutive scoreless innings. Paul Richards caught 34 of those innings and in the process learned from Hubbell that his screwball was such a devastating pitch because it was a change of pace. As a manager Richards insisted that his pitchers attempt to develop a change-up.

Richards batted .160 in limited duty in 1934 and was sold to the Philadelphia Athletics. Owner/Manager Connie Mack installed him as the regular catcher, but Richards hit just .245 and clashed with Mack over his handling of the team's young pitchers. Following the 1935 season Mack traded him to the Class A Atlanta Crackers in the Southern Association.

Atlanta won its second straight Southern Association pennant in 1936. Paul Richards batted cleanup and contributed 14 homers and a .937 on-base plus slugging percentage. He was the only unanimous choice for the Southern Association All-Star team. In 1937—after the Crackers fell to third place—club president Earl Mann named the 29-year-old Richards player-manager. Richards led the Crackers to the pennant in 1938 and was honored as minor league manager of the year by The Sporting News. Atlanta won again in 1941.

Richards was most articulate when talking about pitching and when arguing with umpires. He gained a reputation as an unrelenting intimidator of umpires earning him the nickname, "Ol' Rant and Rave."

When World War II depleted the ranks of major league baseball, Richards—exempt from the draft because of a knee injury—signed with the Detroit Tigers in 1943. From 1943 to1945 he hit a sub-par .236 with 11 home runs. Strong defense and a powerful throwing arm kept him in the majors. Richards also served as an unofficial pitching coach for manager Steve O'Neill and was credited with developing the wild, hot-tempered young left-hander Hal Newhouser into the American League's most valuable player in both 1944 and 1945.

Detroit lost the 1944 pennant on the last day of the season, but won in 1945. The Tigers and their World Series opponents, the Cubs—both with war-depleted rosters— took the series to a seventh game to decide it. In game seven Richards enjoyed the highlight of his major league career when his first inning, bases-loaded double drove in three runs. The battery of Newhouser and Richards went on to beat the Cubs 9-3 for the championship.

Richards spent another year with the Tigers, appearing in 57 games and hitting just .201 in 1946. The Tigers organization recognized his talent for managing and developing young players when they chose him to manage their AAA affiliate, the Buffalo Bisons, in 1947.

With shortstop Neil Berry being lauded as a future major leaguer with the Detroit Tigers, the Hillerich & Bradsby company—maker of Louisville Slugger Bats—came calling.

Neil's signature used on his Louis-ville Slugger bats.

Photo from author's collection

In response to an email request for information, Chris Meiman—Exhibits Director/Curator for the Louisville

Slugger Museum & Factory—responded with the following information:

"Neil signed with us on April 14, 1947 while still playing in Buffalo. It looks like he might have gotten a set of golf clubs out of the deal, which was common at the time. At the time he requested John Antonelli's bat at 34 inches and 32 ounces."

John Antonelli was an infielder and a Buffalo Bison teammate of Neil in 1946. Antonelli had played in the majors with St. Louis and Philadelphia in 1944 and '45 but couldn't stick in the big leagues after the war. It is likely that Neil had been using an Antonelli bat in 1946 and chose that bat, when he signed with Louisville Slugger.

Meiman continued, "From what we've been able to see in the bat record cards, it seems he varied his bats quite a bit. Over his career, Neil used several models. The first bats he ordered were a 'Hank Greenberg' model (35 inches, 34 oz).

"Specifically he used the K55 model (34 inches, 32 oz), the K48 model (34 inches, 32 oz) and the F69 model (34 inches, 32 oz).

"The K55 model was very famous a bit later on as Mickey Mantle used it, as did Rocky Colavito and Ron Cey amongst others.

"The K48 was used by Carl Yastrzemski, Bill Madlock and Ted Simmons.

"The F69 model I believe was Rick Ferrell's model who played just before Neil did. I don't think too many others used that model."

Neil Berry started the 1947 season with Buffalo in a similar fashion as the 1946 season; leading off, playing shortstop, and getting hurt. Neil went 4 for 9 in the Bison's first two games but couldn't go in game three because swelling in his right wrist prevented him from throwing. He couldn't attribute the injury to any particular play or action. X-rays were negative and Neil was back in the lineup on April 26, after missing five games. Eight games later he was hitting .410 (16 for 39) but a pulled groin kept Neil out of eight more games in May. When he returned to the lineup, his defense helped Ted Gray win his first game of the season. W. S. Coughlin reported in the *Courier-Express* that Neil Berry "returned to action at shortstop and uncovered a corking performance of no little help to southpaw Ted Gray when he handled nine chances in the Hans [Honus] Wagner manner."

Neil, still nursing the stubborn groin injury, slumped in June and as his batting average fell so did his place in the batting order. He would bat second or third, or as low as sixth.

Neil recalled, "My manager told me, 'Here's what I want you to do, get a short bat—an inch shorter—get a barrel bat, choke up on it, and if you swing and I think you're goin' for a home run—or if I see your hands down near that knob of the bat—I'm gonna kick you right in the ass.

"Well he's the only guy that ever told me to hit the ball to the opposite field. Everybody else, I gotta pull the ball, pull the ball. Why? That means that you're honest—yeah [an] honest—0 for four, 0 for four, that doesn't sound too good either."

The "Hank Greenberg" model, a 35-inch, 34-ounce bat, is likely the bat that Neil abandoned for a lighter model, after Paul Richards convinced him to choke up and meet the ball. Neil then apparently tried several 34-inch, 32 ounce models. Concerning a lighter bat, Neil recalled, "I found a better way to do that. I took a big drill and I'd drill a hole right down the middle of that sucker, a half inch, three eighths, all according to [how much weight] I wanted to take off. I'd drill it way down to here (pointing out the spot on a vintage

Louisville Slugger). What I did, when I drilled this out, I saved the sawdust. When I got it where I wanted it I took that sawdust with some glue and I mixed it up and I filled that hole full. Then I took a file and I filed it off. All you could see when I got through was a round circle [on the end of the bat]."

Asked if what he was doing with his bats was legal, Neil replied, "No. The reason I did that [is because] the rules say you can't add any foreign substance. I didn't add any foreign substance (apparently forgetting about the glue), I took wood away, then I put it back in—the sawdust—that's why I thought I could get away with it.

"This was in Buffalo, it wasn't in the big leagues. Yogi (Berra) was catching for Newark, and if you looked just right [you could see] that's different wood [at the end of the bat]. That's what Yogi did and I had to throw 'em out.

Paul Richards was a student and a teacher of the game of baseball, but he was also a disciplinarian who expected his players to play the game the right way, or face his wrath. Neil Berry learned this first hand. The Bisons were playing at Baltimore on a windy night. At the plate, Neil swung at a pitch he liked—intending to drive the ball to the opposite field—but he didn't make solid contact and instead lofted a towering popup to the right side. Neil stood at the plate thinking he was an easy out and watched as the first baseman settled under the ball; he watched as the first baseman adjusted for the effect of the wind on the flight of the ball; he watched as the first baseman made a final attempt to catch the wind blown ball, and he saw the ball elude the first baseman and land in fair territory not far behind first base. With Neil's speed he could have been standing on second base—at the very least, he should have been standing on first—but instead he stood too long at home plate. Neil was right about one thing during that play—he was an easy out. The first baseman picked up the ball and walked to first base for the out before Neil—with a last gasp late start—made it halfway down the line.

Normally after making an out at first base a player returns to the dugout and walks down the steps past his manager to the bench. Paul Richards rarely said anything to a player who committed a physical error, but his players knew they would get an earful for a mental error and as mental errors go Neil's was monumental. Looking to avoid the wrath of his manager—and to acknowledge that he screwed up—Neil went back to the other end of the dugout, hopped the rail and took a seat, not daring to look in the direction of his irate manager. Richards didn't move from his perch but Neil knew his comeuppance was coming.

After the game (Neil couldn't remember the score or whether they won or lost) the Buffalo players headed into the visitor's club house. Shortly after Paul Richards walked through and yelled, "Berry! My office! Now!"

Neil sheepishly entered the office and Richards nodded toward the empty chair on the other side of his desk. Neil sat down and waited for the butt-chewing he deserved. While he sat in that chair Neil watched as his manager looked through some papers on his desk; he watched as his manager made a few notes on one of the pages; he started to sweat when his manager looked at him then returned his attention to another menial task. Neil wondered when the tirade was coming as he sat nervously in the chair. After letting Neil sit there for about five minutes (Neil said it seemed like an hour), Paul Richards, without looking up from his desk, said, "Are you ever going to do that again?"

Neil said, "No sir."

Richards said "Ok get outa here."

Neil would have rather had his butt chewed out right away than suffer like he did, waiting in that chair, but Richards knew his players and expertly handled the situation with his shortstop from Kalamazoo.

From an unnamed newspaper article in the Berry scrapbook:

"**Paul Richards Helped Berry** - Neil Berry, the shortstop from Kalamazoo who may become a Tiger regular [in 1948], is grateful to Paul Richards for some hitting advice that has enhanced his chances of making good with the Tigers.

"Like most every young ball player, Neil always used to grab the bat at the very end of the handle and swing for the fences. Last year Richards became Berry's manager at Buffalo.

"'Choke up on that stick,' Richards told Berry. 'You don't have to kill the ball. Just meet it. You're not big enough or strong enough to be a home run clouter. Your job is to get on base.'

"So Berry started 'swinging from the trademark.' But he found the handle of the bat jabbing him in the ribs every once in a while. So he went a step farther than Richards had suggested. He started using a shorter, lighter bat, changing from a 35-inch 34-ounce to a 34-inch 32-ounce model.

"The improvement wasn't really noticeable until after the Berry's baby was born and Mrs. Berry recovered from the serious illness that followed. Little Neil arrived June 18. A week later, Mrs. Berry was well again and the Buffalo shortstop, who had hurried home to be with his wife, rejoined his club.

"From then until the rest of the season, Berry lashed the American apple at close to a .360 average. At the finish, his mark was .299, highest he ever had enjoyed in three years of organized ball. And furthermore, without trying to hit homers, he banged two. The year before, aiming for the distance in the same league, he hadn't gotten any."

The Buffalo Bisons were in sixth place on June 24 with a three game series against fifth place Baltimore scheduled at

Offermann Stadium. A series win would propel the Bisons into fifth place. Neil—with more than baseball on his mind—went 0 for four in the first game.

"[My son's] birth, at birth, in the hospital, they had a little malfunction in the birth. I was playing for Buffalo at the time and I got a telephone call from [Gloria's] dad who was living with us over here on Inkster. He said that she was having a bad time, could I come home? When you get that [message] you don't know what the scoop is so I asked my manager and he says, this is on a Sunday, I remember because we're playin a doubleheader, he says, 'play the first game and we'll see what we can do,' and I thought, well you son of a— I just said my wife's havin' trouble. I played the first game and came in between games like you always do and you change your sweatshirt and sweaty stuff and I noticed on top of my locker was an envelope, a white envelope. I opened it up, it was a one way ticket to Kalamazoo—on a pullman in those days—and a note's in there says you stay as long as you [need to], until your wife feels better, and then come back, of course. That was [from] Paul Richards, my manager. So by the second game I took off for home. Gloria was home then [and when I got there] she was feelin' pretty good and within three or four days she was feelin' okay. The baby, we didn't know about, he was just a big, half pink, squawling kid you might say. We didn't know anything about his future. I got a telephone call from Buffalo on about the fifth or sixth day, from the manager, and I remember him saying, 'I didn't tell ya to stay the rest of the summer. Get your butt back here!' Then serious, 'if your wife's alright we'd like to have you back."

Neal missed six games to be with Gloria after the birth of their first child on June 18, 1947. His first game back was June 30. Buffalo beat Toronto that day and followed that up with a doubleheader win on July 1. The series sweep put the fifth place Bisons over the .500 mark for the first time since the opening days of the season.

Neil recalled, "About the middle of the season Paul Richards, my manager, said, 'you're gonna go with Detroit next year, you know that don't you? I'm not tellin' any secrets out of school, but you are.'

"He helped me a lot, both on the field and mentally too, I mean. When Gloria had the baby he fixed me up and told me, 'you go home,' put me at ease."

Manager Paul Richards—living up to his reputation and "Ol' Rant and Rave" nickname—had been ejected by umpires 12 times by July 12,1947 earning him a five-game suspension. Ejection 13 came in the first half of the first inning of the first game after his return, but the fiery manager had the Buffalo team in the hunt for a playoff berth.

Perhaps Neil Berry's best hitting performance in a Bison uniform was in a double-header win over the league-leading Montreal Royals at Offermann Stadium on July 13, 1947. His only hit in the first game was the hit that counted the most when he connected in the bottom of the ninth with the base loaded and two out. His hit drove home the tying and winning runs for a 2-1 Bison victory. In the nightcap Berry contributed four straight hits—including two doubles—driving in two in a 9-1 Buffalo win.

A clipping titled, "International League Notes", from an unnamed newspaper in the Berry scrapbook opined, "Neil Berry, Buffalo shortstop, came out of a long batting slump with five hits in a recent doubleheader . . . Neil credits a shortened grip with his better showing at the plate, but friends point to the recovery of Berry's wife from a serious illness."

Neil recalled, "I was hitting about .250 or .260, which wasn't too good at that time. That was in June. I went back to Buffalo and I hit well over .300 the rest of the year and finished up the season hitting just [under] .300, which was very good. I got recalled again to the Tigers at the end of the season and I'll always thank the manager for doin' what he did, for lettin, me go home."

The Bisons finished the regular season with a record of 77 wins and 75 losses, good for fourth place and a playoff berth. Buffalo faced the pennant winning Jersey City Giants in a best of seven, first round match up. Buffalo won the first two games in come-from-behind fashion with ninth inning runs to shock the league's top team. The series moved to Buffalo's Offermann Stadium for game three where 10,200 Bison fans saw the Giants score three first inning runs when—according to the *Buffalo Courier-Express*—"Neil Berry and Dutch Meyer muffed a chance to complete a double play," after the first two Jersey hitters reached.

The *Buffalo Courier-Express* went on to report, "Berry came back to deliver one of the outstanding defensive performances of the year by handling 11 difficult chances like an acrobat. Neil furnished the prize play of the game when he rushed at full speed toward center, with his back to the ball, and nabbed a tall fly lifted by Tom Stallcup with Myatt on first in the fifth. The chance for a catch loomed so remote Berry wheeled and whipped the ball to Wasdell at first to complete a double play."

Ninth inning heroics were again in order for the Bisons with two runs to make it a 5-5 tie and force extra innings. Ted Gray pitched a hitless tenth inning paving the way for a 6-5 Buffalo win when they pushed across the winning run in the tenth.

Buffalo completed the sweep with a 7-6 victory, disposing of the league champion Jersey City Giants with four straight one-run triumphs.

The Bison's opponent in the championship series was the Syracuse Chiefs, who had swept their series against the Montreal Royals. After falling behind three games to one, the Bisons came back from a five-run deficit to take game five. Neil Berry's 2-run home run in the eighth put the exclamation point on the 9-5 Bison victory. Buffalo tied the series with 7-4, 12 inning win before the Syracuse Chiefs won the 1947 International League championship with a

Neil Berry is congratulated by his Bison teammates after his 8th inning 2-run home run against the Syracuse Chiefs in game 5 of the 1947 International League championship. Buffalo won the game 9-5 but lost the series 4 games to 3.

Photo courtesy of Linda Spann

10-3 victory in the deciding game.

Neil Berry considered Paul Richards—who also managed Neil in the majors with the Chicago White Sox—the best manager he ever played for at any level. Baseball scholars agree. Richards, who managed in the major leagues for Chicago, Baltimore, and Houston, is thought to be one of the best managers to never win a World Series.

Neil Berry's 1947 stats: .299 Batting Average, 428 AB, 128 hits (including 20 doubles, 4 triples, and 2 home runs), 64 runs, 50 RBI, and 8 Stolen Bases.

Neil had been playing major league level defense for two years in the AAA International League. Would his improved hitting be enough to propel him to the majors in 1948?

With only 400 major league roster spots available, there were over 20 minor league players on tap to fill each of those spots in 1948.

12

Major League Baseball

When Neil Berry Played the Game

1948 to 1954

Baseball's modern era began in 1901 when the American League declared itself a Major League on par with the long-established National League. Eventually, eight teams competed in each league with Boston, Chicago, New York, Philadelphia, and St. Louis fielding teams in both leagues. Aside from some team name changes in the early part of the century, Major League Baseball consisted of these 16 teams; Boston Braves, Brooklyn Dodgers, Chicago Cubs, Cincinnati Reds, New York Giants, Philadelphia Phillies, Pittsburgh Pirates, and St. Louis Cardinals in the National League; and Boston Red Sox, Chicago White Sox, Cleveland Indians, Detroit Tigers, New York Yankees, Philadelphia Athletics, St. Louis Browns, and Washington Senators in the American League.

In 1948 Major League Baseball still consisted of those same 16 teams playing in the same 11 cities (today 30 franchises play in 27 cities).

When Neil played the game train travel was the mode of transportation for road trips. Between series on the road the visiting team often had to catch a train right after a night game, eat and sleep on the train, and play the next day. Depending on the city, hotel accommodations were located such that the visiting players had to take cabs, busses, the subway, or walk from their hotel to the ballpark.

In the National League those ballparks were:

Braves Field (1915-1952), Boston Massachusetts. Home of the Boston Braves, the sprawling, single-deck park was the first with 40,000 seats, and initially had an outfield so expansive that—according to Ty Cobb—it allowed the game to be played "without the interference of fences."

Ebbets Field (1913-1957), Brooklyn, New York. Home of the Dodgers, this historic stadium is where Jackie Robinson debuted in 1947.

Wrigley Field (1914-present), Chicago, Illinois. Home of the Cubs, Wrigley is known for its hand-operated center field scoreboard and ivy covered brick walls in the outfield.

Crosley Field (1912-1972), Cincinnati, Ohio. Home of the Reds, Crosley Field was the site of the first major league night game under the lights.

Polo Grounds (1911-1963), New York, NY. Home of the Giants, the double-deck stadium with an overhanging left field deck had a deep center field and was the site of "The Catch" and the "Shot Heard 'Round the World."

Shibe Park (1909-1952) / Connie Mack Stadium (1953-1970), Philadelphia, Pennsylvania. Home of the NL Phillies and the AL Athletics the park featured a French Renaissance brick-and-arch facade.

Forbes Field (1909-1971), Pittsburgh, Pennsylvania. Home

of the Pirates, Forbes Field contained a small third deck called "The Crow's Nest" and was one of the first concrete and steel parks.

Sportsman's Park (1902-1952) / Busch Stadium (1953-1966), St. Louis, Missouri. Home to the American League Browns (1902-1953) and the National League Cardinals (1920-1966), the park featured a double-deck grandstand running the length of both foul lines.

Neil Berry played in the American League in these parks:

Fenway Park (1912-present), Boston Massachusetts. Home of the Red Sox, the iconic Green Monster wall in left field is the defining feature of the oldest ballpark still in use for Major League Baseball.

Comiskey Park (1910-1990), Chicago, Illinois. Home of the White Sox, Comiskey featured a large symmetrical field surrounded by double-deck stands.

Municipal Stadium (1932-1993), Cleveland, Ohio. Home of the Indians, the stadium was one of the largest ever built. In

Briggs Stadium, Detroit, Michigan

Postcard from Author'scollection

1947 a chain link fence was installed in the outfield bringing the center field home run distance from 470 feet to 410 feet.

Navin Field (1912-1937) / Briggs Stadium (1938-1960) / Tiger Stadium (1961-1999), Detroit, Michigan. Home of the Tigers, the stadium—renamed in 1938 for owner Walter O. Briggs—featured a flag pole that was in play in deep center field and a right field upper deck overhang. In 1948 Briggs Stadium was the last American League ballpark to add lights and play night games.

Yankee Stadium I (1923-1973), Bronx, New York City, NY. Home of the Yankees, the stadium included "Monument Park" in fair territory in dead center field with Monuments of Babe Ruth, Lou Gehrig, and others.

Shibe Park (1909-1952) / Connie Mack Stadium (1953-1970), Philadelphia, Pennsylvania. Home of the AL Athletics and the NL Phillies, the park was home to the first night game in the American League on May 16, 1939.

Sportsman's Park (1902-1952) / Busch Stadium (1953-1966), St. Louis, Missouri. Home to the American League Browns (1902-1953) and the National League Cardinals (1920-1966), the park was the site of a one-day career of the only midget to play major league baseball.

Griffith Stadium (1911-1961),Washington, D.C. Home of the Washington Senators. A unique feature of this stadium was the center field wall that had to be built around five houses and a tree that encroached into the field of play.

Each team had 25 players on their active roster for a total of 400 major league baseball players. Over half of those major leaguers had honed their baseball skills playing American Legion baseball in their youth. When Neil made the major leagues in 1948 only two players—Brooklyn's Jackie Robinson and Cleveland's Larry Doby—were African-American.

There was no amateur draft in Baseball's postwar era. Players were signed by team scouts like Detroit's Wish

Egan. Some star prospects were coveted by multiple teams and got a hefty signing bonus or a new car to get their name on a contract. Wealthier teams—the Yankees and the Cardinals—could outbid other clubs for top talent. Other players signed for little or no money to get a shot at professional baseball.

With only 400 major league roster spots available, there were over 20 minor league players on tap to fill each of those spots in 1948 (compared to 6 minor leaguers for each spot in 1990). The opportunities were few and the competition was intense.

The game, for the most part, was played by the same rules but expectations were very different. The sacrifice bunt and the hit-and-run were used more often to move runners up, but the stolen base wasn't employed nearly as often. Dom DiMaggio led the league with 15 steals in 1950, Jacoby Ellsbury led the league with 70 in 2009.

Starting Pitchers expected to pitch the entire game—including extra innings—and their managers expected the same. There were 938 complete games pitched in 1951, in 1995 there 275. The bullpen was often manned by aging or failed starters, not the specialists of today's game. There was no "Designated Hitter" so pitchers also batted in both leagues. Many of the team's best players played both halves of a doubleheader (both games) with only enough time between games to change into dry underclothes and smoke a cigarette.

When the umpire got a call wrong—he was still right. There was no instant replay, only arguments. Many of those arguments resulted in an early shower for the manager of the aggrieved team.

Teams played a 154 game schedule with true doubleheaders (one ticket, two games) scheduled throughout the season—usually on Sundays and holidays. Tie games—called for darkness or local curfews—didn't count in standings and were replayed if necessary.

The World Series was played between the American and National League pennant winners. There were no divisions, no wild cards, and no playoffs unless there was a first place tie at the end of the regular season (the last year the league pennant winners squared off in the World Series was 1968 when the Detroit Tigers roared back from a three games to one deficit to defeat the St. Louis Cardinals).

In 1950 the average major league player's salary was $11,000 but the average career was only five years. The games stars of course made more money, Hal Newhouser made as much as $55,000 a year and Virgil Trucks was paid $22,000. This was at a time when United States Senators made $12,500 and doctors made, on average, $12,324. Even with the lucrative average salary, when the season was over many players needed to work in the offseason to support their families. Even the stars of game supplemented their incomes by barnstorming around the country, playing against local all-stars and Negro League teams.

Most major league ballplayers were granted one-year contracts by the team that owned their rights. That contract—for more or less money—was largely based on the player's performance the previous year. Players who had a bad year could get sent back to the minors or take a pay cut of up to 25% (the largest pay cut allowed per league rules). There was a time when the Detroit brass considered releasing two-time AL MVP Hal Newhouser after his injury-shortened six-win season in 1951. Their rationale was that they would still have to pay Newhouser $30,000 after a 25% pay cut to get maybe 10 wins in 1952 (Newhouser was 9-9 in 19 starts for the Tigers in 1952).

The only recourse for a player who was not happy with his final contract offer was to hold out for more money and risk losing his position to one of the many rookies waiting for their chance.

When you made the big leagues as a player you felt real good because there weren't many spots.

~ Neil Berry

13

The Detroit Tigers

Making the Majors

1948

While Neil Berry was training to become a Central Fire Control gunner on a B-29 Superfortress in 1945, and honing his baseball skills with the Buffalo Bisons in 1946 and '47, the Detroit Tigers were winning or contending.

Detroit won the American League pennant in 1945 with a war depleted roster, playing against teams with rosters that were likewise depleted with many major league players serving their country during WWII. With some offensive punch from Rudy York and Hank Greenberg—when he returned for the second half of the season—and strong pitching led by Hal Newhouser (25 wins) and Dizzy Trout (18 wins), the Tigers were able to hold off the Washington Senators and then prevail over the Chicago Cubs in a seven game World Series.

In 1946—with the war over—the baseball talent had returned from military service and went to spring training to compete against wartime players for a roster spot. More than 1000 players—including Neil Berry— jammed spring training facilities to compete for the 400 available jobs.

Neil explained, "I knew what the scoop was, they had all these guys back and I hadn't played in the big leagues before, I played in the minors . . .

"I knew I wasn't going to stay with the parent club, with Detroit, in 1946. I knew that."

When the Tigers broke camp they carried only 13 players from their 1945 World Series championship squad. Only 10 remained at the end of the '46 season.

Manager Steve O'Neill's '46 club won 92 games with their top four starters—Newhouser (26 wins), Trout (17 wins), Freddy Hutchinson (14 wins), and Virgil Trucks (14 wins)— combining for 77% of the club's wins. Hank Greenberg was in top form with 44 home runs and 127 RBIs, but the Tigers spent most of the season chasing the Boston Red Sox and finished in second place 12 games back.

In 1947 the New York Yankees won 19 games in a row in July to build an insurmountable lead in the pennant race. Detroit held off Boston to finish second 12 games behind the Yankees. The Tigers suffered a power drought due to the sale of Hank Greenberg to Pittsburg. Roy Cullenbine was the club leader with 24 home runs and George Kell and Hoot Evers had decent years at the plate but only contributed 15 home runs between them.

The same starting mound staff that combined for 71 wins in 1946 could only manage 55 wins in '47. It was an off year for Newhouser (17 wins) and only Fred Hutchinson (18 wins) improved on his win total of the previous year.

With the 1948 season approaching Detroit Tiger manager Steve O'Neill was hoping for a resurgence from his veteran

Ted Gray, Hal Newhouser, Virgil Trucks, Art Houtteman, Fred Hutchinson, Dizzy Trout

From the Author's Collection

pitching staff (Newhouser, Trout, Hutchinson, and Trucks) as well as some help from youngsters RHP Art Houtteman, LHP Ted Gray, and LHP Billy Pierce.

Following their second place finish in 1947 the Detroit Tigers sold 33-year-old first baseman Roy Cullenbine to the Philadelphia Athletics. Cullenbine led the '47 squad with 24 home runs and was second in RBIs with 78. It appeared Steve O'Neill would have to rely on the outfield position—Evers, Wertz, Mullin, and Wakefield—to supply the power in 1948.

The Tigers also released 37-year-old backup infielder Skeeter Webb after the '47 season creating an opening for a middle infielder to back up shortstop Eddie Lake and second baseman Eddie Mayo. The prime candidates for that role were Johnny Lipon and Neil Berry.

SPRING TRAINING

In the spring of 1948 Neil Berry was vying for the starting shortstop position and a spot on the Detroit Tigers 25-man roster, but Detroit had a veteran shortstop in Eddie Lake.

Lake was acquired prior to the 1946 season in a trade that sent Rudy York to Boston. York was expendable with Hank Greenberg back from military service. Lake led the American League in appearances in 1946 (155) and 1947 (158), playing in every game in each year's 154 game schedule and all five tie games that didn't count in the standings. In 1947 he also led the league in errors (43). Lake batted .211 and contributed 12 home runs and 46 RBI in the 1947 campaign.

Maybe the 31-year-old Lake was tired after playing 313 games over two seasons or felt his other contributions merited a better contract than Detroit offered but, for whatever reason, Eddie Lake was a no-show holdout in the spring of 1948.

The soundness of that decision was summed up by James Zerilli, in an article for the *Detroit Free Press*: "[Lake] apparently hasn't studied the team's shortstop setup; otherwise he would be down here working out with the rest of the squad instead of taking part in a cross-country dollar tug-of-war.

"On hand here making baseball hay while Lake rests are Johnny Lipon and Cornelius Berry.

"The latter two are the talk of the camp, particularly Berry. Both have impressed with their fielding finesse. Manager Steve O'Neill said: 'If either can show me a bit of hitting, he could take Lake's place.'

"Lake has to consider Lipon and Berry as serious threats from another angle. The Tigers already have sent both back to the minors twice. That means they can't ship them to the minors again without losing their hold on them."

Eddie Lake's second holdout in three years opened the

Johnny Lipon appears in an advertisement for
ADIRONDACK Bats on the back cover of the May 1949
issue of Sportfolio magazine.

From Author's collection

door for Neil Berry, but it opened the same door for Johnny Lipon.

John Joseph Lipon was born in Martins Ferry, Ohio, in November 1922. His family moved to Detroit when he was seven years old and he developed his baseball skills on Detroit's sandlots and in American Legion ball. Johnny Lipon—10 months younger than Neil Berry—was signed in 1941 by Detroit's renowned scout "Wish" Egan after graduating from Detroit Chadsey High School.

While Neil was starring in three sports as a freshman at Western State Teachers College, Lipon was making a name for himself as a first-year pro with the Class-C Muskegon Reds in the Michigan State League. Lipon batted .359 in 119 games, with 35 homers for the 1941 campaign.

Lipon's success in Class-C ball earned him a promotion to the Class A1 Beaumont Exporters—managed by Steve O'Neill—in the Texas League in 1942. After hitting .301 with three home runs in the larger Texas League parks, he was called up to Detroit on August 10 to help fill in for Bill Hitchcock, who had entered military service.

Johnny Lipon made his major league debut at Briggs Stadium in the second game of a doubleheader against the Chicago White Sox, on Sunday afternoon, August 16, 1942.

In his first major league game Lipon—like a drop of water on a hot grill—was sizzling, going 3 for 4 (all singles), with one run batted in. In the field, he flawlessly handled six chances at shortstop.

"It was not just what he did," wrote H. G. Salsinger of the Detroit News. "It was the way he did it that stamped him as a natural ball player."

The sizzle evaporated over the course of 34 games and 140 plate appearances for Detroit. Lipon finished with a .191 batting average, nine RBIs, and five runs scored for the fifth-place Tigers. He committed 11 errors in 199 chances for a .945 fielding percentage.

After the 1942 season ended Lipon enlisted in the United States Navy and was assigned to the Great Lakes Naval Station, to the Naval air technical training center in Memphis, and on to the Alameda Naval Air Station in California as an aviation machinist mate. In 1945, he was stationed in the Marianas and served as a flight engineer on a transport plane. He also played baseball there. Lipon was discharged on February 11, 1946—seven days after Neil was discharged—and five days later, re-signed with Detroit.

Berry and Lipon were both in Lakeland, Florida for spring training in 1946. Neil impressed all who saw him play that spring—including manager Steve O'Neill—with his masterful fielding and strong throwing arm, but Neil needed to find his hitting stroke and was optioned to Buffalo.

As a returning serviceman, Lipon had to clear waivers before Detroit could option him to the minors. Detroit wanted to keep him so instead of playing every day in the high minors, Lipon rode the bench in Detroit for the entire 1946 season, appearing in only 14 games and getting just 20 at-bats. Johnny Lipon spent all of 1947 with the Dallas Rebels in the Double-A Texas League. He batted .295 with 11 home runs in 150 games. Neil Berry was with Buffalo again in 1947 and finished with a .299 batting average and two home runs. Would one of them seize the opportunity presented by Eddie Lake's holdout, or would Lake report in time to keep the shortstop position? The Detroit press followed the story throughout spring training.

H. G. Salsinger of the *Detroit News* wrote that, "Eddie Lake's job appears lost." In his March 20 article he also wrote, "Cornelius Berry gave an exhibition of shortstopping here yesterday that Lake would find very hard to match and if the Tiger brain trust prefers Johnny Lipon over Berry, he too would do very well in place of Lake." Salsinger advanced the shared opinion of many observers when he stated, "Lipon is the better hitter and Berry the better fielder."

After Neil started well at the plate—hitting nearly .500 in early spring games—*Detroit Times* staff writer, Leo MacDonell reported on March 24, "Neil Berry's big stick may win the regular Tiger shortstop berth for the young recruit up from the Buffalo club here this spring." MacDonell went on to say that Berry "fielded well and revealed extraordinary speed on the base lines."

Eddie Lake finally made it to camp less than a week before the Tigers were scheduled to break camp and play their way north for opening day.

On March 30, Leo MacDonell reported in the *Detroit Times*, "The veteran Lake who must, of course, be considered the regular shortstop until someone takes the position away from him, reported in camp late and his condition as yet is a matter for speculation." In his article, MacDonell proclaimed, "this writer believes Berry will get the call."

Neil roomed with John Lipon and they would often dine together with Eddie Lake and outfielder Pat Mullin.

Neil recalled, "We ate together quite a bit, that foursome. Those three guys were all Catholics. The whole Detroit organization was Catholic, the manager was dyed in the wool Catholic, Steve O'Neill, he never missed mass.

"I remember the restaurant right across the street from our hotel, a big restaurant. [On Fridays] the waiter would come around, 'Can I help you guys?' [I'd say] 'What's the best steak you've got tonight?' They'd look at me—you son of a bitch—cause they all had to get fish.

"I remember John Lipon a lot of times he couldn't take it, especially if he had quite a game in the afternoon because you could get a dispensation. If you played and worked hard a priest could dispense with the fish deal and you could eat meat. So John got this idea, he'd hold the menu in front of his plate—he had a steak on his plate—and he'd say, 'It's a fish, it's a fish, it's a fish.'

"He was a lukewarm Catholic."

As the Detroit Tigers played their way north, with stops scheduled in New Orleans, LA, Birmingham, AL, Atlanta, GA, Little Rock, AR, Nashville, TN, and Pittsburgh, PA— on the way to an opening day tilt in Chicago—the battle for the shortstop position continued. Many believed Neil Berry had won the job in Florida with his outstanding fielding—expected; and his unexpected .481 (13 for 27) batting average. If that was the case Tiger manager Steve O'Neill wasn't confirming it. In MacDonell's *Detroit Times* story, O'Neill was quoted as saying, "It all depends on their showing from now until the start of the season."

James Zerilli, in an article for the *Detroit Free Press,* reporting from Birmingham, Alabama, opined, "One of the contestants in the three-way race for the Detroit shortstop job has moved well in front. He is Neil Berry . . ." Zerilli pointed out that Neil's .500 (17 for 34) batting average was "at least 100 points better than any other regular," and "he has lined the ball to all sectors of the field."

Reporting from Atlanta, Georgia on April 7, Sam Greene of the *Detroit Free Press* wrote in an article titled, Tiger History's Hottest Battle at Shortstop:

"After 37 days of spring training, Stephen Francis O'Neill is still stumped by the question: 'Who'll play shortstop for Detroit this season?'

"Johnny Lipon, exactly six feet tall, and Cornelius Berry, 5 feet 10 inches, are giants by comparison with veteran Eddie Lake, 5 feet 7 1/2.

"Defensively, the two recruits are so nearly even that batting punch could win preference for one or the other. Here again they are locked in a battle that has developed no perceptible margin on either side. On southern testing grounds Lipon has hit more balls hard but Berry has compiled the higher average.

"'It's strictly a tossup between them,' says O'Neill, who probably will delay a final decision until the Tigers finish their preseason tour. This battle is probably the hottest Detroit ever has had for the shortstop job."

The announcement came in Little Rock, Arkansas, on April 13. Leo MacDonell reported in the *Detroit Times,* that Steve O'Neill "made known formally that George Vico will be at first base and Neil Berry at shortstop in the first game's lineup at Comiskey Field." MacDonell also broke the not unexpected news that Hal Newhouser would be the opening day hurler for the Tigers. Johnny Lipon and Eddie Lake also made the team. Neil Berry won the shortstop job but he wasn't done looking over his shoulder.

In a story by Sam Greene that ran in the *Detroit Free Press* on what must have been a slow news day for sports, the headline read, Another Degree Man - Berry is Tiger's Third College Bred Shortstop. In Greene's article, we learn that the other two were Topper Rigney of Texas A & M, who played in the early 1920s, and Skeeter Webb—Steve O'Neill's son-in-law—of Ole Miss, who preceded Eddie Lake in 1945. The article assures the reader that, "In his choice of Berry over Johnny Lipon and Lake this spring, Steve O'Neill was not influenced by the advantages of higher education. He just thinks that Berry can run faster and will hit harder than either Lake or Lipon."

Ironic that Neil Berry would be referred to as "college bred" and a "degree man" after leaving Western State Teachers College at the end of his freshman year because his paper on the chemistry of glass production for his Rhetoric class was not accepted as his own work. That paper didn't keep Neil in school, but it did launch his professional baseball career.

Neil joined Detroit's 25 man roster that included several former teammates from his first year in professional baseball with the 1942 Winston-Salem Twins. Those players were LHP "Tiny" Ted Gray, Outfielder Vic Wertz, and First baseman John McHale. George "Sam" Vico—another '42 Twins teammate—also made the Detroit squad in 1948 as a First baseman.

The '48 squad was also represented by many of Wish Egan's discoveries as a scout including Hal Newhouser, Dizzy Trout, Hoot Evers, Dick Wakefield, Johnny Lipon, Neil Berry, John McHale, Pat Mullin, Stubby Overmire, Art Houtteman, Billy Pierce, and Ted Gray. Egan also signed Barney McCosky and at his urging the Tigers traded McCosky for George Kell in 1946. Thus Wish Egan was responsible for signing or acquiring over half of Detroit's 1948 25-man roster. Eight of those players were home-grown Michigan boys.

THE 1948 SEASON

Manager Steve O'Neill's batting order and starting lineup to open the 1948 season:

SS - Neil Berry

2B - Eddie Mayo

CF - Hoot Evers

LF - Dick Wakefield

RF - Vic Wertz

3B - George Kell

1B - George "Sam" Vico

C - Bob Swift

P - Hal Newhouser

April 20, 1948 - Opening Day. The Detroit Tigers opened the 1948 season on the road against the Chicago White Sox in Comiskey Park in front of 14,801 fans. The national anthem was played and the White Sox took the field. Right-hander Joe Haynes completed his final warm-up tosses and catcher Mike Tresh fired the ball to second baseman Don Kolloway. Umpire Eddie Rommel yelled, "Play ball," and the 1948 season was underway. Detroit's leadoff hitter—rookie shortstop Neil Berry—stepped in to face Haynes for his first major league plate appearance.

Neil Berry had made it, he was in the show. Only 399 other people on the face of the earth could make that claim on this day.

When Neil saw an offering from Haynes that he liked, he swung, and he ran, but his ground ball was fielded by Chicago first baseman Tony Lupien who stepped on first to retire Neil. Eddie Mayo and Hoot Evers followed with outs making it three up, three down for Haynes.

Hal Newhouser followed suit and retired the first three Chicago batters he faced in the bottom of the inning.

The Tigers and the White Sox were still scoreless after two innings. In the top of the third, it was Detroit's other rookie starter's turn for his first major league plate appearance. Sam Vico then did what every kid that ever played baseball dreams of doing, he connected off Haynes for a home run in his first major league AB.

The score remained 1-0 until the sixth inning. In the top of the inning, Mayo doubled and was sacrificed to third. He came home on a wild pitch to put Detroit up 2-0.

The White Sox got on the board in the bottom of the seventh on a Mike Tresh home run, cutting Detroit's lead to 2-1.

In his fourth trip to the plate, Neil made another out leading off the Detroit eighth inning. It was looking like Neil's debut would include an 0 for 4 performance at the plate.

In the bottom of the eighth Chicago tied the score with two singles and a sacrifice fly. It was 2-2 going into the ninth. Chicago's Haynes, who had given up two runs on eight hits, and Detroit's Newhouser, two runs on seven hits, were both still in the game.

Detroit shortstop Neil Berry - 1948

From Author's collection

Vic Wertz flew out to center to start the Detroit ninth. George Kell doubled and Vico walked. Manager Steve O'Neill brought in pitcher Fred Hutchinson (.302 batting average in '47) to bat for his catcher, Bob Swift. He was rewarded when "Hutch" singled to bring home Kell and advanced Vico to second. Jimmy Outlaw was brought in to run for Hutch before Newhouser added an insurance run when he singled to bring home Vico and advance Outlaw to second base.

That was all for Haynes. Chicago's manager Ted Lyons brought in his 43-year-old right-hander Earl Caldwell— pitching in his final major league season—to face 26-year-old Neil Berry—playing in his first major league game.

Youth prevailed when Berry stroked a single for his first career hit and drove in Outlaw for his first career RBI. The experience was dampened slightly when the speedy and exuberant Berry rounded first base too far. After the throw came in behind him he was forced to keep going and was thrown out at second base.

The White Sox got a one-out hit off Newhouser in the bottom of the ninth but could do no more. Detroit won the 1948 opener 5-2. The Tigers also won the next two games. Neil went 3 for 12 (.250) while playing error-free in his first three games in Chicago.

After their success in Chicago, the Tigers headed home to face the Cleveland Indians in their home opener. Detroit lost 8-2. John McHale flew out to centerfield for the last out of the game and the last out of his playing career. He quit the field for the front office after his only plate appearance of the 1948 season. Neil Berry's major league playing career overlapped McHale's by four days.

The Tigers also lost the other two games in the series vs the Indians. Then Detroit went to St. Louis and lost two more games before ending the losing streak at five when they beat the Browns in the last game of the series.

In the middle game of the series against the Browns—an 11 inning, 9-8 loss—Neil went three for six with an RBI and two runs scored. Neil also committed the first error of his major league career and it was a costly one. Hal Newhouser relieved Detroit starter Fred Hutchinson after the Tigers tied the score at 8-8 in the top of the ninth inning. The score was still tied when the Browns came to bat in the bottom of the eleventh inning. Newhouser walked the first man he faced then induced a ground ball to second baseman Eddie Mayo. Mayo fielded the ball and tossed it to Neil—covering second base—for the force out. Neil—attempting to complete the double play—then threw wild to first base and Sam Vico couldn't corral it. Neil's throwing error allowed the Browns runner to reach second base. The next Browns hitter drove in the winning run with a single. Newhouser took the loss—his second of the young season—on the unearned run attributed to Neil Berry's error.

After nine games Neil was batting .270 (10 for 37) in the leadoff spot with five runs scored and four batted in. Then he pulled a muscle in his leg.

Neil related, "You get hit with somethin' and the first [thing] they think is I wonder what that guy in Toledo could do for us, or Buffalo, or Beaumont—yeah they're makin' a telephone call [when I got hurt] and I hadn't even got to the dugout yet. They're already callin' for the guy to come on up. There was always somebody ready to take your place, you didn't mess around."

With Neil slowed by a pulled muscle Detroit didn't need anyone from Toledo, or Buffalo, or Beaumont—they already had Johnny Lipon on the bench waiting for a chance. Lipon started the next seven games and hit .259 (7-27), with seven runs scored and a home run accounting for his one RBI. That was enough for *Detroit Times* writer Leo MacDonell to declare, "With Johnny Lipon's recent fine showing, his battle with Neil Berry for the regular Tiger shortstop berth, the highlight of the club's spring training camp, has been revived." In the Times article, Steve O'Neill was quoted as saying, "I'll use them both. It doesn't hurt to have two good shortstops, does it?"

The Detroit skipper did use them both, at least for a while. Lipon started game one—and Berry game two—of a doubleheader at Yankee Stadium on Saturday, May 8.

Neil recalled, "When we'd go to New York, we had the locker room that the Yankees used to have, they [had] switched to the other side of the field like they do every once in a while. When we got there, walked in the clubhouse, they still had two lockers with locks on 'em, they aren't metal lockers, they're openings, bigger than a locker with kinda like a screen that you couldn't get in. [They had belonged to] Lou Gehrig and Babe Ruth. They kept 'em, didn't use 'em, kept 'em locked. [They were] in our visitors' clubhouse. I thought that was kinda nice. Kinda [gave] you the feeling that there were some big names here."

In the second game of the doubleheader, George Kell broke his wrist when he was hit by a pitch thrown by Yankee right-hander Vic Raschi. Eddie Lake was tapped to fill in while Kell healed, and started the next 13 games at third base.

Neil started the next 17 games at shortstop. That stretch included a 12 game homestand. Detroit's home games were broadcast by WXYZ and announced by former Tiger great Harry Heilmann.

Detroit's sports press had stopped using the "Connie" moniker in their reports, preferring Cornelius or Neil when writing about the shortstop from Kalamazoo. Apparently Tiger broadcaster Harry Heilmann didn't get the memo.

"When I was [in my rookie season] in Detroit they had an announcer who was one of Detroit's famous ballplayers— he became the announcer—and when he first started announcing [my name] he called me Connie. I never liked that name, it was feminine-like. Gloria's sister came over to see us play a game one time, and we went back to the hotel after the game and she saw [him]. This guy's name was Harry Heilmann, a famous ballplayer. He's the guy that took Ty Cobb's place in center field in Detroit. But anyway, she said, 'Mr. Heilmann, would you do me a favor?'—we were standing in the lobby of the hotel—'would you please not call him Connie anymore?' He said, 'I sure will—I won't do it anymore.' He didn't. He was the only guy that ever called me Connie in public."

Author's note: Hall of Fame outfielder Harry Heilmann, played with Ty Cobb for 12 seasons. It was Heinie Manush who took over for Cobb in center field in 1926. Manush won the American League batting title that year beating out Babe Ruth by six points.

On May 25 at Briggs Stadium vs the Yankees Neil was two for four with a double and two runs scored. Neil also committed his eighth and ninth errors of the season when he couldn't handle Joe DiMaggio's ground ball in the first inning or Vic Raschi's grounder in the second. The miscues resulted in three unearned runs and a 5-2 Yankee lead after two innings. Fred Hutchinson was the pitching victim of Neil's miscues and was taken out of the game after two innings. The Yankees piled on against three other Tiger pitchers to win 16-5.

Without an overpowering fast ball, Fred "Hutch" Hutchinson used his control and a menacing stare to amass a 95-71 record—including 81 complete games—with a 3.73 ERA during his ten seasons with Detroit. He pitched in the 1940 World Series and 1951 All-Star game. An anchor of the talented postwar Tigers staff, he won 18 games in 1947. He also finished 18 of the 25 games he started that year. Taking Hutch out of a game often came with consequences.

When Hutch got into trouble, Steve O'Neill would step out

of the dugout and stroll out to the mound to go get Hutch.

Neil recalled, "here comes the manager and [Hutch] would look at him, 'What the hell you doin' out here? You're not gettin' this ball.'

"I heard Freddy Hutchinson say that to Steve O'Neill, our manager. 'Freddy, Freddy,' O'Neill would say, 'Freddy give me the ball,'

"Hutch, 'God damn it,'

"O'Neill, 'Freddy give me the ball.'

"And I've seen Freddy rampage. He'd beat the hell out of the stadium if he could. I've seen him knock out every light, eight or ten of 'em, in the runway underneath the stands.

Hutch didn't limit his wrath to Briggs Stadium.

"I've seen him go into the [visitor's] clubhouse—this was a getaway night—we had our stuff all packed in those circus trunks with the square boxes in there and they'd all fit into the big box. The guys had a lot of their stuff—extra shirts, your jockstrap, extra pair of shoes—packed and he took those and tossed 'em up to the ceiling. There were clothes hanging all over.

"Later he'd apologize. Fred was a good guy but he'd get mad when he got taken out."

Yankee catcher Yogi Berra commented, "I always know how Hutch did when we follow Detroit into a town. If we got stools in the dressing room, I know he won. If we got kindling, he lost."

Neil's stretch as starting shortstop ended on May 28 after going hittless in four at bats and committing his tenth error in the first game of a road trip against the Browns in St. Louis. He was batting .248. The Tigers—at 17 and 18—were in fourth place, seven games behind league leading Philadelphia.

Neil explained, "I told lots of people when I got down—me or anybody else on the team—when you were hitting, and you got down to .250, they were looking for somebody else."

They didn't need to look far. Johnny Lipon started the next six games.

Neil started the following five, including a doubleheader against the Boston Red Sox in Fenway Park on June 6. Neil had one of his best games of the 1948 campaign in the first game—a 5-4 Boston win—when he went 3 for 5, with 2 runs scored, 1 RBI, and his first stolen base of the season. One of his hits was a double off Fenway's 37-foot left-field wall that is only 310 feet from home plate. Simply known as "the wall," it was a tempting target for right-handed hitters. Fly balls that would be outs at the other major league parks would hit off the wall for a base hit, or in some cases a double for speedy baserunners. The wall had been painted green in 1947 giving rise to its recent and now famous nickname, "The Green Monster."

In the second game—after Detroit jumped out to an early 4-0 lead—the Red Sox got to Art Houtteman, scoring six runs in 2.2 innings before he was replaced by Hal White. White got out of the third inning but in the Boston fourth Ted Williams followed a Johnny Pesky walk with a double to deep right-center field, driving in Pesky. That was all for White and while the Tigers made the pitching change, Ted Williams, standing on second base called over to Detroit's rookie shortstop, "Hey meat." Williams then asked Neil Berry if he was proud of his pop up double and proceeded to point out what a real double—the one he just hit—looked like. According to Neil this was all done in good humor and "meat" was a common slight bestowed on rookies, sometimes with references to their ethnicity. Must be Ted Williams didn't know Neil Berry was Dutch.

Neil had this to say about Ted Williams' hitting style: "Ted Williams was a terrific hitter, but I can tell you with a pure heart—no bullshit, serious, not lying—that if I [tried to] hit like he hit, I wouldn't 'have stayed up a month. To hit off your front foot, to hit to all fields—you didn't do that when I played—you pulled the ball, or tried to pull the ball, or acted like you wanted to pull the ball, or you didn't play. You went down [to the minors and] they got somebody that did."

Neil's batting average after the first game of the Boston doubleheader was up to .261 (30 for 115), but he was back down to .248 after going 2 for 14 in the next three games.

Johnny Lipon was hitting at a .293 clip (17 for 58) in his limited action (18 appearances including 14 starts).

With George Kell back in the lineup for the May 31, Memorial Day doubleheader, Eddie Lake was back on the bench. But not for long. On June 8, Lake took over second base for the injured Eddie Mayo and played well enough to earn a platoon with the 38-year-old veteran.

On June 10, after 46 games, Detroit—at 22 and 24—was in fifth place, nine games back of the first-place Cleveland Indians. In their game at Philadelphia that day, Steve O'Neill installed Johnny Lipon as the Detroit Tigers shortstop. Neil Berry would only see six more starts at shortstop in the 1948 season.

Neil said, "I still think that the manager [Steve O'Neill], he was alright, he didn't say anything to me or anything, [but] I think there was a like and dislike there for the first time in my life. The [Detroit] manager was the manager of my roommate for two years—they won everything at Beaumont, Texas—and he wanted John [Lipon] to play shortstop. Now that's just my own opinion. John and I were roommates for six years so you know we got along pretty good, he was my good friend, but he was also the other shortstop."

Neil's new role was coming off the bench to pinch-hit or pinch-run, with an occasional spot start. Ironic that the two players Neil Berry bested—in what the *Detroit Free Press* called, "probably the hottest [battle] Detroit ever has had for the shortstop job,"—were both in the starting lineup, while he rode the bench.

Neil was a spectator for a historic game at Briggs Stadium

when the first night game was played in front of 54,480 fans on June 15, 1948. Detroit was the last American League team to install lights and play night baseball (the Cubs were the only National League team without lights) but club officials hadn't learned from the experience of other clubs and were unsure of when to turn on the lights and start the game. At 9:29 p.m. it was deemed dark enough to turn on the lights

September 20, 1948 - Briggs Stadium, Detroit. Neil Berry showed off his speed when he scored from 1st base in the 1st inning against Boston.

After Neil beat out an infield single with one out, Vic Wertz hit a ground ball off the glove of second baseman Lou Stringer for an error. Berry raced to 3rd base and Stringer's throw got away from 3rd baseman Johnny Pesky who was charged with an error. Berry scampered home and was safe when Sox catcher Birdie Tebbetts couldn't handle the throw from Pesky.

and play. Hal Newhouser pitched a two hit complete game under the lights defeating the Philadelphia Athletics 4-1.

Thirteen additional night games were sceduled during the 1948 season and all drew well helping Detroit set an attendance record of 1,700,000. That record would be broken in 1949 and another new record estabished in 1950.

The streaky Tigers lost 9 of 11 games at home to close out June, then won 10 of the first 12 July games on their way to a 17 and 14 July record. At 46 and 48 on the season Detroit

The same play photographed at almost the same moment from the third base side of home plate. Notice how Tebbetts is attempting to block Berry off the plate before he has the ball which is a violation of the rules.

Author's note: This is the photo Neil Berry signed for me the first time we met.

Both photos from Author's collection

was in fifth place and a distant 10.5 games back of Boston. In a tight race the top four American League teams—Boston, Philadelphia, New York, and Cleveland were separated by only two games in the standings.

By August Eddie Lake had supplanted Eddie Mayo at the keystone corner with Johnny Lipon as his regular double-play partner at the shortstop position. Then on August 24— in a game against the Philadelphia Athletics, at Shibe Park— Lake suffered a season-ending injury. The injury occurred when he took a throw from Lipon as the baserunner crashed into him at second base. Lake broke the third finger of his left hand in two places.

Initially, Steve O'Neill opted for the veteran, Eddie Mayo, to replace Lake at second base. Mayo made O'Neill look prophetic when he went 3 for 5 with three runs scored in a 10-4 Tiger win over the Athletics on August 25. Mayo started the next seven games but could only muster 3 hits in 31 chances (.097), leaving O'Neill pondering his next move.

O'Neill had more to worry about but less to ponder when, on August 29, in the first game of a doubleheader at Yankee Stadium, George Kell's season ended when he suffered a double fracture of his jaw after being hit by a ground ball off the bat of Joe DiMaggio. Jimmy Outlaw, and later Eddie Mayo would man the hot corner for the remainder of the season.

On September 1, the Detroit Tigers—at 59 and 62—were in fifth place, 16 games behind the league-leading Boston Red Sox, and 10.5 games behind the fourth place Philadelphia Athletics. With only 33 games left to play, there wasn't much risk in O'Neill's next move. On September 3—prior to their game at Comiskey Park in Chicago—O'Neill asked Neil Berry, "Ever play second base?"

Neil had not played second base but replied, "I think I can handle it all right."

And handle it he did. In the three game series in Chicago,

he played flawless defense at second base and went 7 for 11, with three walks, batting second in the lineup behind Lipon. Neil had a hand in every Tiger rally in those three games, with Detroit winning twice. He kept it up—going 3 for 8—in a doubleheader in St. Louis, but mustered only one hit in three games—all losses—in Cleveland.

On September 11, the Tigers were back home for a doubleheader vs the White Sox. It was Harry Heilmann Day at Briggs Stadium. Between games, the Tigers honored their long time announcer and former playing great, by presenting him with a solid gold pass, good for all games played at Briggs Stadium. Neil had four hits in nine ABs in the doubleheader and Detroit prevailed in both games.

In his first 10 games at second Neil Berry was hitting .366 (15 for 41). Why Steve O'Neill started Eddie Mayo at second base for the next five games is anybody's guess, but after Mayo batted .243 over those games, Neil was back in the lineup and played the next 23 games at second base—including the 1948 season's final game—the game Neil would later recall as his favorite game as a major league player.

*That was the most exciting game, it made me feel the best.
The victory didn't mean much to us, but they had to jump
on a train that night.*

~ Neil Berry

14

Neil's Favorite Game

Extending Clevelands Season

1948

With a record of 73-50, the Cleveland Indians were a very respectable 23 games over .500 at the end of August 1948 but were trailing both Boston (75-48) and New York (74-49) in the race for the American League Pennant. So far Detroit had held its own against the powerful Indians, winning six games while losing seven.

Cleveland rose to the challenge of the pennant race in September with a 22-6 record that included five wins and only one loss against Detroit.

When asked who was the toughest pitcher he faced in the majors, Neil Berry, without hesitation, replied, "the Cleveland staff." Neil's .222 batting average against Cleveland in 1948 was 44 points lower than his .266 season average.

In 1948 that staff included Gene Bearden (2.43, 20-7), Bob Lemon (2.82, 20-14), Steve Gromek (2.84, 9-3), Satchel Paige (2.47, 6-1), and Bob Feller.

Cleveland scout Cy Slapnicka signed Bob Feller in 1936 for one dollar and an autographed baseball. No word on which signature on the baseball sealed the deal, but Cleveland had the 17-year-old, hard-throwing phenom's signature on a contract. Feller made his first start on August 23, 1936, against the St. Louis Browns. He recorded 15 strikeouts in earning his first career win. He finished the year with a 5–3 record that included a 17 strikeout game in a win over Philadelphia that tied Dizzy Dean's single-game strikeout record.

Some of Bob Feller's career highlights prior to 1948 include:

- In 1938 Feller led the majors with 208 walks and 240 strikeouts.

- On October 2, 1938, Feller set the modern major league record of 18 strikeouts against the Detroit Tigers in the first game of the season-closing doubleheader. Feller (17-11) gave up seven hits and four runs and lost the game to Detroit journeyman pitcher Harry Eisenstat.

- In 1939—for the second consecutive year—Feller led the majors in both strikeouts (246) and walks (142). He also led the American League in wins (24), complete games (24) and innings pitched (296.2).

- In 1940 Feller accomplished a pitching triple crown leading the AL in ERA (2.61), wins (27) and strikeouts (261). His Opening Day no-hitter against the Chicago White Sox is the only no-hitter to be thrown on Opening Day in major league history. Feller's 31 complete games and 320.1 innings pitched also led the majors. He won the Sporting News Player of the Year Award.

- Feller's wins (25), strikeouts (260), innings pitched (343), and walks (194) again led the majors for the 1941 season. He also tossed an AL-best six shutouts on the season.

- Feller's post-war career included his second career no-hitter on April 30, 1946, against the New York Yankees. For the 1946 season, he posted career-highs in strikeouts (348), games started (42), games pitched (48), shutouts (10), complete games (36), and innings pitched (377.1)—all tops in the majors that season. Feller finished 26–15 with a career-low ERA of 2.18.

- Feller's 1947 season included leading the American League in wins (20) and shutouts (5). He led all of baseball in strikeouts (196) and innings pitched (299).

Bob Feller was still a workhorse and a strikeout machine for the Cleveland Indians in 1948. On the last day of the 1948 season he was going for his 20th victory—a win that would bring the AL pennant to Cleveland.

The 1948 Cleveland Indians were one of baseball's greatest teams (they were selected as the ninth best team ever by *The Sporting News* in 2011). They featured six future Hall of Famers: outfielder Larry Doby, second baseman Joe Gordon, shortstop Lou Boudreau, and pitchers Satchel Paige, Bob Lemon, and Bob Feller.

In October, only a three game series against the Tigers at Cleveland Municipal Stadium stood in the way of the Cleveland Indians' first title in 28 years.

"Actually the mental attitude of Cleveland was that if they showed up, they would win," Neil recalled.

Cleveland entered the first game against Detroit on October 1 with a 95-56 record, a game and a half ahead of both Boston and New York, who were idle but would close out the season playing each other. The Indians and Bob Lemon couldn't hold a one run lead and lost when the Tigers rallied for three runs in the ninth inning. With

Detroit playing the spoiler role, Cleveland held a one-game lead with two left to play.

On October 2, Cleveland southpaw Gene Bearden shutout Detroit in convincing fashion 8-0, winning his fifth decision against the Tigers in as many starts. The only Tiger to reach third base in the game was Neil Berry after his single and a couple of ground outs.

The Boston Red Sox also won, eliminating the New York Yankees from the pennant race.

Neil explained, "The way it worked out to the last game of the season was if Cleveland won the ball game they would win the American League pennant. If they lost [and Boston won] they would be tied with the Boston Red Sox. They would have to go to Boston the next day for a playoff game."

The major leagues played a 154 game schedule in those days. Ties—due to games called for darkness or weather—didn't count in the standing and were usually made up over the course of the season, but there was no provision for making up a game with pennant implications after the season ended. That being the case, a Boston win and a Cleveland rainout would leave Boston a half-game back and Cleveland would win the American League championship. The home club—not the umpires—were in charge of the decision to play or not in inclement weather.

Cleveland's colorful owner, Bill Veeck joked that he would call it off when the first cloud was sighted but Veeck did request that American League president Will Harridge send league officials to rule in the event of rain. Harridge complied with Veeck's request but the sun was out and rain never threatened.

On October 3, the last day of the regular season, two games—the New York Yankees at the Boston Red Sox, and the Detroit Tigers at the Cleveland Indians—would determine the 1948 American League champion or result in a one game playoff for the title.

BOSTON - Oct. 3, 1948, At Fenway Park in Boston the Yankees hoped to return the favor and eliminate the Red Sox. To have a shot at the pennant Boston had to triumph and needed the Tigers to knock off the favored Indians.

New York manager Bucky Harris—who had replaced Joe McCarthy as the Yankee skipper in 1947—called on rookie right-hander Bob Porterfield to pitch the final game, while Boston's new manager Joe McCarthy chose the veteran Joe Dobson to keep Boston's hopes alive.

Starting Lineups:

New York Yankees	Boston Red Sox
Phil Rizzuto . . . . . . SS	Dom DiMaggio . . . CF
Tommy Henrich . . 1B	Johnny Pesky 3B
Bobby Brown 3B	Ted Williams . . . . . LF
Joe DiMaggio . . . . CF	Vern Stephens . . . . SS
Yogi Berra . . . . RF	Bobby Doerr 2B
Hank Bauer . . . . . . LF	Stan Spence . . . . . . RF
Charlie Silvera C	Billy Goodman . . . 1B
Snuffy Stirnweiss . 2B	Birdie Tebbetts C
Bob Porterfield . . . . P	Joe Dobson . . . . P

Detroit Tiger ace, "Prince Hal" Newhouser—pitching on short rest after throwing a complete game shutout over the St. Louis Browns—was looking for his 21st win on the final day of the season. Bob Feller was pitching for Cleveland and going for his 20th win of the season. The Cleveland fans were well aware that Feller had bested Newhouser in their three previous head to head meetings and were confident and ready to celebrate. According to Neil the Cleveland newspapers were also confident and predicting a Cleveland victory—especially with Feller going against a Tiger team with two light-hitting rookies at the top of their batting order (referring to Neil and his roommate, Johnny Lipon).

CLEVELAND - Oct. 3, 1948. "There were 74,000 people at the stadium, standing room only. The place was jumpin'. They had firecrackers and noisemakers, they were celebrating already," Neil recalled.

The celebrating fans at Municipal Stadium may have been looking ahead to the Indian's first pennant and World Series appearance since 1920, but celebrations and predictions aside, there was still a baseball game to be played.

Starting Lineups:

Detroit Tigers	Cleveland Indians
Johnny Lipon . . . . SS	Dale Mitchell . . . . LF
Neil Berry 2B	Allie Clark . . . . RF
Vic Wertz . . . . RF	Lou Boudreau . . . . SS
Pat Mullin . . . . . . CF	Joe Gordon 2B
Dick Wakefield . . LF	Ken Keltner 3B
Eddie Mayo 3B	Larry Doby . . . . . . CF
Sam Vico 1B	Eddie Robinson . . . 1B
Bob Swift C	Jim Hegan C
Hal Newhouser . . . P	Bob Feller . . . . P

CLEVELAND - In the top of the first Johnny Lipon started things off with a single to left for the visiting Tigers. Neil Berry laid down a sacrifice bunt to move Lipon into scoring position at second base. Vic Wertz walked but Pat Mullin flew out to left, and Dick Wakefield flew out to center, ending the Tiger threat.

In the bottom of the first Hal Newhouser retired the Indians in order on Dale Mitchell's ground out and Allie Clark's line out, before Lou Boudreau flew out to center.

Detroit 0 - Cleveland 0, after one inning.

BOSTON - The Yankees struck first in the top of the first. With one out Tommy Henrich walked and Joe DiMaggio hit a two out double to bring him home.

Boston got two walks off Porterfield but couldn't bring a run home.

New York 1 - Boston 0, after one inning.

CLEVELAND - Eddie Mayo led off the Detroit second inning with a ground out. Sam Vico singled to right but was caught stealing ahead of Bob Swift's ground out.

In the bottom of the inning, Joe Gordon grounded out to third before Cleveland got their first base runner when Newhouser walked Ken Keltner. Newhouser got out of the inning with a strike-em-out (Larry Doby), throw-em-out (Swift to Lipon, Keltner caught stealing) double play.

Detroit 0 - Cleveland 0, after two.

BOSTON - In the top half of the second inning, Hank Bauer walked and came home on singles by Charlie Silvera and Snuffy Stirnweiss. Porterfield sacrificed the runners to second and third. Phil Rizzuto hit a ground ball to Boston shortstop Vern Stephens who threw home to nab Silvera.

Boston got a hit in the bottom of the inning but failed to score.

New York 2 - Boston 0, after two.

CLEVELAND - Newhouser grounded out to the first baseman to lead off the Detroit third inning, bringing up the top of the order for their second chance at Bob Feller. Johnny Lipon walked and Neil Berry singled to right, setting the table for the heart of the Tigers order. They didn't disappoint (well, they did disappoint the Cleveland faithful). Vic Wertz doubled to left driving in Lipon and moving Berry to third. Pat Mullin was intentionally walked to load the bases, setting up a potential double-play to get the Indians out of the inning . . .

BOSTON - After the Yankees went down in order in the top of the third, Boston's Dom Dimaggio led off the bottom of the inning with a single. While Johnny Pesky was settling in at the plate, Boston's PA announcer updated the Fenway crowd and Red Sox players with news from Cleveland, "Detroit has the bases loaded, one run in, with Dick Wakefield at bat."

Suddenly there were 31,000 Dick Wakefield fans in Fenway park . . .

CLEVELAND - Still in the Detroit third, with the bases loaded, Dick Wakefield spoiled the Indian's strategy with a two run double to left, scoring Berry and Wertz, and sending Feller to an early shower. Sam Zoldak replaced Feller and was greeted with a run scoring single by Eddie Mayo. The Indians again loaded the bases with Tigers on an intentional walk to Sam Vico. Ed Klieman replaced Zoldak on the mound and induced Bob Swift to ground into a second-to-catcher-to-first, inning-ending double play. The bases loaded strategy worked this time, but Detroit had a four run lead and Bob Feller was out of the game.

Feller's final line: 2.1 IP, 5 Hits, 4 Earned Runs, 3 Bases on Balls, 0 Strikeouts.

Detroit 4, Cleveland 0, after three.

BOSTON - Still batting in the bottom of the third, Boston's Johnny Pesky flew out to center bringing Ted Williams to the plate. The Boston PA announcer came on with another update, "Wakefield doubled. Detroit leads three to nothing." Detroit was doing their part. Williams put the Red Sox on the board with a double down the left field line, scoring Dom DiMaggio. Vern Stephens singled off the glove of third baseman Bobby Brown and Williams had to remain at second base. Next up was Bobby Doerr who hit a two-run double to right center. Stan Spence walked and Billy Goodman singled, driving in Doerr with the fourth Boston run of the inning.

Bucky Harris had seen enough and signaled for Vic Raschi to come in for Porterfield. The out-of-town scoreboard in left field was updated to show Detroit 4, Cleveland 0, after three innings. With one out and men on first and third, Birdie Tebbetts came to the plate. His ground ball forced Goodman at second and scored Spence from third. Joe Dobson struck out to end the inning.

New York 2, Boston 5, after three.

CLEVELAND - After Cleveland failed to score in the bottom of the third inning, Detroit was back at it in the top of the fourth. After batting around in the third, Newhouser was again the Tiger leadoff hitter. Cleveland's fourth pitcher of the day, Steve Gromek, struck out Newhouser for the first out of the inning. The top of Detroit order set the table for a second straight inning with a Lipon single and a Berry double (a "pop" double according to the newspaper account in Neil's scrapbook, which explains why Lipon didn't score). Wertz followed with a double to center (a "legitimate" double according to the same newspaper) scoring Lipon and Berry. A walk and a double play ended the top half of the inning.

Cleveland coaxed a walk off Newhouser in the bottom half but otherwise went quietly.

Detroit 6, Cleveland 0, after four.

Prince Hal was cruising through the vaunted Indians lineup. Scoreboard watchers in Boston were pleased. The score remained 6-0 until both teams scored ninth inning runs. In the Detroit half, Johnny Lipon doubled home Vico who had walked.

Newhouser lost his shutout in the bottom of the inning when the Indians scored on single, ground out, and an RBI single.

Hal Newhouser's final line: 9 IP, 5 Hits, 1 Earned Run, 2 Bases on Balls, 3 Strikeouts.

Final Score Detroit 7 - Cleveland 1

BOSTON - The Red Sox finished off the Yankees 10 to 5, and with Detroit's win, moved into a tie with the Cleveland Indians, both teams with 96 wins and 58 losses.

Neil recalled, "I think we got 5 hits from the two of us [Neil and roommate Johnny Lipon] and we beat them 7-1. You could hear a pin drop in that crowded stadium. It just took the bottom right out of them. That was the most exciting game, it made me feel the best. The victory didn't mean much to us, but they had to jump on a train that night."

Newhouser's 21st victory of the season—aided by 15 Tiger hits—sent the Cleveland Indians packing for Boston and the first playoff game in the 49-year history of the American League.

The Indians beat the Red Sox 8-3 in the playoff game and went on to beat the Boston Braves in the World Series, but they almost didn't get the chance due in no small part to a pair of Tiger rookies, including the shortstop from Kalamazoo.

The 1948 Detroit Tigers finished the season with 78 wins and 76 losses, good for fifth place, 18.5 games behind the American League champion Cleveland Indians.

Neil Berry's contribution: SS/2B 87 games, 256 AB, 46 runs, 68 hits, 16 RBI, .266 avg, .952 fielding.

Dr. Stryker told me to grin and bear it.

~ Neil Berry

15

The Detroit Tigers

Red Rolfe Takes Over

1949

In Steve O'Neill's six-year tenure as Detroit's manager, he led the Tigers to only one other second division finish, fifth place (78-76) in 1943, his first year at the helm. His teams followed that with four consecutive first division records; 88-66, good for second place in 1944; 88-65, first place and a World Series championship in 1945; 92-62, second in 1946; and 85-69, second in 1947.

There were no first and second divisions per se; the American and National Leagues each had eight teams, and the teams sorted themselves out each year based on their records. The top four teams were considered the first division; the four also-rans, the second division.

After three second-place finishes and a World Series championship, the 1948 fifth place, second division finish cost Steve O'Neill—the affable, easy-going Detroit manager—his job.

New York manager Bucky Harris was also let go after the Yankees' third place finish. In New York the expectation wasn't just first division, it was first place.

While the Yankees were looking for a new manager they were also shopping for a better defensive catcher to replace Yogi Berra who had split time between the outfield and catching for the Yankees in 1947 and 1948.

Neil Berry shared the following assessment of Yogi Berra.

"What kinda catcher is he? Fair.

"How does he throw? Fair.

"How does he receive? Fair.

"How's he on popups? Fair.

"He ran a little better than you thought he did. Yogi was a little bit faster than [you would think] to look at. He took small steps—he wasn't a very tall guy, 5-7 or 5-8, but anyway he ran better than you thought he would.

"Well how come he's makin' the all-star team? He hit .300, as a catcher, lefthanded.

"I wish you could have seen Yogi hit. He used to drag the bat [like] you see these little kids. I mean little kids— pictures of 'em goin' to Little League practice—and the bat's so big they can't carry it, they drag it behind. That's how Yogi used to come up to the plate, like the bat was too heavy for him, draggin it up there. [Then] he'd get up to the plate and he'd just dare you to throw the ball in range where he could hit it. If you throw that ball near him he's gonna swing at it and he's gonna hit it someplace and you gotta make a play on him. Like a guy said, 'the only place to pitch Yogi is low and behind him.'

"What're you gonna do? He just was a swinger, just dared you to throw the ball by him. He knew he was swingin' wild—he knew that—but he knew how wild to swing."

Talk of replacing Yogi stopped when the Yankees hired the plainspoken, quick-witted Casey Stengel as their new manager. Stengel's famous quotes included, "Managing is getting paid for home runs someone else hits," and "The secret of managing is to keep the guys who hate you away from the guys who are undecided."

Stengel would guide the Yankee dynasty for the next 12 seasons, after all, Casey Stengel knew, "Good pitching will always stop good hitting and vice-versa," and the Yankees had plenty of both.

Stengel liked Yogi and protected him from those who criticized or made fun of his young catcher. Stengel also assigned future Hall of Famer Bill Dickey to work with Yogi on his catching mechanics and his in-game anticipation.

Not one to be outdone in the witty-words-of-wisdom category, Yogi quipped, "Bill Dickey is learning me all his experience."

Malapropism is the mistaken use of a word in place of a similar-sounding one, often with unintentionally amusing effect, but when they are uttered by Yogi Berra they're known as "Berraisms."

Many Berraisms attributed to Yogi weren't actually his and led to this one that was, "I really didn't say everything I said."

He probably didn't say everything that he was credited with saying but on the baseball diamond he really did do everything he did.

What did Yogi Berra do in his 19 year playing career? He made the All-Star team 18 times. He had a career batting average of .285 and had five seasons batting over .300. He was the American League Most Valuable Player in 1951, 1954, and 1955. He was inducted into the Baseball Hall of Fame in 1972 and when he came to a fork in the road, he took it.

Nearly 50 candidates sought the open managerial position

in Detroit, but owner Walter O. Briggs, his son Spike, and general manager Billy Evans—at Spike's suggestion—chose Red Rolfe, a candidate that hadn't even applied.

Robert "Red" Rolfe graduated from Dartmouth in the spring of 1931. The infielder had been scouted by a number of teams, but with a chance to play alongside Yankee greats Babe Ruth and Lou Gehrig—players he had idolized growing up—Red took a six thousand dollar signing bonus to sign with New York on June 25, 1931.

Red Rolfe made it to the majors in 1934, in time to share one season with Babe Ruth and six with Lou Gehrig. Rolfe played third base for the Yankee dynasty teams that dominated the American League from 1936 through 1939, winning the World Series each of those years.

During his 10 year playing career with the Yankees, Red Rolfe batted .289 in 1,175 games and led the American League in doubles for the decade of the 1930s.

Red's older sister, Florence, had introduced Red to Isabel Africa who was visiting the family cottage in the summer of 1928. Red was infatuated with the brown-eyed, dark-haired beauty who was studying to become a dietician at the University of New Hampshire.

They married on October 12, 1934. Red had long suffered from inflammatory colitis, a stomach condition causing his immune system to attack his bowels. After studying the disease, Isabel recommended changes to Red's diet to help the condition, while doctors warned that the stress of a baseball season would aggravate it.

Isabel soon learned how to keep score and properly fill out a scorecard and could quickly calculate her husband's batting average after each at-bat.

Rolfe was an astute student of the game and developed the habit of writing down what pitchers threw in certain situations and other game-day observations in his little black book.

After Rolfe's playing career—cut short by his stomach problems—he coached at Yale for four years before returning to the Yankees as a coach in 1946. Rolfe had his eye on succeeding manager Joe McCarthy, whenever the longtime Yankee skipper was ready to retire. But new owner Larry MacPhail replaced McCarthy with Bucky Harris in 1947. Harris brought in his own coaches and Rolfe took a job with the Detroit Tigers. As Detroit's chief scout, Red was in charge of rebuilding the farm system.

On November 15, 1948, Red Rolfe was named the Detroit Tigers' new manager.

Five days prior to hiring Red Rolfe, Tigers GM Billy Evens traded LHP Billy Pierce and $10,000 to the Chicago White Sox for 33-year-old catcher Aaron Robinson. Evans felt that the Tigers would compete for the pennant in 1949 and needed an experienced catcher to get the most out of their pitching staff. Robinson also batted left handed and would be counted on to reach Detroit's short porch in right field.

Aaron Robinson gave the Tigers what they were expecting when they traded for him prior to the 1949 season but what was unexpected—at the time—was that Billy Pierce would go on to win 211 games, 186 of them for the Chicago White Sox. Detroit Tiger fans will forever consider the Robinson-for-Pierce trade one of the worst in franchise history.

In the spring of 1949 Doctor Homer Stryker's Orthopedic Frame Company of Kalamazoo was—with the success of the cast cutter and oscillating bone-cutting autopsy saw—outgrowing their East Michigan Avenue shop and would soon move to a larger building on Alcott Avenue.

Dr. Stryer—Neil's first American Legion baseball coach—was also conducting his orthopedic medical practice on the fifth floor of Borgess Hospital. Olive McGowan Miller was part of his secretarial team. In the book, *The Stryker Story–Homer's Iliad*, McGowan Miller related that normally "appointments might be two weeks in advance, but if the patient was a baseball player, we must 'get them in somehow.'"

After a year of playing major league baseball, Neil Berry got right in. Neil had been playing basketball to keep in shape during the winter months, but—with spring training only weeks away—he hurt his shoulder going for a loose ball. Dr. Stryker diagnosed the problem and suggested surgery would be his best option. Neil protested that surgery wasn't an option this close to spring training where he would be fighting for the starting job at second base. Wasn't there something else he could do? Yes, there was.

Neil said, "Dr. Stryker told me to grin and bear it."

Dr. Stryker never sent Neil a bill for that advice.

Spring Training

When Neil reported to spring training in 1949, he did grin and bear it, and he did so without telling the Tigers about the injury. In those days—if at all possible—you played through injuries, especially if you were a second-year player fighting for a job. With more than 20 minor-league players available for each major-league position, there were simply too many good ballplayers waiting for their shot to take your place. Not only was Neil's opportunity to be the team's regular second baseman at stake, but he also risked losing his roster spot, and possibly his major-league career, if he didn't "grin and bear it," and play.

A clipping in the Berry scrapbook from an unidentified newspaper quotes Red Rolfe, the new Tiger skipper, concerning the second base competition:

"It is no secret that we tried to improve our second base situation," Rolfe admitted. "Yet, I don't believe we are as bad as we seem to be. Berry hit .266 and that was topped by only three other second basemen in the league—Jerry

Priddy (.296), Bobby Doerr (.285) and Joe Gordon (.280). He fielded .980 and that was bettered only by George Stirnweiss and Bobby Doerr . . .”

The easy-going ways of Steve O'Neil were history. Red Rolfe, set higher expectations for spring workouts and player expectations. He told the press that the Tigers would be the best-conditioned club to leave Florida.

Red Rolfe's proclivity for writing down game-day observations continued during his tenure as field manager of the Detroit Tigers. He kept a private journal with accounts of every game he managed. Rolfe's journal helped him evaluate the capabilities of his own players and also helped him identify weaknesses in other teams that his club could exploit.

All of Rolfe's journal entries as manager of the Detroit Tigers are captured in the excellent book, *The View From The Dugout – The Journals of Red Rolfe*, edited by William M. Anderson.

Red Rolfe was dismayed that Neil Berry came to spring camp nursing a sore arm. From *The View From The Dugout – The Journals of Red Rolfe*, “Berry knew he had a chance to be our regular second baseman. Why didn't he get his arm in shape during the winter? There is absolutely no excuse for any player, especially an infielder, to come up with a sore arm in spring training.”

Neil's shoulder injury kept him from getting his arm in shape in the weeks ahead of spring training and it is likely that compensating for the shoulder led to the sore arm. It didn't matter, Neil was competing with Eddie Lake and two others for the second base job. He wasn't out of the lineup for long.

The spring games started on March 15 and Red Rolfe started keeping notes on player performance in game situations.

From *The View From The Dugout - The Journals of Red Rolfe*:

"Second base

1. Neil Berry

'looked good at second base and hit the ball hard.'

'continues to hit the ball good and he is improving around second base.'

'pivoted on a beautiful double play on a ball deep to short. He looks better in the field every day.'

2. Eddie Lake

'made our club look steadier'"

The press seemed to favor Neil—or felt that Rolfe did— because of his speed.

Detroit Free Press articles by Sam Greene followed the 1949 second base competition:

March 5 - "Red Rolfe's repeated references to the Tigers' lack of speed implies a preference for Cornelius J. Berry as second baseman. Berry is faster than Eddie Mayo or Eddie Lake with whom he shared the position last year."

April 2 - "Edward Erving Lake is leading Cornelius J. Berry by a step in the race to determine Detroit's second baseman. This time next week, or earlier, their positions may be reversed. It is that kind of race. Berry fell behind at the start because of a sore arm. After recovery, the Kalamazoo candidate gained the preference of the rail birds, if not of Red Rolfe, who will make the final decision."

April 8 - "At the doubtful second-base spot, Rolfe tested four candidates in Florida exhibitions before sending Bob Mavis and John Bero to Toledo. He is still alternating the two survivors—Eddie Lake and Cornelius Berry.

"After Lake finished a stretch of six games, Rolfe was asked whether the undersized Californian would open against the White Sox at Briggs Stadium, April 19. 'I don't know yet.' Rolfe answered. 'Berry will get another chance before we get home.'"

Detroit Manager Red Rolfe and second baseman Neil Berry, 1949

Photo courtesy of Linda Spann

April 15 - "Because of his adaptability to changing needs, Cornelius John Berry, of Kalamazoo, will be in Detroit's opening day lineup for the second successive season.

"As a freshman infielder last spring, Berry qualified to start the American League race at shortstop. He earned the preference of Steve O'Neil after a stubborn battle in the south with Johnny Lipon, now his golfing partner and roommate on the road.

"As a sophomore Berry has been named to play second base in the first game of the championship schedule—Detroit vs. Chicago—at Briggs Stadium Tuesday. He has convinced Red Rolfe that he deserves selection over veteran Eddie Lake.

"This is an unusual, if not unique, distinction that has come to Berry—starting his first two major league seasons at two different positions. Each time he was chosen because of an advantage in speed."

THE 1949 SEASON

Manager Red Rolfe's batting order and starting lineup to open the 1949 season:

2B - Neil Berry

SS - Johnny Lipon

3B - George Kell

RF - Vic Wertz

LF - Hoot Evers

C - Aaron Robinson

CF - Johnny Groth

1B - Sam Vico

P - Hal Newhouser

Detroit Second baseman Neil Berry

Photo from Author's collection

The Tigers started the 1949 season by taking two out of three from the Chicago White Sox at home, before splitting two games with Cleveland Indians on the road, and taking two more from Chicago at Comiskey Park. After two losses at Briggs Stadium to the St. Louis Browns, the Indians were in town for a three game series.

Cleveland lefty Gene Bearden continued his mastery over the Tiger hitters, winning 4-1, for his second win of the season. Both his wins came over Detroit and Bearden was riding a personal six-game win streak over the Tigers.

Neil Berry got a leadoff hit off Bearden in the bottom of the first inning. That hit raised his batting average by 20 points because it was only his third hit of the young season. Neil's first hit of the season came in the fourth game, also a leadoff single against Beardon. After 10 games Neil was hitting just .073 (3 for 41). It was Neil's stellar defense over those first 10 games that kept him in the lineup.

The seemingly ageless Satchel Paige was scheduled to make his first start of the season in the second game of the series against Cleveland. Neil was looking forward to playing in front of a home crowd that would include thousands of high school players in town for the Tigers' annual instructional clinic. Then he caught a bad hop in the face during fielding practice and with Neil sporting a black eye and .073 batting average, Red Rolfe decided a few days off might help him with his batting slump.

Neil told *Kalamazoo Gazette* sports editor Jerry Hagan, "There's nothing wrong with my hitting that a couple of good days at the plate wouldn't offset. I've been hitting the ball well enough, but always right at someone."

Eddie Lake started the next 10 games at second base and counted 5 hits in 41 at-bats for a .122 average. Red Rolfe's concern over the offensive weakness of the second base position had been confirmed in those first 20 games. On May 7th Detroit traded seldom-used outfielder Earl Rapp to the Chicago White Sox for infielder Don Kolloway. The Tigers were hoping Kolloway would add some offensive punch at second base. He did, batting .314 in his first nine games.

After Neil was benched, he appeared in only 19 of the next 55 games serving as a pinch hitter, pinch runner, and defensive replacement. He got two hits in nine at-bats during those games, raising his average to an even .100 (5 for 50) for the year.

After 65 games the Tigers (36-29) were in fourth place—percentage points behind Boston—and five games back of the league-leading Yankees. The Cleveland Indians were a game behind Detroit in fifth place.

Neil Berry had contributed little to Detroit's winning record but with George Kell out with a broken toe, and Eddie Lake hitting .103 (9 for 87), Neil got another chance. He started at second base in game 66 on June 28, in the first of a four-game series against the Indians in Cleveland. Neil recorded 4 hits in 13 AB with two runs scored in the series. He would go on to start 76 of the remaining 86 games at second base and the Tigers would make some noise in the 1949 pennant race.

During the season the Detroit ball club was called on by a representative of sporting goods giant A.G. Spalding and Brothers. Being a former major league player, the Spalding rep was granted clubhouse access to speak to the team.

As Neil told it, "In 1949 we're settin in the clubhouse in Detroit and our manager, Red Rolfe, said, 'guys before you go out give me five minutes, I want to introduce you to this guy. He's from High Point, North Carolina and he wants to offer you a deal.'

"So this guy comes in and says I got a ball—not an expensive baseball, but a good ball—that they're gonna sell at the concession stands for a buck or so, two bucks. It's gonna have all the Tigers autographs on the ball, an autographed ball with the whole team. They're gonna sell 'em and we're gonna get a percentage if we sign with that company as a team, not as individuals, as a team. If anybody has signed [with someone else] and won't be on the ball, we couldn't do it. Well, we had a couple of guys like Newhouser—they'd already signed with somebody, so we couldn't do it.

"But the little guy who gave the speech in there, Red Rolfe

introduced him to the team, 'I'd like to have you meet Billy Jurges.'

"[It was] the first time I ever saw him. I look, the guy is like a midget. At that time he was 50 some years old, at least, but he was a little teeny squirt. He's the reason I wanted to play shortstop."

When Neil finally met his boyhood hero—Chicago Cub shortstop Billy Jurges—in 1949, Jurges was forty one years old and working for Spalding and Brothers. During his playing days Jurges—the little teeny squirt Neil met in 1949—was listed at 5' 11" and 175 pounds, slightly taller and heavier than Neil. But when Neil was a kid listening to his hero on the radio, Billy Jurges must have seemed like a giant.

Detroit started July like a bad firecracker, a little fizz but no boom. They lost two of three at home to the White Sox before finishing the homestand with three straight losses to the Indians.

A five game road trip resulted in a win and a loss to the Browns and a win and two losses to the White Sox.

After returning home and losing two out of three to the Red Sox, the Tigers record stood at 42-41, good for fifth place 11.5 games behind the first place Yankees. In the second loss to Boston on July 16, Neil Berry was 2 for 3 with a walk and a run scored. The two hits raised his batting average to an unremarkable .163.

In the second half of July Detroit picked up the pace. They won two out of three from Philadelphia, then swept three games from the Washington Senators before losing two out of three to the Yankees.

Neil went 3 for 5 with a single, double, triple, and run scored in a win over Washington on July 21 at Briggs Stadium. He continued to hit Washington pitching on the road. He was 2 for 4 with a double, a walk and two RBIs on July 26 and followed that with another double and three runs scored in a three for six hitting performance on July 27, both Tiger wins. Neil raised his batting average over 40 points to .209 in two weeks.

After taking three of four from the Washington Senators to start off a 14-game road trip, the Tigers arrived in Philadelphia on July 29 for a four game series against Connie Mack's Athletics at Shibe Park. Detroit's record stood at 51-45, good for fifth place, 9.5 games behind the pace-setting Yankees and a game and a half behind fourth place Philadelphia.

The A's took the first game of the series 5-3 to drop Detroit another game back. Detroit's pitching led the way in the next three contests with three consecutive shutouts over the A's. Virgil Trucks won 11-0, Ted Gray 3-0, and Fred Hutchinson 6-0. Their combined 27 scoreless innings propelled the Tigers into fourth place. In those three games Neil had six hits in 12 ABs—raising his average to .228—but he didn't reach base with a walk.

Next stop for Detroit was Yankee Stadium where Hal Newhouser (10-7) took on the Yankee's Allie Reynolds (11-1) on August 2.

Neil recalled, "Allie Reynolds with the Yankees, he was a mean son-of-a-bitch. Big guy. He was an oil man's son from Oklahoma, a real well built kid. He threw hard and he didn't like what you did to him [with the bat].

"We were playin' in Yankee Stadium one day and [Red] Rolfe told me if you get two balls on ya, crowd the plate a little bit, don't give 'em too much space, get a little closer. He said if they throw [another] ball, get closer yet, crowd the plate right up."

Red Rolfe was trying to help Neil get on base more often. Mixing in some walks could be the difference between leading off—where his speed would be an asset—or batting eighth where his .228 average dictated and where he batted against Allie Reynolds in New York.

The Tigers sent seven men to the plate in the top of the first inning against Reynolds but only scored one run, leaving three on base. Hal Newhouser gave up the tying run on a walk and two singles in the bottom of the inning.

Neil Berry led off the second with a single to center field but was out when Newhouser's attempted sacrifice bunt resulted in a double play. A pop up to short ended the top half of the inning. In the Yankee second a double, a single, and a sacrifice fly put them ahead 2-1.

The Tigers took the lead in the fourth inning when Aaron Robinson homered following a George Kell double. A Johnny Lipon pop up and a Berry ground out was followed by a walk to Newhouser. The inning ended when Yogi Berra threw Newhouser out trying to steal second base.

Allie Reynolds got two quick outs in the top of the fifth inning before things started to go wrong for Reynolds and right for Detroit. With two out, Dick Wakefield walked ahead of Vic Wertz' long home run to right field. Reynolds wasn't happy. Kell then coaxed a walk off Reynolds. A Robinson single and Joe DiMaggio's error put Tigers on first and third. Lipon singled home Kell for the third two-out run of the inning.

Neil Berry came to bat with Robinson on second, Lipon on first, and Newhouser on deck. After taking the first two pitches for balls—and remembering his manager's advice— Neil moved a little closer to the plate. Next pitch, ball three.

"So I can remember Yogi catchin' back there [when] I got ball three on me—no strikes—ball three, so I got up on the plate. Yogi caught the ball on ball three and threw it back to Reynolds. Reynolds, just standin' on the rubber—didn't hardly take a sign—just reared back and threw at me. Hit me on the elbow.

"I said, 'what the hell's he doin? I can't hurt him or anything (with his hitting)' Yogi said, 'he just don't like you doin that. Now you're on first base but you're hurtin'.'

"Hit me right on the elbow, that's the kinda mean guy he was. He got a big kick out of that but why'd he hit ME? If he wanted to hit some of the big guys, hit Wetrz or Evers or Mullin or those guys—the guys that hit home runs once in a while—that's ok, I can see that. But not ME. The worst I could do [to him] is get a walk. He figured I was showin' him up."

Hitting Neil to load the bases with two outs backfired when Newhouser walked to score Robinson. That was the end of the day for Reynolds but not the end of his pitching line. Reynolds was replaced by Fred Sanford who gave up a run scoring infield single to Don Kolloway—batting for the second time in the inning. Tigers 8, Yankees 2 after 4.5 innings.

With Allie Reynolds out of the game there would be no retaliation that day for hitting Neil.

"But we had one guy, Freddy Hutchinson—Reynolds, he had to come to the plate in those days—he came to bat and 'ol Hutch stuck it up his butt too."

Neil Berry walked 27 times in 365 plate appearances (PA) and batted .237 in 1949. That's one walk for every 13.5 trips to the plate. By comparison Johnny Groth—the starter with the closest number of PA—hit .293 in 1949 and was issued 65 walks in 418 PA, one walk for every 6.4 trips. Had Neil walked at the same rate, his 78 hits in '49 would have resulted in a .261 batting average.

Allie Reynolds was remarkably consistent for the Yankees after they acquired him from Cleveland after the 1947 season. He won 16 games in '48, 17 in '49, 16 in '50, 17 in '51, and won 20 games in 1952 at the age of 35. During the 1951 season Reynolds became the first pitcher in the American League to pitch two no-hitters in a season. He walked three when he no-hit Cleveland on July 12, and walked four while no-hitting Boston on September 28. He didn't hit any batters in those games and no batters hit him.

Detroit took two out of three from the Yankees then lost two out of three in Boston. While Detroit was finishing their road trip against New York and Boston, the Philadelphia Athletics were winning five of six against the White Sox and Indians. After their 9-5 road trip the Tigers were in the same position they started, fifth place and a game and a half behind Philadelphia.

After game 120—the first game of a doubleheader against the St. Louis Browns—the fifth place Detroit Tigers had a record of 64-56 and were 11.5 games behind the first place Yankees. Boston, Cleveland, and Philadelphia were still ahead of Detroit in the standings. Detroit won the second game of the doubleheader then reeled off seven more victories, beating New York, Washington, and Philadelphia. The eight game winning streak propelled the Tigers back into fourth place, eight games off the pace.

During the streak, on August 27, Neil Berry had perhaps the finest hitting performance of his major league career. Neil had two clutch hits while going 4 for 4 at the plate, with 2 runs scored, and 2 RBIs, in a 7-6 win over the Washington Senators. The win was Hal Newhouser's 14th of the season and Detroit's sixth consecutive win.

Boston stopped Detroit's streak at eight with a pair of wins at Briggs Stadium. The Tigers won the final game of the three game series to start another streak. The red hot Tigers swept series' against Chicago (3), St. Louis (2), Cleveland (2), and Chicago again (2). After winning 18 of 20 Detroit was a very respectable 82-58 (.586)—24 games over .500—and knocking on the door. Detroit trailed first-place New York by 5.5 games and were 2.5 games behind second-place Boston—with 14 games left to play.

For Detroit to have a chance at the pennant they had to keep winning and hope New York and Boston faltered in the final weeks of the season.

After winning 18 of 20 Detroit had road games with Boston (2) and New York (2). Those four games would provide clarity or—if Detroit could win all four—chaos in the final weeks of the 1949 American League pennant race.

It was clarity that was provided when Detroit lost all four games. The Yankees and the Red Sox would battle for the pennant, while the Tigers and the Indians—now a game and a half ahead of Detroit—battled for third place.

After New York and Boston all but mathematically eliminated Detroit from the race, the Tigers won two road games at Washington and split two games with Philadelphia. Cleveland, meanwhile, was getting the final nail driven in their coffin—losing two each to New York and Boston. Detroit was now a game and a half ahead of Cleveland for third place. Both teams controlled their own destiny; Detroit had six games remaining—three on the road and three at home—all against Cleveland. Cleveland had nine games remaining, with a three game trip to Chicago between the home and away series against Detroit.

Detroit started well taking two out of three in Cleveland. Virgil Trucks won his 19th game of the year with 5-0, five-hit shutout. In the second game, Hal Newhouser dueled Bob Feller but neither was sharp. Newhouser gave up five runs in the first inning but prevailed when Feller gave up eight in five-and-a-third innings before being relieved. Newhouser went the distance after his shaky start. Detroit couldn't figure out Bob Lemon and lost 5-1 in the third game.

At the close of play on September 25, 1949, Boston and New York were tied for first at 93-55.

Detroit was in third place two and a half games ahead of Cleveland. Detroit went home to wait for the Indians who had three games to play in Chicago before closing out the 1949 season in Detroit.

Cleveland swept the three games in Chicago to draw within one game of the idle Tigers. Third place would come down to the final series against Cleveland in Detroit. The third-place math was easy for Detroit—win two games, finish in third place; win one game, tie with Cleveland for third. The math was also easy for Cleveland—sweep the series, finish third.

Almost a year removed from Neil's favorite game in 1948, it would again be Hal Newhouser facing Bob Feller. Neil was 0 for 3 this time and Cleveland second sacker Joe Gordon touched Newhouser for two home runs. Both pitchers went the distance with Feller getting the win in Cleveland's 6-4 victory. The teams were now tied for third place with two games to play.

Boston held a one game lead over New York, also with two to play. They would close out the season playing each other in a two-game weekend series in New York to decide the 1949 American League champion.

Saturday, October 1, 1949 - Cleveland had a promising start in the top of the first inning with their first two batters, Dale Mitchell and Lou Boudreau, drawing walks from Tiger's starter Ted Gray. That brought Detroit nemesis and hero of yesterday's game, Joe Gordon, to the plate. Cleveland's player/manager Boudreau signaled for a hit-and-run and both base runners were off with Gray's next pitch. Gordon swung and ripped a vicious grounder toward Tiger's third sacker, George Kell. For those of you scoring at home, what followed was a 5 - 4 - 3, Kell to Berry to Kolloway, triple play.

The defensive gem would be Detroit's only highlight as Cleveland's Mike Garcia blanked the Tigers, 4-0, giving up seven hits and stranding nine men on base.

In New York, the Yankees were down 4-0 to Boston after three innings but rallied for a 5-4 win setting up a championship showdown on the regular season's final day.

Sunday, October 2, 1949 - A year earlier The Detroit Tigers were a game over .500 (77-76) and 19 games behind the league-leading Cleveland Indians when they squared off in the last scheduled game of the 1948 season. Detroit had nothing to gain, but Cleveland had plenty to lose when a Tiger victory forced them to play an extra game against the Boston Red Sox to determine the 1948 American League champion.

For the Boston Red Sox, the Berraism, "it's like déjà vu all over again," certainly applied with the last game of the season set to determine if they or the New York Yankees would be the 1949 American League champion.

The stakes were much different for Cleveland and Detroit in the final game; Detroit would tie Cleveland for third place with a win, or finish fourth.

In Detroit, Cleveland's Bob Lemon squared off against Detroit's Virgil Trucks. The Indians got three hits and scored a run off Trucks in the first inning. Trucks settled down and kept the Indians off the board until the fifth inning when his own error contributed to an unearned run to go along with the one Cleveland earned. In the sixth inning, it was a passed ball that led to another unearned run, and a 4-0 lead for the tribe.

The Tigers, meanwhile, had done little against Lemon connecting for only three hits over the first five innings. Down 4-0 after the top of the sixth, Detroit got to Lemon in the bottom of the inning. A walk and three consecutive singles accounted for three runs before a Detroit batter was retired. Cleveland replaced Lemon with Bob Feller who gave up a sac-fly for the fourth Tiger run of the inning, before striking out Neil Berry and getting Trucks to pop up for the third out. It was all tied up at four apiece after six innings.

After a scoreless seventh, Cleveland broke things open. Larry Doby hit a home run and a two-out, bases-loaded single off the bat of Dale Mitchell brought home two more. Lou Boudreau drove in the final run after Hal White had replaced Trucks on the mound.

Detroit couldn't get anything started against Feller in their final two innings of the game and the '49 season.

Final score - Cleveland 8, Detroit 4.

In New York, Boston sent 23-game winner Ellis Kinder to the mound to battle with New York's Vic Raschi. After Boston failed to score in the top of the first, the Yankees got Phil Rizzuto home after he tripled to open New York's half of the inning. The score remained 1-0, Yankees, until the bottom of the eighth inning. With Kinder out of the game (lifted for a pinch hitter in the top of the inning), Boston brought in lefty Mel Parnell to face New York's left-handed power threats, Tommy Henrich and Yogi Berra. The move backfired—Henrich homered and Berra singled—and that was all for Parnell. He was replaced by Tex Hughson who induced a double-play ball off the bat of Joe DiMaggio. But he couldn't get the third out of the inning giving up two singles and a walk before Jerry Coleman cleared the bases with a double. Coleman was thrown out at third. The Yankees led 5-0 going into the ninth inning.

In the Boston ninth Ted Williams walked with one out, Vern Stephens singled, and Bobby Doerr tripled to drive them both in. A shallow fly to center didn't score Doerr, but Billy Goodman's single to center did. With two outs, it was up to Birdie Tebbetts to keep the line moving. A base runner would bring the tying run to the plate. Tebbetts was in the same position a year ago, except that his team was facing a much larger deficit. In that winner take all game against Cleveland in 1948 Tebbetts grounded out to third base. In '49 against New York he popped up to first base.

Final score - Yankees 5, Red Sox 3.

On the last day of the 1949 regular season, George Kell was hitting .341, and Boston's Ted Williams was at .344 before the last games were played. Williams did not get a hit in his two official ABs, while Kell had two hits in three official trips to the plate. With Boston's game over Ted Williams' average stood at .343.

Detroit's game against the Indians was in the bottom of the ninth inning. Johnny Lipon batted for Neil Berry and grounded out. Dick Wakefield batted for Hal White and singled bringing up shortstop and leadoff man, Eddie Lake to face Bob Feller. George Kell was on deck, after his two hits, his batting average stood at .343. His final AB against Bob Feller would determine the 1949 American League batting champion. Or would it?

Eddie Lake didn't let it come to that. Lake hit a ground ball to Cleveland shortstop Ray Boone who turned it into a double play to end the ball game with Kell in the on-deck circle. George Kell won the American League batting title with a .34291 average; Williams was second at .34275.

Detroit acquired George Kell from the Philadelphia A's in 1946 and in a career that spanned 15 seasons, he had his best years with the Tigers. Kell batted better than .300 every season from 1946 to 1951. In 1946, while batting .322, Kell struck out just 20 times. In 1947 he made the American League All-Star team for the first time. A 10-time All-Star, Kell batted .306 in 1,795 career games. When his playing days were over, he broadcast Tiger games for 37 seasons. George Kell was inducted into the Baseball Hall of Fame in 1983.

Many consider George Kell to be one of Detroit's greatest players but teammate Neil Berry wasn't a fan.

Kell had a lifetime .969 fielding percentage at third base, but according to Neil, "Hit right to ya, throw a guy out, he could do that. [Kell] could throw good enough to play third base in the big leagues, but his sideways movement wasn't the greatest. [Tiger manager and former Yankee All-star third baseman] Red Rolfe tried to help him and [Kell] told him, 'you manage, I'll play third.'"

Cover of the 1950 Famous Slugger Year Book published by Hillerich & Bradsby Co. maker of Louisville Slugger bats. Cover photos: top left George Kell - 1949 AL batting champion, top right Jackie Robinson - 1949 NL batting champion, bottom left Ted Williams - 1949 AL home run leader, bottom right Ralph Kiner - 1949 NL home run leader.

From Author's collection

Neil acknowledged that Kell, "did get a lot of poop hits (poorly hit balls that barely cleared the infield), I'll say that for him. How he did it I don't know. He was a magician. He did swing the bat pretty good but he couldn't run and his arm wasn't strong, so to put him in the Hall of Fame? He was lucky."

The final 1949 first division standings:

New York Yankees	97 - 57	.630	-
Boston Red Sox	96 - 58	.623	1.0
Cleveland Indians	89 - 65	.578	8.0
Detroit Tigers	87 - 67	.565	10.0

Back on top in the American League, the New York Yankees were also World Series champions in 1949 beating the Brooklyn Dodgers four games to one.

Losing three in a row and third place to archrival Cleveland was hard to swallow for manager Red Rolfe and Tiger fans but in their first year under Rolfe, the Tigers improved by eight games and were back in the top division.

In his second big league season Neil Berry started 90 games at second base and fielded .970. At the plate he contributed 78 hits in 329 AB for a .237 average. He scored 38 runs and knocked in 18.

Baseball pundits predicted that—if Detroit could fill a couple of holes and the pitching held up—the Tigers would make a run at the pennant in 1950.

Detroit started filling those holes on December 14, 1949, when they traded pitcher Lou Kretlow and $100,000 cash, to the St. Louis Browns for second baseman Jerry Priddy.

Damn it was close.

~ Neil Berry

16

The Detroit Tigers

Pennant Contenders

1950

The acquisition of Jerry Priddy was expected to solve Detroit's problem at second base. At that time the "problem" was Neil Berry and Eddie Lake, but the real problem was that no one who had played second base since Hall of Famer Charlie Gehringer, was—well—Charlie Gehringer. The six-time all-star with a .320 lifetime batting average during an 18-year career had also won the batting title and MVP honors in 1937. He was a hard man to replace but the 30-year-old veteran Priddy was coming off the 1949 season with a .290 batting average and had connected for 11 home runs and driven in 63—not Gehringer numbers—but a definite improvement over light hitting Berry (.237), and Lake (.196).

Neil said, "When they made second base available, that's good, then they wanted to get someone with more experience, Jerry Priddy, they got him, and I had to go learn how to play third base. Why? Just in case, so you can play second, short, third. Well, okay, so they kinda baited me along there 'cause they wanted to keep me 'cause I could do all three of 'em. But I didn't get a chance to play regular anymore, I had to wait for someone to get hurt. It kinda got to a point where it wasn't any fun anymore."

The Tigers also traded under-performing (.206, 6 HR, 19 RBI) outfielder Dick Wakefield—a $50,000 bonus baby when he signed in 1941—to the New York Yankees for left hand hitting first baseman Dick Kryhoski. The Yankees were hoping Wakefield could recapture the magic that resulted in a league-leading 200 hits and 38 doubles while batting .316 in 1943, the year he made his only all-star appearance. Wakefield appeared in three games for the Yankees in 1950 and three games for the New York Giants in 1952 before ending his once-promising career.

Spring Training

A 1950 spring training clipping from an unnamed newspaper in the Berry scrapbook reads:

"With Jerry Priddy at second base and Johnny Lipon at short, Berry fully realizes he has no chance to break into the lineup.

"And he doesn't like it. He let us know that. As he explained it: 'I know I'm slated to warm that bench all year. I know my only chance to play is if someone gets hurt. Otherwise, I'll either pinch-hit or pinch-run occasionally, but I don't like looking forward to that prospect. I'd feel better if they traded me to some other club where I could play regularly. Or send me somewhere so that I could be in the lineup every day. After all, I'm not getting any younger.'"

Going into spring training in 1950 the Tiger's infield was considered set with newly acquired prospect Dick Kryhoski expected to supply more power at first base, and newly acquired veteran Jerry Priddy being hailed by manager Red Rolfe as "the best second baseman we have had since Charlie Gehringer."

George Kell was a fixture at third base and the shortstop job was Johnny Lipon's to lose. Lipon's play over the first 16 spring games suggested he might do just that. At the very least it opened the door for Neil Berry to compete for the shortstop position.

The headline for the *Detroit Free Press* article read, "Berry May Supplant Lipon at Short"

In the article *Free Press* sports editor, Lyall Smith pointed to Lipon's seven errors in 19 games and quoted Manager Red Rolfe saying, "I'm going to give Berry a chance. We must tighten up our infield defense."

The article goes on to report, "It has been no secret in camp this year that unless Lipon hit consistently his job would be endangered. Not that Berry is expected to hit any better than Lipon. He isn't.

"Yet, Rolfe figures that Berry is a better fielder and is faster than Lipon.

"He has indicated for several weeks that if the rest of his regulars hit well, he would be willing to sacrifice the extra hits Lipon might make for the fielding ability and speed of the slender, fast-moving Berry as leadoff man.

"The Tiger board of strategy believes that Berry will be able to make plays that Lipon often misses. Those are on ground balls hit to the right of the shortstop toward third.

"Lipon has shown a definite deficiency at that spot. Berry's speed gets them. Lipon proved off his .290 average in 1948 that he is a much better hitter than Berry.

"But despite unlimited opportunity this spring, he has failed to cement a job that was considered to be his personal property when the team encamped here one month ago."

Whether Neil had a legitimate shot at displacing Johnny Lipon at shortstop, or the reported competition was just a way to spur on Lipon, ultimately the Detroit manager chose the prospect of more offense—including an occasional home run—from Johnny Lipon over tightening up the infield defense with Neil Berry.

It was well reported that Detroit's second-year manager Red Rolfe, the former Yankee, had a penchant for home runs and extra-base power. *Detroit Free Press* sports editor, Lyall Smith wrote, ". . . through all his press conferences, formal or impromptu, is woven the theme of his days with the New Yorkers. And that theme is power.

"He passes over batting averages with hardly a second glance. But extra-base hits, power, a long ball, a cluster of home runs—that's where his emphasis lies."

THE 1950 SEASON

Manager Red Rolfe's batting order and starting lineup to open the 1950 season:

SS - Johnny Lipon

2B - Jerry Priddy

3B - George Kell

RF - Vic Wertz

LF - Pat Mullin

CF - Johnny Groth

1B - Dick Kryhoski

C - Aaron Robinson

P - Fred Hutchinson

Neil Berry started the 1950 season on the Detroit bench. While Neil watched and seldom played the Tigers won six of nine April games then went 16 - 9 in May. Detroit won 15 of their first 18 games in June to propell them into first place. After losing three games at home to fifth place Washington the Tigers—at 37 and 18 (.673)—were still in first place, one game ahead of the New York Yankees.

On June 23 the Yankees were in town for a four game series. The first game was one of Detroit's 14 night games under the lights and 51,400 fans showed up.

Ted Gray started but didn't last long. The Yankees blasted four home runs and scored six runs in three innings. Hank Bauer connected off Gray in consecutive at bats in the first and third innings. Yogi Berra and Jerry Coleman also homered off Gray. He was replaced by Dizzy Trout before recording an out in the fourth inning.

Down 6 - 0 after three and a half innings, Detroit went to work in the bottom of the fourth. With one out Johnny Groth and Don Kolloway singled. Bob Swift walked to load the bases. Dizzy Trout then unloaded them with a grand slam, his first home run of the year. The Tigers weren't done. Jerry Priddy hit a two-out solo shot. George Kell followed with a single ahead of a home run by Vic Wertz. Hoot Evers—batting for the second time in the inning—closed out the fourth inning scoring with a home run of his own. After the four home run barrage against three Yankee pitchers the Tigers led 8 - 6.

The Yankees weren't done either. Joe DiMaggio homered off Trout in the seventh to make it 8 - 7. In the eighth inning Tommy Henrich hit the sixth home run of the game for the Yankees. His two-run shot of Trout put New York back in the lead 9 - 8. Fred Hutchinson got the final outs in the eighth and after the Tigers didn't score in the bottom of the inning, Hutch got DiMaggio, Berra and Mize in order in the ninth.

In the bottom of the ninth Vic Wertz hit a one out double to center field putting the tying run in scoring position for Hoot Evers. Evers teed off on a Joe Page fastball and hit it over DiMaggio's head in center field driving in Wertz. While DiMaggio was chasing down the ball Hoot Evers was flying around the bases. By the time DiMaggio coralled the ball and got it to Phil Rizzuto, Evers had circled the bases for an inside-the-park home run and a 10 - 9 Tiger victory.

On a night that saw 10 home runs find the stands in Briggs Stadium, the game was decided by the 11th home run of the night, the one that didn't leave the park.

Detroit won three of four games from the visiting Yankees to build a three game lead. The Tigers remainded in first place—leading by as many as 4.5 games—throughout July and well into August.

Neil appeared in only 22 of the Tiger's first 105 games—18 times as a pinch-runner (scoring five runs), and four times as a pinch hitter. He was 0-5 with a walk in his six plate appearances. He had seen only five innings of defensive duty at second base after pinch-running for Jerry Priddy.

Through the games of August 10, Neil was primarily a spectator while the first place Tigers built a three and a half-game lead over the Cleveland Indians and a four game lead over the Yankees.

On August 11, in the second game of a doubleheader at Sportsman's Park in St. Louis, the Tigers pounded out 13 hits but scored only one run in a 2-1 loss to the Browns. Not only did Detroit lose a seemingly winnable game but they also lost shortstop Johnny Lipon with a spike wound after he stole second base in the fifth inning. He was replaced by Neil Berry—the speedy, seldom used, utility infielder.

Neil's first start of the 1950 season would come in Detroit's next game on August 15—in game 107—against the Cleveland Indians. He played shortstop and batted eighth, going 1 for 4. Hal Newhouser was the tough-luck loser when Al Rosen homered in the bottom of the ninth to tie the score 2-2. In the Indians tenth—with runners on second and third—Detroit Manager Red Rolfe had Newhouser intentionally walk a batter to set up a force play at the plate. Rolfe and the Tigers got the ground ball they needed. The ball was fielded cleanly by Berry but Robinson needlessly came off the plate to catch his throw home and the winning run scored.

Neil Berry was 1 for 3 in his next game, a 4-1 win over the Indians.

Next up were the Chicago White Sox—in Detroit for a two-game set. In the first game, Neil committed an error when he dropped a throw from the catcher on a steal attempt. It would have been the third out of the first inning and the Sox used the extra out to score two unearned runs. Neil made up for the defensive lapse by going 2 for 4 at the plate with a run scored and an RBI in Detroit's 6-2 win.

In the next game—an 8-3 win over Chicago—Neil was 1 for 3, with three RBIs and a run scored. Defensively he committed his second error of the season but he was also part of three double plays with Priddy and Kolloway.

After a day off the St. Louis Browns were in town for a four-game set. Neil continued to hit well going 4 for 11, with two walks and three RBIs in the first three games. Detroit won the opening game of the series, 6-0, behind Art Houtteman's dominating, one-hit shutout.

A doubleheader with the Browns followed on August 20. In the first game, Detroit was trailing 4-1 in the sixth inning. After a one-out walk to Johnny Groth and a two-out walk to Neil, Charlie Keller doubled. Groth scored, but Neil—believing there was only one out—stopped at third base. The rare mental error by Neil drew the wrath of his manager but the Tigers recovered to win 5-4 before dropping the second game of the doubleheader, 6-2.

On August 21, Dizzy Trout pitched Detroit to a 7-1 victory in the fourth game of the series. Neil went 0 for 3 after hitting safely in all seven of his prior starts while filling in for Johnny Lipon.

After their game, Detroit caught a train for New York, the first stop of a four-city, 12 game road trip. The first game of a three-game series at New York was scheduled for the next day. The Detroit Tigers were in first place after the games of August 21, 1950, 3.5 games ahead of the second-place New York Yankees.

With only 42 games left on the schedule, this was an important road trip. The Tiger coaches, players, and most serious fans of a contending team knew what they needed to do.

Neil explained, "If you can just split with the guys you need to split with, and beat the guys underneath you, you got it made."

In 1950 the guys the Detroit Tigers needed to split with were the other three teams that shared the American League's first division. In the American League, the first division was always (or so it seemed) the Yankees and three other teams. In 1950, Red Rolfe's second year as manager, the Detroit Tigers were one of those teams. The other two were the Boston Red Sox and the Cleveland Indians.

The teams in the American League's second division— "the guys beneath you," that you needed to beat—were the Washington Senators, Chicago White Sox, St. Louis Browns, and the Philadelphia Athletics.

"We had an eastern trip to make—Boston, New York, Philadelphia, and Washington. We had a meeting [and figured] if we could split with New York and split with Boston, we'd have it made. Then [go to] Philadelphia and Washington—we beat 'em all year long—easy, not easy, but I mean we were supposed to beat 'em and we [usually] did."

"[On this trip] we played Boston and New York—New York first, then Boston—then went to Philadelphia and they beat our butts, then Washington beat us."

Neil was still in the lineup, subbing for the injured Johnny Lipon, and went 0 for 4 in the first game against New York and 1 for 2 with a sacrifice in the second game, both losses. Lipon was back in the lineup for the third game and contributed three hits, two runs, and an RBI in Detroit's 6-3 win. During that ten-game August stretch that Neil started at shortstop, he hit .294 (10 for 34) with two runs scored and seven batted in. The Tigers won six of those games, but with Johnny Lipon back in the lineup, Neil Berry was back on the bench. In his utility role, Neil would see only limited action during the remainder of the 1950 season.

August 23, 1950 - Yankee Stadium, New York. Two play-ers are on the ground and a third is on his way down in this force play at second base in the 3rd inning. Tiger second baseman Gerry Priddy kneels as he watches Tiger shortstop Connie Berry toss to first after forcing Yankee shortstop Phil Rizzuto (on ground). Berry made play on Hank Bauer's slow roller but failed to get Bauer at first. Yankees won 7-5 to take second straight game in current series with league-leading Tigers.

AP Wirephoto from Author's collection

After losing two out of three to the Yankees, it was on to Boston where the Tigers and the Red Sox split a short two-game series. After dropping two of three to Philadelphia, and three of four to Washington—teams they were supposed to beat—the Tigers limped home with a 4 and 8 record for the road trip.

After their poor showing on the road, the Tigers were two games behind the surging Yankees, but there was a month of baseball yet to be played and Detroit would be playing 23 of their final 30 games at home in Briggs Stadium.

The Tigers started their September home stand by sweeping a two game series with the White Sox then taking two out of three from the Browns. Two games with Cleveland rounded out the home stand.

The Tigers do some late season scoreboard watching from the dugout and they're not happy to see the Yankees post a win in the tight race for the Amerciam League pennant.

Standing left: Hal Newhouser

Others foreground to back: Neil Berry, Johnny Lipon, Fred Hutchinson, and Pat Mullin (leaning forward).

Photo from Neil Berry's scrapbook

In the first game Hal Newhouser beat Cleveland's Early Wynn 5-3 for his 13th victory of the season. The win—combined with New York's loss to Boston—left the Tigers a half game back of the Yankees.

The second game, on September 7, was a slug fest. Art Houteman didn't make it out of the first inning giving up seven runs (six earned) on six hits. Four of those hits were singles but most of the damage came from Al Rosen's 34th home run—a two run shot—and Bob Feller's three run homer, his second of the season. Fred Hutchinson came in to get Ray Boone—batting for the second time in the inning—to retire the side.

Bob Feller's second home run of the season was the seventh of his career and helped stake the Indians to a seven run lead before the Tigers came to bat. Feller may have been overconfident with the big lead he had a hand in securing but his home run would be the highlight of his short day. Feller got Don Kolloway to ground out before giving up a single to Johnny Lipon. After a George Kell double, a Vic Wertz single, and a Hoot Evers triple, three runs were home for the Tigers and Bob Feller was done for the day. The Tigers pushed another run home—charged to Feller—against reliever Jesse Flores. Cleveland 7, Detroit 4, after one.

Detroit got two runs off Flores in the third when Hoot Evers drove in both runs with a double. The Tigers tied the score in the fifth on a Jerry Priddy home run off Al Benton, the third of five pitchers the Indians would use that day.

In the top of the sixth the Indians regained the lead with three runs off Hutchinson and Hal White. Two of the runs were unearned due to Hutch's two errors in the inning. In the bottom of the inning Detroit got two runs back—both unearned—after a walk, an error, and Hoot Evers second triple and fourth RBI of the game. Cleveland 10, Detroit 9, after six.

The Indians added a run in the top of the seventh for a two

run lead that lasted until Hoot Evers tied the score with a two run homer—his fifth and sixth RBI—in the bottom of the eighth.

After neither team scored in the ninth inning, the game that didn't want to be won was tied at eleven. The game so far had produced 22 runs on 25 hits—including four home runs, two triples, and five doubles—against nine pitchers and each team had committed three errors.

In the top of the tenth with one out Ray Boone was safe on an error by Kell. Detroit's fourth pitcher Hank Borowy—who came on for Hal White to pitch the eighth—got a ground ball for the second out bringing Larry Doby to the plate. Doby connected for his 22nd home run of the year putting Cleveland ahead 13-11.

For Detroit most of the offense that day came off the bat of Hoot Evers with a double, two triples, and a home run— good for six RBI—in his five ABs so far. Evers only needed a single to hit for the cycle. His chance would come in the tenth inning.

Hitting for the cycle is when a batter hits a single, double, triple, and home run—in no particular order—in the same game. In the 55 year history of baseball being played at the corner of Michigan and Trumbull—in Bennett Park, Navin Field, or Briggs Stadium—only eight players have hit for the cycle. The last player to do it was Boston's Joe Cronin in August 1940. The last Tiger to hit for the cycle in Briggs Stadium was Charlie Gehringer on May 27, 1939.

Trailing by two runs Vic Wertz led off with a single off Marino Pieretti, Clevelands fifth pitcher of the game. Hoot Evers was up next for what was likely to be his last plate appearance of the game. The Detroit fans—aware of the cycle possibility but also hoping for a game tying home run—serenaded Evers with their familiar refrain, a long drawn-out H..o..o..o..o..t. Evers lined a fair ball to left field and—down by two and with Wertz running ahead of him—gave no thought to stretching the hit into a double.

The single gave Evers his cycle and also gave Detroit two on with nobody out. Johnny Groth then walked to load the bases for Jerry Priddy. Priddy hit a ground ball that resulted in a force out at home plate for the first out. Next up with the bases still full of Tigers was Joe Ginsberg whose line drive to center field was caught for the second out but scored Wertz from third base. With two out Charlie Keller was brought in to pinch hit in the pitcher's spot. Red Rolfe told Neil Berry to be ready if Keller reached base. Keller's single to center brought Groth home from second with the tying run. Berry replaced Keller at first base and was in the game long enough to be forced out at second base on Kolloway's ground ball.

After 10 innings, the three hour, 25 minute game was declared a 13-13 tie—both teams had trains to catch. The game would be replayed if necessary (it would be). The tie didn't count in the standings but the player stats did count including Hoot Evers cycle.

While Detroit and Cleveland were playing a game that didn't count in the standings, the Boston Red Sox beat the Yankees in another slug fest 10-8.

The first division standings after the games of September 7, 1950:

Team	W-L	W%	GB
Detroit	82-48	.631	–
New York	83-49	.629	–
Boston	82-51	.617	1.5
Cleveland	80-54	.597	4.0

The Tigers caught the Yankees and also caught their train to Chicago where they won three of four games from the White Sox on the short road trip. Back at Briggs Stadium Detroit beat Washington twice and were in first place by a half game over the Yankees.

The Tigers then lost two out of three to the Yankees and lost two games to Boston to drop to third place 1.5 games off the pace in the tight race for the American League pennant.

A three game sweep of Connie Mack's Philadelphia Athletics righted the ship and after play on September 21, the Detroit Tigers—14-6 so far in September—and the New York Yankees were tied for first place with identical 91- 53 records. The Boston Red Sox were two games back and Cleveland was a distant seven back. Detroit had been in first place for a total of 110 days and were 38 games over .500 but now there were only 10 games remaining to determine the 1950 pennant winner and World Series participant from the American League.

New York's final ten game schedule started and ended with Boston, a two-game set in New York and two games to close the season in Boston. In between, both teams had games with second division teams—Washington, and Philadelphia—looking to play the spoiler role. In this pennant race New York and Boston would settle their own business.

The Detroit Tigers had six games left against their perennial rival Cleveland Indians, starting with a three-game road series at Municipal Stadium, and ending the 1950 season with three games at Briggs Stadium. A four-game home series with the lowly (54-90) St. Louis Browns was sandwiched between the clashes with Cleveland.

The winning formula Neil spoke of, "split with the guys you need to split with and beat the guys underneath you," had been in play all season and was how the Tigers got to the final ten games in a first-place tie with the Yankees. Detroit's record so far against first division teams was 31-29 (11-11 vs NY, 12-10 vs Boston, and 8-8 vs Cleveland with 6 left to play). As for the guys underneath, Detroit was 60-24 against second division teams.

Cleveland—all but mathematically eliminated, at seven games back—was intent on spoiling Detroit's bid for the

American League pennant and pitched Bob Feller against Detroit's Hal Newhouser in the first game of the series.

Newhouser gave up a two-run homer in the first and the Tigers got an unearned run off Feller in the third. The Indians got the run back in the bottom of the inning with a double and single for a three to one lead. It stayed that way until Detroit's Don Kolloway hit a two-out, two-run homer in the top of the ninth to tie the game. The Tigers' elation for Kolloway's heroics was short-lived, when Joe Gordon, Cleveland leadoff batter in the bottom of the ninth, touched Newhouser for the game-winning home run.

In the series second game, the Tigers couldn't recover from a Larry Doby grand slam in the third. Five Tiger pitchers couldn't hold off Cleveland who added five more runs in the seventh contributing to the 10-2 final. After two losses in Cleveland and a New York win over Boston, Detroit was now a game and a half out of first place with eight games to play. They needed a win in the final game of the series.

The third game was a pitching duel between Detroit's Ted Gray and Cleveland's Bob Lemon. Lemon helped his own cause with a fourth inning home run. Johnny Lipon squared things with his first home run of the season in the seventh. The score was still tied 1-1 when Cleveland came to bat in the bottom of the tenth inning. Lemon led off with a triple to right center. Rolfe had Gray walk the next two Indians to load the bases and set up a force play at home. Larry Doby fouled out to first baseman Don Kolloway for the first out. Then with one out and the bases loaded, Luke Easter hit a ground ball to Kolloway who fielded the ball, touched first base and threw home to catcher Aaron Robinson. Robinson could have easily tagged Lemon for the third out, but he didn't realize Kolloway had touched first base for the second out, removing the force play at home.

The Tiger's third loss in a row to the Indians left them two and a half games behind the first place Yankees, who had won their two-game series with Boston.

Detroit returned home desperate to win and hoping New York would falter. Both teams played second division teams leading up to the final days of the season. The Tigers won three of four from St. Louis, and the Yankees took three of four from Washington and split two games with Philadelphia.

That left Detroit with three games to play at home against Cleveland, while New York would close the season with two games against Boston who had been eliminated from contention with a doubleheader loss to Washington. Detroit's only hope was to sweep the Indians and hope for a Boston sweep of the two games with the Yankees. A win in their first game with Cleveland while the Yankees were idle left Detroit two back with two to play.

Detroit's Ted Gray and Cleveland's Bob Lemon were matched up again for the first game but this one was no pitching duel. Gray didn't make it out of the fifth inning while Lemon cruised through the Tiger lineup giving up six hits and winning his 23rd game of the season, 12-2.

The 1950 American League pennant race was over. Detroit and Cleveland split the final two meaningless games. Detroit finished the season with a 9-13 record vs Cleveland.

The New York Yankees won 98 games to win the American League pennant. They finished 60-28 against the second division—while Detroit was three games better at 63-25—but the Yankees had the best record against a first division opponent with a 14-8 mark vs Cleveland. There are a lot of "ifs" when you play 154 games and miss winning the pennant by three, but if Detroit and New York had both split 11-11 with Cleveland—Detroit would have won the pennant. The difference in performance against the Cleveland Indians was one of the stories of the 1950 pennant race.

Neil remembered, "Awe God, we came home and closed the season with Cleveland and the Yankees slipped in ahead of us. Damn it was close."

Damn Yankees? No. Damn Indians.

Detroit won 95 games in 1950 surpassing the league win totals of their pennant-winning clubs of 1907 (92), 1908 (90), 1935 (93), 1940 (90), and 1945 (88). In the Detroit Tigers 49-year history, only the 1909, 1915, and 1934 squads won more than 95 games.

The team's outstanding performance earned Red Rolfe manager of the year honors in the American League.

The New York Yankees went on to defeat the Philadelphia Phillies four games to none in the 1950 World Series.

Following the 1950 season Connie Mack—the tall tactician— retired as manager of the Philadelphia Athletics after 50 years at the helm. Since joining the American League in 1901 the A's had only had Connie Mack as their manager. Instead of the traditional team uniform other managers wore, Mack dressed in a suit. He wore a derby or bowler hat instead of a ball cap. From the dugout, he would wave a rolled up scorecard to position his outfielders.

Connie Mack won 3,731 games but he also lost 3,948. He piloted the Athletics to nine American League championships and won five World Series titles in eight appearances, but he also suffered last-place finishes 17 times. It is extremely unlikely his records for wins and for losses will ever be broken because it is even more unlikely the owner of a major league franchise will ever manage their own team for 50 years.

While the Detroit Tigers were battling the New York Yankees for the 1950 American League pennant, American troops were battling the forces of international communism in Korea. Soviet-backed North Korea's invasion of the pro-Western Republic of Korea was the first military action of the Cold War. Over the next year, 516 inductees from Kalamazoo County were sent to Korea. Neil's brother Carl, who served as a pilot in World War II, was stationed at a training base in Africa during the Korean War.

Unlike World War II, US involvement in the Korean War

did not have a large impact on baseball. Fewer major league players served in the military during the Korean War than during World War II. Notable exceptions included Boston's Ted Williams, Brooklyn's Don Newcombe, New York Yankee Whitey Ford, New York Giant Willie Mays, and Detroit's Art Houtteman.

I figure Neil never will be rated a power hitter, but these new bats should help him punch the ball through for base hits.

~ Red Rolfe

17

The Detroit Tigers

Back to Mediocrity

1951

After nearly winning the pennant in 1950, the Detroit brass mostly stood pat and would go with much the same team in 1951 but with Art Houtteman in the Army and an aging starting staff, the Tigers did pick up some insurance when they selected LHP Gene Bearden off waivers from the Washington Senators. Then in May Detroit traded RHP Saul Rogovin to the Chicago White Sox for LHP Bob Cain.

During Neil's off-season, he and Gloria welcomed their second child into the world on January 27, 1951. They named their cute little bundle of joy, Linda. A few weeks later Neil packed for Lakeland Florida and another spring training with the Detroit Tigers.

Neil Berry's contribution to the 1950 campaign was a .250

batting average (10 for 40), with 6 walks, 9 runs scored, and 7 RBIs. He appeared in 39 games. After being little more than a spectator during Detroit's 1950 pennant run, Neil was looking for more playing time in 1951.

Standing 5' 10" tall and tipping the scale at 168 pounds, Neil Berry was built for speed, not power, but he couldn't steal first base. Neil needed to find more punch from his bat to get more ABs (at-bats) from his manager.

Spring Training

The shorter bat seems to help me swing with more power.. . .

~ *Neil Berry*

It is not clear which 34 inch, 32 oz Louisville Slugger model(s) Neil used during the 1950 campaign, but in spring training 1951, Red Rolfe—in an attempt to get more production out of Neil's bat—came up with a bat of his own design for Neil to try.

An *Associated Press* report by Charles C. Cain from Lakeland, Florida stated that "Neil Berry could be the secret weapon in the Detroit Tigers attack this year if Manager Red Rolfe's ideas pan out.

"The Tiger pilot devoted a lot of time this winter to trying to figure out a way of trying to step up the hitting power of the Kalamazoo-born Berry.

"The results showed on opening day of spring practice when Red called Berry aside and presented him with two 'bantam' bats.

"They are short, chunky affairs about 31 inches in length compared with the usual 34-35. They are eight inches in circumference at the end and four inches at the handle.

"The bats, made on specifications drawn up by Rolfe, even bear the name of the Tiger Manager."

The article quotes Rolfe as saying, "I figure Neil never will be rated a power hitter, but these new bats should help him punch the ball through for base hits."

After his initial tryout with the bats, Neil offered this evaluation for the AP article, "The shorter bat seems to help me swing with more power and coordination than I had before and every drive feels better too."

That was a wise assessment for a utility infielder who's manager had designed a bat specifically for him.

The Tigers stumbled their way to a 4-16 record in Florida before leaving to play their way north for an opening day matchup with Cleveland at Briggs Stadium. George Kell caught a spike in his hand and was sidelined, giving Neil Berry a stretch of spring training starts at third base. Second baseman Jerry Priddy told the *Detroit Free Press* that Berry was playing third base "like he always played there." After five games at third, Neil—using the Red Rolfe designed bat—was leading the team with a .407 spring training batting average (11 for 27).

The Tigers closed out the exhibition season with an 11-2 win over the Louisville Colonels. Notwithstanding the last spring game, spring training 1951 was not a good one for the Detroit team that had contended for the American League pennant in 1950. The Detroit organization, players, and fans were saddened to learn of the death of their long time, outstanding scout Aloysius "Wish" Egan. Egan passed away on April 13 after a two year battle with cancer. Egan boys currently on the Detroit roster were Hoot Evers, Johnny Groth, Johnny Lipon, Pat Mullin, Saul Rogovin, Art Houtteman, Joe Ginsberg, Dizzy Trout, Ted Gray, Hal Newhouser, and Neil Berry. Egan was also instrumental in securing the trade that brought George Kell from Philadelphia to Detroit. Missing from the Detroit roster was Egan signee Billy Pierce. The left-handed hurler who was traded to the Chicago White Sox after the 1948 season.

Detroit finished the 1951 spring exhibition slate with a 7-20 record. George Kell still wasn't ready to go and Eddie Lake had been sold to the Yankees on April 5, so Neil Berry got the opening day nod at third base, his third different opening day position in his first four years in the majors (shortstop 1948, second base 1949), but this time he knew—regardless of how well he performed—it was temporary. When George Kell was ready, George Kell would play.

THE 1951 SEASON

Manager Red Rolfe's batting order and starting lineup to open the 1951 season:

SS - Johnny Lipon

3B - Neil Berry

1B - Don Kolloway

RF - Vic Wertz

LF - Hoot Evers

CF - Johnny Groth

2B - Jerry Priddy

C - Joe Ginsberg

P - Hal Newhouser

Detroit followed up their poor spring showing with a slow start to the 1951 regular season, losing two at home to the Indians, and losing two of three in Chicago (with Billy Pierce winning the rubber match after Detroit's first win of the season). After winning the first game of the series against the Browns in Detroit, the rest of the series was rained out. Rain and cold weather was the story of April with only eight games played in 14 days resulting in a 3-5 April record.

When the Chicago White Sox came to town on April 28, George Kell was ready to play. Kell had a hit, two walks, and a stolen base, helping the Tigers beat Billy Pierce. In the six games that Neil Berry played while Kell convalesced, he hit .263 (5 for 19), with three walks, in the cold and miserable spring conditions in Detroit and Chicago.

Detroit's record on May 3, after a loss to Boston, stood at 4 wins and 7 losses. A mid-May win streak with 12 wins in 15 games was followed by a stretch of 12 losses in 13 games. After winning eight of the next nine games the sneaky Tigers were 25-23 and in fifth place in the standings.

On June 27, after defeating the first-place Chicago White Sox, the Tiger record stood at 31-30 and would be the last time the team was above the .500 mark for the 1951 season.

The All-Star Game was played in Detroit on July 10, 1951, but the game was overshadowed when—the day before the game—baseball and fans of the game learned of the death of longtime Detroit broadcaster, and former Tiger star outfielder, Harry Heilmann. The game began with a moment of silence in Heilmann's honor.

Harry Heilmann (HOF 1952) was one of the best right-handed hitters in the history of the game. He won four batting titles (1921, 1923, 1925 and 1927), and topped the .400 mark (.403 in 1923) to become one of the dominant players of the 1920s. Heilman credited Ty Cobb—who he beat out for the 1921 batting title—for teaching him how to become an elite hitter.

In 1934—after a 17-year major league career—Harry Heilmann was hired by WXYZ to handle the play-by-play responsibility on broadcasts of Detroit Tigers games for the Michigan Broadcast Network. Through the 1941 season, Heilmann was part of an unusual broadcasting arrangement. Heilmann's broadcasts anchored the Michigan Radio Network that stretched across Michigan, while Ty Tyson did play-by-play separately on WWJ for metropolitan Detroit. In 1942, the Tigers gave exclusive broadcast rights to WXYZ with Heilmann as the sole announcer.

Heilmann was the voice of the Tigers in 1940 and 1945 when the Tigers won the American League pennant and won the 1945 World Series over the Chicago Cubs. He became known for his story-telling and for his knowledge of the game. Heilmann's down-to-earth, factual broadcasts, and familiar voice was a mainstay in homes all over Michigan and the Midwest during the baseball season. His tendency to drop the letter "r" from the end of words, resulted in Hal Newhouser as "Newhousa" and Bob Feller as "Fellah." After an outstanding play, Heilmann would pause and let the cheering crowd fill the airways before saying, "Listen to the voice of baseball."

Harry Heilmann was the only voice of baseball that many Tiger fans knew. That voice fell silent on July 9, 1951, when Heilmann succumbed to lung cancer at the age of 56.

Ty Cobb, Heilmann's teammate and rival for the batting crown, visited him in his last days with news that Heilmann had been elected to the Baseball Hall of Fame. The news pleased Heilmann but it wasn't true. Cobb knew Heilmann would get in and wanted him to have that moment before he passed. Harry Heilmann was elected to the HOF the following year.

George Kell and Vic Wertz started the All-Star Game for the American League and both hit solo home runs but it was the National League that brought the power with four home runs and won 8-3.

After starting the first six games of the season, filling in for George Kell, Neil Berry started an additional 33 games—alternating with Johnny Lipon for several stretches at shortstop—and appeared in 28 others during the 1951 season.

The 1951 season was not going well for the Tigers as a team or for Dizzy Trout who was on his way to a league leading 14 losses against only nine wins.

Neil Recalled, "Dizzy Trout was pitchin' one day and I booted a ball or somethin' and he said something to me on the field, like when you gonna catch a ball, or somethin'

[like that.]

"Got back to the bench and Hutch said, 'What'd Diz say?' I don't know, some smart remark. 'Well you tell him to kiss your ass.' Hutch didn't go for that shit. Good guy. Good guy to have on your team.

"I don't know if Hutch kinda liked me or not but anyway he asked me on two or three different things that I didn't [think] a guy of his talent and longevity, his stature—he was well thought of in the league. Anytime there was a league board for rules and regulations, he was on it.

"Anyway we were in New York one day and he said, 'Neil how would you like to go see a show tonight?' He'd usually

August 1, 1951 - Yankee Stadium, New York. Neil Berry made the third out of the 1st inning attempting to steal 3rd base on a strike 'em out (Vic Wetz) throw 'em out (Yogi Berra to Bobby Brown) double play. Detroit won the slugfest 9-8.

Photo from Author's collection

go with Hoot Evers, him and Hoot were just like brothers. He didn't say anything about Hoot but said, 'I got a deal here. Have you seen . . .'"

Neil paused his story and thought for a few seconds, "oh what's the name of the musical . . . Mary Martin . . . (Neil singing) 'I'm gonna wash that man right out of my hair . . .' South Pacific!

"Hutch said, 'how'd you like to go see South Pacific? Mary Martin retired you know, last week.'

"For two or three years she did that every day, played the lead. Hutch told me a funny thing happened, I got a telephone call from a girl I went to high school with and she's takin' Mary Martin's place. She wanted to know if I wanted to go to the show and bring a friend. So he took me to the show and introduced me to the girl. I can't remember her name (Martha Wright)."

With a large number of games being played in the afternoon, there was time in the evening to take in a show, go to a club, or go to a favorite restaurant.

Neil related, "Eating is actually a big part of being on the road. You find a good place, find an odd place, find a place nobody else's at, or a new place, or a place that's got a name and nobody knows it.

"Some of those places are so good. Across the street from our hotel in New York, every so often on a Friday they'd have lobster. If you ate two—they weren't real big ones—if you ate two, you got the third one free."

Players also knew where to go—or not to go—based on advice from other players. Yogi Berra's famous advice concerning a particular restaurant, "Nobody goes there anymore, it's too crowded."

Neil continued, "[There's also] the place you didn't have to find, 'Hey why don't you guys go to so and so,' and you know it because of the name and you go and you're usually disappointed.

"One of the places all the Yankees used to go—Joe DiMaggio, Mickey Mantle, the little lefthander, Ford, and the second baseman, Billy Martin—what the hell was his name, he was a Yankee booster. Every time he was in there people wanted to get their picture taken with him. Jack Dempsey's. I'll bet ya anything those three or four guys didn't pay for their food there."

Neil was the starting shortstop for both ends of a doubleheader against the St. Louis Browns in Sportsman Park on Sunday, August 19, 1951. Detroit won both games while Neil got only one hit in the first game and went 0-4 in the second game. It was that second game in St. Louis that added a historic story that—as long as the game is played—will forever live in baseball lore. Neil Berry witnessed it all from his shortstop position.

The St. Louis Browns had been acquired by Bill Veeck (rhymes with wreck) in 1951. Veeck had previously owned the Cleveland Indians from 1946 to 1949 but was forced to sell the team to settle his divorce from his first wife.

During his ownership of the Cleveland franchise, he was responsible for signing Larry Doby in 1948, the first black player to play in the American League. Before Doby's first game Veeck had his play/manager Lou Boudreau introduce Doby individually to each of his new teammates, three of those teammates chose not to offer Doby a hand to shake. Very soon after, those three were no longer Cleveland Indians. Veeck also signed Satchel Paige making the seemingly ageless hurler the oldest rookie in major league history.

Bill Veeck thought going to a baseball game should be fun and was an innovator when it came to promotions. While league officials frowned, the fans cheered the antics of Max Patkin, the "Clown Prince of Baseball" when he appeared in the coaching box at Cleveland's Municipal Stadium.

Veeck, who had lost a leg during the war, would self-promote by using his wooden leg as sight gag—after lighting a cigarette, he would roll up his pant leg and use the ashtray he had carved into the leg—but he never used the leg or the pain that accompanied his multiple surgeries, as an excuse.

It was Veeck's Indians that the Tigers pushed into a one-game playoff for the pennant in 1948, a game Cleveland won before dispatching the Boston Braves for their first World Series title since 1920.

After Veeck married his second wife Mary Frances Ackerman in 1950, he got back into baseball when he bought a majority stake in the St. Louis Browns in 1951. The Browns and the St. Louis Cardinals had shared Sportsman's Park—the Cardinals were the Browns tenants—for three decades but Veeck wanted the St. Louis market to himself and was hoping to drive the popular Cardinals out of town. Veeck hired former Cardinal greats Rogers Hornsby and Marty Marion as managers, and Dizzy Dean as an announcer and he decorated Sportsman's Park exclusively with Browns memorabilia. But the Browns were a bad team (58-96 in 1950) and Bill Veeck had to rely on something other than baseball to bring in the fans.

After a road trip that ended in Detroit on August 12, 1951, the Browns were 34-75 and in last place in the American League. Bill Veeck needed to come up with something to keep the fans coming to the ballpark.

After the Browns split a two-game series with Cleveland, Detroit was in town for a four-game series, including a Sunday doubleheader on August 19.

Detroit won the first game, 5-2, defeating the Browns best pitcher, Ned Garver. Detroit pitcher Gene Beardon scattered seven hits and Neil contributed a double and scored a run.

Between games of the doubleheader Veeck served cake and ice cream to the crowd and entertained them with an assortment of acts including the now-familiar antics of Max Patkin, the "Clown Prince of Baseball." The between game festivities concluded with the presentation of a giant birthday cake celebrating the American League's fiftieth anniversary. All at once a midget in a Browns uniform popped out of the cake. The crowd cheered as the 3 foot, 7 inch, Eddie Gaedel took a bow and showed off his 1/8 jersey number.

In the second game, the Tigers left two men on base in the first inning and didn't score.

In the Browns half of the first, outfielder Frank Saucier—making only the second start of his short career—was scheduled to leadoff against Detroit hurler Bob Cain. Frank Saucier could hit minor league pitching. In three minor league seasons, he batted .380 and was the minor league batting champion in 1949 with a .446 mark while playing for the Wichita Falls Spudders, the Browns B league affiliate. Saucier had quit baseball prior to the 1951 season after he struck oil in Oklahoma but was lured back by Bill Veeck and debuted on July 21.

While Detroit pitcher Bob Cain took his warm-up tosses, Saucier took his practice cuts in the on-deck circle. When plate umpire Ed Hurley signaled to play ball, Browns manager, Zack Taylor, called the surprised Saucier back for a pinch hitter. Out trotted Eddie Gaedel, number 1/8, all of a yardstick plus seven inches tall.

Bill Veeck had signed Gaedel to a major league contract for $100 a game and notified American League headquarters by telegram on Friday night, knowing there wouldn't be anyone there to read it until Monday morning.

Hurley consulted with crew chief, Joe Paparella, and after the Browns manager showed them a valid contract and a copy of Veeck's telegram, they had no choice but to let Gaedel bat.

During an impromptu meeting at the mound, while the umpires were determining that Gaedel was under contract,

Neil recalls Tiger catcher Bob Swift advising his pitcher to "try and keep the ball down" if they let Gaedel hit.

Gaedel was under orders from Veeck to leave the bat on his shoulder and under no circumstances was he to swing at a pitch. He also had Gaedel spread his feet and bend over making his already small strike zone even smaller. Tiger catcher Bob Swift tried his best to present a target for his pitcher but Cain was wary of throwing too hard and lobbed his pitches to Swift. Gaedel walked on four pitches and was immediately replaced with pinch-runner Jim Delsing. Gaedel walked back to the dugout while waving his cap to the cheering crowd.

Frank Saucier told The New York Times in 1991. "Eddie came back to the dugout and sat down beside me. I said, 'Eddie, you were kind of showin' it up a little bit there, weren't you?' 'Man,' he said, 'I felt like Babe Root.'"

Frank Saucier had one hit in 14 ABs in 1951. He served his country in the Korean War in 1952 and never returned to baseball. He was making too much money in the oil business.

Eddie Gaedel's line for the game and, as it turned out, his career: One Game, one Plate Appearance, 0 At Bats, 0 Hits, one Base on Balls.

Eddie Gaedel holds the record for the shortest man to ever play major league baseball. He is also tied with a number of others for the shortest career in major league history. The next day American League President Will Harridge, with the full support of the commissioner of baseball, voided Gaedel's contract and banned "midget" players from the game, determining that their continued participation "comes under the heading of conduct detrimental to baseball."

Bill Veeck mocked the decision by humorously demanding a ruling on whether New York Yankee shortstop Phil Rizzuto, at five foot six, was a short ballplayer or a tall midget. Ironically, despite the negative reaction to Veeck's stunt by

August 20, 1951 - Briggs Stadium, Detroit. In a game against New York Neil Berry tripled to centerfield off Yankee starter Eddie Lopat in the 3rd inning. Neil beat the throw from Joe Dimaggio to 3rd baseman Bobby Brown. Umpire Charlie Berry (no relation) is on hand to make the safe call.

AP Wirephoto from Author's collection

both leagues and the commissioner's office, it came at a time when owners feared losing their audience to the new medium of television and gave baseball a much needed shot in the arm. It got people talking about the game of baseball.

1951 was the last year that Yankee great Joe DiMaggio played. The Yankees' last series in Detroit started on August 20. In that game—a 6-3 Tiger win—Neil Berry was two for four including his first triple of the year.

Joe DiMaggio's last game in Detroit fell on August 22.

*August 20, 1951 - Briggs Stadium, Detroit. Neil Berry—
after hitting a 3rd inning triple—raced home on Par
Mullin's fly out. Yankee catcher Yogi Berra is late with an
attempted tag. Umpire Eddie Rommel makes the safe call.
The Tigers won the game 6-3.*

Photo from Author's collection

Neil Berry—with another triple—and Joe DiMaggio both
drove in two runs for their team in Detroit's 7-6, 12 inning
win. DiMaggio's final hit in Briggs Stadium was an eleventh
inning single to left field. DiMaggio's last-ever-out in Briggs
Stadium was a ninth inning pop up to Neil Berry.

Detroit was out of the pennant race and was destined to
finish in the second division but they did have an opportunity
to avenge last year's disappointment at the hands of the
Cleveland Indians, who knocked the Tigers out of the race

in the final days of the 1950 season. When Cleveland arrived in Detroit for a three-game series on September 21st, they were a half-game behind the American League-leading Yankees and had beaten Detroit in 16 of the last 17 meetings.

When the Indians left town after a three game Tiger sweep they were 2.5 games back and never recovered.

Detroit ended the disappointing 1951 season with a 73-81 record, 25 games behind the first place New York Yankees, and 22.5 games behind their 1950 club.

Neil Berry appeared in 67 games (starting 39) and posted a .229 batting average in 157 at-bats in 1951

.

The 1951 postseason featured three teams and they were all from New York. The Yankees prevailed in the American League but the Brooklyn Dodgers and New York Giants had to complete a three game playoff to determine the National League pennant winner.

On the last day of the season both teams won one run games to finish the regular season tied at 96-58. It had been predetermined that a first place tie would be played off in a three game series.

Game 1 at Brooklyn's Ebbets Field was the first game ever broadcast on the radio coast to coast. Bobby Thomas was the hero for the Giants with a two run homer in the Giants 3-1 win. The short series then moved to the Polo Grounds— the Giant's home park—for game two and, if necessary, game three. The Dodgers thumped the Giants 10-0 in game two to tie the series and make it one game for the pennant.

After seven innings game three was tied at one run apiece. In the top of the eighth the Dodgers got to Giant starter Sal Maglie for three runs on four hits, a wild pitch, and an intentional walk. With a 4-1 lead Dodger starter Don Newcombe got three straight outs in the bottom of the inning.

Brooklyn didn't score in the top of the ninth, but they had a three run lead and were three outs away from the pennant and a World Series matchup with the Yankees.

The Giants had other ideas. They were four runs away from a pennant, but had only three outs to work with. The first Giant batter against Newcombe in the ninth was Al Dark who reached on an infield single. Don Mueller followed with a single to right advancing Dark to third base. After a Monte Irvin pop up for the first out, Whitey Lockman hit a line drive double to left center field plating Dark to make it a 4-2 game and moving Mueller to third. With one out and men on second and third, Dodger skipper Chuck Dressen brought in Ralph Branca to face game 1 hero Bobby Thomson. On an 0-1 count Bobby Thomson hammered a low line drive to deep left field. The ball cleared the fence as Giants radio announcer Russ Hodges famously screamed, "The Giants win the pennant! The Giants win the pennant! The Giants win the pennant! The Giants win the pennant!" Hodges almost went hoarse shouting the legendary refrain a total of eight times but his unabashed excitement is part of the reason Bobby Thomson's pennant winning walk-off home run will forever be known as the "Shot Heard 'Round the World."

After their dramatic come-from-behind win in the National League playoff the Giants lost the World Series to the Yankees four games to two.

Neil Berry was up and I just fired my trouble ball—three in a row for three called strikes.

~ Satchel Paige

18

The Detroit Tigers

Detroit's First 100 Loss Season

1952

Detroit GM Billy Evans lost his job because of the club's dismal performance in 1951 as did farm director Ray Kennedy and club secretary Clair Berry.

Red Rolfe was retained to manage the 1952 squad, while new GM Charlie Gehringer went to work paring down Detroit's $552,000 payroll—the second highest in the league behind the New York Yankees.

On February 14, 1952, Gehringer made his first trade as Detroit's GM when he sent LHP Gene Bearden, LHP Bob Cain and 1B Dick Kryhoski to the St. Louis Browns for C Matt Batts, LHP Dick Littlefield, OF Cliff Mapes and 1B Ben Taylor. A lot of players changed uniforms but the trade was by no means a blockbuster. The Browns got the best of it when Bob Cain won 12 games in 1952.

Spring Training

On January 17, the Tiger ballclub mourned the passing of their owner, Walter O. Briggs, age 74. His son, Walter Owen "Spike" Briggs Jr., took over as franchise president. A month later head groundskeeper, Neal Conway, collapsed and died in Lakeland. Art Houtteman's wife and daughter were involved in a car accident on their way back to Michigan resulting in the death of his 7-month old daughter. These tragedies cast a pall over Spring Training in 1952 and foreshadowed a disastrous 1952 season.

Neil recalled, "Mr. Briggs died while I was still playin' for Detroit, then the young guy took over. I don't think he cared for baseball—it was something he inherited—the son, Spike they called him. Spike Briggs and everything changed. Inside the clubhouse changed. Little things changed. They used to buy all our sanitary hose, they never counted the towels [before], a lot of little things. Bats, you used to be able to order a dozen bats if you wanted to, not any more, not since Spike took over. It seemed like he tried to get rid of the team and the team played like that too."

Neil told the *Kalamazoo Gazette,* "I think my main asset to the Tigers at present is that during the four years I have been with them I've played short, second, and third. So instead of having to keep three utility men on the bench for those positions, they keep just one—me."

As far as Red Rolfe was concerned the starting shortstop job was up for grabs and would go to either Johnny Lipon or Neil Berry if either showed they could hit consistently. A sore arm at the start of spring training put Neil on the shelf for a time but when he got a chance he hit enough and displayed superior defense to once again supplant Johnny Lipon at shortstop.

After trading for Taylor, Mapes, and Batts GM Charlie Gehringer wanted to see them in the lineup.

THE 1952 SEASON

Manager Red Rolfe's batting order and starting lineup to open the 1952 season:

SS - Neil Berry

3B - George Kell

1B - Ben Taylor

RF - Vic Wertz

LF - Pat Mullin

CF - Cliff Mapes

C - Matt Batts

2B - Jerry Priddy

P - Dizzy Trout

Neil Berry started on opening day for the fourth time in five years. Back at shortstop, the job was his to lose and lose it he did. After six games with only two hits and a .133 batting average, Johnny Lipon started game seven.

The Tigers lost their first eight games—five on the road— to open the 1952 season before erupting for a 13-0 win over Cleveland. Art Houteman gave up one hit and a walk in the best pitching performance of the young season. Ted Gray followed that with a six hit, five walk, 1-0 shutout of the Indians to sweep the short two game homestand at Briggs Stadium.

Back on the road for nine games against Boston, New York, Philadelphia, and Washington, the Tigers lost six, won two, and tied one leaving them in last place with a 4-14 record.

Back home Detroit lost three of four to the White Sox and had split the first two games of the series against Washington.

Virgil "Fire" Trucks—looking for his first win of the '52

season—was scheduled to pitch the rubber match.

In 1950 a pulled tendon in his right arm limited Trucks to 48.1 innings and three wins before he decided to follow the doctor's advice and shut it down for the rest of the season.

Coming back from the 1950 season ending injury Trucks posted 13 wins with 89 strikeouts in 153.2 innings—including five complete games in his last six starts—in 1951.

After their disappointing 1951 season, the Tigers were counting on Trucks to help them rebound in 1952.

On May 15, 1952 while many Detroiters were downtown enjoying a parade for visiting General Douglas MacArthur, only 2,215 fans showed up for the Tigers game against the Washington Senators.

Virgil Trucks set the side down in order in the first inning. Bob Porterfield—pitching for the Senators—gave up a walk to George Kell but got out of the inning when Pat Mullin and Vic Wertz couldn't advance him.

In the second inning Trucks worked around Jerry Priddy's fielding and throwing errors to retire the Senators without a hit.

Trucks and Porterfield matched each other giving up no-hits and no-runs through five innings.

In the top of the sixth Trucks hit Jim Busby after two were out. He then picked Busby off first base, but Busby was safe at second on Priddy's third error of the day. Trucks got the final out stranding Busby at second base. Porterfield gave up the first hit of the game, a harmless two out single to Kell.

In the bottom of the seventh a Vic Wertz double was wasted when he was picked off second base.

In the top of the eighth Trucks gave up his only walk of the game but Washignton couldn't do anything else. Through eight innings Virgil Trucks had hit two batters and walked one, but hadn't given up a hit. Porterfield had given up three hits—including an eighth inning, infield single to Trucks—but hadn't allowed any runs.

In the top of the ninth inning Trucks induced a fly ball from Busby for the first out, a Jackie Jensen grounder to first base for the second out, then struck out Mickey Vernon.

Virgil Trucks pitching line after nine innings of work, 9 IP, 0 Hits, 0 Runs, 1 BB, 7 SO, but the game was still a scoreless tie. Vic Wertz took care of that with a two out, walk-off home run to deep right field to secure Truck's no-hitter and win it for the Tigers.

Virgil Oliver Trucks was born in Birmingham, Alabama on April 26, 1917. He was the fourth of 13 children with eight brothers and four sisters.

By the age of 10, Virgil was playing youth baseball, and advanced through the American Legion leagues during his high-school years as a strong-throwing infielder and outfielder.

He signed with the Detroit Tigers as an outfielder in 1937 but Detroit pigeon-holed the contract (a practice of not submitting contracts to major-league baseball) and didn't assign Trucks to a minor league affiliate so Trucks decided to play semi-pro ball, where he first tried his hand at pitching.

Trucks earned his "Fire" nickname in 1938 while pitching for the Andalusia Bulldogs. He also earned a reputation as a strikeout artist by setting a record for the most strikeouts in a season in Organized Baseball with 420. Trucks was 25-6 with a 1.25 ERA, and pitched two no-hitters for the Bulldogs.

After Detroit resecured their rights to Trucks he pitched his third no-hitter for the Tigers' Class A-1 Beaumont Exporters in 1940. After spring training in 1941 Trucks was optioned to the Buffalo Bisons where he led the league in strikeouts with 204.

Trucks made his major-league debut on September 27, 1941 at Briggs Stadium coming in in the top of the fifth inning with the Tigers down 8-4 to the Chicago White Sox.

Trucks gave up four hits and two runs and also allowed a Sox player to steal home (stealing home on a rookie while up 8-4? Must be the White Sox didn't read the unwritten rules).

Two months later, Pearl Harbor was bombed and Trucks wondered what was next for him and his baseball career. Trucks made the Detroit squad in 1942. He was inconsistent early but ended up leading the team with 14 wins and had a 2.74 ERA.

He topped that in 1943 with 16 wins and a 2.84 ERA in 202.2 innings pitched.

In 1944 Trucks enlisted in the Navy and pitched for Mickey Cochrane and Great Lakes Bluejackets, the best major league team not playing in the majors. Trucks won all four of his decisions; cumulatively, he was 10-0 with 161 strikeouts in 113 innings.

After aggravating an injured knee, Trucks was discharged near the end of the 1945 baseball season. After rehabbing his knee he met the Tigers in St. Louis to play the final two games of the season. The Tigers needed a win to secure the pennant and chose Trucks to start the first game. Trucks gave up one run on three hits in 5.1 innings. Hank Greenberg's grand slam with two outs in the ninth won it for Hal Newhouser in relief. The win made the second game against the Browns unnecessary.

In the World Series against the Chicago Cubs, Virgil Trucks—on the roster because returning servicemen could join their team at any point and still be eligible for the World Series—won game two with 4-1 complete-game victory. The Tigers prevailed in seven games over the Cubs to take the '45 World Series.

Trucks struggled to gain his prewar form, winning 14 games in '46, 10 in '47, and 14 in '48. He rebounded in 1949 with 19 wins, a 2.81 ERA after his best ever start to a season. He led the league with 153 strikeouts. Trucks attributed his success to new manager Red Rolfe and pitching coach Ted Lyons. He also pitched in, and won, his first All-Star Game.

Detroit followed Trucks no-no with a three game losing streak before winning five of nine to close out May.

On June 2nd, mired in last place at 13-27—10.5 games behind the league-leading Boston Red Sox—Detroit pulled the trigger on a blockbuster trade with Boston in an attempt to right the ship. The Tigers sent Johnny Lipon, Hoot Evers, George Kell, and Dizzy Trout to the Red Sox and received Pitchers Fred Hatfield and Bill Wright, Outfielder Don Lenhardt, Shortstop Johnny Pesky, and First Baseman Walt Dopro in return. This blockbuster trade shocked the baseball world as well as the players involved. The enormity of this trade is demonstrated by the fact that eight of the nine players in the trade were regulars for their team.

The key player in the deal for Boston was George Kell. The Red Sox needed a hitter to replace Ted Williams who had been called back to active duty in the Korean War. Kell, by his own admission, was no Ted Williams but he would be a solid bat in the middle of the Boston lineup.

The deal was actually completed very late at night on June 2. The teams agreed to announce the trade the next day. Detroit had just finished a series in Washington and Red Rolfe was responsible for telling the players about the trade on the train en route to Philadelphia where the Tigers were scheduled to take on the Athletics. That was fine for everyone but George Kell who drove with his wife from Washington to Philadelphia. George's younger brother, Everett "Skeeter" Kell was a rookie second baseman with the A's and their parents were in town to see their boys play.

Unable to get in touch with George, Dizzy Trout—just before he left for Boston—contacted Kell's brother and asked him to break the news. George Kell—who had hoped to finish his career in Detroit—was shocked, but he didn't let that affect his play for his new team.

Johnny Lipon—Neil's good friend, roommate, and competition for the shortstop position—was gone to Boston, but Neil Berry was still stuck in a utility role behind newly acquired veteran shortstop Johnny Pesky.

On June 9, 1952, without fanfare, the Tigers signed a 21-year-old shortstop out of the University of Wisconsin for $55,000. Harvey Kuenn, at 6'2, 187 lbs was not the power hitter his size suggested but the line drive hitter with doubles power convinced the Tigers to out bid 11 other teams for his services. Detroit assigned Kuenn to the Class B Davenport Tigers.

After Detroit's three games series in Philadelphia, the Tigers boarded the train to Boston. They stayed at the Hotel Kenmore in Boston a short five minute walk from Fenway Park. Only once during the five-game series did the Tigers return to their hotel as winners. Boston's George Kell was 9 for 18 at the plate for his new team.

After winning only 23 of their first 72 games the Tigers made another mid-season change when they fired Manager Red Rolfe and coach Dick Bartell on July 5th. Pitcher Fred "Hutch" Hutchinson was named as Rolfe's replacement.

There were very few bright spots for the Detroit organization or Tiger players in 1952. One of those bright spots came from first baseman Walt Dopro, one of five players acquired from the Red Sox. On July 14 Dopro had five hits—all singles—in five at-bats in an 8-2 Detroit win over the Yankees in New York. Dopro followed that with four singles in four at-bats in the first game of a doubleheader in Washington on July 15 making him nine for nine in his previous two games. In the first inning of the second game Dopro came to bat against righty Bob Porterfield with the bases full of Tigers. Dropo cleared the bases with a triple for his tenth consecutive hit. His eleventh consecutive hit was a single off of Porterfield in the top of the third.

Only two players in the game's modern era had ever connected for 12 consecutive hits. Cubs catcher Johnny Kling did it in 1902, and Boston third baseman Pinky Higgins tied Kling's record in 1938. Higgins had his 12 hits in 14 plate appearances with two walks mixed in during the streak. Walks do not count as an at-bat so his 12 hits in 12 at-bats qualified as consecutive hits.

Walt Dropo's next at-bat came with one out in the top of the fifth inning against lefty Lou Sleater who had relieved Porterfield. Dropo doubled to left field to tie the major league record for consecutive hits with 12. Dropo's chance to break the record came in the seventh inning but his foul pop fly landed in the catcher's glove instead of the seats and the streak was over. Dropo did add a ninth-inning single to finish 8 for 9 in the doubleheader. Before Dropo's hitting rampage he was batting .265. After 13 hits in 14 at-bats, his average stood at .296.

Only three players have come close to this record in the past 20 years. The Yankees Bernie Williams had 11 consecutive hits in 2002, a feat that Boston's Justin Pedroia matched in 2016.

Houston Astro Jose Altuve had 10 consecutive hits in 2018. Major League Baseball doesn't add asterisks to its record book but I'll add one to this book. *Altuve's hit streak came during the Astros sign-stealing shenanigans in 2017 and 2018. The Astros used a video camera in center field to capture the opposing catcher's sign to the pitcher. An Astro player or team staffer watching the live feed would then signal to their batter what pitch was coming.

That makes 12 hits in a row—without cheating—that much more amazing.

Neil Berry also had his best days at the plate for the 1952 season in July, on the road.

On July 16 at Griffith Stadium in Washington Neil had three hits—including a double—in 5 at bats with two runs scored and three batted in to lead the Tigers to a 9-0 win.

He followed that up on July 20 in the first game of a double header at Shibe Park in Philadelphia going three for four with a triple, two runs scored, and two RBIs in an 8-7 loss to the Athletics.

Detroit started August with two losses at home to the Boston Red Sox before Art Houtteman pitched a 6-0, four-hit shutout for his sixth win of the year on August 3. Neil Berry led the Tiger attack with an RBI triple and run scored in the first and an RBI single in the fourth. He also contributed a walk and a sacrifice bunt.

On Tuesday, August 5, the last place Tigers limped into St. Louis with a 36-67 record, 25 games behind the league leading Yankees and 5.5 games behind the seventh place Browns. There was no question that Detroit was going to finish in the second division. The only question to be decided for Detroit in the last 50 games of the 1952 season was if they would finish last or if they could overtake the Browns for seventh place.

Detroit's Ted Gray lost to Bob Cain and the Browns 5-1 on Tuesday but the Browns were starting Satchel Paige—a baseball relic at 46—on Wednesday. If the Tigers were looking forward to hitting against Ol' Satch, they shouldn't have been.

Leroy "Satchel" Paige—the seemingly ageless righthander who had pitched for more teams at every level than any player in history—was in his second year with the Browns in 1952. Bill Veeck first brought Paige to the big leagues with the Cleveland Indians in 1948 on his Paige's 41st birthday. He won six games for Cleveland that year helping the Indians win it all but Cleveland released Paige prior to

LeRoy "Satchel" Paige with Cleveland.

the 1950 season. Paige was out of the majors in 1950 but Bill Veeck gave him another chance with the St. Louis Browns in 1951. Satchel Paige was still a big draw and Bill Veeck needed to draw fans.

Satchel Paige's pitching heroics were established well before his belated opportunity in the recently integrated major leagues.

As a gifted young hurler Paige worked for a series of Negro League teams, starting with the Chattanooga White Sox—at the age of 20—and progressing to bigger, better clubs in Birmingham, Baltimore, Cleveland, Pittsburgh and

Kansas City. Drawing fans was crucial in the Negro Leagues and Satchel Paige was the biggest drawing card in the League. In order to be available for more games Paige was often pitched for only three or four innings before he was taken out. Too short an appearance to be credited with a win but long enough to be stuck with a loss. Best estimates of Paige's record in the Negro League is 103-61, with 1,231 strikeouts and 253 bases on balls.

The Negro Leagues had an off season—and off days—but many of the game's black stars—or entire teams—barnstormed across the country between games and seasons. One such barnstorming stop for the Kansas City Monarchs was Kalamazoo, Michigan on a Thursday afternoon in October 1941.

In anticipation of the upcoming game against city champion Sutherland Papers, the *Kalamazoo Gazette* reported that, "LeRoy (Satchel) Paige, the Negro Bob Feller, will be the feature attraction in what is Kalamazoo's biggest ball game since Paul Dean and the St. Louis Cardinals played here four years ago."

The Monarchs won, 6 to 3, over Sutherland. Paige pitched his customary three innings and gave up two runs and two hits, including a run scoring single to 19-year-old Neil Berry.

Eleven years later, on August 6, 1952, Satchel Paige—pitching for the St. Louis Browns—got a rare start at Sportsman's Park against the visiting Detroit Tigers. Virgil Trucks started for the Tigers and both pitchers were throwing a shutout through nine innings. Neil Berry had a hit and a walk off Paige in his first four plate appearances. His fifth time facing Paige came in the top of the tenth inning.

In his autobiography, *Maybe I'll Pitch Forever*, Satchel Paige told it this way:

"I got a little worried in the tenth, though. The Tigers loaded the bases on me with nobody out.

"They sent in Johnny Pesky to pinch-hit against me and

Johnny was one of those .300 hitters.

"Clint Courtney, my catcher, came out real fast. 'Be careful here,' he told me.

"'Ol' Satch knows when to be careful, don't you worry.'

"I was careful. I wanted this game. I'd pitched too many innings in it to give it away.

"I pitched my fast sinker and Johnny Pesky pounded it into the ground and we got a force-out at home plate.

"There was one out and no run in yet.

"Johnny Groth came up. I fired hard and low to him and he grounded into a force play at home plate, too. Two out and no runs in.

"'That's the way,' Clint yelled at me. 'We're almost home.'

"I figured we were home. Neil Berry was up and I just fired my trouble ball—three in a row for three called strikes. I was out of the inning without a run scoring.

"In the eleventh and twelfth I fired zeros at Detroit again and in the last of the twelfth we won it."

Satchel Paige hadn't pitched a complete game in the majors leagues since 1949. The 46-year-old Paige's pitching line on this August night, 12 IP, 7 hits, 0 runs, 2 BB, 9 SO. His "trouble ball" that he used to strike out Neil Berry was said to be so slow that hitters thought it may never arrive.

In 1952 Satchel Paige won 12 games against 10 losses with a 3.07 ERA in 138 innings pitched. Paige led the American League in games finished with 35 and had 10 saves.

Paige would pitch one more season with the Browns in 1953 before being released by the Baltimore Orioles prior to the '54 season.

Satchel Paige—at the age of 59—made his final appearance in the major leagues with the Kansas City A's in 1965. On September 25, with 9,289 in attendance at Municipal Stadium, Paige started against the Boston Red Sox. In his three innings of work he gave up one hit—a double to Carl Yastrzemski.

In 1971 Satchel Paige was the first vintage Negro Leaguer to be voted into the Baseball Hall of Fame.

Detroit won only 14 of their remaining 49 games after losing to Satchel Paige on August 6. The Tigers were swept by the Browns the next day then played the White Sox seven times in a row and lost six times.

A Sunday loss to New York at Yankee Stadium left the Tigers at 41-81 and 30 games behind the league leading Yankees.

The next day, Monday, August 25 it was Virgil Trucks turn on the mound in Yankee Stadium.

So far in the 1952 season Virgil "Fire" Trucks was either red hot—with a no-hitter, a 1 hit shutout, and two other wins giving up a run in each—or a smoldering ember, losing 15 games with little spark from his teammates.

On that Monday afternoon Trucks was up against the Yankees Bill Miller.

Miller started the game by striking out Johnny Groth and Johnny Pesky. After a walk to Fred Hatfield, Walt Dropo flew out.

After a Mickey Mantle popup and Joe Collins strikeout, Trucks worked around an error by his catcher, Matt Batts, that allowed a runner to reach, to get Yogi Berra on a fly to right.

In the second inning Miller gave up a single to Batts and Trucks retired the side in order.

The Tigers went down in order in the top of the third and Phil Rizzuto led off the bottom of the inning for the Yankees. Rizzuto hit a ground ball to Tiger shortstop Johnny Pesky.

Pesky fielded the ball but couldn't get a grip on it. By the time he threw to first base Rizzuto was called safe on a close play. The official scorer—the NY Times John Drebinger— scored it an error by the shortstop. Bill Miller successfully sacrificed Rizzuto to second base bringing Mantle to the plate with one out. Trucks walked Mantle before a ground out by Collins put Rizzuto and Mantle in scoring position on second and third base. Trucks struck out Hank Bauer to get out of the inning.

After Miller set down the Tigers in order in the top of the fourth Trucks took the mound to face Yogi Berra, Gene Wooding, and Loren Babe. Trucks noticed that the error on the scoreboard had been changed to a hit—the first of the game off Trucks—by John Drebinger, the official scorer.

What Trucks didn't see as he went about his business of retiring the Yankee batters, was the sportswriters in the pressbox getting on Drebinger for changing the error to a hit.

Trucks and Miller continued to battle—each man with a single hit against—through six innings.

Meanwhile, Drebinger decided to reconsider his error-turned-hit call and went to the source. Drebinger called down to the Detroit dugout and spoke with Johnny Pesky. Did the baseball stick in your glove—justifying a base hit— or did you mishandle it for an error? Pesky assured him that he mishandled the ball for an error and Drebinger was satisfied.

In the top of the seventh inning Detroit got to Miller with a Dropo double and a run scoring single by Bud Souchock to take a 1-0 lead. Trucks got the Yankees in order to end the seventh.

In the eighth Miller gave up a walk and single but got out of the inning when Trucks was thrown out at the plate.

When Virgil Trucks came out for the bottom half of the eighth inning the scoreboard had been changed to reflect the scoring change. The third inning Rizzuto hit was changed back to a Pesky error and Trucks realized he was now throwing a no-hitter. Trucks struck out Billy Martin then got a pop up and fly ball to end the eighth.

In the Yankee ninth Trucks got Mickey Mantle (strike out), Joe Collins (line out to CF), and Hank Bauer (ground out 2B to 1B) to end the game.

During the worst Detroit season on record Virgil Trucks reclaimed his fire long enough to pitch his second no-hitter of the 1952 season.

Trucks finished the '52 season with five wins and 19 losses. In his five wins he pitched 43.2 innings and gave up two runs (.41 ERA). In his 19 losses he gave up 85 runs in 153.2 innings (4.99 ERA).

Before Trucks accomplished the feat, Johnny Vander Meer—in consecutive games—and Allie Reynolds were the only pitchers to throw two no-hitters in the same season.

The trades, a new manager, Dropo's hit streak, and Trucks two no-hitters ultimately didn't help.

Detroit finished last and ended the season a whopping 45 games behind the first place Yankees who won their fourth straight World Series in seven games over the Dodgers.

The 1952 Detroit club won only 50 games, while losing 104—the first time ever that the Tigers lost 100 or more games. They finished a distant 14 games behind the seventh place St. Louis Browns.

Art Houtteman—back from Korea—won nine games but led the league with 20 losses.

Hal Newhouser—after accepting a 25% pay cut—made 19 starts in 1952. He went 9-9 with a 3.74 ERA, and eventually lost his starting spot to young Billy Hoeft. Newhouser's final victory of the season on September 25—a six hit, eight strikeout complete game against the Browns—was the 200th win of his career. It turned out to be his last as a Tiger.

Harvey Kuenn—after hitting .340 in 63 games with Davenport—was called up on September 6. Detroit manager Fred "Hutch" Hutchinson liked what he saw and started Kuenn at shortstop—moving Pesky to second base—in 19 of Detroit's 20 remaining games. In those 19 games Kuenn only struck out one time in 85 PA while compiling a .325 BA

Maybe Hutch had a hunch about Neil Berry's future when he penciled Berry's name on the lineup card at shortstop for the final game of the 1952 season. In the season finale at Briggs Stadium against the Cleveland Indians Neil was 3 for 5 at the plate—raising his season average to .228—with a run scored and an RBI. It was the last game in a Tiger uniform for the shortstop from Kalamazoo.

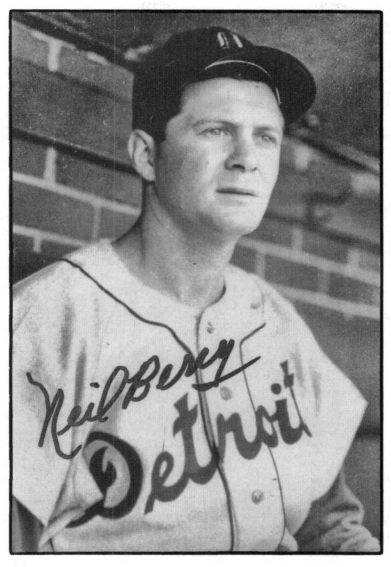

You've gotta get the breaks, you gotta be in the right place at the right time. When Charlie Maxwell signed with Boston, Ted Williams was playing left field. What chance is Charlie going to have to play left field? You have to get traded, you have to get with another ball club.

~ Neil Berry

It may be a good break to get away from Detroit where I've been classed as a utility man.

~ Neil Berry

19

Traded to the Browns

St. Louis Browns & Chicago White Sox

1953

After Detroit's disastrous '52 campaign house cleaning was in order. On October 27, 1952, Neil Berry was traded by the Detroit Tigers along with Outfielder Cliff Mapes and $25,000 to the St. Louis Browns for slugging Outfielder Jake Crawford. Crawford led the Eastern League with 27 home runs in '52 and appeared in 11 games for the Browns in September. The trade didn't pan out for Detroit, those 11 games Crawford played with the Browns was ultimately his entire major league career.

In December Detroit released Bob Swift and traded Johnny Groth, Virgil Trucks, and Hal White to the St. Louis Browns for infielder Owen Friend, leftfielder Bob Nieman, and catcher Jay Porter.

In January Don Kolloway was traded to the Philadelphia Athletics.

The Tiger's 1953 team didn't have a single starting position player that was a member of the 1950 squad that came close to winning the American League pennant. They did have some pitching left from that near-championship club with Art Houtteman, Ted Gray, and Hal Newhouser, but Houtteman—along with catcher Joe Ginsberg—were traded away in June.

Detroit would field a different team of veteran players in 1953 but did have 22-year-old Harvey Kuenn at shortstop and an 18-year-old kid fresh out of Southern High School in Baltimore. Al Kaline debuted on June 25, 1953. The player that would come to be known as, "Mr. Tiger" had seven hits in 28 AB in 1953. One of those hits was off the St. Louis Browns' Satchel Paige.

Veteran lefty, 32-year-old Hal Newhouser only made it into seven games for Detroit in 1953. He was 0–1 with a 7.06 ERA when Detroit released him on July 22.

Newhouser considered himself retired but former Tiger teammate Hank Greenberg—part-owner and GM and of the Cleveland Indians—offered him a chance to make the '54 club as a reliever. Newhouser accepted Greenberg's offer and helped Cleveland to their legendary 111 win season. Pitching primarily in long relief, Newhouser won seven games and saved seven others, posting a 2.51 ERA in 46.2 innings pitched.

Hal Newhouser made two appearances in 1955 before he retired from his playing career. Newhouser remained in baseball for several decades working as a scout for the Orioles, Indians, Tigers, and Astros.

THE ST. LOUIS BROWNS

The Browns won the American League pennant in 1944 when many of the league's top players were in the military during World War II (Detroit won under the same circumstances in 1945). The Browns lost the '44 World Series four games to two to the National League's St. Louis Cardinals, their rival for baseball supremacy in St. Louis.

In the post-war years through 1952, the Browns were firmly entrenched in the American League's second division. With 94 losses they finished in sixth place in 1948, finished last in 1947 and 1951, and finished seventh in '46 with their high-water mark in wins at 66. The Browns also finished seventh in '49, '50, and in 1952 when they finished 14 games ahead of the Detroit Tigers.

During this period being traded to the often cash-strapped Browns was like baseball purgatory—you were still in the major leagues but your career was on the downswing. Bill Veeck—who purchased the Browns in 1951—couldn't afford to field a competitive Browns Team with dwindling attendance due to their own mediocrity and the popularity of the Cardinals. Brown players that were having good years and up-and-coming minor league talent were often traded to contending or rebuilding teams for cash and journeyman players.

After the rival Cardinals were purchased by St. Louis-based brewery Anheuser-Busch in 1952, Bill Veeck realized he would not win the franchise battle to have the Browns be the only team in St. Louis. Veeck started looking into his options for moving the Browns but didn't formally announce that the '53 season would be the last season for the Browns in St. Louis.

In preparation for moving the Browns, Veeck also sold Sportsman Park—owned by the Browns, rented by the Cardinals—to August Anheuser "Gussie" Busch Jr. who renamed the park Busch Stadium prior to the 1953 season. Bill Veeck still held out hope that the American League

owners would approve moving the team to Baltimore—
with Veeck owning a controlling interest—and held on to
the $800,000 he got for Sportsman Park to set up the new
franchise.

Neil Berry looked at his trade to the Browns as an
opportunity. Neil told the *Kalamazoo Gazette*, "If I could get
away to a good start and have a good year, it could mean a
lot to my baseball future. It will be something different, a
challenge. Really, I'm eager to get going and see what I'll be
able to do."

Writing about the '53 Browns upcoming spring training
in San Bernardino, California, the *Kalamazoo Gazette*
reported, "[Berry] joins a squad that numbers nine other
ex-Tigers on its roster ... Pitchers Bob Cain, Dick Littlefield,
Marlin Stuart, Virgil Trucks, and Hal White, Infielder Dick
Kryhoski, and Outfielders Johnny Groth, Don Lenhardt,
and Vic Wertz.

The Gazette opined, "Neil won't be lonely, but he has a job
cut out to grab off an infield spot, and he's played everything
but first base."

Spring Training

The St. Louis Browns spring training was held in San
Bernardino, California in 1953, 2200 miles from Kalamazoo.

As Neil told it, "Vic Wertz called me and said I'm gonna buy
a new Pontiac and I'm gonna drive it to Riverside, California.
That's where we had spring training that year. That's where
we lived, at the Mission Inn in Riverside, but the ball field
was in a little dinky town near there (San Bernardino). It
took us about a half-hour to get there, from the Mission Inn
to the ball field. Every morning we took a bus over there.
Anyway, he said I'm coming through Kalamazoo, do you
want to ride with me to spring training? What we're gonna
do is, I'm gonna pick you up in Kalamazoo and were gonna
go to Chicago and pick up Johnny Groth and Dick Kokos—
he's an outfielder—and the four of us will go in my new

Pontiac to Riverside.

"Everything was fine, we were having a lot of fun but we got into [New Mexico] about nine o'clock in the morning—the sun had come up of course—and it started getting dark, sorta dark and dusky. So we stopped at a gas station—it was a convertible by the way—and made sure the top was all buttoned-down and stuff and the guy says there's a dust storm comin'. [It was] noon [when] we stopped in this little town—it was right after lunch—we couldn't see anymore. It was pitch dark at mid-day, that's how black it was. We asked the guy [at the gas station] where a hotel or motel was. We couldn't see nothin'. We [asked] about one of the guys taking the car and cleaning it because even though the top was buttoned down it was still sandy inside. You started to chew it when you talked. It was pitch black and I mean just as black as midnight with no stars or moon or anything. When you're out in the desert there's no lights. All the cars had stopped. We happened to be in Clovis, New Mexico. I can remember that particular night we didn't know what the hell we were gonna do. We can't just sit here and twiddle our thumbs and we knew damned well if we started drinking beer that's not gonna be good. So we got to the hotel and started asking questions and guess what—they were having the state basketball championship that night. Two Indian schools from reservations were playing basketball in town that night, so we went to the basketball game."

The guys made it to the Mission Inn without further incident but Vic Wertz's brand new Pontiac convertible showed signs of wear from the dust storm they passed through.

During spring training the guys woke up one morning to find snow on the ground. According to Neil, "it had snowed like a son of a gun. Vic Wertz and I were eating breakfast and waiting for the bus thinking we had the day off. After breakfast, the bus was there. Where we goin'? We're goin' to the ball field. Gee, we can't go there, [the] snowflakes

March 7, 1953 - St. Louis Browns Training Camp, San Bernardino, CA. Neil Berry shows off his whirl-and-throw double play form for the camera man.

Photo from Author's collection

[were] as big as silver dollars.

"The *Sporting News* had a picture of a snowman the guys had built at the ball field. We played ball there that afternoon at four o'clock. The sun came out, the snow melted, it was a little damp but we played an exhibition game against—I forget who it was."

Satchel Paige—with 12 wins and 10 saves in 1952—was still a big draw and would be on the '53 roster regardless of what he did in Spring Training.

From his autobiography, *Maybe I'll Pitch Forever*:

"I went back to spring training . . . and I got there just in time to go to San Francisco for an exhibition game. Man it was cold there. Before the game, Marty Marion told me to warm up.

"'It's too cold for that,' I told him.

"'But I got you scheduled to pitch here, Satch, and you got to pitch. You'd better warm up.'

"That's what I did. I went into the clubhouse and got warm. Then I came out.

"'I'll take three throws now and we can start,' I told Marty.

"I tried it a few innings and it was so cold I couldn't get my hand in my glove.

". . . Marty pulled me. 'Maybe since you're out of the game you'd like to go over and give that young kid some pointers?' Marty asked me, pointing to a rookie we had on our club.

"'I like to help those young men,' I said, 'but I've been carryin' youngsters like them so long I think I'll have to put 'em down.'

"'Why do you keep pitchin' then?' Marty asked me.

"''Cause of money and women," I said.

". . . Marty didn't ask me any more questions that night."

The young rookie pitcher Satchel Paige declined to carry on that cold day in San Francisco could well have been the 25-year-old lefty that the Browns purchased from the Brooklyn Dodgers in February for $50,000. Tommy Lasorda won 14 games with a 3.66 ERA for the AAA Montreal Royals in 1952 but—unlikely to crack Brooklyn's roster in 1953—was expendable.

Tommy Lasorda was heartbroken to leave the Brooklyn organization that he thought of as family. He was also astonished when he learned that someone was willing to pay fifty grand to get him.

Lasorda pitched well enough in spring training to earn a spot with the Browns but there was a problem. On the train ride east Bill Veeck informed Lasorda that he couldn't afford to pay Brooklyn the $50,000 so he was returning him to the Dodgers. The Dodgers sent him back to Montreal where he had his best year yet winning 17 games.

In his three year major league playing career—with Brooklyn ('54 and '55) and Kansas City ('56)—Tommy Lasorda appeared in 26 games, pitched 58.1 innings, and did not record a win but he was destined to have a Hall of Fame career as the manager of the Los Angeles Dodgers. In his twenty one years at the helm for the Dodgers, Lasorda was twice manager of the year, won four NL Pennants and two World Series titles. He was inducted into the Baseball Hall of Fame in 1997.

On March 25 the Browns signed free agent third baseman Bob Elliott.

Neil reminisced, "It was quite an experience I had that spring training. I didn't play much baseball, none of us did cause we didn't have a very good team. We played everyday but we didn't do too good but we had a lot of fun and a good bunch of guys. We had Bob Elliott. He was a good ballplayer. In fact, I think in 1946 in the All-Star game or World Series—

he played for Pittsburg at that time—he was Most Valuable Player."

Bob Elliott was a six-time All-Star during his career—three times with Pittsburgh ('41, '42, '44) and three times with the Boston Braves ('47, '48, '51)—and was the National League MVP in 1947.

Prior to the start of the season the Browns and the Cardinals played a three-game "City Series" in the stadium they shared.

"We played the Cardinals [and] we beat 'em two out of three in the city series. They had a lot better team than we did, but anyway we had Satchel [Paige] and I guess they always had a banquet at the Chase Hotel—which is a big hotel in St. Louis—and they wouldn't let him in. We said if you don't allow Satchel—because of the color deal—you're not gonna get any Browns. Evidently they had a meeting and 'that's ok, he can come.' So he was there and we had a good banquet."

THE 1953 SEASON

Neil Berry's utility player tag stuck and that was his role when the Browns opened the 1953 season versus the Detroit Tigers at Busch Stadium on April 14, 1953. The Browns Virgil Trucks—with the help of former Tigers Johnny Groth and Vic Wertz—shut out the Tigers in a Browns 10-0 win in front of 11,804 fans.

After the home opener, the Browns hit the road for a series in Chicago, Detroit, and a single game in Cleveland. The Browns split two games with the White Sox before sweeping three games from the Tigers at Briggs Stadium. The Browns 5-1 start in 1953 had them all alone in first place. A loss in Cleveland left them tied with the Yankees for first place on April 23rd.

Neil Berry got into his first game as a St. Louis Brown— as a defensive replacement at third base—on April 25th in a loss to the Chicago White Sox. The loss knocked the Browns out of a third-place tie with the Sox.

Neil recalled, "[Bob Elliott] was a big guy. They called him 'Sarge.' He and I hit it off together and we became good friends. We went out to dinner a lot, in fact we went across the bridge [to East St. Louis] so much that the guy takin' the toll just waved us through. He knew we were ballplayers.

"But anyway, we'd take Satchel's jeep. He bought a regular Army Jeep—Army surplus—he bought one of those and had it painted pure white. Then someplace he bought two horns this long (Neil indicated how long)—air horns for semis—and mounted them on the front of that Jeep. He'd blow that horn, you'd look around, it sounded like a semi on the highway but it was Satchel in that white Jeep. He'd blow it so hard [that Jeep] almost went backwards.

"We're sittin' in St. Louis one day and Bob Elliot said, 'you like ribs?' Yeah. 'how 'bout you and I take Satch's jeep and get some ribs.'

"Bob was a good enough friend, he'd say, 'How 'bout borrowin' the jeep tonight?'

"Satch said 'go ahead.'

"Elliott would say, 'Well you better let us use it because if you drive it you're gonna ruin it because you can't drive.' Ol' Satchel, he'd say, 'Shee—it'

"Elliott would say, 'You can't. Every time you come in here I'd ask how'd you do today Leroy, cause you can never stop, you're always bangin' into a guy.

"They used to get on each other like that.

"Anyway, Satchel'd give him the keys. So we took that thing—this place was still in St. Louis but it was in a bad part of town—and we pulled up down there, parked a little ways from it and walked back. It was a small—maybe 30 ft. front—restaurant. Walked in and the tables were like card tables with checkered tablecloths. I'd say the whole place had eight or nine tables, then they had booths along the side. Along the back was a big pit where they were grillin', you could see it.

"So we sat down and here comes this real fat colored gal. She got from about here to there from us and she turned 'round and went back to the kitchen. She came back out with a stack of small autograph books. She said, 'I knows you's ballplayers, which one is which?' We told her we were with the Browns. There it is (the Browns autograph book). She had other ones she showed us. She had presidents, movie stars, ballplayers, football players, basketball players in these books. She had teams and she had the Browns, and sure enough there were a bunch of guys in it and we signed it for her.

"She asked us what we'd have, we said ribs. We got a plate of ribs and a beer for just a couple bucks and the ribs, so many of 'em that they hung over the edge of the plate. God were they good.

"I don't know why I didn't gain more weight because I could eat pretty good."

On May 5, the 9-9 Browns were in sixth place, a half-game behind the White Sox, and one game behind the fourth place Philadelphia Athletics. Then, on a rainy night in Busch Stadium—in front of only 2,473 fans—Browns rookie right-hander Bobo Holloman made history.

Alva Lee "Bobo" Holloman broke into professional baseball with the Chicago Cubs organization in 1946 and worked his way through the minors including a stint at the Cubs' Double-A affiliate, Nashville Vols. It was in Nashville that the "Bobo" nickname stuck when the Vol's owner remarked that Holloman reminded him of American League All-Star pitcher, Bobo Newsom.

The Cubs gave up on Holloman and he eventually landed

with the Syracuse Chiefs (unaffiliated) of the International League in 1952.

During the '52 season, Holloman was 16-7 with a 2.51 ERA in 183 innings pitched. He pitched 12 complete games in spite of losing a month when he had an appendectomy. He allowed the fewest hits (123) of any pitcher in the International League that year.

In October 1952 Syracuse traded Bobo to the St. Louis Browns and he made the '53 club at age 30. Browns Manager Marty Marion had Holloman slated for relief duty. He made his major-league debut on April 18, one of six pitchers that followed starter Don Larson—also making his major-league debut—in an 8-7 Browns victory over Detroit.

Holloman wasn't effective coming out of the bullpen. In his 5.1 innings in April Bobo allowed five runs on 10 hits and his ERA stood at 8.44. Despite his slow start Bobo considered himself a Starting Pitcher and lobbied his manager to give him a start. Marty Marion finally relented, Bobo Holloman would start his first major league game on May 6, 1953, against the Philadelphia Athletics.

What played out that day was one of the most unexpected pitching performances in Major League Baseball history. Bobo Holloman—in the first start of his major league career—pitched a no-hitter. No one in the modern era (since 1901) had pitched a no-hitter in their first start, and no one has done it since.

Holloman's game was far from perfect. Six batters reached base, one on his own error on a ground ball in the fifth inning, the others on walks. Three of those walks occurred in the ninth inning when Bobo—likely feeling the pressure of the situation—walked the first two hitters he faced. He was saved by a 2B–SS–1B ground ball double play that advanced a runner to third base with two out. Bobo then issued his third walk of the inning before a fly ball to deep right field ended the game and wrote Bobo Holoman's name in the record book.

Almost as improbable as Holoman's pitching performance was his hitting. Bobo was two for three—both singles—with three RBIs.

Holloman won two more games in ten starts in 1953—his only year in the majors—and his two hits and three RBIs were the only ones of his short major league career.

Bobo's no-hitter is the only one ever pitched in Busch Stadium—home to the Browns and Cardinals in 1953, and home to the Cardinals until 1966.

Alva Lee "Bobo" Holloman's improbable pitching performance on May 6, 1953 will be forever known in St. Louis Browns' baseball lore as "Bobo's No-No."

Bobo Holloman wasn't the only pitcher on the Browns roster that would have an inconceivable pitching performance during their career.

Don Larsen was 15 years old when his family moved to San Diego in 1944. Don attended Point Loma High School where he became a star in basketball and baseball. He declined offers to play college basketball but when Browns scout Art Schwartz offered the 17-year-old right-handed pitcher an $850 bonus Larsen signed with the St. Louis Browns.

Larsen was sent to Aberdeen in the Class-C Northern League where he pitched two seasons for the Pheasants. He won 17 games in 1948 and was promoted to the Globe-Miami Browns in the Class-C Arizona-Texas League to start the 1949 season. He was promoted to Class-B Springfield midseason. In 1950 he played for the Wichita Indians in the Class-A Western League.

In 1951 Larsen, 22, was drafted into the U.S. Army where he spent two years during the Korean War in a Special Services unit at Fort Shafter, Hawaii playing baseball. Larsen was discharged in 1953 and went to spring training with the

San Antonio Browns. After pitching well for San Antonio he was promoted to the major-league Browns.

The 23-year-old Larsen stood 6-feet-4 and weighed 215 pounds when he made his major-league debut on Saturday, April 18, 1953, in the first game of a doubleheader against the Detroit Tigers at Briggs Stadium. Larsen pitched shutout ball for five innings before the Tigers got to him in the sixth, scoring three runs to take the lead. Browns manager Marty Marion used six relief pitchers—including Bobo Holloman and Satchel Paige—to secure an 8-7 Browns win and a no-decision for Larsen.

Neil recalled, "In St. Louis one day [St. Louis Browns coach, Bill Norman] asked me if I wanted to do him a favor, he had [catcher] Clint Courtney and he had [another catcher he didn't want to use], 'I gotta get somebody to warm up a guy down in the bullpen, he wants to try a [new] pitch.' He was just a coach at the time—Marty Marion was the manager—Bill was just a coach, but it was his job to take care of this guy.

"The guy wanted to work on a slider. He doesn't know how to throw a slider. He knows how but he's just gotta practice. Will you take him down in the bullpen and catch him for 15 or 20 minutes. So I did. [Don Larsen] was a big guy, about six-four, he had a good arm, pretty good pitcher, but he was straight as a string and didn't have anything else, but he developed."

Don Larsen finished his 1953 rookie season with the Browns with a 7–12 record, 4.16 ERA, and 96 strikeouts in 38 games, 22 of them starts. Larsen beat the New York Yankees with a four-hit complete game on September 17. Larsen also had two saves in '53 including a two inning save on September 22 to secure the great Satchel Paige's last major league win.

After the Browns relocated to Baltimore for the 1954 season, the Orioles lost 100 games and Larsen led the league in losses with 21. He only won three games, but two of them were against the Yankees, impressing Yankees manager Casey Stengel. Larsen was acquired by the Yankees as part of a 17 player trade in 1955.

Larson was 9 - 2 with a 3.06 ERA in 19 games—13 starts—for the Yankees in 1955. In his only World Series start against the Brooklyn Dodgers that year, Larson gave up five runs in four innings—including home runs to Roy Campanella and Gil Hodges—and took the loss.

During the 1956 season, Larson started 20 games and appeared in 18 others, going 11 - 5 with a 3.26 ERA. The Yankees again faced the Dodgers in the World Series and Don Larsen started game two at Ebbets Field. Larsen was wild—four walks and hit in 1.2 innings—giving up five runs. Due to an error with one out in the second, all the runs were unearned. He ended up with a no-decision after a total of seven Yankee pitchers—including Larson—gave up 11 walks, 12 hits, and 13 runs in a 13-8 Dodgers victory.

Nothing Don Larson did in the regular season or in his previous World Series performances hinted at what he would do on October 8, 1956, in game five of the 1956 World Series.

With the series tied at two games apiece, the Dodgers called on game one winner, right-hander Sal Maglie. Maglie won game one 6-3, scattering nine hits and four walks while striking out 10 Yankees in a complete game performance. He did better than that in game 5—another complete game—when he allowed only two runs on five hits, but this day belonged to Don Larson.

Don Larsen beat Maglie and the Dodgers that day when he pitched the only perfect game in World Series history. He never waved off his catcher Yogi Berra, and only needed 97 pitches to dispatch the National League champions. The Dodgers came close to getting a hit in the second inning when a hot shot ground ball off the bat of Jackie Robinson deflected off the glove of third baseman Andy Carey to shortstop Gil McDougal. McDougal fired the ball to first baseman Joe Collins who kept his foot on the bag while stretching to catch the ball. The throw nipped Robinson by a half step.

A perfect game is defined as a game in which a pitcher (or combination of pitchers) pitches a victory that lasts a minimum of nine innings in which no opposing player reaches base. Thus, the pitcher (or pitchers) cannot allow any hits, walks, hit batsmen, or any opposing player to reach base safely for any reason. Fielders cannot make an error that allows an opposing player to reach a base. Perfect is 27 up, 27 down. There have been only 23 perfect games in Major League Baseball history.

After the Browns unexpected 5-1 start to the season, and the improbable Bobo's No-No, the Browns—with a 10-9 record—would not be over the .500 mark again during the 1953 season.

Neil Berry got his first starts in a Browns uniform on Sunday, May 24 playing both halves of a doubleheader. In the first game Neil had an RBI triple off Early Wynn for the Browns only run in a 5-1 loss to Cleveland. In the second game Neil was three for five with a double and a run scored. The Browns scored eight runs but Bob Cain and Don Larsen gave up nine runs on 10 hits and six walks.

Neil started for the third game in a row the next day against the White Sox. He drove in two runs but the Sox prevailed 7-5. Neil also started the second half of doubleheaders on May 30 and May 31. In his five May starts Neil was batting .368 with a double, two triples, three runs scored, and four RBIs but Manager Marty Marion chose not to start Neil for the next eight games.

Neil started the second half of a doubleheader on June 10, and after going two for four was batting an even .400 for the season. At the end of the day the seventh place Browns were 19-33, 19.5 games behind the league leading Yankees, and seven games ahead of last place Detroit.

The Browns were living game-to-game, paycheck-to-paycheck, and with the mounting losses came dwindling attendance. To keep the club afloat Bill Veeck sold his Arizona ranch and also sold players that played well enough to arouse interest from other clubs.

On June 12 the Browns sold Willy Miranda to the New York Yankees. The next day they traded Bob Elliott and

May 17, 1953 - Yankee Stadium, New York. Browns' Neil Berry scores from second on Clint Courtney's pinch hit single in the 10th inning. Catcher Ralph Houk waits for the throw. The Umpire is Eddie Hurley. The Yankees scored two in the bottom of the 10th to win 6-5.

New York Mirror Staff Photo from Author's collection

Virgil Trucks to the Chicago White Sox for Darrell Johnson, Lou Kretlow and $75,000.

On July 23, eleven weeks after pitching a no-hitter, Bobo Holloman was sold to Toronto (International League) for $7,500.

Neil appeared in 57 games—including 23 starts—for the 1953 Browns.

Reflecting, Neil said, "I don't think I had a very good shot—in the big leagues—as far as building up a batting average. It takes a little time and [that's] the worst thing in the world for an 'in case man'—that's what we called 'em—in case someone drops dead you get to play.

"A utility infielder, all you do is sit on the bench until the seventh, eighth inning, then, anyone see where my glove is? Why? You're goin' in as a pinch runner or to play for somebody. You got everything to lose and nothing to gain.

"A lot of times you don't get any times at bat. All you can do is make an error and lose the ball game. You go in to play defense—they got you just to play defense—and when you can't play defense you ain't worth a damn. If you happen to get a hit, that's fine but they don't put you in there for that."

Neil came off the bench to pinch run and/or play defense 34 times. In those 34 appearances—games he didn't start—Neil had a single AB in seven games, two AB in two other games, and one game with three AB. He had 2 hits in those 14 scattered AB for a .143 batting average.

In the 23 games Neil started he had 26 hits in 85 AB for a .306 average.

Neil Berry didn't like Browns' manager Marty "Mr. Shortstop" Marion. Maybe the feeling was mutual and led to Neil only starting 23 games, or maybe only starting 23 games—while batting over .300—was why Neil disliked Marion. In any case Neil's spot on the bench was a warm one as he watched the Browns lose. They were consistent losers against the top division with identical 5-17 records against

New York, Cleveland, Chicago, and Boston. The only team the Browns beat consistently during the '53 season was Detroit, going 15-7 against the Tigers. In their last year in St. Louis the Browns were a dismal 54-100 and finished last in the American League.

The last game Neil Berry started for the Browns in '53 came in Chicago against the White Sox on August 19. Going into that game Chicago manager Paul Richards—Neil's manager in Buffalo—had the Sox in second place 7.5 games behind the first-place New York Yankees.

Neil had a good game that day at the plate going 2 for 5 with a walk raising his season average to .286. He started a double play and turned another from his second base position in the field. The Browns won 4-3 in 10 innings.

CLAIMED BY THE WHITE SOX

On September 1, 1953, Neil Berry was selected off waivers by the Chicago White Sox. On September 8, the St. Louis Browns purchased Johnny Lipon from the Boston Red Sox to fill the roster spot created by Neil's departure.

As Neil told it, "Paul Richards was managing the Chicago White Sox, and he knew about me [from] when I played for him in Buffalo, and at that particular time the White Sox were [eight and] a half games outta first place with the Yankees, and he had nobody on his team, the White Sox, who could play second, short, or third, which I had played all three positions. So he made a deal with Bill Veeck who was the owner of the St. Louis Browns. If he could get me on a lend/lease basis—if I could go to Chicago and play for the White Sox, cause I could play all three positions [and] they had no one, and they were in a battle for the pennant—if I could come there with the stipulation I could go back to the St. Louis Browns the next season, that was fine. So I go to the White Sox and play.

"Minnie Miñoso was there but he wasn't playing third base, Bob Elliot was playing third. Miñoso was a hell of a ballplayer. He could go like hell, he had a good arm, and he was a scrapper."

Cleveland owner Bill Veeck originally signed Orestes "Minnie" Miñoso in 1948. After dominating performances for San Diego in the Pacific Coast League in 1949 and 1950,

Miñoso made the Indians squad out of spring training in 1951. Although Miñoso could play multiple positions he couldn't crack Cleveland's veteran starting line up.

On April 30 the win-now Indians traded Miñoso to the Chicago White Sox in a three-team trade that also involved Philadelphia.

When Miñoso took the field at Comiskey Park on May 1 against the New York Yankees it was the first time a black man wore a Chicago White Sox uniform. Miñoso wasted no time winning over the fans when he homered in his first at-bat off the Yankees Vic Raschi.

Before long Miñoso was the toast of the town. Whenever Miñoso reached base, the Comiskey Park crowd would chant, "Go! Go! Go!" Sox fans even gave him his own day later that season, marking the first time the White Sox had ever honored a rookie in this manner.

For the 1951 season Miñoso hit his way to a .326 average, second in the American League, and ran wild leading the league in triples (14) and stolen bases (31). He made his first of seven appearances in the All-Star Game and was second—behind the Yankee's Gil McDougald—for Rookie of the Year honors.

The White Sox now had a top-of-the lineup hitter to pair with emerging star Nellie Fox and the Go-Go Sox that would challenge the Yankee dynasty throughout the '50s—and win the pennant in '59—were starting to take shape.

In the mid-1950s Latino players were still a novelty in the big leagues. In a game against the Yankees, Casey Stengel had a Latino player—utility infielder Willie Miranda—curse at Miñoso, hoping to distract him when he was up to bat. Miranda, with a menacing pose, let fly a barrage of *curse* words that only he and Miñoso understood. Miñoso played along, shaking his fist at Miranda and replying in an equally intimidating tone, he accepted Miranda's dinner invitation for later that night. Miñoso then hit a game-winning triple.

Minnie Miñoso played for 17 seasons in the major leagues—11 with the White Sox—but his career numbers, .298 batting average, 1136 runs, 186 home runs, and 1023 RBIs, did not earn him a spot in the Baseball HOF.

Thought by many to be among the best baseball players not enshrined, Miñoso was also passed over by the Committee on African-American Baseball, a special panel formed to open the Hall of Fame to overlooked and underappreciated stars of black baseball.

The White Sox did honor Miñoso by retiring his number 9 in 1983 and erecting a statue of him outside their park.

Concerning his first encounter with Miñoso when he joined the White Sox, Neil related, "When I checked in there, I emptied my bag out in front of my locker, Miñoso was a couple of lockers down from me, and he looked and he started laughin'. A guy says what you laughin' at and he says, 'small feets.'

"Me, you lookin' at my shoes?—which were only size five—and he says, 'Nobody steal your shoes, you got small feets.'"

"When I got to Chicago, Paul Richards said, 'If I see you tryin' to swing for a home run I'm gonna kick you right in the ass.' What do you mean? 'I don't want you swingin' for the fences, I want you to hit the ball like Nellie Fox.'

"[Nellie Fox] wasn't that good of a second baseman. He was a pretty good [fielder] but he couldn't throw. I found that out just by listening to the guys when I joined the club. [At second base] you could knock the ball down, it could hit you in the chest and you could pick it up and still throw a guy out. He was a good little ballplayer but what he did with the bats, he got himself what they call a bottle bat."

In the spring of 1951, the Chicago White Sox were training

in Pasadena, California where second baseman, Nellie Fox, was trying to earn a spot on the 1951 squad. The left hand hitting Fox was also experimenting with a shorter, thicker, "bottle" bat at the urging of Chicago hitting coach, Doc Cramer, and manager, Paul Richards. Fox, at 5' 10" and 160 pounds (similar in size to Neil) showed a lack of power in 1950— .247 average, no home runs, 30 RBIs in 130 games— but he had a knack for making contact, striking out only 17 times in 457 ABs.

With the bottle bat, Cramer was able to get Fox to quit trying to pull the ball and he soon started lining the ball to all fields. Winning a roster spot and the starting second base job, Nellie Fox had a breakout season in 1951 and would go on to a Hall of Fame career.

"Richards thought you could develop that so he made me buy a dozen of those bottle bats. It didn't work. You practice all your life a certain way . . . this just felt so odd."

Neil appeared in five games in September for the White Sox. He had one hit in his eight at-bats and played error free defense in his three starts at second base.

Chicago didn't catch the Yankees and was overtaken by Cleveland to finish in third place.

For the fifth year in a row the New York Yankees won the World Series again beating the Brooklyn Dodgers.

For three seasons and part of a fourth, three different Detroit managers had Neil Berry and John Lipon in a revolving door at shortstop hoping one would hit enough to claim and hold the position. The trade that brought Johnny Pesky over from Boston settled the issue for the remainder of the '52 season but the 33-year-old Pesky was nearing the end of his career. If the Tigers were looking to Pesky to bridge the gap until Harvey Kuenn was ready they didn't need to worry. There was no gap left to bridge.

After Kuenn's September performance in 1952 he made the team at shortstop during the spring of 1953. There was no need for Harvey Kuenn to look over his shoulder. He hit .309 in April and never looked back. At the end of the 1953 campaign Kuenn led major leagues in PA (731), AB (679)—an American League record—and hits (209) on his way to a .308 average. Kuenn was selected to play in the All-Star Game (1st of eight appearances) and won Rookie of the Year honors in the American League.

Harvey Kuenn was a fixture at shortstop for Detroit for the next four years. Between 1952 and 1955 Kuenn started 365 games in a row with the only exception being the last game of the '52 season when Neil Berry started.

Kuenn was moved to the outfield in 1958. After adjusting to his new position he won the batting title in 1959. His .353 average that year was 27 points higher than second place finisher Al Kaline. In 1960 the Tigers were looking for more power and traded Harvey Kuenn to the Cleveland Indians for Rocky Colavito and his league leading 42 home runs. The trade—finalized two days before the start of the 1960 season—was the only time the batting champion was traded for the home run champion.

The United States avoided a larger war with Russia and China—and possibly WWIII—when an armistice was reached with North Korea in July 1953, but not before some 5 million soldiers and civilians had lost their lives in the Korean war.

We played a couple of exhibition games against the Japanese team. The first ones to come over here to play. They were good students, eager to learn.

~ Neil Berry

20

Traded to the Orioles

Baltimore Orioles & Kansas City Blues

1954

Bill Veeck attempted to move the Browns from St. Louis, to Baltimore after the 1953 season while retaining principal ownership but he was blocked by the other owners. It soon became apparent the owners—many of whom were angry about the midget he signed and other publicity stunts he pulled—would not approve any deal that kept Bill Veeck in a controlling role.

Neil played for Veeck's Browns for most of the 1953 season and recalled, "Bill Veeck was a nice guy. He wanted to do the best he could 'cause he was a promoter. A lot of the things he wanted to do didn't fit in with the other guys, the old owners. It was a hobby to them, it was their little babies— their ball team—they didn't wanna exploit them.

"[Veeck] wanted to make money out of [his team] like it

was the fourth of July all the time. God, the things he used to do. [After the first game] you'd walk out of the clubhouse, go down the runway, come up out of the dugout and what the hell's happening? There's no infield there, it's covered in plywood. The whole field is covered in plywood hooked together underneath for a basketball game—the Harlem Globetrotters. They put two baskets up and they played 20 minutes or so between halves of a doubleheader. First you got a doubleheader, then [between games] the Harlem Globetrotters are playin' basketball against the Boston Whirlwinds, then they'd have fireworks afterwards. This all in one night."

Neil also recalled that, "Bill Veeck sure had a beautiful wife—nice girl—[she] used to sit down and drink a beer with the guys in the tavern. When do you get that from the wife of the owner? At the motel they had beautiful big bar and the guys'd be settin' in there and she'd come in, 'Hey, you mind if I have a beer with you guys?' and sit down and drink a bottle of beer with the guys. That's pretty nice and made the family look good [but] Bill would [jokingly say], 'Hey, what you guys tryin' to do?' But he was a nice guy, a real—to me—a guy's guy."

Bill Veeck finally accepted his alienation by the other owners and sold his share of the Browns to a group of investors with Baltimore businessman Jerold Hoffberger— brewer of National Bohemian beer—being the largest shareholder. The American League owners approved the sale of the team and then approved the move to Baltimore.

When Browns moved to Baltimore they were renamed the Orioles. The name change was intended to distance the new franchise from the Browns' history.

Other teams that relocated in the 1950s retained their nickname in order to maintain a sense of continuity with their past including the Brooklyn/Los Angeles Dodgers; the New York/San Francisco Giants; the Boston/Milwaukee/Atlanta Braves; and Philadelphia/Kansas City/Oakland Athletics.

The new Baltimore Oriole franchise started making moves to further distance themselves from the Browns.

November 1953 - Released Manager Marty Marion.

December 1953 - Traded LHP Bob Cain (4-10, with 6.23 ERA for the Browns in '53) to the Philadelphia Athletics for veteran RHP Joe Coleman and unproven LHP Frank Fanovich.

February 1954 - Released Satchel Paige who—at 46-years-old—pitched 117.1 innings in 1953.

Prior to the start of the 1954 season Baltimore also released or traded away LHP Harry Brecheen (5-13 with a 3.07 ERA), Roy Sievers (.270 BA in 92 games), and Jim Dyck (.213 BA in 112 games).

In an unrelated transaction Joltin' Joe Dimaggio—two years removed form his Hall of Fame career with the Yankees—married America's sex symbol, the blond bombshell Marilyn Monroe on January 14, 1954.

Still on their honeymoon in February, they stopped in Korea so Marilyn could entertain the troops. She did 10 shows in four days for more than 100,000 vocally appreciative soldiers.

Back at their hotel room Marilyn excitedly told her husband, "Joe, it was wonderful. They loved me. You've never heard such cheering."

An amused DiMaggio—a nine time World Series champion—replied, "Yes, darling, I have."

Ultimately the timing was off for the two American icons and the Dimaggio/Monroe marriage only lasted the equivalent of one baseball season. They were divorced in October, 1954.

Neil Berry was hoping to stick with the White Sox in 1954 and play a full season under his favorite manager, Paul Richards. Instead—on February 5, 1954—he was traded by the Chicago White Sox along with Outfielder Sam Mele to the

Baltimore Orioles for Outfielder Johnny Groth and Infielder Johnny Lipon, both former Detroit Tiger teammates.

Baltimore Orioles Spring Training

Neil recalled, "The only thing I didn't like at that time, Jimmy Dykes became the manager of Baltimore. When [the Browns] went to Baltimore they hired Jimmy Dykes. I didn't like Jimmy Dykes' attitude. He was an old-timer and everything was, 'that's not the way we did it.' He didn't give a crap because that was gonna be his last year as manager.

"The first thing he did in Spring Training he split the squad—took all the old guys and let them work out in the morning—and took all the younger guys in the afternoon, which is a crock of crap.

"He wasn't a mixer, he kept aloof with the guys. One of the old-timers, Jimmy Dykes was a third baseman I guess [but] he wasn't a good manager, didn't care if you won or lost. I didn't like that."

Jimmy Dykes was an old-timer. His major league career began in 1918 for Connie Mack's Philadelphia Athletics. He played second and third base for the A's for 15 years then— following the 1932 season—Mack sold Dykes (along with Al Simmons and Mule Haas) to the Chicago White Sox for $100,000. Dykes was a player/manager for the White Sox until 1939—his last year playing—and was manager until the team lost 20 of their first 30 games in 1946.

Major league baseball was still five years away from racial integration in 1942 but Dykes allowed two black players to try out for the White Sox. He was particularly impressed with one of the players but ultimately didn't make either player an offer. Had he signed the 23-year-old black kid that had so impressed him, Jackie Robinson would have been under contract to the Chicago White Sox four years before he was signed by Brooklyn's Branch Rickey.

Dykes took over for Connie Mack—the long-time manager

of the Philadelphia Athletics—after the 1950 season. He managed the A's for three seasons before he was let go after a seventh place finish in 1953. The Browns-turned-Orioles wasted no time in tapping Dykes as their manager for 1954.

"We went to Yuma for spring training with Baltimore. Anyway the manager said he wanted some guys so he picked—he didn't pick the best ballplayers, don't get me wrong—he picked a team to go to L.A., Los Angeles. At the time it was the Cubs [AAA team] called the Los Angeles Cubs. That's where all the Hollywood stars go, that's their home team. Anyway [we went there] to play three days of benefit games for some kids deal in Hollywood.

"Jimmy Dykes was our manager. Why he picked me, I don't know. Anyway I went to play an all-star team from around that area. Los Angeles, San Diego had a couple of kids, anyway a good team to play. Our team was of course all from the [Orioles].

"We played there then we played a couple of exhibition games against the Japanese team. The first ones to come over here to play. They were good students, eager to learn.

"It was funny because they came over here to learn baseball and they had about five or six guys, between innings, they just stayed out there. One by third base, one by second, like the umpires. They'd be near them with clipboards and if somethin' happened—and we did a couple of things to try to unnerve them you might say—you had to go out and explain it to them. Like faking a guy off third base to see if the pitcher would balk. He did. He stopped his motion and stepped back off—uh, time, what?—he scored [from third base]. Once [the pitcher] starts his motion he can't stop, you've gotta go through with [the pitch].

"It was a lot of fun and the way those guys were so attentive. Fundamentally, they were coming along pretty good but they were never gonna be good outfielders because they can't throw that good, [not] like our guys. The infielders, they could run and throw but the outfielders lacked that strong arm.

"The funny part was the Japanese guys are not very well endowed, physically, if you know what I mean. We had a catcher named Babe Martin—Boris Martinovich actually—who was a catcher quite a long time in the big leagues, and he was hung like a horse. We noticed because we all used one big shower room at the clubhouse. We were just waiting there smoking cigarettes and watchin', watchin' these little Japanese guys while our guys would come in and flip their towels off to go naked into the shower, and watched [their reaction]. We said, 'wait 'till Babe Martin comes in . . . here he comes.' the Japanese guys almost jumped off the floor when they saw him."

THE 1954 SEASON

"We had a wonderful inaugural, opening day in Baltimore. They had four or five hundred thousand people, the whole town turned out, lined the streets, and my God the girls in the third and fourth floors in the buildings, confetti, and the streets were lined triple deep. They treated us like kings.

"In Baltimore, two of the best roomies you could have, Vic Wertz and Vern Stephens, the three of us got an apartment. Two nice guys and they accepted me as a little pea-head and we got along fine—ate together, drank beer together, and got a car from the owner together.

Concerning Jimmy Dykes, Neil said, "I didn't like his attitude, he wasn't gonna play me anyway. I got to play a couple of games or something. We had a terrible team—we had some good ballplayers—I don't think he was a good manager, that's all."

Jimmy Dykes managed one season in Baltimore and presided over a team that won 54 games and lost 100.

In 1960 Jimmy Dykes was managing the Detroit Tigers and—on August 3—was involved in one of the most bizarre trades in major league history. The Detroit Tigers traded their manager, Jimmy Dykes, to the Cleveland Indians for their manager, Joe Gordon. No players or future considerations were involved. It was straight up manager for manager, Dykes for Gordon.

In five games and 10 plate appearances for the Baltimore Orioles, Neil Berry had one hit and a walk. He played flawless defense handling 13 chances without an error.

Traded to the Yankees

On May 11, 1954, the Baltimore Orioles traded Neil Berry with Jim Post (minors) and Outfielder Dick Kokos to the New York Yankees for Infielder Jim Brideweser.

"So we started the season there and I played, then they made a deal with the Yankees and, I forget how many guys went, but I was traded to [Yankee farm team] Kansas City, which at that time was in the minor leagues—triple-A—the American Association. They had a pretty good team there, four or five guys made the majors."

In 1954 the Blues were the American Association defending

Neil moved around a lot in 1953 and 1954, playing for the St. Louis Browns, Chicago White Sox, Baltimore Orioles, and Kansas City Blues.

Photo courtesy of Linda Spann

champs having won the pennant in 1952 and 1953. Neil Berry was expected to take over for Brideweser at shortstop for the Blues but as reported by the *Kansas City Star*, "just before leaving Baltimore he was struck on the right shoulder by a ground smash off the bat of Philadelphia's Bill Renna. By the time he arrived in Kansas City he was unable to throw." Neil was taken off the active list and recuperated at home. He rejoined the Blues on June 14, and was batting .273 after seven games at shortstop. Then a leg injury sidelined Neil again. The injuries caused Neil to contemplate retirement but he played out the season. The Blues finished 68-85 and in seventh place. 1954 was their last year in Kansas City.

"So I finished the season with Kansas City. In the minor leagues, your season ends about September twelve. In the big leagues, they don't end until October first or second. I'm through with my year at Kansas City and I was told that they wanted me to go to New York.

"Well, I knew enough about baseball after all this time, I wasn't eligible for the World Series. You had to be on the team by a certain date, on the parent team by a certain date to be eligible to play in the World Series. I wasn't [on the team by that date], so I'd play until the end of the season then I'd go home and they'd play in the World Series. So I said, 'No, I don't want to do that.' They said, 'What are you gonna do?' I said, 'My season's over. My contract called to finish the season at Kansa City, right?' Yes. 'I think I can go home and I can fish for two or three weeks and you still have to pay me, because my contract was originally with Baltimore, you have to pay me another two, three weeks. Why should I go to New York and work for nothin' you might say, I'm already gonna get paid, but I can't play in the World Series. I can't get any cut of the World Series [money]. If I coulda got a cut of the World Series I might've done it.'

"So I said I'm goin home. [They said] 'You can't do that.' I said, 'Watch me.' I came home.

Neil was right about the timing. He would not have been

on the Yankees roster in time to be considered for their World Series roster and wouldn't have received any share of the World Series money. The Yankees had played in the five previous World Series so it made sense that Neil would have considered the World Series aspect when he contemplated the possibility of being called up in 1954. As it turned out the Yankees won 103 games in 1954—more games than any of the previous five years—but came in second to the sensational Cleveland Indian team that won 111 games.

"I found out later on that the old manager, before Casey Stengel, before World War II, the Yankees had a manager who lived just outside of Buffalo. One of their famous managers (Joe McCarthy), he used to come to the games in Buffalo all the time, when I was playing in Buffalo and watched me play. He recommended that the Yankees buy me. [I guess] he liked the looks of me, I don't know, but I still didn't want to go to the Yankees. I didn't want that, so that was it."

Neil chose not to play out the rest of the season with the Yankees, an opportunity that may have allowed him to demonstrate that he could still play major league defense and show off his speed. If he hit at all during a brief stint with the Yankees he may have raised his trade stock for 1955 but—at this point in his life—Neil had other priorities.

"Underneath it all, about the middle of the season, I often laid awake nights thinking to myself, 'my little wife is home taking care of Skip, all by herself, with another little girl, Linda, all by herself. I don't think that's fair.' So I say, 'that's enough, I'm not gonna put her through that anymore.'"

Neil Berry's refusal to report to the New York Yankees at the end of the 1954 season was the end of his professional baseball career. He left without regret and on his own terms, but the Yankees hadn't given up on Neil just yet.

After the 1954 season the Kansas City Blues moved to Denver. The 1955 Denver Bears owned Neil's contract and wanted him to report to spring training.

The *Kalamazoo Gazette* reported, "Denver carried very few players over from the Kansas City Blues when the franchise shift was completed, and Berry was one of them. He can play almost any position in the infield and the Bears still consider him a valuable asset. Berry wonders why their contract offer didn't match their apparent desire for his services."

Neil asked Denver to release him so he could play semi-pro ball with the Ausco's team in St. Joseph, Michigan. Denver refused to release Neil and put him on the restricted list when he didn't show up for spring training.

"So . . . I stayed home and at the end of the year, they said, 'well, now do you want to go to spring training [next year] with Ralph Houk?' [Houk] who later became manager of the Yankees, was managing Denver. Denver, at that time, belonged to the Pacific Coast League, which was triple-A, which was good. 'He would like to have you come and play in Denver.' I said 'no, I'm not gonna go, I wanna stay home with my wife.'

"Well, I stayed home and this, that, and the other thing, and the season, just before it started, I got a telephone call [from the Yankees], 'If we send a scout to Kalamazoo, to talk to you, would it do any good to talk to you, and you might wanna sign?' [I told him] you can send him to me if you want to and he said, 'okay, we're sending Mickey Cochrane.'

"Mickey Cochrane used to be a catcher for Detroit, who was now working for the Yankees. He was working for the Yankees and he's a Hall of Famer for the Tigers. He said, 'He will be in Kalamazoo and he'll meet you in the bar at the Burdick [Hotel] at two o'clock.' Well, I knew who he was because I belonged to Detroit all these years before and he was a big star when I was a kid [and he was] playin' for Detroit. Well, I thought that would be pretty nice meeting Mickey Cochrane, one-on-one, so I went down there, and when I got there Mickey wasn't in too gooda shape. That's all I'm gonna say, but I know it wasn't the ice cubes. He said,

'Neil, we'd like to have you come and play in Denver.' I said, 'I don't want to, I'm gonna stay home.' He said, 'We can do this, and we can do that, and the Yankees might call you up.' I said, 'I don't want to.'

"He said, 'Where do you want to go?' I [told him] there's one place, I talked it over with my wife, there was one place I would have gone, possibly, San Diego (in the Pacific Coast League). [San Diego] was managed by a friend of mine, and had four or five players on the team that I had played with, good friends.

"The Pacific Coast League, at the time, was the only league in baseball that had an unlimited pay scale. All the other ones had a limit, you could go so high and that was it. We had guys in the Pacific Coast League making more money than guys in the big leagues. That was the place to play [minor league ball] in those days. Now Denver dropped out of that league. Well, Denver was a little off the beaten path as far as the Pacific Coast League. All the teams on the Pacific coast were in California and up the coast. So the deal there was you played five days or six days in a row and then you got a day off every week, to travel. And they flew all the time in California, so if we were playin' in San Diego, we'll say, and the next game was in L.A., how long does it take to fly from San Diego to L.A.? You're there in no time. So everybody wanted to play in the [Pacific] Coast League, the weather was beautiful, you had beautiful ballparks, you had an off day, good playing conditions. San Diego is the only team that I would have possibly gone to."

Another reason players liked the Pacific Coast League (PLC) was the controversial "no-draft" clause. Unlike any other minor league, a player in the PLC could elect to sign the no-draft clause to waive the possibility of being drafted by a major league team.

In the July, 1952 issue of *Sport* magazine, Kevin "Chuck" Connors said, "By signing the 'no-draft' clause I can help determine my immediate future and my post-baseball career, which is of vital importance, too.

Connors explained, "I enjoy making all sorts of public appearances. Since I'm now exempt from the major-league draft, local organizations can count on scheduling me months in advance. These appearances help swell my bank account. One of my routines is 'Casey at the Bat.'"

Neil was well aware of the benefits of playing in the Pacific Coast League, "A lot of guys made some good contacts there. Look at [the TV series] *The Rifleman*, he was just a damned first baseman for Chicago for a year or so, went to a banquet and recited 'Casey at the Bat,' the next thing you know he's in the movies."

Chuck Connors was originally signed by the Brooklyn Dodgers in 1940 and was sold to the Chicago Cubs in 1950. He appeared in 66 games at first base in 1951 for the Cubs, but only hit .239. Connors signed with the Los Angeles Angels of the PCL in 1952.

Connors, at 6'5", was one of a very few ballplayers who played both major-league baseball and pro basketball (with the Boston Celtics in 1946-47). He quit baseball after the 1952 season to concentrate on his acting career. His best known role was Lucas McCain in the TV show *The Rifleman*, which ran for five years, from 1958 to 1963.

Neil had no intention of going into show business, but the weather and playing conditions in the Pacific Coast League were enough to keep Neil in the game a little longer.

"So, I told [Mickey Cochrane] I'd like to go to San Diego, and he said, 'we'll see what we can do.' I said, 'okay, you see what you can do.'

The Yankees got back with Neil to let him know they were unable to trade him to San Diego. It seems the Yankees wanted too much money or talent in return. That was the spring of 1955 and was Neil's last opportunity to play professional baseball. His professional playing days were over; he knew it and now the Yankees knew it too.

I'm taking over a team who was so far in the basement you gotta look up to see the bottom.

~ Neil Berry

21

Berry Replaces Rowe

Managing the Montgomery Rebels

1958

After his major league playing career was over, Neil Berry was living on Inkster Avenue in Kalamazoo with his wife, Gloria, their kids Neil Jr. (Skip) and Linda, and Gloria's father.

Neil played semi-pro ball and softball, and—along with ex-pro Jim Mellinger who played for the St. Louis Cardinals, New York Yankees, St. Louis Browns, and Baltimore Orioles—owned Sportsland, a sporting goods store located in the Portage Plaza.

Neil's brother Carl was still a Captain in the Army Air Corps in 1956 when he stopped by for a visit. Neil recalled their conversation, "Carl said he finally got a deal, 'I'm gonna get stationed near home, O'Hare field in Chicago.'

"I said, 'What are you gonna do there?' [He told me] they have a couple of squadrons there that fly out of O'Hare to the [Soo] locks.

"He was a Flight Leader and he would take a young, new guy up to go through whatever they had to go through, then they'd come back to O'Hare."

On October 10, 1956 two U.S. Air Force F-86 Sabre Jets collided over Lake Michigan. The Lake freighter S/S Ernest T. Weir rescued one of the pilots after he spent three hours in the water. Several other ships in the area participated in an unsuccessful attempt to locate the second pilot.

As Neil told it, "I had a sporting goods store at that time in Portage. Two guys come in one day—pulled a staff car in front of the store—they came in, 'you Neil Berry?' Yeah. 'We have some bad news. Your brother just went down in Lake Michigan. We can't find him.'

"He was flying' with this kid and I don't know what the kid did but they said the kid zigged when he should have zagged and smashed my brother right in the cockpit and he couldn't get out. The kid got out."

The sporting goods store was doing well and Neil enjoyed talking baseball and other sports with everyone who came through the door.

Then as Neil told it, "In 1958 I got a telephone call and it's Detroit. And it's an old guy (Bill Norman) who was a coach at St. Louis [when I played there], who was now the manager of Detroit, and he said, 'Neil, how would you like to manage?' And I said, 'where Bill?' He said, 'Schoolboy Rowe is managing Montgomery, Alabama but he's sick. He's sick and we need a guy to manage. How'd you like to manage Montgomery?' I [told him] yeah, that might be fun.

'How about your wife?' I know Gloria, she'd follow me right down there, kids and all. So he says, 'I'll tell ya what. You get your stuff together, get yourself on a plane, and get down there to Montgomery cause [Schoolboy] doesn't feel too good.'"

Lynwood Rowe and Cornelius Berry shared a January 11 birth date with Rowe being 12 years Berry's senior. Lynwood picked up the nickname, "Schoolboy" and pitched in the major leagues for 15 years. Cornelius was dubbed, "Connie" before his sister-in-law asked the Detroit Tiger announcer, Harry Heilmann, to please call him Neil.

Lynwood "Schoolboy" Rowe compiled a lifetime record of 158 wins against 101 losses. He pitched in three World Series and was named to three All-Star teams. His best year was 1934, winning 16 consecutive decisions en route to a 24-8 record and 3.45 ERA for the Detroit Tigers. In Game 2 of that year's World Series, he retired 22 consecutive batters en route to a 12-inning, complete-game victory over the St. Louis Cardinals. In Game 6, Rowe pitched another complete game but was outpitched by Paul "Daffy" Dean and took the loss. St. Louis won the series four games to three over the Tigers. Rowe finished fourth in the American League's 1934 Most Valuable Player voting behind teammates Charlie Gehringer and the winner, Mickey Cochrane. In 1935, Schoolboy Rowe won 19 games with a league-leading six shutouts and was selected for the American League All-Star team. The Tigers won their second consecutive American League pennant. Rowe posted 2.51 World Series ERA but lost both of his starts. He did win Game 3 in relief of Elden Auker and Chief Hogsett and the Tigers took the series four games to two over the Chicago Cubs.

Schoolboy could also hit. He had a .303 batting average with eight doubles, two home runs, and 22 RBIs in 1934. In 1935, he hit .312 with three home runs and 28 RBIs. In his 15-year big league career, Rowe had 153 RBIs and hit eighteen home runs, good for 14th best in major league history for a pitcher.

Rowe was dominant for the Tigers again in 1936, with 19 wins, but in 1937 and 1938, arm trouble limited him to 31 and 21 innings.

Schoolboy mounted a comeback and his 16 wins and 3.46 ERA helped the Tigers win the 1940 pennant. Rowe finished seventh in that year's AL MVP vote but had an abysmal World Series, getting clobbered in both his starts. The Tigers lost the series to the Cincinnati Reds in seven games.

Detroit sold Rowe to the Brooklyn Dodgers in 1942, and after winning only one game, he was sold to the Philadelphia Phillies in 1943. Finding his old form, Schoolboy compiled a 14–8 record and a 2.94 ERA for the Phillies and finished fourteenth in the National League MVP voting. Like many players, Rowe served in the military during World War II and missed the 1944 and 1945 seasons, and like many of the game's stars, he kept playing baseball. Schoolboy was assigned to the Great Lakes Naval Training Station where his former teammate, Mickey Cochrane, put together an All-Star baseball team that included Schoolboy, Bob Feller, Johnny Mize, and Billy Herman. Schoolboy pitched and played the outfield while leading the team with a .446 batting average. In 1944 the Great Lakes team won 48 games and lost only 2, going 11–1 against major league competition. In 1946, fresh off two years of military baseball, Rowe returned to the Phillies in top form. He won eleven games that year and posted a career-low ERA of 2.12. Another good year in 1947 earned Schoolboy the last All-Star nod of his career. The Phillies released Schoolboy Rowe after the 1949 season and he finished his pitching career in 1950, in the Pacific Coast League, with San Diego.

After Schoolboy Rowe's playing career ended, he was a coach and scout for the Detroit Tigers and in 1958 he was managing their class D farm club, the Montgomery Rebels of the Alabama-Florida League. The Rebels were not a good baseball team at the beginning of the '58 season and the best Schoolboy could do was coax them to 10-17 start before he became too ill to manage.

Neil Berry had not crossed paths with Schoolboy Rowe until he took over as manager of the Montgomery Rebels in May 1958, less than three years before Rowe's death at age 50.

"So I get out to the airport here and I get on a plane. I had to go to Detroit. Well, the plane from here—I don't even remember what that was—but I get into Detroit and they've got a great big one and I flew to Cleveland, [then on] a little smaller one, from Cleveland I flew down to Atlanta, a little smaller one, and I land someplace. You know by the time I got to Montgomery I was in like a piper cub.

"I finally got to Montgomery. So I got there and of course, I called [home], 'everything is fine, yeah, but I've got a terrible team, honey. Where they got these guys I don't know. I think they're 13 games in the basement and I haven't even started yet.'

"Well, Schoolboy Rowe was there when I got there and he said, 'Neil, I feel sorry for ya.'

"Boy that's nice, he feels sorry for me. He's going home to his wife and I'm taking over his team who was so far in the basement you gotta look up to see the bottom. So I take over and we work out and I say to myself, 'Where in the hell did these kids learn to play ball like that. They can't do anything.'

"I got a telephone call from my little girl and she says, 'we're comin down.' I said, 'you are?' 'Yep' 'When?' 'Quick as I can get this thing packed up.' Well, we had a brand new little Oldsmobile 88, a brand new little sucker, it was silver with a black roof. By God, in a couple of days, here she pulled into the ballpark down there with that nice little car, the little shit drove that thing all the way down there with two kids and the whole back end full of stuff. I said, 'you make it all right?' 'Why sure. What do you think, I can't drive?' She was a good driver.

"I had a nice air-conditioned apartment. In fact, it wasn't an apartment, it was a little house behind another house and it was very nice. About two or three blocks from the ballpark, nice neighborhood, and so we stayed there all summer. The kids liked it. It was just so hot that if you didn't have air conditioning you were gonna die. It was cool enough at night to play ball, it was all night games. It was a nice ballpark and she came to all the games with the kids. They ate peanuts and popcorn, and watermelon, and we stayed there all season.

"That's where Linda (Neil's seven-year-old daughter) says, 'Hey Dad, you know what Mr. Morris told me?' Mr. Morris was the groundskeeper, he was head of the grounds, the baseball field and across the street, the football field where they play the Senior Bowl.

"'You know what Mr. Morris told me?' They had gone over to his house to swim in their pool,

'[He told me] don't you ever call them colored people because they're n_ _ _ _rs (n-word). Is that right Dad?' I said, 'no, don't do that.' 'Why?' What am I gonna tell her? I said, 'well, it's not nice to do that.' 'Okay.'

"That's the way they thought about it. He was a nice guy, Sam Morris was, but he was born and raised in Montgomery."

Back to baseball, Neil explained, "So I was lucky that in June I got six or seven, maybe more [new players], they only allowed 16 on the team there, I got about half of them All-American kids from college. I got a couple from Florida State, I got one from Tennessee, I got one from Alabama, I got another from Auburn, [so] I had a pretty good nucleus, in June. That's the time they say they start shaking the leaves in these teams up here. In other words triple A, double A, [single] A, B, C, D, they start shaking the tree and what falls off goes to the next league [down]. So we got some kids from a higher league to come down. I got a couple of pretty good kids there. We were so far back [but] we missed the playoffs by a game. From then on through the rest of the season, we missed the playoffs by one game and I thought I did pretty good."

In 1958 Neil Berry managed the Montgomery Rebels to a 55-44 mark but couldn't overcome their 10-17 start under Schoolboy Rowe. Montgomery's 65-61 record was good for fifth place, nine games back of league champion Selma Cloverleafs, and 3.5 games out of fourth place and qualifying for the playoffs. The Rebels .556 winning percentage under Neil, extrapolated to the entire 1958 season, would have been good for third place.

"So, I thought, well I don't know if I'm gonna manage next year or not. [Then] I got a letter from Detroit that they had—I don't know how many teams—but they chopped it down to six minor league teams, 'cause of money, I guess. Toledo was their number one, and they had a team in Texas, Kentucky, and a couple in Pennsylvania. Down to six teams and they had guys who had managed for the Tigers for six, seven years already in the minors. Well, those are the guys that are gonna keep their jobs. That's just common sense and fairness."

That was the end of Neil Berry's short managerial career and also the end of his connection in any official capacity with Major League Baseball.

Neil Berry's sports career was documented in three large scrapbooks that his highschool sweetheart—and later his wife—Gloria maintained. The scrapbooks tell a career story that began when a *Kalamazoo Gazette* clipping of the first game of the 1936 Kalamazoo Central football season was pasted on the first now fragile page of the first scrapbook. The Gazette's game coverage noted, "Young Dale[*sic*] Berry, who was promoted to the varsity squad only Friday night, showed considerable promise in his ball-carrying efforts and in his ability to pass."

Twenty two years later, in 1958, "Berry Replaces Rowe" was the final headline pasted in the nearly full third and final scrapbook.

Epilogue

I know one thing, I've had many years of experiences that, to me, are important sometimes. To other people, oh God, all he does is shoot the breeze, but I've been around a couple county fairs and a hog show. I've been to a lot of places, I've met a lot of people . . .

~ Neil Berry

"I don't think there's too many people that have met as many celebrities as I have, movie stars, presidents and governors, and big wheels here and there. Just lucky, I was in the right place, right time."

Two of those big wheels Neil was lucky enough to meet were famous Generals;

- General George C. Marshall coordinated Allied operations in Europe and the Pacific during World War II and was hailed as the organizer of Allied victory by Winston Churchill. Marshall served as Secretary of State from 1947 to 1949, and was responsible for the Marshall Plan for Europe's post-war rebuilding. That success was recognized with the 1953 Nobel Peace Prize.

- General Claire Chennault was the Commander of the Fourteenth Air Force in China. During World War II, his elite fighter squadron became known as the Flying Tigers.

One thing both Generals had in common—a fact that won't be found in any history book—is that Neil Berry bummed a cigarette off each one of them when they met.

Neil recalled, "There's a fella that got his name in the paper a few years ago, he was the hero of the whole world. Hell, he was standing there [when we met] and I asked him for a

410

cigarette. George C. Marshall, he put in the lend lease deal with Germany after the war. I was at a banquette with him at the hotel where the downtown quarterback club had their weekly or monthly luncheons and we were invited because at the time we were in first place. He happened to be there, not for the meeting, and I [asked him for a cigarette] because I had a reputation of bein' a jerk and askin' [important people for a cigarette].

"I asked General Chennault for a cigarette. General Claire Chennault was the guy who saved Burma with his P-40s and P-41s, P-38s–whatever the hell he had. Claire Chennault, he saved them because he had his own little air corp to fight the Japanese. I met him, [not] met him—he didn't come there for me—I just run into him at the railroad station in St. Louis, Missouri.

"But I used to do that just for the hell of it. I started it down in Midland when we had a colonel come out to watch me give physical training, not me, watching the class. I had about 30 or 40 of his officers out there who had to take callanetics. So we got through with the callanetics and I'm on the stand. I jump down off the stand and the colonel and his two or three guys were standing there, and when you get through callanetics for 15 minutes you can play softball, horseshoes, anything. We were standing there getting them dispersed to whatever they wanted to do. He's standing there and lit up [and I asked], 'Do you have another cigarette sir?' 'Oh, sure.'

"Well that started [people talking]. 'You know that god damned Berry?' 'What?' 'He borrowed a cigarette off Colonel so and so.' 'Oh, how come he did that?' Because he was smokin' and I didn't have any, that's why you dumb cluck. Well, it got to be fun and so I did that."

After managing the 1958 Montgomery Rebels, Neil, Gloria and the kids moved back to Kalamazoo and the Inkster Ave. home they shared with Gloria's father.

Neil continued to operate Sportsland for a time but

eventually closed the business when it became apparent that he wouldn't be able to compete with the large department stores that were opening in the area. He then worked installing gymnasium floors in high schools and colleges. As a member of the carpenter's union, Neil and a helper built forms for the cement foundation of Kalamazoo Valley Community College. Before his retirement from the carpenter's union he worked in a government job for Kalamazoo County, building desk counter tops and doing other light carpentry and repair work.

In a 1993 interview Neil was asked about Derek Jeter's chances of playing in the major leagues.

Derek Jeter played shortstop for Kalamazoo Central and was named the top high-school player in the country by Baseball America in 1992, his senior year.

The New York Yankees drafted Derek Jeter in the first round of the 1992 draft. Five teams passed on Jeter allowing the Yankees to grab him with the sixth pick. One of the teams that didn't pick Derek Jeter was the Houston Astros who had the first overall pick. A Houston scout had been following Jeter and was convinced that the Astros should take him with their first pick and lobbied the Houston brass. Worried that Jeter would demand a larger signing bonus than they were willing to pay, Houston selected Phil Nevin instead. The Houston scout who had pushed so hard for Jeter quit his job with the Astros in protest. That scout was a former teammate of Neil Berry, Tiger Hall of Famer, Hal Newhouser.

Neil's response about Jeter's chances . . . "He was awfully lucky. I hope he makes it. What makes it tough on a kid like that is they give him $800,000 . . . that used to mean he'd be starting in left field or center field or right field for the Yankees either this year or next year. That doesn't mean anything anymore, but the pressure they put on these kids . . . I mean they give him all that money and send him out. Sure, he isn't going to make it for quite a time, maybe he'll never make it, we don't know. That's why I hope he goes to school. It takes a lot of politics, it takes a lot of luck. You've gotta get the breaks, you gotta be in the right place at the right time. If they don't like the way you comb your hair, they can say, 'I don't like that kid.'"

The Yankees liked the way Jeter combed his hair and the other shortstop from Kalamazoo made it to the major leagues in May, 1995 at the age of 20. Derek Jeter went on to a Hall of Fame (2020) career with the New York Yankees.

At age 65 Neil took up golf at his wife's urging. His first ever golf shot landed 6 inches from the hole on the short par 3, No. 1 at Kalamazoo's Red Arrow course. The story of this golf shot seems to have changed a bit over time, like a fish story in reverse. Instead of the fish getting bigger with each telling the golf ball has gotten closer to the hole.

Neil became an avid golfer, joining his wife and friends visiting many courses throughout the area, but tennis was the game for daughter Linda, and later her daughters, Sarah and Lizzie. Before enactment of Title IX—which prohibited discrimination on the basis of sex in education programs including athletics—Linda's high school did not have a women's tennis team. In a May 1999 *Kalamazoo Gazette* article about the Berry family's sports tradition, Linda said, "I learned tennis and played it at the city parks." Linda became a member of the "Hodgman Girls" who were coached by the late Dr. A.B. Hodgman. The Hodgman Girls competed in state and national competitions and won three national city championships. Linda Berry teamed up with Kathy Dombros in doubles and the pair rose to rank of No. 7 in the U.S. in under-16 doubles.

Linda (Berry) Spann's daughters also excelled at tennis. Sarah was a class B No. 1 singles champion in high school at Gull Lake before playing for Ferris State University, leading the team to a No. 14 national ranking in her final year. Lizzie had just won the Wolverine Conference No. 3 singles championship when the gazette article was written.

According to Linda, Neil "is big on golf," but when his daughter and granddaughters get a racket in his hands, "I think he enjoys (tennis) more than he might want to admit. But he's more proud of what Sarah and Elizabeth have achieved than any of his own accomplishments. He's that kind of a person."

Neil was honored as a charter member of the Kalamazoo Central Athletic Hall of Fame in 2003. Also posthumously honored in the ten member inaugural class were Central coaches Eugene S. Thomas and Fred (Dutch) Zuidema,

both influential men in Neil's prep sports career.

After taking over for Gene Thomas in 1939, Fred Zuidema would go on to coach Kalamazoo Central football for the next 14 years. One of Zuidema's best teams were Southwestern Michigan Conference Co-Champs with Muskegon in 1949. His '49 squad mirrored Thomas' 1938 squad with an 8-0-1 record. The '49 squad scored 158 points while allowing opponents only 25. This too, was remarkably similar to the '38 teams production of 157 points and allowing 36. Bill Crouch and George Heinrich were first team All-State performers on the '49 team.

Zuidema also served as Central's athletic director for 13 years until his death in June 1961. At a halftime tribute during Central's game with Benton Harbor that October, Central High School principal Eugene Thomas introduced the newly-established Fred B. Zuidema Memorial Award to be presented each spring to the senior who is considered the most outstanding in scholarship, sportsmanship, and athletic proficiency. A moment of silence in memory of "Dutch" Zuidema was then observed. Kalamazoo Central's Zuidema Gymnasium is named in his honor.

Gene Thomas served as Kalamazoo Central principal for 20 years, holding that title longer than anybody in school history, and retired in 1965. Thomas died in 1970 at age 70. Today the Maroon Giants play football in Eugene S. Thomas Stadium.

Neil lost his biggest fan and the love of his life when Gloria—his wife of 66 years—passed away on February 1, 2009. A few years later Neil moved in with his daughter Linda.

I was introduced to Neil in October 2013 when he was 91 years old. His playing career ended a year before I was born, but we got on like old friends. We both wondered why so many major league ball players couldn't bunt.

Neil was having health issues and found himself in the

Emergency Room one winter night in January shortly after his 92nd birthday. He had recently had surgery and his left hand and arm had unexpectedly swelled so his daughter Linda got him in the car and drove to Borgess Hospital. At 92 Neil Berry was no longer the fleet footed all state back that ran, passed, and punted Kalamazoo Central to a state championship in 1938. He didn't have the range he had when he was the sure-handed shortstop who starred on Kalamazoo's American Legion teams and didn't have the throwing arm he had when he broke into the major leagues with the Detroit Tigers in 1948. Neil had added quite a bit of weight and gray hair framed his still handsome face, but his memory for detail was as sharp as it had ever been. Neil tended not to let an opportunity to share a story pass even when the listener was an unsuspecting nurse.

"What are you here for tonight Mr. Berry?" the young nurse asked.

"Well my hand isn't supposed to be all puffed up like this and Linda thought we should have it looked at right away," Neil responded.

"Can you tell me your date of birth?"

"January 11, 1922"

"Have you been here before Mr. Berry?"

"Yes I have but in the original hospital building."

"Who did you see?"

"That guy," replied Neil pointing to a nearby hospital bed.

"I'm sorry Mr. Berry, do you know which doctor you saw?"

"I saw the doctor whose name is on that bed, Dr. Stryker. He was a doctor here. He had an office on the second floor."

"Ooookay. When did you see Dr. Stryker?" asked the surprised nurse.

"It was 1949 or maybe 1950 but I know it was February because spring training was starting in a couple of weeks. I hurt my right shoulder—my throwing arm—playing basketball. If the Tigers knew I was playing basketball I would have been fined and if I couldn't play I might have been out of a job. Dr. Stryker was my first coach in Legion ball and he had been a pitcher for the University of Michigan, so I thought I'd go see him about my arm."

Later on, at another appointment with a different nurse, Neil shared that he had been a major league ball player. This nurse with no frame of reference to guide her concerning this revelation asked Neil if he knew Babe Ruth. Neil told her no, he didn't know Babe Ruth and he hadn't met George Washington either.

Eventually Neil required dialysis on a regular basis so we met at the clinic and often watched replays of the previous night's Tiger game. We'd talk baseball, current affairs, and whatever else was on his mind.

Linda's text message on a Tuesday morning in August, 2016 alerted me to the fact that her dad was back in the hospital, ". . . his health is declining quickly. At this time he may not be able to continue dialysis." Neil had already missed it Monday and may not be well enough for Wednesday's session. "If dialysis is stopped, he won't live too much longer . . . of course he would love to see you."

I arrived at Neil's room as the hospital Chaplain was just about to leave. He thanked Neil for the story. I asked the Chaplain which story.

"The one about his wife and family. They seem to have been a common thread throughout," the Chaplain said. I agreed.

Linda left the room to make some phone calls while Neil and I talked. An attractive woman entered the room, the stethoscope around her neck identifying her as a doctor. She greeted Neil and introduced herself to me. So as not to be mistaken for family, I introduced myself as Neil's friend. The doctor asked Neil if it was ok to have a discussion in my presence. He said it was. In a professional and compassionate manner the doctor talked to Neil about what was going on with him and what was inevitable. She told him it was time to let nature take its course. Neil understood and thanked her. After she left I was at a loss as to how to continue our conversation but Neil wasn't.

"Did you see her skin? Perfect. Smooth as a baby's butt" Neil said.

I agreed with Neil's observation and after a silent moment, Neil matter-of-factly said, "It's nice to have someone to talk to when you're dying."

I'm not sure if he meant me or the doctor.

An hour or so after Linda was back in the room I left not realizing that this would be our last conversation. Neil thanked me for coming and as I turned to leave said, "Bill, you're my best friend." I was touched and thanked him for saying that. As I was leaving the room Neil added, "my other friends are all gone, but I can name every one of them."

I walked away wondering if he was doing just that.

That night Neil had his bed moved closer to the window. The view included Upjohn Park and the roof of his boyhood home on Walter Street.

Neil Berry passed away peacefully on the evening of August 24, 2016. His funeral was held on August 30. Linda asked me to speak at the funeral and I can only hope that I spoke the right words and told the right stories to honor Neil Berry, the shortstop from Kalamazoo.

Later that night 24-year-old JaCoby Jones made his Major League debut at third base for the Detroit Tigers. His first Major League hit was a go-ahead RBI double to right in the sixth inning, giving the Tigers a 4-3 lead. The Tigers added on and came away with an 8-4 victory over the White Sox at Comerica Park. Neil would have liked JaCoby Jones.

Afterword

In 2017, I attended the Michigan History Conference in Sterling Heights, Michigan, to hear William M. Anderson—author, historian, and Detroit Tiger fan—discuss his book, *The Detroit Tigers, A Pictorial Celebration of the Greatest Players and Moments in Tigers History*. After the presentation, when it was my turn to have him sign my copy of his book, I shared with Mr. Anderson that I too was writing a book and it was about the shortstop from Kalamazoo. Anderson looked up from the book he was about to sign and—to my surprise—said, "Neil Berry?"

William Anderson had interviewed Neil for his book, *The View From the Dugout, The Journals of Red Rolfe*. Anderson suggested that that book would be an excellent source of primary information for my book. He was right.

I knew the title of this book, *The Shortstop from Kalamazoo*, would not bring to mind Neil Berry for most baseball fans, but now that you've read the book, should a discussion transpire about the shortstop from Kalamazoo, you can impress the participants by asking, "which one?"

Bibliography

BOOKS

Anderson, William M. The View From the Dugout, The Journals of Red Rolfe. Ann Arbor: The University of Michigan Press, 2006

Bak, Richard. A Place for Summer, A Narrative History of Tiger Stadium. Detroit: Wayne State University Press, 1998

Breneman M.D., James C. with Hagar, Dave. The Stryker Story, Homer's Iliad. Kalamazoo: Phil Schubert & Associates, 1992

Dunbar, Willis F. Kalamazoo and how it grew. Kalamazoo: Western Michigan University, 1959

Krantz, Les. Reel Baseball, Baseball's Golden Era, The Way America Witnessed It. New York: Doubleday, 2006

Marshall, William. Baseball's Pivotal Era 1945-1951. Lexington: The University Press of Kentucky, 1999

Massie, Larry B. & Schmitt, Peter J. Kalamazoo The Place Behind the Products. Sun Valley: American Historical Press, 1998

Paige, Leroy (Satchel) as told to David Lipman. Maybe I'll Pitch Forever. New York: Doubleday & Company, 1962

Plaschke, Bill with Tommy Lasorda. I Live For This. New York: Houghton Mifflin Company, 2007

Veeck, Bill with Ed Linn. Veeck–As In Wreck. Chicago: The University of Chicago Press, 1962

MAGAZINES

Connors, Kevin (Chuck). as told to Sexauer, Chuck. "I'll Stick With The Coast League." Sport, July 1952, pp 22-25

420

Hirshberg, Al. "George Kell's Big Year." Sport, October 1952, pp 39, 78-79

Newcombe, Jack. "Road Trip Diary." Sport, August 1954, pp 30-32, 74-77

SCRAPBOOKS

The Neil Berry scrapbooks 1936-58. Privately owned by Linda Spann.

NEWSPAPERS

Articles from the following newspapers are included in the Neil Berry Scrapbooks:

Detroit Free Press

Detroit News

Detroit Times

Kalamazoo Gazette

Twin-City Sentinel

Winston-Salem Journal

WEBSITES

https://www.baseball-reference.com

Baseball Stats and History

https://sabr.org

Society for American Baseball Research

https://en.wikipedia.org

Wikipedia The Free Encyclopedia

espn.com

Index

A

Altuve, Jose 356

Anderson, Captain 72, 133, 205, 207, 296, 419

Aybar, Eric 190

B

Babe, Loren 362

Baker, John 190

Baker, Merle 22

Balch, Vern 116, 131, 152

Bartell, Dick 355

Bass, Mike 116, 131

Batts, Matt 348–350, 349, 350, 361

Bauer, Hank 284, 286, 318, 322, 362, 363

Bearden, Gene 281, 283, 300, 332, 348

Beck, Zinn 193

Bench-jockeying 170, 171, 235

Bengoechea, Adam 173

Benton, Al 50, 55, 59, 60, 65, 67, 68, 83, 132, 324, 415

Bero, John 297

Berra, Yogi 5, 6, 8, 9, 222, 242, 273, 284, 291, 292, 304, 310, 318, 338, 339, 345, 361, 362, 380

Berry, Carl 12, 35, 330

Berry, Clair 348

Berry, Neil

  Always throwing something at something 30

  Bright's disease 53

  Bummed a cigarette 410

  Dart-ass 34, 38, 48, 70

  Dogs while growing up 26

  First ever golf shot 413

  Fruit tree larceny 36

  Gloria fishing all by herself 45

  Hey meat story 274

  His good friend Walter 207

  Kalamazoo Central Athletic Hall of Fame 414

  Meeting Gloria 39

  Mr. Thomas would like to see you 47

  Needed B-29 gunners 214

  Play on Sunday? 115

  School pictures 20

  Summer job 33

  The dog, Major 32

  Vine Junior High 38, 39, 45

  Why can't we get married? 209

  Youngest professional baseball club 179

  Young Neil 18

Berry, Umpire Charlie 344

Betzel, Bruno 187

Birmingham Black Barons 150

Blanchard, Bill 85, 88, 92, 93, 96, 98

Bockelman, Jack 54, 59, 60

Boone, Ray 311, 324, 325

Borowy, Hank 325

Boudreau, Lou 282, 285, 308, 310, 340

Branca, Ralph 347

Brenly, Bob 190

Brideweser, Jim 396, 397

Bridges, Tommy 134, 152

Briggs

Spike 349

Walter O. 110, 194, 253, 293, 349

Brown, Bobby 284, 287, 338, 344

Brown, Mace 228

Burge, Lester 231

Burris, Herb 114, 119, 126–129

Busby, Jim 351, 352

Busch Stadium 252, 253, 368, 374, 376, 378

C

Cain, Bob 332, 333, 342, 343, 348, 349, 357, 369, 381, 392

Caldwell, Earl 269

Campanella, Roy 380

Carey, Andy 380

Cates, Nady 161, 162, 167, 174, 177, 178, 183, 187

Cavanaugh, Ken 115, 131

Chapman, Ben 167–171, 177, 178, 235

Chennault, General Claire 410

Chicago American Giants 121, 122, 149

Chicago Cubs 6-8, 21, 28, 29, 105, 110, 150, 158, 164, 169, 174, 175, 182, 185, 190, 191, 194, 223, 226-228, 239, 250, 251, 256, 276, 336, 353, 356, 376, 394, 401, 404

Clark, Allie 140, 151, 285

Clarke, Everett 118, 121, 123, 124, 128, 131, 148

Cleveland Indians 101, 134, 154, 169, 180, 196, 198, 250, 269, 275, 280, 282, 283, 285, 288, 289, 299, 301, 309, 313, 319, 321, 327, 329, 340, 345, 357, 364, 367, 389, 396

Cobb, Ty 21, 251, 272, 336, 337

Cochrane, Mickey 30, 196, 201, 353, 399, 401, 404, 405

Colavito, Rocky 240, 389

Coleman

Bob 90, 92, 114, 119, 128, 129, 131

Jerry 310, 318

Collins, Joe 361-363, 381

Columbia Cleaners 114, 115, 117, 130, 131, 150, 151

Comfort, Reeves 62, 67, 77, 83, 98

Comiskey Park 152, 197, 252, 266, 278, 299, 386

Connors, Kevin "Chuck" 400, 401

Conway, Neal 349

Cooper, Walker 201

Corstange, Ester 33, 34

Coughlin, W.S. 232, 241

Courtney, Clint 360, 379, 382

Cramer, Doc 388

Crawford, Jake 366

Cronin, Joe 227, 325

Cross, Willard 81, 82, 214

Crowe, Miles 115, 120, 124-126, 128, 129, 131

Cullenbine, Roy 194, 257, 258

Cuyler, Kiki 96, 105, 106, 154

D

Dark, Al 347

Davis, Ben 189

DeHammer, Dana 115

Dickey, Bill 168, 292

DiMaggio

  Dom 254, 284, 287

  Joe 169, 170, 203, 272, 278, 284, 285, 304, 310, 318, 340, 344, 345

Dobson, Joe 284, 288

Doby, Larry 253, 282, 285, 286, 309, 325, 328, 340

Doerr, Bobby 284, 287, 296, 310

Dopro, Walt 354, 355

Drake, Earl 69

Drebinger, John 362

Dressen, Chuck 347

Durden, Chauncey 167, 168, 174, 177

Durian, Richard 108

Durrett, Red 231

Dykes, Jimmy 393, 394-396

E

Easter, Luke 328

Eaton, Zeb 230, 232

Ebbets Field 170, 235, 251, 346, 380

Egan, Aloysius Jerome "Wish" 91, 92, 96, 97, 101, 106, 113, 153, 154, 163, 177, 254, 261, 266, 334

Elliott

  Bob 373-375, 382

  Gilbert 179

Paul 62

Engelman, William P. 22

Evans, Billy 293, 294, 348

Everhardus, Herman 41, 51, 52, 65, 83

Evers, Hoot 7, 257, 258, 266, 267, 299, 305, 318, 319, 324, 325, 326, 334, 335, 339, 354

F

Fanovich, Frank 392

Faudem, Frank F. 199

Feidorek, Stan 62

Feller, Bob 134, 153, 201, 281, 282, 284, 285, 286, 287, 307-311, 324, 328, 337, 359, 405

Fitzgerald, Ray 116, 131, 140

Fleckenstein, Harold 62

Fleugel, Jim 22

Flores, Jesse 324

Flying Dutchman

  Berry, Neil 51, 54, 65, 79, 83

  Berwanger, Jay 40

  Everhardus, Herman 41, 51, 52, 65, 83

Ford, Whitey 44, 52, 131, 230, 331, 340

Forster, Ivan 131

Fort Custer 147, 150, 151, 157

Fox, Nellie 386, 387, 388

Foxx, Jimmie 227

Franks, Herman 231

Friend, Owen 366

G

Gaedel, Eddie 342, 343

Galer, Runt 120, 122, 125

Garcia, Mike 308

Garrison, Wilt 186

Garver, Ned 341

Gehrig, Lou 168, 227, 253, 271, 293

Gehringer, Charlie 30, 110, 314, 316, 325, 348, 349, 404

Georgion, George 108

Gilbert, Louie 22, 179

Gill, Coach John 141-144, 146

Gilman

    Art 125

    Gerald 54, 60

Ginsberg, Joe 326, 334, 335, 367

Goodman, Billy 284, 287, 288, 310

Gordon, Joe 12, 282, 285, 286, 296, 308, 328, 396

Goslin, Goose 30

Graham, Hugh 122, 125

Gray, (Tiny) Ted 34, 171-173, 179, 182, 196, 197, 234, 241, 247, 258, 266, 303, 308, 318, 328, 329, 334, 350, 357, 367

Greenberg, Hank 30, 110, 134, 135, 150, 156, 170, 201, 240, 241, 256, 257, 259, 353, 367

Greene, Sam 264, 265, 297

Green Light letter 202

Groggel, Kurt 62, 90, 98, 99, 100

Gromek, Steve 281, 288

Groth, Johnny 299, 305, 317, 318, 320, 326, 334, 335, 360, 361, 366, 369, 374, 393

H

Hagan, Jerry 69, 71, 74, 79, 122, 130, 153, 300

Hamrick, Ray 230, 231, 232

Harridge, Will 283, 343

Harris, Bucky 228, 230, 237, 284, 287, 291, 294

Hartnett, Charles Leo (Gabby) 28, 226-228, 232, 235, 236, 237

Hatfield, Fred 354, 361

Haynes, Joe 266, 267, 269

Hegan, Jim 285

Heilmann, Harry 21, 271, 272, 279, 336, 337, 404

Helmer, Hale 54, 67, 81, 82

Henrich, Tommy 284, 285, 310, 318

Herman, Billy 28, 29, 41, 51, 52, 65, 83, 108, 201, 227, 231, 405

Hiatt, Ray 115, 124, 127, 131

Higgins, Pinky 152, 222, 223, 356

Hill, Bill 17, 43, 61, 116, 119, 125, 131

Hitler, Adolf 110

Hobbs, Roy 29

Hodges, Gil 380

Hodges, Russ 347

Hoeft, Billy 363

Hoffberger, Jerold 391

Hogue, Bobby 166, 167, 173, 175, 176, 178, 179, 182, 195, 196

Holloman, Alva Lee "Bobo" 376-379, 383

Homer in the Gloamin' 228

Hornsby, Rogers 341

Houk, Ralph 382, 399

House of David 121, 130, 132-134, 152

Houtteman, Art 234, 236, 258, 266, 274, 320, 331, 332, 334, 349, 357, 363, 367

Howland, Bill 54, 67, 75, 83, 84

Hubbell, Carl 196, 227, 238

Hubert, Dick 60, 62, 67-72, 75, 77, 84, 85, 108, 143, 179

Hughes, Dale 127, 129

Hughson, Tex 310

Hurley, Ed 342, 382

Hutchinson, Freddy 257, 258, 269, 270, 272, 273, 303, 305, 317, 318, 323, 324, 355, 364

Hyames, Coach Judson 22, 114, 124-126, 130, 144, 149, 152, 153

I

Independent leagues 114

Industrial league 113, 117, 118, 124, 127

Irvin, Monte 347

J

Jensen, Jackie 352

Jeter, Derek 412

Johnson, Kenny 90, 92, 95, 119, 123, 126, 174, 175, 383

Jones, Bob 54

Jones, Chuck 67

Jurges, Billy 28, 29, 227, 302

Jurwiak, Chester 60, 81, 82, 83

K

Kalamazoo

First Christian Reformed Church 13

I've Got a Gal in Kalamazoo 157, 208

Sara Woolley 157

Paper City 10, 15, 114, 122

Upjohn Park 3, 11, 18, 21, 22, 30, 34-36, 38, 41-43, 47, 51, 53, 65, 68, 72, 75, 77, 108, 109, 113, 118, 418

Walter Street 11, 18, 21, 32, 33, 418

Kalamazoo Central 4, 22, 23, 27, 42, 47, 48, 50, 52, 55-60, 62, 64-69, 71-74, 77-83, 104, 105, 109, 117, 136, 144, 151, 154, 155, 408, 412, 414-416

Kaline, Al 367, 389

Kansas City Monarchs 152, 153, 359

Karchunas, Al 115, 131

Kean, Bill 115, 126, 131, 152

Kell, Everett "Skeeter" 354

Keller, Charlie 320, 326

Kelley, Gerald 103, 104

Kell, George 2, 231, 257, 266, 269, 271, 275, 278, 299, 301, 304, 308, 310-313, 316-318, 324, 325, 334, 335, 337, 350, 351, 354, 355

Kelly, Earl 139, 140

Kelly, Joe 102, 149

Keltner, Ken 285, 286

Kinder, Ellis 310

Kline
  Jim 116, 125
  Tris 119
Kling, Johnny 223, 356
Klosterman, Augie 115
Koch, Wally 115, 122, 123
Koenig, Mark 227
Kokos, Dick 369, 396
Kolloway, Don 267, 300, 305, 308, 318, 320, 324, 326, 328, 335, 367
Kribs, Dave 129, 138, 140, 149, 150, 152
Kryhoski, Dick 315, 317, 348, 369
Kuenn, Harvey 355, 364, 367, 388, 389
KVP (Kalamazoo Vegetable Parchment) 15, 42, 113, 114, 120, 123, 125

L

Lake
  Eddie 222, 223, 237, 258, 259, 262-265, 271, 275, 278, 296, 297, 299, 300, 301, 311, 314, 334
  Mike 164, 173, 176, 179
Landis, Judge Kenesaw Mountain 201
Larsen, Don 378-381
Lasorda, Tommy 373
Legion Blues 31, 87, 114, 127
Legion Juniors 87, 89, 90, 92, 94, 97, 99, 102-105
Legion Maroons 53, 86, 87, 89, 97, 99, 101, 103, 114

Lemon, Bob 281, 282, 307, 309, 328, 329
Lenhardt, Don 354, 369
Lester, Bob 115, 118, 231
Lewis, Pete 192
Lines, Bill 62, 85
Lions Club Tournament 108
Lipon, John 154, 192, 222, 223, 258-266, 270, 271, 274, 275, 278, 279, 284, 285, 286, 288, 289, 298, 299, 304, 311, 315-317, 319, 320-324, 328, 334, 335, 337, 349, 350, 354, 355, 385, 388, 393
Littlefield, Dick 348, 369
Lockman, Whitey 347
Lorentzen
  Deane 43, 109
  Frank 16, 43, 109, 110, 138-140, 151, 172, 199, 342, 343, 392
  Gloria 2, 39, 43, 44, 45, 92, 109, 118, 137, 154, 157, 208, 209, 210, 211, 213, 214, 217, 220, 245, 246, 271, 332, 402, 403, 408, 411, 415
Louis, Joe 111
Lowe, Rusty 218
Lupien, Tony 267
Lyons, Ted 269, 354

M

Maartens, Johnny 49, 54, 56, 59, 60, 62, 88, 116, 119, 127, 129, 131, 149
MacDonell, Leo 263-265, 270
Mack, Connie 5, 238, 251, 253, 303, 327, 330, 393

MacPhail, Larry 294

Maglie, Sal 346, 380

Mantle, Mickey 240, 340, 361-363

Manush, Heinie 171, 272

Mapes, Cliff 348, 349, 350, 366

Marion, Marty 22, 23, 341, 372, 377, 379, 381, 383, 392

Marks, Jack 67, 73, 85, 101, 104, 119, 124, 129, 131, 140, 153

Marshall, General C. 410

Martin, Babe 395

Martin, Billy 88, 179, 192, 225, 232, 339, 340, 363, 395

Maskin, George 82

Mathews, Jim 178, 179

Mavis, Bob 297

Maxwell, Charlie 146, 365

Mayo, Eddie 258, 266, 267, 270, 275, 278, 279, 285-287, 297

Mays, Willie 6, 180, 181, 198, 331

McCarthy, Joe 284, 294, 398

McCosky, Barney 266

McDougal, Gil 380

McHale, John 82, 163, 164, 167, 171, 173, 175, 176, 179, 193, 194, 195, 225, 236, 266, 269

McKee, Harold 86, 88-92, 97-101

McKinley, Will 19, 54, 56, 58-60

McLain, Bill 62, 98

Mesick, Mr. 109, 143, 145

Metzger, Bob 115, 131

Midget game 342

Miller, Bill 48, 157, 208, 294, 295, 361, 362

Miñoso, Minnie 385-387

Miranda, Willy 382, 386

Mitchell, Dale 186, 285, 308, 310

Mize, Johnny 201, 318, 405

Moceri, Joe 159, 176, 179, 199

Moerman, Bill and George 88, 108, 120, 149

Molenaar, Tom 108

Monroe, Marylin 392

Mueller, Don 175, 347

Mueller, John 159

Mullin, Pat 258, 263, 266, 285, 286, 305, 317, 323, 334, 345, 350, 351

Murray, Don 159, 175, 179

Myer, Buddy 169

N

Nagy, Steve 176, 185-189

Newcombe, Don 331, 346, 347

Newhauser, Harold 92, 94-96, 101

Newhouser, Hal 96, 113, 134, 196, 201, 239, 255-258, 265-267, 269, 270, 277, 284-286, 288, 289, 299, 301, 303-308, 319, 323, 324, 328, 334, 335, 337, 353, 363, 367, 412

Nieman, Bob 366

Norman, Bill 379, 403

Notre Dame 23, 163

O

Olander, Coach Milton 22

O'Neill, Steve 222, 224, 238, 257-259, 261, 262, 264-266, 269, 271-273, 275, 278, 279, 290, 291

Outlaw, Jimmy   269, 278

Overmire, Frank (Stub)   151, 266

Owens, Jesse   110

P

Paige, LeRoy (Satchel)   153, 281, 282, 300, 340, 348, 357-361, 367, 372, 374, 379, 392

Paparella, Joe   342

Par, DeWitt   72, 345

Parnell, Mel   310

Parsons, Dixie   165, 198

Partlow, Roy   231, 232

Patkin, Max   340, 342

Pedroia, Justin   356

Peifer, Fred   152

Perk, Lyle   41

Pesky, John   177, 184, 274, 276, 284, 287, 354, 355, 359-364, 388

Peterson, Pete   159

Phelps, Leon   149

Pierce, Billy   232, 258, 266, 294, 334, 335

Pieretti, Marino   325

Pivonka, Big Joe   123

Polo Grounds   6, 7, 180, 251, 346

Pool, Clarence   108

Porterfield, Bob   284, 286, 287, 351, 355, 356

Porter, Jay   366

Priddy, Jerry   296, 313-320, 322, 324, 326, 334, 335, 350, 351

Purnell, Benjamin   132, 133

R

Radulovich, John   159, 163, 173, 175, 176, 179, 225

Ramona Park   113, 115, 117, 131, 150

Ranney, Charles   67

Rapp, Earl   300

Raschi, Vic   271, 272, 287, 310, 386

Read, Buck   22

Reeves, Jack   60, 62, 67, 77, 83, 88, 98, 122, 123

Remington, Dick   79, 80-82

Reynolds, Allie   303-305, 363

Rhabe, Nick   179

Rhodes, Dusty   181

Richards, Paul   237-239, 241-246, 249, 385, 387, 388, 392

Rickey, Branch   231, 393

Rickey, Branch Jr.   187

Riggs, Lou   231

Righter, Glen   22

Rigney, Topper   152, 265

Rizzuto, Phil   177, 184, 284, 286, 310, 319, 322, 343, 361-363

Roberts, Robbie   174, 179, 184

Robinson
  Aaron   294, 299, 304, 317, 328
  Eddie   285

Rockne, Knute   23

Roe, Dallas   60, 62, 88

Rogell, Billy   110

Rogers, Packy   230

Rogovin, Saul   332, 334

Rolfe, Robert (Red)   168, 198, 290, 293-301, 303, 311, 313, 316, 317, 319, 321, 326, 328, 330, 332-335, 348, 349, 350, 354, 355, 419

Rommel, Eddie   267, 345

Roosevelt, President Franklin D.   201, 202, 231

Root, Charlie   226, 227, 343

Rosen, Al   319, 324

Ross, Dave   88, 114, 118, 119, 120, 126-131, 149, 152, 153

Rowe, Schoolboy   30, 152, 196, 201, 402-406, 408, 409

Ruth, Babe   21, 165, 168, 226, 227, 253, 271, 272, 293, 417

S

Sain, Johnny   196

Salsinger, H.G.   261-263

Saucier, Frank   342, 343

Schilling, Curt   189, 190

Schindler, Bob   49, 54, 60

Schmeling, Max   111

Schoendienst, Red   197

Schrier, Neil   108

Scott, Coach Donald   61, 62, 85

Shank, Harold   41

Sherman, Jack   55, 58, 77, 98

Shoup, Don   152

Siker, Miss   145

Silvera, Charlie   284, 286

Simmons, Al   227, 240, 393

Slapnicka, Cy   101, 281

Slater, Emko   116, 124, 127-129, 131, 141, 143, 144, 152

Slaughter, Enos   197

Sleep, Sum   116, 120, 123, 125, 127

Smathers, Punk   114, 115, 118, 119, 121-123, 126, 128-131, 134, 152

Smith
  Hilton   153
  Lyall   316, 317

Sommers, Gerald   67

Soules, Clair   56, 88

South Pacific   339

Sowers, Ray   68, 69, 81, 82

Spahn, Warren   196

Spalding, A.G.   29, 301, 302

Spann, Linda   1, 63, 67, 70, 76, 84, 85, 116, 160, 206, 215, 236, 248, 298, 396, 413

Spence, Stan   284, 287, 288

Spurgeon, Fred   22, 154

Stengel, Casey   292, 380, 386, 398

Stillwell, Ken   96, 98, 101, 102, 104, 139, 140, 143

Stirnweiss, Snuffy   284, 286, 296

St. Louis Cardinals   91, 107, 153, 155, 250, 359, 368, 402, 404

Stoops, Art   125

Stringer, Lou   276

Stryker, Dr. Homer   43, 86-89, 103, 113, 290, 294, 295, 416, 417

Stuart, Marlin   369

Sutherland Paper Co.   16, 26, 42, 112, 114-132, 144, 148-153, 359

Swift, Bob   266, 269, 285-287, 318, 343, 366

T

Tabacheck, Martin   179, 192, 225, 232

Taborn, Al   62, 67, 69, 71, 83, 140

Taylor, Ben   348, 350

Taylor, Zach   342

Tebbetts, Birdie   2, 165, 276, 277, 284, 288, 310

Terpening, Thaxton   62

Terpstra, Bennie   33

Thomas, Bobby   346

Thomas, Coach Gene   22, 23, 46-51, 54, 57, 60, 65, 66, 70, 72, 75, 77, 78, 83, 159, 346, 414, 415

Thompson, Francis (Piff)   62

Thompson, Fresco   187

Tiefenthal, Harlun   98, 100, 104

Tighe, Jack   158, 159, 164, 165, 195

Timmerman, George   125, 126, 153

Travis, Bob   88, 92, 108, 149, 155

Tresh, Mike   267

Trout, Dizzy   196, 256, 257, 258, 266, 318, 320, 334, 337, 350, 354

Trucks, Virgil   1, 255, 257, 258, 303, 307, 309, 310, 350-354, 359, 361-363, 366, 369, 374, 383

U

Unser, Al   164-166, 171, 175, 178, 179, 183, 186-188, 191, 198, 199, 212, 213

Unwritten rules   186, 189, 353

Upjohn Park   3, 11, 18, 21, 22, 30, 34-36, 38, 41-43, 47, 51, 53, 65, 68, 72, 75, 77, 108, 109, 113, 118, 418

V

Vanderberg, Bill   98

Vander Meer, Johnny   363

Vander Molen, Andy   108

VanKeuran, Paul   41

Van Lente, Red   116, 131

Veeck, Bill   283, 340-343, 357, 358, 368, 369, 373, 382, 385, 390, 391

Verlander, Justin   190

Vernon, Mickey   352

Vico, George   159, 171, 176, 179, 265-267, 269, 270, 285-288, 299

W

Wade, Jake   174, 178

Wadsworth, Senator   107

Wagner, Honus   21, 241

Wakefield, Dick   213, 258, 266, 285, 287, 304, 311, 315

Warren, Bruce   13, 54, 60, 67, 71, 75, 80, 81, 83, 196

Watson, John   49, 54, 60

Webb, Skeeter   222, 258, 265

Webster, Neil   88, 92, 94, 96, 120

Welaj, Lou   193

Wertz, Vic   179, 180, 181, 197, 198, 225, 229, 236, 258, 266, 269, 276, 285-288, 299, 304, 317, 318, 324-326, 335, 337, 350-352, 369, 370, 374, 395

Western State Teachers College   10, 21, 25, 83, 114, 136, 137, 140, 141, 143, 261, 265

Westgate, John 22

White, Hal 274, 310, 311, 324, 325,
     366, 369

Wieczorek, Chester 232

Will, George 190

Williams, Bernie 356

Williams, Stewart 159

Williams, Ted 159, 197, 201, 203,
     274, 284, 287, 310-312, 331,
     354, 356, 365

Wolthuis, Hubert 108

Woodling, Gene 201

Woolley, Sara 157

Wright, Bill 354

Wright, John 231

Wynn, Early 324, 381

     Y

Yastrzemski, Carl 240, 361

York, Rudy 30, 256, 259

     Z

Zeller, Jack 192, 195

Zerilli, James 259, 264

Zichterman, Herman 108

Zuidema, Coach Fred "Dutch" 46,
     78, 83, 414, 415

Made in the USA
Middletown, DE
02 September 2021